# THE POWER OF SPORTS

# MICHAEL SERAZIO

# THE POWER

## MEDIA AND SPECTACLE

# OF SPORTS

**NEW YORK UNIVERSITY PRESS**
New York
www.nyupress.org

References to Internet websites (URLs) were accurate at the time of writing. Neither the author nor New York University Press is responsible for URLs that may have expired or changed since the manuscript was prepared.

Library of Congress Cataloging-in-Publication Data
Names: Serazio, Michael, author.
Title: The power of sports : media and spectacle in American culture / Michael Serazio.
Description: New York : New York University Press, [2019] |
Series: Postmillenial pop | Includes bibliographical references and index.
Identifiers: LCCN 2018037667 | ISBN 9781479887316 (cl : alk. paper)
Subjects: LCSH: Mass media and sports—United States. | Sports—United States—Sociological aspects. | Sports in popular culture—United States.
Classification: LCC GV742 .S47 2019 | DDC 070.449796—dc23
LC record available at https://lccn.loc.gov/2018037667

New York University Press books are printed on acid-free paper, and their binding materials are chosen for strength and durability. We strive to use environmentally responsible suppliers and materials to the greatest extent possible in publishing our books.

Manufactured in the United States of America

10 9 8 7 6 5 4 3 2 1

Also available as an ebook

*For Lucy, future Padres fan—*
*you are our greatest blessing*
*and we root for you above all*

# CONTENTS

Ignoring [mediated sports] today would be like ignoring the role of the church in the Middle Ages or ignoring the role of art in the Renaissance; large parts of society are immersed in [it] . . . and virtually no aspect of life is untouched by it.

—**Michael Real**, sports scholar

# KEEPING THE FAITH

## The Elementary Forms of Sports Life

We recognize that sport is the religion of the western world . . . So we decided to use the Olympics, the most sacred ceremony of this religion, to make the world pay attention to us.

—**Black September Organization** on its 1972 Munich Games attack

**T**OWARD THE END

# OF MY GRANDFATHER'S LIFE,

we did not—beyond genetics—have a great deal in common. He was six decades older and lived 2,500 miles west, on the other side of the country. But I loved him dearly, yearned to connect, and wanted to have something to talk about when I dialed him up every few weeks. So we talked, as many men do, about sports. Specifically, we talked about what, besides family, might have been the last vessel that united us in faith and love: our hometown San Diego Chargers.

We harrumphed about local sportswriters' pulling their punches in covering a perennially disappointing franchise; griped about team ownership trying to shake down taxpayers for a sweetheart stadium deal; and lamented the infestation of advertising that was consuming sports media. But we also reminisced fondly—stories of my grandfather taking my uncles to games at the old Balboa Park field and my own dim, sweet memories of the 1994 season. Whenever I was back in town, I felt an inexplicable urge to pick up a cap or a shirt with the lightning bolt logo on it. After my grandmother passed, I recall my mother remarking that fall seemed to go faster for Pops because football was in season; it got him through the week and filled the days with something to think about and look forward to. I suspect that, though the details will vary for other teams' fans, the fundamental texture of this ambivalence—economics and culture pulling us in different directions—will feel true and familiar. What mattered most is that my grandfather and I were talking, period. Nowadays, that is no small accomplishment.

In an era of cultural fragmentation, political polarization, and the relentless distraction that comes with living amidst media abundance, sport represents one of the last institutions of unifying mass ritual—bringing together enormous audiences, focused on the present, live moment.[1] In that, it retains a timeless "totemic" cultural power long ago revealed to be at the core of religious worship, but given new import in the DVR and smartphone age. Yet, conversely, that power is being strained, co-opted, and artificially manufactured. A variety of media convergence trends are revolutionizing the way that sports are packaged for us: an explosion in opinion-oriented, "hot take" journalism formats; branded content commercializing and corrupting new frontiers; and social media accelerating news cycles and displacing traditional gatekeepers. And because—not in spite—of its escapist value and its (allegedly) apolitical sheen, sports can smuggle in powerful but subtle ideological messages about inequality, war, and labor, even as signs of racial activism reemerge. Simultaneously, the shifting dynamics of gender roles and masculine power, writ large across society, are being reflected in the experiences of female sports journalists, the coverage of violence against the male body, and the ascendance of analytics as a labor ideal.

Through in-depth interviews with dozens of high-profile leaders and professionals in sports media and journalism as well as those in the business and marketing of sports, *The Power of Sports* explores, maps, and critiques the cultural production of today's lucrative, ubiquitous sports landscape. The book is about how sports explain and reflect life in contemporary American culture: our spiritual experience, technological disruption, commercial greed, economic disparity, military hawkishness, and manhood ideals. If we hold up a mirror to sports, we see the realities of the nation staring back at us—despite what those myths of "escapism" might like to suggest.

At my grandfather's funeral, my cousin brought up to the altar a faded blue Chargers hat that Pops had worn for many years, and it rests today on my aunt's fireplace mantle as a reminder of him. Sport thus helps us endure in every sense of the word—existentially, palliatively—but it does so at an enormous cost and without naïveté among stakeholders about the value and purpose of the spectacle. This book is an attempt to understand that "medium," that social glue—its causes and consequences: economic, political, and cultural. Many of these dimensions and issues of sport's power have held true for decades—even centuries—but the subject feels newly urgent today given the transformations both within and beyond: the media evolution, market necessity, and ideological consequence embedded in the games and the wider societal upheaval, discontent, and contestation that swirls beyond the boundaries of simple play. As former NBA commissioner David Stern told me:

> It's a natural flowing dynamic: You build a building where 18-to-20,000 perfect strangers come together for the communal purpose of rooting the home team onto victory, where people who sometimes don't even know each other are high-fiving a spectacular shot or a winning performance. As life gets more impersonal, as we retreat into our homes and we get—we order our food, we get our EKG, we buy our cars, we do a tremendous amount from the comfort of our smart devices in a chair at home—the last places that people are likely to gather are going to be . . . houses of worship and houses of sports worship. No doubt about it.[2]

## THE BOX SCORE

The spectacle is, simply put, big-time. Perhaps the defining feature of sports culture over the last quarter-century has been how it has ballooned in slow motion before our eyes: more interest, more outlets, more money. Ours is an age of sporting excess right down to the amount of statistical information that now crawls across the ticker updates during TV broadcasts. Depending on which estimate one consults, the global sports industry is pegged somewhere between $200 and $700 billion.[3] Given that this was, by one count, 60 percent more than the value of the film market, News Corporation overlord Rupert Murdoch not long ago observed, "Sport absolutely overpowers film and everything else in the entertainment genre."[4] Within the United States, nearly a quarter of all Americans spend money at least once a month on sports, contributing to nearly $70 billion worth of tickets, broadcast rights, sponsorships, and apparel.[5]

That figure has been projected to grow by another $10 billion over the next half-decade, thanks to a media rights bubble that has yet to burst and has proven mostly immune to the traditional gravity of financial cycles: The past decade saw three straight years of double-digit growth, following a whirlwind of major TV deals.[6] Fans' voracious appetite for sport has pushed it to the center of the pop culture buffet; just a few years into the new millennium, the explosion of networks (and sub-channels) dedicated to airing sports content meant that viewers could pig out on some 645 hours per week.[7] Of the 25 highest-rated broadcasts in American television history, 22 have been sporting events and, on average, sports-related newspaper stories online outhit all other subjects combined.[8] The intensity of that attentiveness made the NFL into an unparalleled economic juggernaut and, for a time, the most popular and powerful television programming of any kind. By 2016, league games accounted for 60 of the top 100 Nielsen scores and Super Bowl XLVIII set a record with 112 million viewers, which was broken only by Super Bowl XLIX, naturally, which saw 114 million Americans tuning in.[9] And pro football is not alone in this recent dominance: At the peak, in 2015, 93 of the top 100-rated American TV shows in a single season were live sports programs—up from just 14 in the top 100 a decade before.[10]

The durability of sports' widespread, mainstream popularity—at a time in mediated culture when such blockbuster successes, especially on television, are ever harder to come by—has been a boon to providers pushing the product. ESPN is, by far, the "worldwide leader" in cable revenues, pulling in nearly $8 per household in monthly subscriber fees and representing, at one point, the "principal cash spigot" for parent corporation Disney, when it topped out with some $10 billion in earnings.[11] It was called, at that time, "the most valuable media property on the planet," and as former CEO Michael Eisner joked, "[Disney] would not exist without ESPN. The protection of Mickey Mouse is ESPN."[12] Live sport is, simply put, the biggest reason your cable bills have exploded (and, fittingly, if you do like sports, chances are decent it's the only reason you haven't cut the cord yet). Beyond ESPN, regional sports networks are also some of the most expensive channels for distributors to maintain in the lineup, and sports programming is said to be "keeping the lights on" at ABC, CBS, NBC, and Fox, accounting for more than one-third of all ad sales.[13]

Although awash in revenues, sports media are not, necessarily, awash in profits (an issue vexing ESPN especially). Acquiring all that live content has become more expensive than ever, with sports rights exceeding half of all TV programming costs.[14] This is what's making leagues, teams, and players fantastically wealthy and American football is, as usual, the apotheosis of such excess. By mid-decade, the NFL was bringing in $13 billion in annual revenue, with commissioner Roger Goodell ravenously aiming to double that figure within

10 years.[15] Franchise values had already doubled under his tenure, with 20 of the 50 most valuable teams worldwide hailing from the league, including the top-ranked $4 billion Dallas Cowboys.[16] (It should be caveated, however, that winning is not necessarily everything when it comes to revenue generation—rather, as we'll see shortly, something deeper and more enduring actually churns all that commerce. Coming off a 4–12 campaign, for example, the Cowboys' net worth still grew by 25 percent and the similarly woeful New York Knicks—they of the .390 winning percentage—posted their own 20 percent increase.)

It's not just the NFL, though, that is finding its boats lifted by this rising tide. Even at the "amateur" level (the great Orwellian doublespeak of sports labor economics), coffers are flush, with the top 20 college football programs pegged at a collective $3 billion value.[17] Football—as the vast majority of the world knows it (i.e., soccer)—remains by far the single most lucrative sport, registering some $35 billion in annual revenues, as the rights to England's elite league have skyrocketed 3,000-fold over a half-century.[18] Even baseball, regularly lamented as a fusty cultural relic, seems hardy enough on paper, raking in a record $10 billion in revenues, with more than a third of its teams recently ranking first in prime-time home markets.[19]

Clearly, then, sport still makes it rain. And sport's apparent immunity from macroeconomic gyrations also makes it a fairly sure thing as an entertainment investment; not only has there never been a crash in the sports media market (unlike other industries such as tech or housing, it just keeps going up), but even in the midst of the last cataclysmic global downturn, sports' 7 percent growth rate still exceeded that of almost every nation's GDP.[20] In sum, little seems to have changed since communications professor Robert McChesney declared, some 20 years ago, that sport was "arguably the single most lucrative content area for the global media industry."[21] What is curious, though, is just how much of this commerce seems built upon

and stimulated by a fundamental economic (if not cultural) irrationality; this is manifest in the accommodation of swindling cartels,
the production of profligate venues, the staging of lavish mega-events,
and the thoughtless consumption of branded merchandise.

## IRRATIONAL EXUBERANCE

"Sports is a way of life, like eating. People say, 'You should pay to feed
the homeless.' But the world doesn't work that way."[22] So sayeth Carl
Pohlad, late owner of the Minnesota Twins—and a member of the
rarefied elite that stands to gain from that spending—encapsulating
the way in which the attachment to sports drives all those revenues
and grossly disfigures public priorities. That attachment is the reason
why, in the 1970s, the only paved road in southern Sudan apparently
led from the airport to a stadium.[23] That attachment is the reason
why, of 340 Division I colleges, only 23 athletic departments actually
operated in the black and, at Rutgers, a $20-million-a-year sports
deficit was allowed to eat into library costs, faculty hires, and student fees.[24] Owner Art Modell of the Baltimore Ravens (and crusher
of dreams in Cleveland) put it even more bluntly than Pohlad: "The
pride and presence of a professional football team is far more important than thirty libraries."[25]

None of this makes sense from a "rational" standpoint, but the
cultural logic of sports, I submit, overwhelms any fidelity to rational
judgment. A. J. Maestas, CEO of Navigate Research, a sports marketing agency, explains further: "The marketing world, for the most
part, and the sports marketing world in particular, now has woken
up to: You know, it isn't about a rational trade-off with fans with
season tickets or yelling at a television screen because a 23-year-old
doesn't go left versus right. It's very irrational. It's very emotional. . . .
That means the rules of classic economics don't necessarily apply. . . .
I think that the lesson is that people's motivation, especially related

to marketing and completely related to sports, is emotional. Not economic: cost-benefit, reward-incentive, risk-reward. It's just not. It's communal and tribal and emotional."[26]

Cities are just as prone, collectively, to that magical thinking as the individual fans that populate them and therefore vulnerable to the emotional exploitation leveraged by sports' stakeholders. Nowhere is this more apparent—and appalling—than in the construction of sports venues. Recall that, up until the 1950s, most sports facilities were paid for by team ownership; by the 1990s, however, that ratio had flipped and more than three-quarters of arenas and stadia were being publicly financed.[27] Some $10 billion in municipal largesse was diverted to subsidize venues in the first decade of the 21st century and 2017 capped an "unprecedented" three-year period where $17 billion was spent to create or improve stadia; in just one recent example, the Minnesota Vikings were able to extort from residents half the cost of their $1 billion U.S. Bank Stadium (with its apparently necessary "state-of-the-art corporate suites").[28] Why is it so rare that a local government or referendum voters will oppose team demands for new or renovated facilities?

On one hand, the basic laws of supply and demand (more cities want franchises than leagues provide) means that those franchises can negotiate from a position of inherent strength, while cities can only and ever "play defense" against threats to elicit tax credits, property rights, luxury seating renovations, and unsold ticket compensation, among other perks.[29] Those supply-and-demand conditions are distorted thanks to a monopoly advantage few fellow industries enjoy. Following a 1922 Supreme Court ruling, Major League Baseball and, later, other leagues were granted immunity from anti-trust laws, affording these cartels near total control over both the allocation and placement of franchises.[30]

One might expect more teams to go around, given Americans' insatiable appetite for sports and steady population growth—and were professional sports a theoretically "freer" market, there might well be—but, with the artificially depressed supply, cities are all the more likely to acquiesce to blackmail for those extravagant subsidies.[31] One expert argues that, because of those factors, big-time sports leagues have "established [themselves] as some of the most powerful firms in the history of America."[32] (And as detailed later in this chapter, it is the same monopolistic structure of production that fortifies sport against the forces of consumer fragmentation that have so besieged other pop industries and American culture overall; in other words, without that cartel swindle, the "field" for forging community might be impossibly spread asunder.)

Franchises are, moreover, merely mirroring a broader corporate pattern evidenced across industry sectors, by extorting public capital and government welfare with regular threats to pull up stakes and move elsewhere.[33] Indeed, "strip-mining" cities in this fashion becomes even easier if teams don't actually *own* their own home fields, while those municipalities that are most ripe for abandonment (i.e., blighted and cash-strapped) can usually least afford to compete with sexy rival suitors across state lines.[34] In the most infamous instance of infidelity, when Mayflower moving vans squirreled away the Baltimore Colts' equipment to Indianapolis under cover of night, it was not for lack of local love; the team had set a regular season attendance record just months earlier.[35] Fans are loyal to their teams—irrationally so and often to a fault, given the economic realities that so consistently betray them.

To be certain, though, it is not only sticks, but carrots as well that drive stadia economics—benefits touted that typically turn out to be more magical than monetary. During the stadia boom of the past few decades, projects were often packaged as urban "renewal"—an antidote to years of inner-city decay and white flight to the suburbs. Conventional wisdom held that a quirky, charming ballpark complex like that of Camden Yards could spark a downtown renaissance, drawing tourist interest, entertainment venues, and retail chains: Call it the city-as-theme-park planning schemata.[36] And here was yet one more triumph of branding—a way for cities to project, through spectacle, an air of cosmopolitan liveliness in the global competition for capital.[37] Having a "big league" team somehow symbolizes and communicates the (apparently very necessary) image of being a "big league" city—that shopworn cliché that mayors and other self-interested boosters (like financers, developers, and other members of the local business elite) often drop when spinning constituents on multimillion-dollar boondoggles.[38]

Yet the research findings are unequivocal: It simply doesn't add up. According to Robert Baade, a leading scholar of sports economics, stadia and arenas (which often fall prey to higher construction costs and yield lower rent and tax revenues than estimated) make almost "no significant impact" on cities—providing, at best, a minor bump to the local economy or, more likely, detract from existing competitors, as all that entertainment spending would simply happen elsewhere in town.[39] Adding insult to injury, teams are now abandoning "old" new stadiums at an accelerated pace—the kind of wasteful planned obsolescence long endemic to consumer goods like iPhones but seen recently with the Atlanta Braves disposing of Turner Field after just 19 years and the Texas Rangers finding Globe Life Park inadequate after 22 years.[40]

A similarly illogical and fraudulent game of economics also plays out in the hosting of global competitions. Cities will pay a small fortune—typically, upward of $100 million—to bid for the privilege of paying a large fortune to host the Olympics (including a $15 billion tab for London, $40 billion for Beijing, and $50 billion for Sochi).[41] Enormous investments are made in facilities that then usually sit unused—the "badlands of modernity," as they've been aptly called—and, contrary to boosters' claims, tourism actually *goes down* during these mega-events, making profit improbable and financial burden inevitable.[42] Justifications here, too, tend to hinge on the ethereal and ephemeral, with promoters hyping an "improved national spirit and mood" and "greater social inclusion"—qualities that are, by definition, immaterial and incalculable even as they are accompanied by a multibillion-dollar price tag.[43]

Yet, as I will argue, this collective effervescence *is* true, real, and necessary, though perhaps not at the foolhardy economic cost it tends to elicit. The identity of a team *is* a source of unrivaled symbolic power—and therefore *also* a means of capital manipulation. Given the intimidating emotional hold that teams retain over followers, it becomes harder to formulate a civic identity through other, more productive and public urban emblems.[44] A polis can, regrettably, imagine itself (and its health) more easily through a playoff berth than those "thirty libraries," to borrow Art Modell's callous comparison.

And even if you haven't signed off on an (economically) wrongheaded stadium deal, you've likely felt the weight of this illogic any time you've ever made a purchase of branded sneakers or other sports-logoed merchandise. This was the real genius of Nike founder Phil Knight: He realized that he wasn't even "in the shoe business. . . . He was in the entertainment business."[45] The power and allure of those $100 Air Jordans is wholly imaginary and symbolic rather than material and functional; most consumers at the checkout register neither contemplate the bleak conditions of sports merchandise production nor can they actually (consciously, rationally) believe that, in purchasing them, they, too, can fly "like Mike," even as this is precisely the con job that all branding is predicated upon.[46] And because fans worship, blindly, at this altar of sports myth—myself included—Nike doesn't actually need to "make shoes," as its SEC filing reveals, but rather makes *meaning*.

As with other apparel companies in the $170 billion sporting goods industry, its symbolic labor force (e.g., M.J., and Nike's agency of record, Wieden+Kennedy) add the "real" value and reap the cushiest rewards here, not those who are subcontracted to make the actual, *tangible* goods for "slave wages, forced overtime, and arbitrary abuse," as Knight himself once acknowledged.[47] We think not of that exploited garment worker in Dhaka when interacting with the Swoosh or Chicago Bulls logo that she sewed on, but rather of the seductive wonderment and social power those icons supposedly offer us in the developed, postmodern world.[48] (Much the same whitewashing and willful ignorance occasionally accompanies the production of sports facilities, too: When the 2022 World Cup kicks off in Qatar, global attention will no doubt be focused more on the pitch than those migrant worker deaths that went into constructing it.[49])

Thus, as should be clear by now, sports are big money—a "highly lucrative, multi-branched transnational economy of enormous scope and influence" and an increasingly central component in the "culturalization" of contemporary economics.[50] And, yet, as also shown here, all that commercial exchange appears to be dependent upon a somewhat "fuzzy math"—one that does not add up when considered in the empirical, verifiable language of cost-benefit (for nations, cities, and consumers). It seems like we do not act *financially rationally* in the presence of sport—but why is that?

## THE SPORTS TOTEM

The answer—and the esoteric essence of fandom—might just be found in a context far removed from sports.[51] Almost precisely a century ago, Émile Durkheim, a pioneering figure of early sociology, pondered along similar lines. He wrote in the wake of the industrial revolution and the tumultuous reshuffling of culture that it had wrought—a zeitgeist perhaps not so far removed from our own, as the increasing specialization of economic roles within the division of labor threatened to tear traditional communities apart and freight individuals with the dread of what he called "social anomie": that feeling of normlessness, disorder, and alienation that seems to characterize and plague the modern age.[52] Durkheim felt that individuals needed to be stitched together by "a strongly held common morality . . . a strong *collective conscience*" and he endeavored to explain how complicated societies cohere—how, in short, we manage to get along.[53]

To do so, Durkheim went back to the beginning: religion in its simplest form, digging through accounts of "primitive" cultures like the Arunta tribe of Australia, hoping to excavate ancient sources of the ties that bind.[54] His theoretical conclusion, as revealed in *The Elementary Forms of Religious Life*, remains as profound and relevant today as it is elegantly efficient: Whenever a society worships a divine form, it is, in fact, also simultaneously worshipping itself.[55] Religion is not, then, about the "cosmic order" (despite the claims of religious authorities); it is about *social* order and the imagined bonds that unify a group.[56] Through faith, we transcend atomistically rather than metaphysically, for religion is, ultimately, the "enduring source" of—and, indeed, invention for—"human social identity and fellowship."[57] As more recent surveys have shown, it remains "the single most important repository of social capital."[58] For Durkheim, this all hinged on what he termed the "totem":

> On one hand, it is the external and tangible form of what we have called the totemic principle, or god. But on the other, it is the symbol of that particular society we call the clan. It is its flag; it is the sign by which each clan distinguishes itself from others, the visible mark of its personality, a mark that embodies everything that belongs to the clan in any way. . . . The god of the clan, the totemic principle, must therefore be the clan itself, but transfigured and imagined in the physical form of the plant or animal species that serve as totems.[59]

In other words, religious totems, while officially symbolizing deities, also implicitly offer vessels for fellowship, licenses to congregate together. As human beings are social creatures, there is something universal—and still enduring—in that tribal yearning. Yet community is often more abstract and imagined than concrete and identifiable. The totem, then, gives believers a physical representation, legitimation, and coordination of that need for identity and unity: a Star of David hung from one's neck; a Ganesh figurine placed on the dashboard; the St. Christopher medal that's tucked inside my wallet. Theological justifications are really just incidental; what matters is that through our faith in these common artifacts—and participation in the rituals that surround them—community is forged. As an emblem of and for the group, the totem helps differentiate insiders from outsiders.[60]

Durkheim acknowledged, however, that because religion's centrality was waning and fewer collective practices yoke tribes together, "many modern, social institutions are religious in character."[61] What totems, therefore, survive and persist in contemporary American culture? The Red Sox. The Packers. The Lakers. And so on.[62] Rereading Durkheim's depiction of aboriginal practices, one can't help but be struck by the ancient echoes of today's fandom habits: "It often happens that the whole clan does not reside in the same place . . . [but] its unity is felt even without any geographical basis."[63] Think here of the jersey-clad fan diasporas fanning out to NFL Sunday Ticket bars every autumn. "In most societies, the child has the same totem as his [parent]."[64] Recall how routinely we speak of being "born" into a particular fandom and treat those who change allegiances to rival teams with the same ostracism familiar to heretics and apostates. "Totemic images are not only reproduced on the walls of houses . . . they are also found on the bodies of men. . . . It is imprinted on their flesh. . . . It is a general rule that the members of each clan try to give themselves the external appearance of the totem. . . . When the totem is a bird, the individuals wear feathers on their heads."[65] Behold, the grandstands at Philadelphia Eagles, St. Louis Cardinals, and Chicago Blackhawks games—replete with drunk weirdoes in bird costumes.

Moreover, the underlying theoretical functionality is similarly uncanny, as one British sociologist finds in his study of soccer hooligans: "This love which the lads feel for their team is simultaneously also love for the feeling of solidarity which they experience every time they attend the game and participate in the communal practice of drinking and singing. Just as Durkheim suggested aboriginal tribes worship their society through the totem, so do the lads reaffirm their relations with other lads through the love of the team. . . . The team and the love invested in it is a symbol of the values and friendships which exist between the lads."[66]

Sports are, in short, a force that gives us meaning.[67] Michael Novak, a philosopher and theologian, makes this case most romantically; the language of sports, he observes, is saturated with religious terms like "sacred, devotion, faith, ritual, immortality, and love"; in its symbolic recreation of a "cosmic struggle" for an uncertain survival and "the hunger for perfection" (and ascetic preparation it demands), sport drives one "in some dark and generic sense 'godward.'"[68] Former Washington Redskins head coach George Allen might well concur; as he once stated: "Winning is living. Every time you win, you're reborn. When you lose, you die a little."[69]

The "godward" arc that Novak invokes suggests that sports can serve as a vehicle for existential elevation in a fashion that faith formerly fulfilled.[70] Nike advertising has, in particular, delivered these "homilies . . . of transcendence" over the years, constructing sport as a "conduit to another level of consciousness" and a "secular salvation or redemption" in an otherwise cynical era.[71] But beyond transcendence, sport also furnishes faith's traditional projections of probity; supplying something clear-cut, an "oasis of stability" that simplifies quandaries of right and wrong amidst the pluralistic ambiguity of a complex, messy world.[72] We imbue our favorite franchises with a kind of "moral superiority" and, in turn, sports discourse informs us "what the sources of evil are [and] . . . who the agent of evil is" and the "means by which" it can be overcome (e.g., beating the Raiders).[73] "I think that people look at athletes and see, like, better versions of themselves," *Sports Illustrated* senior writer Greg Bishop tells me. "They see things that they wanted to be or things they wanted to do."[74]

To sum up, then, sports and religion are, theoretically, "soul mates," as athletes, fans, and believers alike "recite similar liturgies," "divide the world into winners and losers," "require total commitment of body and mind," and are "bathed in myth and sustained by ritual."[75] The ultimate point of those rituals is, once more, togetherness: "the feeling of collective participation and sharing of concerns and powers beyond the potential of the individual human," as sports scholar Michael Real discerned of Super Bowl socialization.[76] And that practice of sports religion actually turns out to be literal for some: More than a quarter of all Americans believe God has some role in determining who wins a game; another quarter have prayed to God to help their team; and more than half think that God rewards athletes of faith with success and health.[77]

Indeed, if religion and sports seem inseparable today, it is because it has always been so. When Pierre de Coubertin, founder of the modern Olympic games, "insisted repeatedly on the religious character" of the competition he had revived, he was, in fact, channeling an ethos evocative of his antediluvian forbearers: "For me, sport is a religion with church, dogma, cult . . . but especially with religious feeling."[78] Far from peculiar, this nexus between sports and religion has been explicit and strong throughout much of human history.[79] From the first day of the ancient Olympics being reserved exclusively for pantheistic ceremony to Native American tribes constructing athletic spaces next to religious temples, the prehistoric world offers no shortage of examples and linkages.[80] (The Redskins' coach

Allen would find ample evidence for his aforementioned analogy of losing as death: Certain players in Aztec and Mayan matches were apparently beheaded and had their hearts cut out upon a sacrificial altar after the game. Talk radio absorbs those impulses nowadays.) Assorted ball games were an essential part of Easter season rituals in medieval Europe and the muscular Christianity movement of the 19th century found Victorians enthusiastically theorizing that "strenuous athleticism, physical dexterity, [and] symmetrical muscularity" was critical to "Christian manliness"—a curious theological equation of physical heath as indicative of moral health and vision of Jesus as bodybuilding messiah (e.g., "Blessed are those who can bench 200").[81]

Rare has been the religion that took a puritanical aversion to sports as secular distraction, though, more recently, some radical Islamist groups have banned soccer and punished enthusiasts for precisely that reason.[82] Much more common has been an unabashed embrace: owners like those of the Colorado Rockies and Orlando Magic aggressively marketing "faith days" to mega-churches; a public prayer preceding the national anthem at Oklahoma City Thunder games; Christian sports books like those of Tony Dungy and Tim Tebow ascending the bestseller lists; the Vatican sponsoring a sports talk radio program in the hopes that soccer might lure wayward Italian Catholics back into the Church; and Pope Francis launching an interdenominational sports conference called, appropriately enough, "Sports at the Service of Humanity."[83] (This, too, came at a commercialized price—the event was subsidized by almost $2 million in sponsorships.[84]) By contrast, running back Arian Foster hesitated to admit his own atheism, for fear of losing endorsement opportunities.[85]

Yet all of this sports-sited fervor is happening while religion, as traditionally conceived, is supposedly dying. That's what the secularization thesis holds, at least: that when societies modernize—as seen

acutely in Western Europe—"religious institutions, actions, and consciousness" dwindle.[86] In America, church membership peaked in the
1950s and an array of participation measures of formal faith ritual
(e.g., Bible studies, Sunday schools) evince a similar decline in the
years since, along with more "surfing" across congregations by potential adherents.[87] The latest Pew statistics find that nearly a quarter of all Americans—some 56 million people—are now religiously
unaffiliated, including a sharp decline in self-professed Christians, as
each generational cohort seems to identify less religiously than its
predecessor.[88] Clearly, religion has, over the course of several centuries, lost its monopoly on cultural life and the public square, no longer so collectively defining reality and forming the basis of identity
as it once did.[89] And, yet, as Durkheim probed more than a century
ago, "If religion provided moral solidarity in the past, and if religion
has been in a continuous state of decline, what will take its place in
the future?"[90]

The answer provided here is sports culture—the definitive "civil"
or "folk" faith of our time that fills the vacuum created by the decline of traditional religion.[91] Given that, on Sundays, almost three-
quarters of Americans are likely to be in church or watching football
(or doing both), even the magazine *Christian Century* conceded
that the NFL had basically become "America's newest indigenous
religion."[92] Moreover, many of the responsibilities that once fell to
formal religion and the church—"an alternative family, a support
system as well as a system of meaning . . . the moral instruction
of children, the ritual differentiation of men and women, the worship . . . of a common divinity . . . and the national and international
experience of collective bonding around that divinity"—now reside,
most conspicuously, within the purview of sport.[93] Which means
that, as critic Steve Almond points out (in his manifesto *Against
Football*, no less), "the only spiritual adhesive strong enough to unite
Americans, a modern temple in which neighbors join together during

Sunday services to slake fierce and ancient longings once served by the Church" might just be sports.[94]

## A CULTURE IN FRAGMENTS

Perhaps a "values vacuum" has been created whereby many people feel alienated, no longer believing deeply in anything, identifying with anyone, or feeling committed to any cause outside the immediate interests of themselves and their significant others. An opening exists, therefore, for enterprising parties to engage in the "consciousness" trade . . . to help supply the meaning and commitment that rapid social change under . . . postmodernity ha[s] evacuated from many lives. But what phenomenon has the emotional force to bind symbolically the fragmenting constituents of society . . . especially where there is abundant critical self-reflection, cynicism and a seeming "exhaustion" of novelty? Not surprisingly, the answer . . . is media sport.[95]

I, of course, concur with sport scholar David Rowe here, but before fully engaging the potential of that prescription, those problems that plague postmodernity might well be further enumerated and elaborated: in particular, the persistent disquiets of alienation, polarization, and fragmentation. As to the first, Americans are accustomed to hearing regular reports of diminishing public trust in all manner of large social institutions: Congress, public schools, corporations, the media, and, in fact, organized religion itself.[96] Simultaneously, sociologist Robert Putnam has charted a wide range of post-1960s measures showing a feeling of communal breakdown across the U.S., including declines in membership in local groups, neighborly trust, and "the sense of shared identity."[97] Indeed, it is revealing that Putnam chose a sports practice—*Bowling Alone*—for his book title as the metaphor with which to index and illustrate civic vitality (or lack thereof).[98] Broadly speaking, community has, over many millennia, gone from a "fixed given," defined by spatial limits to a flexible, voluntary, "deterritorial[ized]" social product, with populations ever more mobile and migratory, either by choice or necessity.[99]

Our politics and culture, it is regularly lamented, also divide us. The notion of America as a polarized electorate is, by now, that rare shared truth that Republicans and Democrats can agree upon in an age of fake news and alternative facts. For the better part of 50 years, there has been a steady rise in partisanship to the point that Pew calls it "the defining feature of early 21st century American politics," as centrists dwindle, networks and neighborhoods ideologically self-sort, and negative opinions of political opponents ossify.[100] Some wonder if these trends relate to the ascendance of "information cocoons"—our increasing capacity to filter out opposing views and contrary representations of reality as news arrives via cable channels, blogs, and other social media.[101] Communication theorist James Carey once beautifully likened reading a newspaper to "attending a mass," in that the specific, ephemeral information distributed through it was far less important than the cultural power of a having a common worldview represented and ratified by it.[102] If true, the slow death of daily newspapers could leave localities bereft of not just an investigative watchdog but equally a communal glue.

And, yet, fragmentation is evident not only in public affairs but equally across popular culture: I speak here of the entertainment cocoons that define our time. Smartphone distractions seclude us *Alone Together* in social settings; the digital delivery and algorithmic targeting of pop content has splintered taste beyond blockbusters, once broadly cast to mass audiences, and into the "long tail" of smaller, niche interests.[103] (Netflix, with its vast and particularistic library, is the quintessential example of this, consuming one-third of all Internet traffic during peak hours.[104]) This explosion of media options available to consumers likely means that cultural sensations seem less "sensational" than they might have a generation ago (in terms of audience size, industry revenues, etc.) and a canon of relatable references and collective memory accumulated through newspaper readership, terrestrial radio hits, and network shows is that much harder to come by.

Spotify carries an infinitely larger variety of artists and sub-genres than the shelves of Sam Goody could ever shoulder and television executives can only reminisce fondly about the late 1970s when, pre-cable, 90 percent of the U.S. population was tuning into just three channels during prime time. Unlike the "enforced similitude" that broadcast TV's ubiquity furnished American culture—and the way it pieced together a coherent mosaic of "national identity," not to mention Baby Boomer collective memory—in today's profusion of choice, flexibility and abundance, the most popular shows like *Big Bang Theory* and *NCIS* are lucky to draw 10 percent of U.S. households, which would have put them at risk of cancellation in the 1980s.[105] Indeed, "the defining trend of media in our lifetime is fragmentation [and] . . . as media content has become ever more individualized and on-demand," writes Michael Mulvihill, senior vice president at Fox Sports, "increasingly, we are each a demographic of one."[106]

Moreover, besides shrinking audiences for fragmented content—the *M\*A\*S\*H* finale, for example, drew 106 million viewers (in fewer TV homes in 1983) as compared to the equivalently esteemed *Mad Men* finale, which drew just 5 million—the bewildering complexity of that content perhaps repels casual consumption and therefore common conversation.[107] Prestige franchises of the last two decades like *Lost*, *The Wire*, and *House of Cards* are far more confusing and time-demanding, narratively speaking, than the episodic or even serialized hits of previous eras.[108] One cannot "simply" drop in on the *Game of Thrones* season finale and appreciate it as a cultural form without significant investment beforehand (and, in my case, a Wikipedia connection and pad of paper to keep notes). Game 7 of the NBA Finals, in terms of comparatively attainable dramatic pleasure, would seem to be considerably less befuddling to those who did not watch the first six.[109] For all of its well-lauded merits, then, the scripted storytelling style of our cable-digital era forecloses easy access and thus looser affiliations as and with other fans. Peak TV is great for art, but less so for widespread social communion. "I think we, in this very fragmented society, need things like that," veteran sportswriter Robert Lipsyte laments in an interview. "If we don't have general magazines, we don't have general popular TV shows, our music fragments us, our sexuality, certainly our politics . . . but not the games themselves—there's something very positive in that."[110]

## WHERE TRIBES STILL AMASS

Supreme Court Chief Justice Earl Warren once remarked, "I always turn to the sports pages first, which records people's accomplishments. The front page has nothing but man's failures."[111] Warren's sentiments echo the religious themes identified earlier—that sport remains a beacon for hope and the scaffolding for such belief in progress. But it also suggests that sport might represent a countervalence to the postmodern theory that, amidst a crisis of cultural relativism and the collapse of former sources of authority, "metanarratives" are now otherwise in decline.[112] These metanarratives, which represent the accumulation of smaller stories articulating a grand, universal, and eternally enduring idea about human experience within particular ideological contexts (e.g., an Absolute Truth that Christianity, Marxism, or scientific objectivity profess and provide), have been increasingly under assault from particularistic incredulity.[113] More recently—and more partisanly—some detect an outright "epistemic breach" in U.S. news culture, whereby massive amounts of Americans embrace a tribal, conspiratorial thinking that rejects "mainstream institutions devoted to gathering and disseminating knowledge (journalism, science, the academy)—the ones society has appointed as referees in matters of factual dispute."[114] As one media scholar observes, "In such a world all the traditional institutions that provided the social cement of modern life—most notably the family, the church, the factory or company, mass media, and the state—are nothing but bargaining chips in our individual negotiations with the forces of change that sweep contemporary life. People cannot simply rely on parents, priests, professionals, or presidents anymore—they have to go out and construct their own narrative."[115]

And, yet, sports remain recalcitrant, mostly, to this narrative of metanarrative decline.[116] No one scoffs at the objectivity of sports page box scores as "fake news"; a game was played and it had an observable outcome we (usually) agree not to disagree about, at the level of empirical verifiability. Broader than that, though, sport remains a vessel for the simulation of enduring faith and truth when other news tends to troll for our cynicism and resignation. Sports are, after all, timeless as a cultural practice: No society in human history has ever existed without them in some form.[117] They are also fairly universal (soccer, especially): perhaps the "only global idiom apart from science"—a language that, because it is encoded in the body, "transcends linguistic" divisions and can be communicable across the widest possible range of nations and cultures "with virtually no dissent, opposition, or challenge."[118] And sport is also embedded *in* our language itself—with as many as 1,700 oft-used metaphors derived from the field of play found in English—framing how the world is seen, not least in the sense that life itself is a kind of "game."[119] The structure of sports are, therefore, an exercise in power that helps define a society's values; they offer "cultural texts" that generate "meta-social commentaries," which this book will attempt to unpack for the contemporary American moment.[120]

Sports' massiveness—in terms of (literally) still aggregating masses amidst those forces of fragmentation—is a considerable part of that power, delivering office water-cooler moments that persist in popular culture and offering the "glue of collective consciousness" that the acid of modern life has otherwise dissolved.[121] One national survey of U.S. fans finds that more than three-quarters believe that sports brings together "people from different walks of life" (and half of fans rely upon sports as "a link between generations" in their families).[122] The NFL, in particular, has self-consciously sought to style itself as "a rare national site of unity, stability, and inclusiveness" from the tumultuous 1960s onward—a "lingua franca by which men of vastly different beliefs and standing could speak to one other"—to the point that one league executive can credibly claim, "We're really in the business of aggregating America around events and around our game. There are fewer and fewer places where you can do that [and] if you can . . . you are going to be more and more valuable."[123]

Quite simply, the most people in the history of humankind to share the same experience, at the same time, are audiences for recent international sporting events.[124] Over the course of two weeks in 2012, more than 150 million tweets were exchanged about the London Games; two years later, 90 percent of Dutch households watched Holland's World Cup semifinal and some 30 million Chinese viewers awoke at 3 a.m. to catch the final match.[125] Domestically, 88 percent of Americans call themselves sports fans (with 68 percent saying that being a fan of their favorite team is a "very" or "somewhat" important part of their lives) and, even for those who aren't, sports media remains "an inescapable reality, forming part of the context of every American's life."[126]

A review of the demographic profile of American sports fans shows that, despite this ubiquity, they are also disproportionately likely to be male, black, and have played sports as a youth.[127] Unsurprisingly, research from both here and the United Kingdom has found that parents and families are critical for nurturing sports participation as a "normal part" of daily life.[128] Similarly, studies have shown over several decades that peers and friends, families, and fathers, in particular, tend to be some of the key influences that socialize a person into fandom—a finding that holds true, globally, from Canada to Australia to Greece.[129] In an important book on the psychology of sports fans, Daniel Wann and colleagues found that the most common motivations and pleasures for spectators included: pure entertainment value; excitement and arousal; the chance to spend time with others; the self-esteem boost furnished; the grace and beauty of athletic movement; the diversion from daily life; and the utility for family gatherings.[130] When it comes to particular favorite teams, Wann concludes that, of dozens of possible reasons, fans' allegiances stem primarily from a fundamental psychological desire for "belonging and affiliation" and "to feel part of distinctive groups."[131]

Clearly, as discussed earlier, the antitrust exemption that sports leagues wield to maintain their cartel power is a key factor in staving off the cultural fragmentation that has so splintered other pop culture industries asunder. Yet there is also something uniquely deep, tribal, and even existential in sport's capacity to unify—an anti-"centrifugal" force against other dimensions of identity that divide, "transport[ing] fans and players alike into another realm of consciousness."[132] On one hand, it epitomizes what political historian Benedict Anderson has called "imagined community," in that believing in a shared identity is more important than actually knowing all the members of that group conjured.[133] But sometimes the ineffable materializes and gooses the believer with chills; ESPN *Outside the Lines* reporter Kelly Naqi evocatively conjures this sentiment in (unknowingly) Durkheimian terms:

When the Red Sox finally won the World Series [in 2004] and I was living in New York City and I still probably walked out the next day with my Red Sox cap and Red Sox shirt. I saw—more than any other time in my life in New York City—a ton of people with Red Sox stuff on. It was, like, you're proud to be one of them, like, "You're one of me. I'm one of you." You give each other that nod, like, "Yeah, we won." Even though, we—I—had nothing to do with this team except that I have poured hours of my life into watching them and listening to them on the radio. . . . There is this connection and there is this escapism: We're all in it together.[134]

Naqi invokes here a curious, though not at all unusual, pattern to sports fandom: that merging of personal identity with team identity. Like war, sport's power is unique in its ability to generate an explicit identification with those on the "battlefield."[135] When fans talk about their favorite team, language belies logic—that "we" community of followers (united really only as consumers of a copyrighted cultural product) becomes one and the same, "inseparably intertwined," with the professionals at play.[136]

Players certainly spin this yarn in post-game interviews (e.g., "We feed off [the crowd's] energy. They feed off us."); franchises sell it explicitly in commodified form (as elaborated further in chapter 3); and philosophers rhapsodize about its sonic essence (e.g., "cheering 'transform[s] individuality into communion'").[137] In short, they're called Manchester *United*—not Manchester *Atomized*—for a reason. And, yet, even amidst all these pieties of devotion, we are still just as often fair-weather wimps at heart: Some years back, social psychologists reported the landmark, albeit obvious, finding that fans wear team merchandise and use "we" more after victory than defeat, because a sports team's success enhances one's own public self-image and sense of worth.[138] (More interestingly, subsequent studies have found that, after watching our favorite team win, we tend to overestimate our *own* ability to tackle challenging physical, mental, and social tasks.[139])

According to one scholar, sport teaches us to think in those tribal terms that bifurcate a black-and-white world of good versus evil; it teaches us that "the tribe is the paramount unit of social order, the enemy is other neighboring tribes; they cheat and thus are less than human."[140] That mentality colors fans' perceptions and capacity to grasp objective reality. One classic example of this is an experiment from the 1950s that showed students at Princeton and Dartmouth the exact same game between the two schools, with Princeton students identifying more fouls committed by Dartmouth players and vice versa.[141] Perhaps these tribal loyalties run deep because, historically, the sports club was a key factor in the "structure of feeling" among blue-collar communities—an origin story of civic pride.[142] Or perhaps the human being is a "rooted beast," needing to express, outwardly, that "rooting" through sports, especially when the enduring American ideal and historical experience of geographic mobility is constantly "uprooting" her, anonymously westward and from city to city; the team totem therefore enchants us with the prospect of permanence, even as all else that is solid seems to melt into thin air.[143]

So perhaps it is that—the most basic of human dreads, mortality—which drives us into the arms of sports community. This might well explain my grandfather's hat still resting on my aunt's fireplace mantle. In one intriguing experiment, researchers found that, when prompted to think about death, fans expressed even greater hope and faith that their teams would win it all, suggesting that we are driven to associate with institutions and cultural groups that live on to help cope with the persistent, anxiety-inducing finitude of our own existence.[144] In that sense, it doesn't really matter whether our teams win or lose on the field; as long as the totem survives, so do we.[145] Our fidelity to it stitches us not just across space, but equally binds us in time, as former ESPN reporter Bonnie Bernstein explains:

> One of the things that's sacred in sports to me is the family bonding that sports creates and extends from generation to generation. My parents were raised differently than my grandparents were raised. . . . We're going to raise our kids differently than we were raised, but I think one of the common threads is sports. It brings us all together,

it provides a platform for family members—to share stories of their memories when they were watching those teams. It provides rich, historical context that can be shared among everybody in a family. And that's the one thing that I love.[146]

## THE SACRED POWER OF LIVE

Above all, sport tells us what time it is. Its temporal quality is essential to its cultural power: the ability to anchor participants (players and fans alike) in the present moment; to concentrate a vast, shared psychic energy on events unfolding before us *right now*. It orients observers; synchronizes schedules; coordinates collectivity. "Most of the time, we are time travelers—we are either worried about the future or worried about the past. But how many times are we actually in 'the now'?" asks John Rowady, president of rEvolution, a sports marketing and media agency. "Sports . . . is 'appointment now.' You just are naturally drawn to 'the now' and you exist there for a while. . . . It's really hard to get into 'the now' such a complex world. . . . [And] it's lucrative to be in 'the now.'"[147]

Indeed, "the now" is incredibly powerful and valuable, both economically and culturally. Attendance (either in person or through mediated means) at "the now" is especially lucrative for advertisers—making it a marketable commodity—and never more so than in a DVR-time-shifted era (more on this in chapter 2).[148] But "the now" is also existentially critical for living through asynchronous postmodernity, when people seek mindfulness, individually, and co-presence, socially, against the onslaught of distraction, multitasking, and disjuncture of time and space.

An increasing truism of contemporary pop culture (and an oft-heard sales pitch from providers of it) is that you can watch whatever, wherever, *whenever* you want; but with sports, you can't—and that's a good thing. It resists being on demand, temporally at least, and instead demands our "collective co-presen[ce]" at specifically sched-uled intersections with it and each other.[149] Waxing poetic on that experience of sports' "sacred time," the philosopher Novak writes, "At moments of high intensity, there seems to be no past, no future. One experiences a complete immersion in the present, absorption in an instantaneous and abundant now."[150] This is deeply Zen; it also makes mad bank. Cultures (and advertisers) *need* this complete and utter absorption in that present mind-state that psychologists term "flow." "I think that's one of the reasons I love sports," writes then–*Grantland* staffer Brian Phillips. "Suddenly, there's two seconds left in the fourth quarter and the Hail Mary is diving toward the end zone, and for that little stretch, the world is pure event."[151]

Few cultural practices can achieve the wonder of "pure event" and communal immediacy on such a grand scale—the feeling that, as the scroll of history unfurls, almost everyone, momentarily, seems to be on the same page. Sport can do so, because it is, at its core, unreal. Cultural historian Johan Huizinga makes this argument in his influ-ential theory of play: that play is defined by the freedom to engage in it (i.e., being superfluous, it can be postponed and resumed at will); that play occupies an "interlude" from daily life and takes place in a special, temporary world carved out from ordinary reality; and that play "creates order," by proffering clear, tidy, black-and-white con-clusions whose definitude often evades us otherwise in an ambiguous moral universe.[152] After all, the main, and perhaps only, distinction between the sports fan and non-fan is that the former buys into the (utterly irrational, frankly ridiculous) illusion that it actually *matters* who wins the game.[153] Because of that, paradoxically, sport is both totally useless and extraordinarily valuable as a cultural good. "It allows you to feel real emotional investment in something that has no actual, real-world consequences," writes *New York* editor Adam Sternbergh. "You will feel actual joy or actual pain . . . in relation to events that really don't affect your life at all."[154]

Historically (and relevant to the thrust of this particular chapter), religion has been the "primary vehicle for human forms of play," as both religion and play alike have aims on ecstatically transcending everyday existence—those mundane mental states and atomistic social structures that divide and depress us.[155] The sports page and sports broadcasts on television arguably create a reassuring regularity and consistency in society against the backdrop of distressing news and current affairs: The world may seem to be on fire and full of uncertainty, but the games go on, just as they always have.[156] Big games like the Super Bowl offer especially "sacred" markers that protrude from the "'profane monopoly' of secular time," providing a "needed psychic relief from the tedium of western linear time."[157] Against that momentum of "traditionless modernity," sports "satisfy the most persistent hungers of the human heart—for repetition."[158] Baseball, in particular—in the words of former commissioner Bart Giamatti—"keeps time fat and slow and lazy."[159] (This, as we'll see later, has become sports' problem, as well.) What matters, religiously, is that the ritual participants are gathered here, together, in "the now."

That description (and prescription) was essential to sociologists' Daniel Dayan and Elihu Katz's notion of "media events"—those special, large-scale occasions when modern societies feel united through the mass broadcast of "preplanned history."[160] For Dayan and Katz, TV was the answer to Durkheim's century-old concern about the loss of "social solidarity."[161] Such has been the thrilling power and potential of broadcasting since its debut, demonstrated when 300 million radio listeners around the world tuned into the 1936 Olympic Games.[162] These media events fix eyes on a "ceremonial center," commanding simultaneous and universal attention and legitimating the myth that "there is a centre to the social world and that, in some sense, the media speaks 'for' that centre."[163]

Most importantly, these media events are live—guaranteeing "a potential connection to our shared social realities as they are happening."[164] In other words, if content is foregrounded as live, it implies that something is real, authentic, and true, countering any inherent suspicion of mediated illusions—that the tableau has been merely arranged for the camera's eye.[165] The specter of performance-enhancing drugs might have tainted the purity of fans' faith in athletic accomplishment but—in an age of spin and pseudo-events—performance amidst uncertain outcomes still makes sports the original "reality TV" genre.[166] As Chris Dufresne, college sports columnist for *the Los Angeles Times*, summarizes: "What makes covering sports, watching sports, different and bankable—what you cannot ever change about what we do is that it's the last unscripted event: You don't know how it's going to end. That's what makes it better and time and time again, it always comes through—the last second, the Hail Mary, the home run. When you don't know how something's going to end—you can't market that, you can't create that in a lab. . . . People will tune in to see how and they don't know—that's the elixir. That's what makes it different."[167]

## GETTING INSIDE THE SPECTACLE

In a way, though, *The Power of Sports* is precisely that: a book about the creation, representation, and marketing of that "elixir." It is a production-side study and analysis of the cultural and political implications of mediated sports based upon in-depth interviews with journalists, broadcasters, advertisers, and businesspeople. Such a project like this has not been undertaken especially frequently.[168] Much as there is a bias among news folk against sports journalism as a dismissible "toy department," some find similar "disciplinary discrimination" among scholars and, when sports media has gotten academia's attention, it has been more from social scientists' quantitative instruments than the humanistic approach undertaken here.[169] Moreover, there has been, within that approach, a textual emphasis in studying the subject relative to an industrial focus, perhaps in keeping with the overall inclination in media studies: Texts are easy to find; producers harder to track down. Yet as sports scholar Lawrence Wenner advises, "We need to look under the hood of mediated sports more carefully. Critical studies of production context and reporting, and marketing, sponsorship, and promotion in their socioeconomic context, need far greater attention. . . . In the future, we will need to prioritize getting access to sport organizations and media organizations as they fashion their sport-centered product."[170] This is a modest attempt to look under that hood.

As some of the primary "definers" and "propagat[ors]" of sports ideology and culture, journalists and broadcasters will obviously play a prominent role in such an analysis and various scholars have noted the need for more work on the sports newsroom, and the professional norms and occupational pressures found there, as I pursue.[171] Yet it is not just scribes and anchors that construct the spectacle that is contemporary sport; business interests and marketers, too, play a critical and interdependent role in buffing up its shiny packaging. Here, too, the extant scholarship suggests that, despite being "an important site for the analysis of power relations, cultural politics, and cultural representation," the production of sports advertising and sponsorship have been somewhat overlooked.[172] The book will thus critically investigate the influence of advertising and PR on the sports landscape, particularly in chapter 3—looking at the "roles and viewpoints of the cultural gatekeepers involved in the decision-making processes of creating these marketing strategies" (similar to my first book, *Your Ad Here*) and how they imagine and interpellate the market segments targeted.[173] Finally, *The Power of Sports* seeks to add to our knowledge of how digital media transformations are impacting professionals in the business (see chapter 2, especially) and how "taken-for-granted" "institutional structures" within sports production might reproduce gender disparities (the focus of chapter 4).[174]

To be certain, production and consumption of media texts are always and ever intertwined, as the creator (e.g., journalist, advertiser) has in mind certain assumptions about the receiver (e.g., audience, fan) and vice versa.[175] But, historically, the former has gotten shorter shrift, as one study of the *Sports Illustrated* swimsuit issue concludes: "Producers' intentions and practices . . . do influence the ideological power of the media. The way producers shape the content and structure of media texts does influence consumer interpretations."[176] In the case of, say, pro football, where its mythic qualities are not inherent but rather consciously "crafted," those "values and associations seem natural and enduring precisely because of this careful planning."[177] Hegemony, in short, "requires hard work."[178] This is a study of that hard work, through the eyes of the professionals who contribute to it, and the forms of cultural, political, and gender hegemony achieved because of it.[179]

To that end, sports are, in many ways, the least interesting thing about sports. Rather, what makes sports compelling is what they can tell us about *non*-sports contexts and issues—and I'll be scrutinizing that fraught and complicated intersection of sports, media, and politics (acutely in chapter 5).[180] Following sport scholar Garry Whannel, I believe that "the big questions of our time are not about sport, but the questions about sport should concern how it relates to those big questions."[181] Just as anthropologist Clifford Geertz sought to access larger cultural meanings in Bali from the cockfight he observed—and others have used, say, Michael Jordan as a window into the "broader social, economic, political, and technological concerns" of his era— I'll be trying to tack back to that same big picture throughout these pages.[182] I am particularly indebted to David Rowe's *Sport, Culture, and the Media* as a precedent-setting template for this project, hoping to similarly focus on and analyze these "wider social transformations and trends," and the reader of footnotes will notice the (already) extensive use of it.[183]

For in and of itself, the game is, of course, totally meaningless; but, ironically, it is *because* of its meaninglessness that it can serve such an important function for meaning-making. *Because* of the cultural fragmentation and political polarization that otherwise alienates postmodern lives, sport is more important than ever as a site of social debate and intellectual exploration. By looking at sports, we can see and critique issues and trends far from the field of play, relating to religion, journalism, digitalization, commerce, celebrity, feminism, masculinity, violence, labor, inequality, militarism, activism, and, of course, identity and community. This is sports' not-so-hidden power. And as is probably already evident from this opening chapter, the approach will be equal parts romantic celebration and scathing critique; those looking for either, exclusively, will be by turns gratified and disappointed. But I could make sense of sport no other way than engaging it through this complicated, contradictory ambivalence.

Rowe concludes, "As seasons have extended and competitions proliferated in deference to the media hunger for sport—and to sport's appetite for media money—the prospect of creating a media sports culture complex that defies the constraints of time and space—just as the first factory owners began to do in the eighteenth century—approaches closer."[184] In thinking about ways (and through whom) I might try to get "inside" that factory, it quickly became apparent that a very wide range of interlocking stakeholders were involved: "Jockeying for strategic position and power, media companies, sports organizations, clubs, player agents, athletes, and increasingly active audiences are all engaged in an intense struggle for the material and cultural possession of sport."[185] Besides players and fans, I reached out to members from just about all of the aforementioned categories. (The former seemed comparatively inaccessible and, frankly, inadequate to meta-level conversations about the representation of their labor; the latter has been—and will continue to be—studied aplenty by other scholars.)

Following closely the approach that Rowe and his co-author, Brett Hutchins, employed for *Sport beyond Television*, this work is based upon in-depth interviews with dozens of industry professionals and I echo their justification and treatment here: "Rather than treating industry actors as if they possess the keys to unlock the mysteries of media sport development, we regard them as having to negotiate uncertain circumstances over which they strive to give the appearance of control. Most crucially, this method supplies difficult-to-find background information and analysis that rarely appears in news and technology media sources, and enables discussion of emerging issues that require consideration. . . . Such engagement provides valuable insight into the motivations, thinking, and decisions helping to structure the media sport industries, as well as the sources of tension and disagreement in different parts of the sector."[186]

One of the main reasons that media studies scholars often opt for textual analysis or audience-side reception is that accessing the producers of that content is, well, plainly difficult.[187] An "uneasy relation" and "degree of mutual suspicion" has long characterized the regard for scholarly critics among media professionals (and perhaps justifiably so, as suspicion is built into the critic's lens; heaven knows, I ask for advance forgiveness from my interviewees if any of the ensuing analysis offends).[188] And even when we do gain access, interviewees can be "guarded" or defensive and it can be difficult for them to articulate that which seems like common sense, such as the "rules and conventions of production."[189] All of these challenges proved true along the way for this project as well. (Interviewees' tongue-tied-ness was especially apparent when conversations turned to hegemonic masculinity, an article of almost universal faith among critical scholars, but one that proved baffling to process and discuss among those regularly reproducing the representations that uphold it).

In terms of access, my efforts would be considered respectable as batting average, though wince-worthy as free throw percentage: I reached out, almost exclusively by e-mail and through online sites, to 174 potential contacts (i.e., people and organizations) and ultimately secured 57 interviews for 42 hours of semi-structured conversation.[190] Because, as noted prior, the sports spectacle is created by such a wide range of parties, I talked to writers and editors, anchors and producers, marketers and clients, and teams and agents, trying to sample a variety of perspectives on their professional experiences vis-à-vis the subjects to be discussed here. Some were new to the business; others retiring soon; some were deeply rooted at a local level; others had a national profile (though I did tilt slightly toward Boston-based media, given access to and familiarity with my regional market).

This was not a "representative" sample, in any quantitative, social science sense of the word, but I did try to canvas widely across media formats and positions about common themes, trends, and threads rather than exclusively zero in on just, say, newspaper columnists, sideline reporters, advertising creative directors, or player representatives (to name a few of the sub-categories one will find among my sample). I did not limit myself deliberately to mainstream American sports (e.g., baseball, football, and basketball), though the parochial nature of my sports knowledge inevitably gravitated toward those fields of play (knowledge that is itself a product of bias in the content produced for fans); moreover, many other scholars from beyond the U.S. have covered their respective territories far better than I could ever hope.[191]

Therefore, I will make a number of claims about sports media and culture that are circumscribed specifically to the American context but may well have thematic overlaps to situations abroad. (And the slippery, fast-moving nature of this subject made currency an ongoing challenge; interviews were conducted in 2015 and 2016 and the manuscript was being finalized for copy editing in spring 2018, but I fully expected many details might well change swifter than academic publication cycles allow. By the time you read this, dramatic events—particularly with Trump, the NFL, and the anthem—will surely have intervened.) Given the traditional white male-ness of the sports media, I did consciously "oversample" women and persons of color, so as to enrich insight for chapters 4 and 5, particularly. Although varying widely (and *semi*-structured, at best), the interviews were largely guided by questions about media- and commercial-induced change in interviewees' work and how broader contemporary issues intersected with it (e.g., politics, gender).

Finally, before setting out, one last, brief note on style. A few years back, one influential scholar, reflecting on the "poverty of discussion in the public domain" about sports, implored colleagues to "engage with wider audiences both within and beyond academia."[192] That certainly is the humble ambition here. Readers will find a book steeped in academic references and scholarly research, if they choose to go digging in the extensively footnoted sources, but I've tried to borrow a more journalistic, readable (and, admittedly quote-heavy) vernacular so as to avoid inhibiting access with intrusive esoterica. Whether or not that shot drops, you'll have to be the ref.

One of the things they tell you when you start at ESPN is to think of it as "infotainment."
—**Linda Cohn**,
*SportsCenter* anchor

# POWER PLAY

## The Transformations in Sports Journalism

I don't think our audience really wants the facts. They want their opinions validated. In that respect, it's good for my business, because I am in the opinion business, but as a journalist, there's part of me that grits my teeth a little bit, because it's so different than how I was trained to be.
—**Jemele Hill**,
then–*SportsCenter* anchor

FROM ITS EARLIEST DAYS,

# AMERICAN SPORTS JOURNALISM

has been defined by complicated allegiances.[1] In the 19th century, the printing press helped transform sport from local folk culture, which had been mostly amateur and participatory, to mass spectacle more professionalized and spectator-driven.[2] By the time *The New York Journal* established sports as a recurring newspaper section in the 1890s, and standalone magazines like *The Sporting News* debuted, a national passion was thriving.[3] The nature of that love affair—steeped in the totemic experience theorized in chapter 1—would both benefit and inhibit its potential as a journalistic form.

By the 1920s, sports coverage was deemed "indispensable" to growing readership, driving a quarter of all newsstand purchases.[4] Broadcasting's arrival only hastened the forces of economic collusion. By luring American audiences with baseball and college football games, sports became the bait for selling radio sets; the same held true with television in the 1950s and, more recently, high-definition upgrades.[5] "Sport was helping to make television and television was helping to make sport," declared Mark McCormack, founder of the powerful sports management agency IMG.[6] In the

1970s, as the number of sports programming hours doubled, TV networks began to envision themselves as "copromoters" of the events alongside their league partners.[7] And thanks to corporate deregulation and satellite expansion, sports talk radio boomed, with advertisers covetous of the lucrative (read: white male) listenership.[8]

The advent of ESPN in 1979 solidified the ubiquitous sports media landscape we take for granted today: a 24-hour, singularly focused cable channel that would beget multiple TV networks, radio affiliates, film series, and even theme restaurants.[9] As then-CEO Steve Bornstein framed the ambition, "[ESPN] had to be a way of life for people, with as many angles into their lives as possible. I wanted ESPN to replace the word 'sport' in the dictionary. And the only way to do this was to be everywhere."[10] By and large, having made good on that aim, as ESPN goes, so goes the world of American sports journalism. Moreover, the history of contemporary sports also traces a broader tale of media distribution and economics, for so many technological breakthroughs—across cable, satellite, the internet, and social media—have been partly borne of fan demand for sports content.[11]

This chapter examines the symbiotic intersection of sports and journalism against the backdrop of some fundamental questions about power: the power of technology, money, and organizations to influence the norms and practices of media professionals. It begins by chronicling the business arrangements and inherent structural biases embedded in content that aims (and often fails) to satisfy both journalistic necessities and entertainment ambitions. It then situates the effects of digital convergence on sports production within the now-limitless information environment: how to accommodate the maelstrom of participatory, outsider voices; how to keep pace with the viral speed of social media news cycles; and how to strategize spreadable, multiplatform (i.e., click-bait) output. The chapter concludes by illuminating both the "hot-take industrial complex" that has overrun sports with cost-cutting, opinion-oriented imperatives and the full dis-intermediation of independent journalism heralded by those new media venues and ventures.

## OF SYMBIOSIS, SYNERGY, AND SYCOPHANTS

In the early years of this co-dependency, journalism helped "legitimate" sport as a wholesome cultural tradition, especially against the backdrop of prevailing puritanical suspicion.[12] Better still, few other for-profit industries enjoyed as much free publicity, as the press furnished leagues with a regular means of communicating with customers.[13] That coverage ignited interest which begat more coverage: a virtuous cycle (from the perspective of sports stakeholders) cultivating among audiences "a sense of caring, of attachment to major-league sports and athletes and even to corporate brand names," as sports media scholar Mark Lowes discerns. "Without this emotion generated by the media, the sports business would collapse."[14] Succinctly put, sports journalism helps *make* fans—and makes those who sell to them fabulously wealthy.

In exchange, the media reaped its own bounty. Starting in the 1970s, when the networks had long weekend programming slots to fill, and in the years since with cable offshoots, sport has lent itself as a ready resource for vast content needs.[15] Compared to other scripted television options, the cost of putting on all that content is relatively cheap, in terms of dollars outlaid to hours assured (not counting, of course, the increasingly astronomical rights fees), and the leagues provide a predictable infrastructure to deliver and report on it.[16] Money-wise, sports media, unlike the games themselves, was not a zero-sum game: For a long time, everybody won. Garry Howard, then–senior editor of the *Milwaukee Journal Sentinel*, diagrams the transactional nature of this dependency as he experienced it: "When the Green Bay Packers . . . won the Super Bowl in 1996, went back to the Super Bowl in 1997, we had record profits, record revenue at the [paper]. We sent over 25 people to the Super Bowl. . . . We had a separate section that ran . . . every single day for a week, filled with ads. We were able to monetize that at that time, because we had all the information."[17]

He is, of course, speaking from a different, albeit not-too-distant media ecology of journalism—pre-internet, pre-Craigslist—when newspapers were more flush from advertising and still retained local information monopolies within analogue parameters. Advertisers, it should be noted, literally afford the size and scope of the news hole along with helping determine what content gets pushed into it, in the sense of being biased toward sports that attract (mostly male) attentiveness.[18] "If a team advertises big time in our paper, we'll cover them more. . . . It's a hand-feeding-my-hand kind of thing. That will happen. Not if it's a major team—we'll cover them anyways," explains Filip Bondy, a columnist for *The New York Daily News*. "But if it's a question of the NYCFC or the Red Bulls or the New York Liberty or more marginal teams or even the Brooklyn Nets or the New York Islanders—those are the teams that, if they advertise in our paper, we will cover them more."[19] That commercial imperative to aggregate large, valuable audiences also explains sports journalism's limited field of view when it comes to amateur play, which doesn't add up so profitably (and therefore doesn't get column inches or broadcast hours assigned to it); rather, economic logic serves the promotional necessities of mainstream, professional, major-league providers first and foremost.[20] If, say, a National Field Archery Association meet falls in the forest, it doesn't make a (mediated) sound. This is probably well obvious to sports fans, but it nonetheless raises questions about the media's incentives, impartiality, and inclinations toward what—and who—is covered and therefore valued.

Front and center in this enduring quandary of journalistic allegiances is ESPN, befitting its documented designs on ubiquity. It has long tried to maintain a problematic, perhaps irreconcilable, balance of covering the same content that it shells out billions to be able to broadcast.[21] On one hand, shows like *SportsCenter*—ostensibly a news program and thought by some to be "the gold standard in television sports journalism"—are also synergistic promotional vehicles to hype upcoming games (the rights to which are often owned by ESPN and its corporate cousins).[22] On the other hand, when controversy crops up, the network's business obligations theoretically run contrary to any adversarial aspiration to dig up dirt.[23] For this reason, an anonymous insider at the company acknowledges, "ESPN serves two masters—entertainment and journalism, information—and depending on the day, we're probably only serving one of those. We can't be purely journalistic because we have too many business interests with the subject we're supposed to cover objectively."[24]

Nowhere has this conflict of interest been more problematic than in the company's dealings with the NFL. Probably most infamous was ESPN's initial role in—and subsequent withdrawal from, at the apparent behest of league leadership—the *Frontline* "League of Denial" documentary that investigated the concussion crisis.[25] Because many assumed the decision to drop out just might have been motivated by the $2 billion annual deal ESPN holds for *Monday Night Football* rights, "League of Denial" reporter Mark Fainaru-Wada lamented, "It was not a good time for anyone who believed in journalism at ESPN."[26] Yet this was not the only instance of treating the NFL with kid gloves. The network earlier pulled *Playmakers*, its scandalous, semi-fictionalized portrait of league life, upon then-commissioner Paul Tagliabue personally phoning its parent CEO at Disney. As one ESPN executive said in response, "We're not in the business of antagonizing our partners. . . . To bring [*Playmakers*] back would be rubbing it in our partner's face."[27] Journalism, however, *should* be in the business of antagonism—and "afflicting the comfortable" means targeting an institution that has its sights set on $25 billion in revenues.

The flip side of this apparent "pay-for-play" arrangement is the conspicuous absence of attention accorded to non-rights partners—notably, the NHL, which is exiled in the midst of a 10-year-relationship with NBC. ESPN openly admits that it devotes less airtime to hockey than it lavishes on the other major American sports, based upon "fan engagement and research."[28] Such a defense ignores the fact that, given its size and ubiquity, ESPN can, more or less, create its own gravitational pull and *set*—as much as merely *reflect*—the sports agenda. If it doesn't talk hockey, "the nation doesn't talk about hockey either."[29] More likely, business objectives trump any claims to "objective" audience accommodation, as *SportsCenter* anchor (and unabashed hockey enthusiast) Linda Cohn candidly explains: "That's NBC and it's their product. So, ESPN, they say to themselves, 'Well, why should we push this product for them to go watch NBC? Why should we tell these stories?'"[30] (NBC's sports network has made the exact opposite calculation, focusing heavily on NHL and English Premier League coverage and ignoring baseball and basketball; as its chairman, Mark Lazarus, drily remarks, "We knew what rights we had and we based a strategy around them."[31])

To be clear, these critiques of conflict of interest are hardly novel and the network's response seems to have become, in turn, pro forma. Toeing an official line that "policies and procedures" are in place to assure the separate operation of newsgathering and rights ownership, ESPN executive John Wildhack adds that they're "direct" with leagues in communicating that they take "very, very seriously" both "business arrangement[s]" and the obligation to be "thorough, professional, and comprehensive."[32] Another ESPN leader name checks the old "church and state" philosophical ideal within journalism—citing the literal partition on the Bristol campus where rights negotiations are housed apparently separately from reporting personnel.[33]

Others, however, have acknowledged the impossibility of achieving that critical autonomy. ESPN founder Bill Rasmussen muses,

only slightly hyperbolically, "Of course, we pay [leagues] 220 billion dollars, why wouldn't we fawn over them?"[34] More biting is
long-time *New York Times* columnist Robert Lipsyte, who likened
his 18-month tenure as ESPN ombudsman to being "a piano player
in a whorehouse" and found this conflict "embedded in ESPN's
DNA"—from "routine 'self-censorship'" to "the fact [that] everyone
internalizes [business considerations], and factors it in."[35] Jemele Hill,
website columnist and former *SportsCenter* anchor, articulates that
internalization:

> I think you realize that what you say will bang with a much louder
> drum because of where you are. . . . If I criticized Roger Goodell
> while I was with the [*Orlando*] *Sentinel*, [he] may never see the col-
> umn. If I do it at ESPN, it's going to come across his desk. That's
> something that you have to keep in mind. . . . You also do have to
> understand that, because there are business ties, not [just] with the
> NFL, but with a lot of places.[36]

Hill's former co-host Michael Smith, who cut his teeth at the
*Boston Globe*, has also acknowledged that "[Jemele and I] joke that
we used to be journalists. . . . It's been a long time since I've been a
journalist. . . . I'm an entertainer. The E in ESPN stands for entertainment."[37] To be charitable, it's probably unfair to single out ESPN
as somehow unique within sports journalism in terms of its fidelity
to digging (or lack thereof) and its show business sensibility; rather,
ESPN is emblematic of those patterns in evidence across many other
media venues. For example, Hill notes that, during her tenure at the
*Sentinel*, the Orlando Magic heavily advertised and that "in a one-
pro-sports town, a team like the Magic has leverage . . . As a newspaper, you've got to get along with that organization . . . I don't think
the reporting was ever compromised, but it was something that was
definitely in the back of everyone's mind."[38] Newspapers are, thus,

not immune to the influence of business-side benefactors, though U.S. television probably represents a more susceptible medium when it comes to compromised content.

Take the Greg Hardy scandal, for instance—the Dallas Cowboys defensive end who brutally assaulted an ex-girlfriend, earning him a 10-game suspension from the NFL, though only the website *Deadspin* obtained and ran the police photos.[39] Nicole Holder's ghastly, battered body—like Ray Rice's knocked-out fiancée—somehow threatened a multibillion-dollar league's image. And yet: "You will not see on any network, on any broadcast, a really in-depth discussion of Greg Hardy . . . because we're partners with [the NFL]," CBS sportscaster Lesley Visser admits. "The game is kind of sacrosanct. . . . CBS is not non-profit. When they put the game on, they get enormous ratings. They charge great advertising rates. And they don't spend seven minutes discussing Greg Hardy."[40]

Similarly, discussing his ABC affiliate's *Patriots All Access* exclusive interview show, sports anchor Mike Lynch notes, "Subconsciously, somewhere in your brain, you think twice, three, or four times before being critical of a team. I think it handicaps you—no question."[41] Regional sports networks within the U.S. (specifically those that have local rights deals with franchises) seem to be especially prone to such conundrums and calculations. There is, of course, a very long tradition of "homer" announcing—that is, shameless sycophancy in presenting the product—stretching back to baseball radiocasts of the 1930s.[42] But this reframes professional norms away from any semblance of objective ideals. Here's how Sarah Kustok, the Brooklyn Nets reporter for the YES Network, describes that mentality and posture:

It's less digging for stories. You obviously always have to keep things in mind of how the teams want a story put out, turning things into a positive spin. You need to be kind of watchful of how exactly you

frame stories. . . . For me, I feel like it's still, in some ways, [like] being part of the team. . . . At times, it's challenging. . . . Making sure
you stay in accord with what is expected out of you, in terms of
working for the team, but also that you're being as unbiased or fair
as possible, and still covering a story, and staying true to your journalistic responsibility.[43]

This is, plainly, not an easy balance and her ambivalence here tes-
tifies to the weight of conflicting impulses for someone put in the
awkward position of journalist-cum-spokeswoman. I heard much
the same from another sideline reporter, Tina Cervasio, who has covered the crosstown Knicks for the MSG Network: "Sometimes you
do run into [from bosses], 'That was too negative. We need to find
the positive.' It may be a postgame question or story you want to do:
'Well, we can't do that story—it really focuses on where the short-
comings are. Find another story.' You do run into that."[44]

Cervasio had worked in a similar capacity for NESN, covering the Boston Red Sox, and it's worth digressing into some detail
about the operations there from Russ Kenn, the man who coordinated production of game broadcasts for nearly a decade. Although
he acknowledges that his crew didn't "really consider ourselves
journalists"—a Sox broadcast is, rather, "somewhat of a public service" in his estimation—their uninhibited access nevertheless produced problems every so often: "We would see things on the plane or
something, over their shoulder, and we would be privy to things that
other people in the media would not be and so there was a sort of,
you know, a resistance to share any information we obtained outside
of the normal ways of getting information."[45]

This protocol extended to game editing, as well: Both the unusual
(say, a fight between players that their cameras caught in the dugout)
and the routine (Manny Ramirez not hustling groundouts or John
Lackey rolling his eyes at teammates' errors) would draw reprimand

from the team if NESN ran the unflattering footage. Kenn therefore struggled with the dilemma of representing the team accurately (even if in a poor light), but over time, settled on a code of norms that ran roughly like this: If an incident or action was visible from fans' seats in the ballpark, it was fair game to relay on TV (and, thus, clubhouse or plane fodder was deemed off-limits to disclose). The flip side of this cozy arrangement? "I think some players and a couple of managers used NESN as a platform, as a sort of safe haven in some ways, where they could get their message, you know, unfiltered, knowing that we would run pretty much the whole interview or the whole entire sound bite as compared to [other media]."

For all of these reasons and examples, American sports journalism has long labored under the stigma of being the "toy department" of the newsroom.[46] Fundamentally, the task of the sports journalist is in inextricable collusion with those running the business of sports: She helps manufacture "the illusion" that the game result actually matters.[47] Beneath that abstract mandate, though, there are a variety of ways in which the practice of sports reporting seems to further exempt itself from codes of objectivity and has been, as veteran scribe Frank Deford once lamented, "traditionally held to less rigorous professional and editorial standards" than those expected of other journalistic genres.[48] For instance, beat writers, admits one pro football beat writer, sometimes have a hard time covering certain sensitive stories and need a columnist—or even investigative reporter summoned from outside the sports desk—to "parachute" in and tackle a tough subject.[49] "You feel somewhat freer," concurs Kevin Blackistone, *Washington Post* columnist, of that non-beat role. "You feel less beholden to the team of athletes you may be covering."[50]

This is, of course, a source-reporter problem common across the news landscape, but it seems exacerbated when covering the fields of play, given the paucity of sources making the news in a given night. The persistence of "cowering, deflated, non-question" interview softballs—especially those lobbed by broadcast reporters performing stenography at post-game news conferences—probably doesn't aid the profession's cause (e.g., the clichéd query framed as "Talk about X" or "How big was Y?").[51] But, most of all, that absence of an "investigative sports journalism" tradition might be attributed to sport's inherent and seductive escapist sheen and the ensuing institutional instinct, perhaps, to not take too seriously, by way of resources, that which is ultimately just a game.[52] It is sport's dual function in staging that diversion (and building community, too) that seems to excuse it from the practice of journalistic scrutiny; "real" news must, somehow, go somewhere else in the paper or broadcast, as the scholar Lowes critiques: "The sports section exists apart from real news as a fantasy world, one of pleasure and escape from everyday life, and it shouldn't be sullied with reportage critical of the major-league sports industry. . . . Were journalists to challenge this state of affairs they wouldn't be fulfilling their role as head cheerleaders for the major-league sports business. Remember, it is their job to 'keep the dream alive'—to construct an imaginary 'us' around major-league sports."[53]

Another relevant factor might be the teeming ranks of former athletes turned media members telling those quasi-journalistic tales. Bill Rasmussen, ESPN founder, recalls from the early days of the network there being a "gee whiz," awestruck reverence when they first solicited an NFL veteran to the set in Bristol.[54] That deference has continued in the years since. Once installed as experts on broadcast panels, these retired jocks deliver "athlete-friendly platitudes," reliably devoid of any detachment or distance; indeed, it is their (beholden) insider credentials that get them seats on the set in the first place.[55] One might call this the "Mike Golic-ization" of American sports journalism. And the cultural narrative about sports—both through their ephemeral commentary and the accumulated wisdom and taken-for-granted norms of that coverage—is thus ventriloquized through these ex-players; it has the grizzled authority of having lived through the subject. (Interestingly, a case might be made that political journalism—on TV, at least—has been similarly co-opted, with former consultants and partisan insiders now populating debate panels and taking up time that was once devoted to more "straight" news reporting.) Lipsyte gleaned the potential peril of this during his time as ombudsman: "They're never going to point at any kind of systemic abuse—they're part of the industry. . . . At ESPN, what you tended often to see was the intimidating factor of these big handsome jocks looking at the real sportscaster, the professional sportscaster . . . and imply on air, and then telling them off air—this has come up—'Hey, what the fuck do you know? You never played the game.'"[56]

Would it be any surprise, then, if media personnel, endowed with a less jock-ish build and résumé, felt bullied into deference if not outright adoration? Stuart Scott, the late *SportsCenter* anchor, reportedly embraced linebacker Ray Lewis as he was under fire during Super Bowl media day questioning about murder allegations, and scoffed of the probing journalists: "Hey, Ray, fuck them, man."[57] (Lewis would dodge the rap and later land a seat, beside Scott, on ESPN's *Monday Night Football* team.) Quarterback Peyton Manning received a standing ovation from the CBS Sports production team during a meeting before his final Super Bowl appearance and, given Manning's promotional savvy and commercial ubiquity, no doubt has his pick of plum media jobs in retirement.[58]

"There's been a certain blueprint established for a lot of opinion shows in having former athletes," explains Jemele Hill. "The majority of them—they don't have much to say. A lot of them don't want to tick off their buddies they used to play with. Some of them are angling for jobs still in their respective professional leagues."[59] Coaches are even more susceptible to this "revolving door," as ESPN's talent head put it: "This is halfway house for coaches. We build up relationships and we have better access when they go back to coaching."[60]

(And the revolving door swings both ways: Sports PR offices are often populated by ex-journalists who can exploit their network of contacts, well-honed "news sense," and "media logic" to manipulate the needs of former colleagues.[61])

This pattern is not limited to those past their playing days. Two of ESPN's more infamous lapses of recent judgment came at the hands of then-current stars. LeBron James was given license to choose his interviewer for and pocket the advertising revenue gained from his "The Decision" free agency infomercial (ESPN's second-highest-rated program that year); the network's *Bonds on Bonds* series similarly offered the eponymous baseball slugger "final approval" of content.[62] It's hard to imagine CBS or CNN tendering similarly generous conditions to a government leader or business executive—or, at least, it should be.

"There's a form of hagiography that goes into being a sports journalist—there's an expectation of heroism that is built into the narrative, as we present it," says Gary Hoenig, former editorial director of *ESPN The Magazine*. "There's a sort of air blowing into who these people are. It's what we fill the time with when they're not playing."[63] That template typically reaches its sappy apotheosis during Olympic coverage when, in an effort to introduce and create (bankable) attachment to otherwise unknown athletes in unmarketable sports, NBC ratchets up the sentimental puffery to tearjerker heights.[64] But even working the daily grind, the apparent default setting for a sports reporter is to chase down "an inspirational story," rather than casting the scene in more banal terms.[65]

All of these patterns of professional practice can be discerned because sports—particularly televised American sports—are situated at the uncertain intersection of journalistic objectivity, entertainment spectacle, and dramatic storytelling.[66] Should one be soberly realistic, as might be expected of a hard news print reporter, or theatrically inflated, as befitting a show business performer?[67]

Historically, when entertainment indulgences have run up against journalistic temperance, in the "hierarchy of [professional] values," the former has routed the latter—which, I would argue, is driven overwhelmingly by the lucrative nature of sport as a represented commodity-subject within the news and, as fans, our desire for totemic communion in the experience of consuming it.[68] Sports (i.e., players, teams, and leagues) and media providers don't really *want* objectivity, it seems.[69]

This makes for a paradoxical and challenging *self*-conception on the part of individual journalists—ambivalent, as one veteran wrote in his memoir, whether they are called to be "reporters, critics, analysts, investigators, fabulists, moralists, comics, or shills for the games that make us possible."[70] Moreover, despite the veneer of glamor, there can be a surprising amount of disgust felt (not least from the subjects being covered). As *Deadspin* founder Will Leitch explains, "The job itself is very demoralizing—you just go and sit and talk to people that are younger than you, better looking than you, make more money than you, and think you're a pain in their ass and stupid and all you're trying to do is mess up their lives."[71] And, he adds, "You do it while they're naked in front of you."

Back at the newsroom, the "toy department" derision hangs in the air, where some editors view sports as a "necessary evil"—that is, among the most widely read sections but held in less esteem than other, more noble beats.[72] "The sports department didn't have very much respect as far as journalism was concerned," Garry Howard discovered when he started at the *Trenton Times*. But by the late 1980s, he recalls, "Sports was starting to be the kind of place where you could not only make a great living, but at the same time, you could also make a great profit for your paper."[73]

Perhaps no one knows this better than the last media mogul himself, Rupert Murdoch, "the single most important player in the entire sports business," who has famously deployed sport as a (self-described) "battering ram" for other properties in his imperial expansion of News Corp; Murdoch maintains a tradition of focusing intently on the sports department whenever he takes over a newspaper, seeing it as critical to boosting circulation and luring advertising revenue.[74] Most curiously, upon taking the helm at *The Wall Street Journal*—an institution with a tradition of in-depth excellence and glancing (at best) athletic coverage—he reportedly gave the newsroom two brief marching orders: "Shorter stories, more sport."[75] Thus, the devil's bargain that animates sports journalism: It is profitable and popular enough to invite synergy and even self-censorship across a variety of institutions and organizations—making it a blessing and a curse, simultaneously.

## MANAGING ACCESS AND AUTONOMY

By the turn of the 21st century, then, one critic had concluded that American sports journalism and advertising were fast becoming indistinguishable.[76] Then, as now, a huge part of the problem revolves around issues of access and autonomy for those who cover players, teams, and leagues. Among my interviewees, there was an almost universal sentiment that direct access for reporting had gotten more difficult, even as those they are reporting on are far more "accessible" to the public through social and owned media channels. Beat writers are being squeezed by agents, sponsors, and organizations, who wield ever greater leverage over the athlete sources they need to supply the content.[77]

Much of this is no doubt due to the sheer number of flacks working crosswise to objective ends (personnel additions that can be afforded given the revenues pouring in). Overall, the U.S. Department of Labor now reports almost five PR professionals for every one journalist still in the news business.[78] Print scribe Kevin Blackistone estimates that, specifically within sports, that imbalance has escalated "threefold" over the course of his three-decade-long career.[79] This buffer is driven, above all, by the imperative to "preserve a corporate-friendly image," NPR's *Only a Game* host Bill Littlefield complains.[80] Absent longstanding relationships, it becomes harder and harder to get the access necessary to do a story—and it is *because* of those insider relationships that the content that does get produced often precludes critical autonomy.[81]

"[Organizations are] limiting that kind of time that we get to spend with the athletes and giving it to their own people—or not even to anybody—and, yeah, the product suffers," acknowledges Fluto Shinzawa, the *Boston Globe*'s Bruins beat writer. "They have more influence on the outcome—absolutely."[82] There is a distancing and formalization of contact with player sources; simultaneously, PR personnel have routinized a steady flow of inoffensive information to subsidize the otherwise handicapped work of sports journalists.[83] NFL teams, for instance, maintain a fairly regimented in-season weekly schedule for when coaches, coordinators, and quarterbacks are allowed to take the podium and face the press: "There was a time when I could go down and sit in a coach's office and conduct an interview with them—that's all gone," notes one veteran anchor. "The teams have taken over the how and where interviews will be conducted."[84]

This management strategy seems to be a notable reversal of power, protocol, and orientation relative to an earlier era when one ethnographer found teams and leagues bending over backward "to make it *easier* for reporters to do their job" in the hopes of winning more promotional ink than competitors in the sports section.[85] According to Yahoo! Sports NBA writer Marc Spears, franchises have also, over the years, sold off advantageous courtside seating that had previously been reserved for media personnel, thus taking them out of earshot (and adding new ticket revenue to the coffers); he also describes the increasing presence of North Korea–style "minders" who sidle up alongside to listen in during postgame interviews: "They're just so paranoid. . . . It's almost like, 'Ok, we can't censor you, but we're going to make you uncomfortable and make the player uncomfortable, too, so you don't [get] anything [he] shouldn't say.'"[86]

In Oklahoma City, the sports media reports a very deliberate effort by officials with the NBA's Thunder to create a culture where "no one has a personal relationship with any of these guys," including, in one instance, star Kevin Durant being pulled away, literally, before he could show off a new tattoo to a reporter in the midst of some casual chit-chat.[87] Enforcement of such restrictions was not always so fraught. Kelly Naqi, who joined ESPN in the 1980s, reminisces about visiting locker rooms in the aftermath of Magic Johnson's HIV announcement, "And I would ask players, 'Has Magic's announcement affected how you approach—how you have relations with women?' [They] could answer that [back then]. That's, like, an insane question to ask someone post-game now—that PR person would call the head of ESPN to complain."[88]

Again, because of the limited number of sources a sports journalist can rely upon (there are relatively few positions on the field of play compared to other beats and still fewer stars among those), the fear of "ostracism" remains especially acute.[89] "They don't need us as much as they used to," concedes *New York Daily News* columnist Filip Bondy.[90] As recourse, sports journalists find that an inordinate amount of time is spent buttering up agents to get player access—"selling [them] on why this is a good idea for [their clients]," explains *Sports Illustrated* senior writer Greg Bishop. "A team would never put a player in front of me for an hour. . . . They would monitor me as much as possible and that's just kind of my day-to-day dance."[91] His colleague Michael Rosenberg echoes these sentiments, reminiscing: "I think in 1978, you just called and said '*Sports Illustrated* is coming to town' and they rolled out the red carpet for you. . . . Now, it's like, look, these guys can do something for an hour and get 50 grand for it. . . . I've got to convince them why they should talk to me instead of either doing that or talking to the 49ers website that they . . . air whatever [the player says]."[92]

As an investigative reporter might say: Follow the money. Sport *can* bully journalism because the former is still lucrative and represents a revered cultural authority; the latter seems less and less so with each passing year and opinion poll that finds low public regard for the "fake news" that is (allegedly) the American media. In turn, this exacerbates the distinction between "insiders" and "outsiders" that seems to be another defining feature of sports journalism today. ESPN often peddles itself, rhetorically, as having insider authority—selling, for example, exclusive premium content on its website under that exact header wording—and the NFL openly acknowledges, "Since ESPN helps pay the NFL's bills, they get better access."[93] Team network reporters like Sarah Kustok of YES find that access is even easier than when she was at ESPN: "Because [players] do know and understand that your angles, at the end of the day, is keeping the team in mind. . . . They feel like they might have a little bit more control with you than they do with other journalists. . . . [Their] mindset [is] that you're more part of the team than part of the media."[94] To maintain that access, some journalists might downplay a particular story or issue and not "tick somebody off" in the hopes that, "when it comes time for a big interview, the agent or the player will go to you, because you gave them the break on something else."[95] Thus, insider access has become, in the aftermath of industry-wide digital and economic disruption, the last advantage of the legacy journalist, as *Boston Globe* beat writer Fluto Shinzawa explains:

> I know there [are] thousands of people who can probably write better than me and probably know hockey better than me. They have the technology to put out whatever kind of writing or video

or whatever. . . . So, I have to take advantage of what I have: the access. The person at home who is more knowledgeable about these things—they can't go up to the athlete or the coach or the GM and ask them questions that they want to ask. . . . I have to take advantage of that every time and every opportunity that I get. . . . This is perhaps driving our readership.[96]

In turn, a revolution of sorts among outsider sports journalists arose—those that are "free to take shots" because they're "not afraid of being banned from the press box," as ESPN's ombudsman observes.[97] Perhaps no institution is more representative of that technology and tone than *Deadspin*—a website that announces, in its masthead tagline, that coverage is "without access, favor, or discretion." Fittingly, given its trademark irreverence, *Deadspin* was founded by Will Leitch in response to the lack of media attention given to a (pre-dogfighting) lawsuit accusing Michael Vick—quarterback demigod of Nike commercials and *Sports Illustrated* cover stories—of intentionally spreading a venereal disease (and coining one of the sleaziest nom-de-clinics of all time, "Ron Mexico").[98] "There's no way ESPN is going to touch that story with a ten-foot pole," an insider divulged to Leitch, who suspected promotional collusion at play.[99] He expands on this in an interview:

> I could do [*Deadspin*] without going in a press box. That allowed me to write uncomfortable things, because these guys and women in the press box every day, they face these people every day. It's going to be hard for the Atlanta Falcons beat reporter to say, "Hey, Michael Vick, tell us about your herpes testing." He's going to get yelled at by the PR person. . . . It's just like with any other job, when you're doing it day to day, you can't help but identify with the people you see every day at your job, even if you should theoretically have an adversarial relationship.[100]

To be certain, that motto ("without access, favor, or discretion") is a bit of a "self-serving idea," as former *Deadspin* editor-in-chief Tommy Craggs acknowledges, since the site could never dream of having the resources to cover sports like the mainstream news organizations it so frequently skewers.[101] But there is clearly truth in Craggs's contention that "access is compromising and having relationships with powerful sources who have vested interest in certain stories being covered in a certain way is a hugely compromising arrangement and that is the nature of being a mainstream beat reporter of any kind."

Against the backdrop of that hagiographic sports media deference, *Deadspin* scored assorted scoops over the years like Manti Te'o's dead girlfriend hoax, Brett Favre's sexting photos, and Greg Hardy's police records, breaking scandals that other, more compromised (or "tasteful") outlets either missed or avoided.[102] Similarly disruptive and influential, TMZ has laid low domestic abuser Ray Rice, serial philanderer Tiger Woods, and unreconstructed racist Donald Sterling; like Leitch, managing editor Harvey Levin saw "an opening for coverage by an outsider, free of potential conflicts of interest"—which is perhaps possible since TMZ's parent company, Time Warner, has fewer major rights entanglements with leagues it sought to disrupt.[103]

The notion that new technologies and online platforms offer opportunities to contest official, mass media-endorsed narratives is, of course, not unique to sports journalism as a storyline of institutional liberation in the 21st century.[104] Bloggers across the spectrum of content often derive their authority from precisely that *absence* of establishment credentials.[105] Their "amateur" status is what helps corroborate their authenticity as content creators in this space: appearing artless in maintaining an independence from any corporate affiliation that might suggest selling out and pulling punches.[106] "I like the distance of not having a press pass, because it allows for me to be critical . . . and allowed for a real opinion rather than getting to know these guys," says Tas Melas, who co-founded a popular pro basketball podcast that eventually got picked up as a TV show for the NBA network (though he emphasized that, early on, *not* getting paid for that work enabled their freewheeling style and secured their credibility).[107] And even though he has now gained that insider access, he prefers not to host players regularly on set, believing it might dull his edge: "I would start liking these people and I think it would be difficult to separate jobs from friendships."

Beyond these ideals of adversarial independence, outsider sports media also tend to adhere to a more casual, partisan, and irreverent tone that contrasts the formal, neutral, and self-serious pretense of traditional journalistic coverage. *Deadspin*'s Leitch quite consciously sought to bridge that gap between how fans "actually talked about sports" versus how they were typically written about and broadcast to them: a less "phony" or "stodgy" ethos, as Melas similarly describes for his own podcasts.[108] Melas attributes this more relaxed style to the "DIY" aesthetic endemic to the podcasting and blogging world: "We look different—we don't have chiseled jaws and we're not in a three-piece suit." They are often not jocks, much less rich; indeed, they tend to look more like *fans*.

Probably no figure is more singularly responsible for that evolution than Bill Simmons—online columnist turned ESPN (and, later, HBO) mini-mogul. Simmons's "nonprofessional status" and "intentionally undisciplined, biased, and interactive" approach was well suited for the texture and tone of the internet's "immediacy and informality."[109] Defying journalistic norms, Simmons demonstrated, earliest and perhaps still most definitively, that "fans do not need conventional journalists"—inspiring a generation that followed, including Melas himself, who cites Simmons's "fan-centric perspective" as influencing his work.[110]

As Marshall McLuhan might posit, the medium is, to some extent, the message here: Unlike other areas of news coverage, sports content is largely contained within the contests themselves, visible to (and, therefore, contestable by) all; a beat writer who sits through a season's worth of games is, theoretically, no more capable of or qualified to represent and relay that content to other fans than a blogger at home.[111] (Especially when that beat writer has been banished to the rafters—literally and figuratively—in terms of PR forces foreclosing access.) Some even suggest that youthful totemic allegiance might represent a new crucible of credibility, just as (grown-up) insider access once upheld authority: "For your branding," says one 30-year newspaper veteran, "you establish yourself as an expert on Team X because you rooted for team X when you were eight years old."[112] In other words, you can trust Simmons because he's loved the Sox his whole life, not because he's been trained to cover them objectively or even has the means to do so.

As might be expected, the reaction to this generation of digital rebels from the mainstream sports establishment has been, at times, frosty. "It's one thing if somebody sets up a blog from their mother's basement in Albuquerque . . . and they're a pathetic get-a-life loser, but now that pathetic get-a-life loser can piggyback onto someone who actually has some level of professional accountability," veteran NBC sportscaster Bob Costas ranted at one point. "It's just a high-tech place for idiots to do what they used to do on bar stools."[113] In an interview, Costas further elaborates: "A large percentage of what passes for the sports media today consists of people who have no interest in actually having access. They'd rather sit at home and write something off the top of their heads," he says, more or less echoing *Deadspin*'s mandate. "And people, who because they have no access or because they don't have to show up, they don't really have to be accountable, either."[114]

In discussions with sports reporters at more "legitimate" news organizations, *Deadspin*, TMZ, and the like were sometimes specifically scorned for being able to pay for information, which was beyond the scope of others' journalistic ethics (though, one might quibble, payment in the form of media rights' deals secures that routine access for some of those same reporters in the first place).[115] Yet when teams usurp greater power over the public representation of their images, the need for—and authority found in—those insider interlocutors in the mainstream press fades; these punkish outsider digerati are, as such, equally a response to the collusion and control that PR forces have achieved. And the technological context for these dynamics deserves more direct examination.

## WHAT DIGITALIZATION HATH WROUGHT

It's the ultimate reality television—I know people always say that, but the difference is, with reality television, it's contrived, it's scripted, or it's sort of playing to the cameras. Whereas in sports, you get that incredible, authentic, real moment as it's happening. . . . You're in the moment, just overwhelmed with suspense—waiting to see what happens next. And I guess you can pause your remote and go get a sandwich or whatever you want to do, but nobody's going to do that, like they would with a regular show. . . . And that's the one thing that sports—live sports—is always going to have as an advantage over television shows: That it's happening now . . . and nobody wrote the outcome ahead of time.[116]

In chapter 1, I identified an enduring—literally "timeless"—power that sports afford: a culture of synchronicity and contemporaneity amidst the countervailing forces of fragmentation and disjuncture. But that live-ness ought to be recontextualized, given the massive technological changes and media economics reshaping American sport. That "power of now" was recognized at ESPN very early on and built into their production routine; they pioneered the "whip-around theory" of live look-ins, whereby a highlights show would ideally cut into as many big games as possible and "never let a close game end without our cameras being on live," according to network founder Bill Rasmussen. At that time in the early 1980s, when box-score knowledge of the previous night's events didn't arrive until the next morning (and two days later for West Coast games), "It was a base of creating a sense of urgency . . . All of a sudden, we were giving people this live information and it became more and more urgent for them."[117] Fast-forward four decades and you find ESPN president John Skipper declare, with staccato fervor: "We believe in live. We believe in live. We just think at this point with technology and people's expectations and the ability to get instant information, we believe in live."[118]

There is, thus, an apparently widespread belief within the media industry (one that leagues are, of course, happy to sell) that live sports rights—particularly for the NFL—can make or break a network. Fox is thought to have taken off only when they made a splashy bid for an early 1990s contract; CBS's "entire schedule kind of cratered" when they lost it a few years later; and, as *SportsBusiness Journal* media reporter John Ourand puts it, "The NFL deal is really what built up ESPN to the monster that it is today."[119] Indeed, broadcaster Chris Berman echoed that getting *Sunday Night Football* rights was the second "biggest thing" to happen to the network—topped only by ESPN getting on the air in the first place.[120] "When we got the NFL," *Outside the Lines*' Kelly Naqi recalls, "it was like, all of a sudden, ESPN was legitimized as a sports network."[121] Globally, sports rights exclusivity has probably powered the pay-TV model more than any other programming genre, enabling "deep-pocketed, vertically-integrated" media conglomerates to lure upscale audiences into their subscription package fold.[122]

Yet what might have been impressive about live sports in earlier decades has become essential and perhaps even unsurpassed as an attractive content feature nowadays. One cannot overstate just how much my interviewees stressed its importance in our time-shifting, on-demand age. It is a widely shared article of faith that live sport is, as *Ad Age* called it, "one of the last DVR-proof offerings on TV, an arena where 'mass market,' 'reach' and 30-second spots still mean something"—all of which has pushed sport to the forefront of advertising strategy.[123]

By one recent count, 99.4 percent of sporting events are consumed live.[124] This comes at a time when more than half of TV watching is now delayed, either through DVR or video-streaming subscriptions (a figure that rises to almost three-quarters among millennial audiences).[125] That makes sport not just the "last bastion of live viewing" and subsequent "social currency," in ESPN executive John Wildhack's view; it is also thought (hopefully, at least) to represent a "bulwark" against cable cord-cutters who can find online, legally or illegally, most of the content they desire otherwise.[126] Live is such an enticing and valuable production facet that it is being exported and exploited in even non-game domains. The NFL, knowing this quality is "television catnip," pushed its college draft to prime-time hours and CBS now similarly hypes and packages its "Selection Sunday" suspense at the start of the NCAA men's basketball tournament.[127] "I am constantly amazed at how much interest people have [in this]," marvels network executive Sean McManus. "There is no athletic competition, but there is great interest in what a group of men sitting in a hotel room decide."

For media companies, therefore, "[Sport is] the one place they think they can keep themselves going by owning these rights—they need a place where that's safe," admits a former ESPN leader.[128] Moreover, ESPN views the captive audiences for its live events as critical to carry forward momentum into its other studio and news shows—even those that do not immediately follow the telecast, but can nonetheless be synergized, horizontally, down the line. "You hope that that [game] audience can recycle into the morning when we're talking about it during our talk show," explains Dan Stanczyk, associate producer for ESPN Radio. "If we have a game on radio or we have a game on TV, we're hoping that they're promoting our talk show the next morning. That's where you get your new audiences."[129]

For years, the NFL was the primary beneficiary of these economic forces: As the linear TV audience shrank overall, its still-dominant product within those narrower confines became that much more valuable.[130] By contrast, over the first five years of this decade, advertiser commitments to scripted fare and reality TV declined by some $700 million.[131] Brad Brown, former vice president for marketing at Anheuser-Busch (a non-niche product if there ever was one), says that sports gradually became "one-stop shopping" for his whole brand: "It allows for about as efficient a buy from an advertising perspective, still to this day."[132] In that sense, sports content might be theorized as the last throwback to an earlier mass media era, as Terry Lefton of *SportsBusiness Journal* summarizes by way of AMC analogy: "My whole wrap on this is that Don Draper is alive and well in the world of sports. . . . We do all these things that people used to do and look back on fondly: We aggregate big audiences; we produce expensive commercials; put them on in expensive time slots. Very few other things on any kind of TV—particularly linear—can do that. We are Don Draper."[133]

That said, while contemporary sport still preserves many of the cultural and economic capacities that have long held true of television's power—namely, mass audiences watching live—it is equally clear that digitalization is dramatically reformatting the institutions that represent it (thanks to a "series of unceasing convulsions," as *Sports Illustrated* put it).[134] In *Sport beyond Television*, an analysis of how those new media technologies are reshaping the delivery and experience of contemporary sports culture, Brett Hutchins and David Rowe liken the past decade to the 1950s, another "birth of a new media sport order," when TV began to dominate the landscape.[135]

Although digital platforms represent a serious threat to the hegemony of TV-driven distribution, it is not yet a mortal threat; just as radio didn't die out (but instead adapted and accommodated a competitor medium's rise), so, too, can we assume that a comparable adjustment might unfold today. But until that's resolved, the old order is deeply unnerved. "[Media] consumption has changed so quickly, it's scary," admits the president of one of New York's regional sports networks. "Scary because we're heading into the unknown, but exciting because we're building something new and transforming into something that's not exclusively a linear TV business."[136]

Above all, two primary interconnected patterns—adjectives, really—seem to have imprinted themselves on that digital media landscape, from the vantage point of professionals trying to cope with its rhythms: *more* and *faster*. This is felt particularly by sports journalists who operate within a competitive, speedy, multidimensional environment that demands constant "content and comment" from them.[137] In today's media boiler room, there is no off switch. The accelerated interplay of sources, platforms, and audiences has restructured how reporters go about gathering and disseminating sports news.[138] Simultaneously, as journalistic institutions like the daily (printed) newspaper wane, sport is being viewed across the media industries as a supposedly "killer app" that can draw consumers into conglomerate revenue streams and secure that most prized and evasive of commodities nowadays: human attention.[139] But how are journalists, media companies, marketers, and others involved in the business of sports strategizing that time-shifted, co-created, multi-screened relationship—and what are the professionals supposed to do *with* all these noisy amateurs now making their voices heard?

This is a riddle that is, of course, at the heart of not just sports but all American media industries in the 21st century—journalism, advertising, entertainment—and how it gets answered will go a long way toward determining the survival of the corporations that produce that content. When Gary Hoenig launched *ESPN The Magazine*, for example, in the late 1990s—a decade before "Web 2.0" became a fleeting buzzword for the potential power of user-generated content—the imperative to adapt was already top of mind: "I wanted a magazine that recognized that the news—as something a magazine could publish—was becoming irrelevant. That to try to be a 'news magazine' in the context of the emergence of digital media was silly."[140]

For sports media professionals, perhaps the foremost complaint—or advantage, depending on one's perspective—regards the sheer volume of content that is now available and can (and should) be navigated. What had been a broadcast ecology of information scarcity has given way to a landscape of "digital plentitude," radically transforming the "content economy" of mediated sports.[141] In Europe—certainly more so than within the United States—free live sport via public broadcasting had long been the norm; the advent of subscription-based cable, satellite, and digital delivery there and elsewhere has proliferated platforms, along with economic impediments to universal access.[142]

Reflecting on his more than 40 years in the business, player agent Leigh Steinberg identifies this trend as the most significant factor accelerating sports' evolution: "The explosion of networks driven by cable and satellite television meant that all of a sudden there were 300 and, now, more networks fighting for the same space that was once occupied by three major networks. What it did to sports is exponentially more games telecast, exponentially more highlight shows, analysis shows, commentary, features—by 50-fold of what existed before."[143] Similarly, when asked what factor was most decisive in the NBA's fate during his three-decade-long watch, former commissioner David Stern identifies the proliferation of media platforms that enabled the league to grow from the tape-delayed finals games of his early years to instantaneous ubiquity.[144]

For players, too, this variety of new channels has been advantageous in terms of building their "brands"; one agent, David Cornwell, gave the example of a female professional soccer player that he represents who would rarely score minutes on a traditional broadcast network, but could now pursue niche (e.g., cable and digital) contexts for profile-raising, promotional purposes.[145] Cornwell adds, however, that this is a double-edged sword: "In the old days, you didn't have sufficient outlets to broadcast the image of your client and now . . . there's too many to control."

In turn, the effects of that plentitude on both media professionals and institutional strategies might be tallied kaleidoscopically through the various anecdotes shared with me during interviews: From different corners, we see the NESN coordinating producer demanding more and more of Red Sox players' time for pre-game promos; the radio talk show host finding his program's agenda routinely being hijacked by the relentless churn of the "Twitterverse"; the newspaper columnist that no longer has to actually, physically, leave the office to do reporting now that press conferences can be streamed directly to his desktop; the sidebar, on-screen "run down" teasing upcoming segments during *SportsCenter*, in a desperate bid to retain eyeballs amidst abundant alternatives; and a network affiliate anchor trying to cover Tom Brady—who goes months without talking to the media—by "monitoring [his] Facebook page every day. . . . A picture of him dressed up like a dragon taking his kids out on Halloween? Boom—that makes it on the air."[146]

More content to produce; more content to keep track of. This seems to be the widespread refrain—a cyclically, cynically exhausting escalation of input and output. And it is that entire participatory scrum—with athletes and fans equally taking part on social media—that journalists and media companies are tasked with (and seem bedeviled by) brokering. Just a half-decade after blogging was born as a medium, one could already choose from more than 350,000 sports-related incarnations for content.[147] A mere 2 percent of linear television content is sports-related, yet sports represent, by one count, some 60 percent of the conversation on Twitter.[148] Thus, in 2016, Facebook rolled out its "Sports Stadium" platform to try to harness the 650 million users that it claims identify as fans—and "harnessing" is precisely the most apt verb to articulate media company ambitions in the social space.[149] That which appears uncontrollable might just be co-opt-able; for all the talk of the "democratic" upshot of new media, viewed from another perspective (admittedly, more top-down), it can also be seen as a whole lot of free labor going around.[150]

This is partly because the conditions of digital plentitude bespeak a "voracious appetite for media content and an imperative that this content be cheap," as sports scholar Garry Whannel diagnoses.[151] *Bleacher Report*, a digital media subsidiary of Time Warner and a top-10 website in its category for traffic, offers an instructive example. It hosts local, user-generated content at sub-sites focused on fans' favorite teams and sports worldwide. Yet as revealed by one aspiring writer there (who was "rewarded" with $200 for 500 articles that pinged 3 million page views), its CEO sees sportswriting going through the same industrial pangs that convulsed pop music just a few years prior: from powerful gatekeepers and tight distribution (i.e., of the newspaper era, where fans had nowhere else to go for hot takes, save for a few stray columnists per city) to the blog and social media model where content becomes "more nameless and faceless in the sense that people are interested in reading good content and they're caring less and less about where that content comes from."[152]

That free labor invitation and ideal more or less embodies a range of sports media tactics and institutions. From ESPN's executive suite, interactivity is viewed as a way to forge "a deeper and closer connection" with the brand and its network talent.[153] Fan content is, further, conceptualized and exploited as a "real time focus group"—a way to gauge and react to audience buzz as it unfolds around the "digital water cooler."[154] Sources ranging from the Big Ten Network to CSN–New England report that production strategy has been profoundly upended by the opportunity to solicit and integrate that second-screen input through polls, tweets, comments, and the like.[155] Individually, sideline reporters are now explicitly encouraged by bosses to engage their social media following through Q-and-A give-and-take (and, in the inevitable event of asinine feedback, "whether you agree [with them] or not: [to say] 'ooh, that's an interesting point'").[156]

The effectiveness of this kind of fluid programming strategy—in terms of popularity, to say nothing of subjective "quality"—remains an open question and ongoing experiment, even for practitioners employing it: "It's fine and everybody loves to see their tweets on TV and it generates social media interaction, but you wonder when you're watching it, is this interesting?" ponders Spike Eskin, program director and co-host at WIP Philadelphia. He instructs his radio personnel to therefore very quickly summarize only the best incoming online comments and, when filling in on the graveyard shift, he'd use the commercial breaks to beg those responding on Twitter to actually *call* into the show: "They would be talking about what I was talking about on the air and part of me would be like, 'Come on here, man—it's midnight. There's nobody on the phone—could you please call?'"[157] As player agent David Cornwell summarizes of these conditions and imperatives: "One thing the [media] beast has to be done is be fed. It has to be fed content. It used to have to be fed content every twenty-four hours, now it needs content every twenty-four seconds."[158]

Indeed, for journalists, there is a broad agreement that the pace of their work has accelerated and they attributed that primarily to the influence of social media, specifically Twitter, which has to be frantically monitored: "It also forces you to be wary of anything and

everything that could happen at any time and sort of that obligation to go ahead and constantly be checking or to be wary of, 'Are
we going to find this out tonight?' 'When is this going to break?'"[159]
Social media has, moreover, revolutionized temporal routines: from
nightly highlights or the morning paper as the slower-paced, deci-
sively spaced checkpoints for breaking news to a constant, unpre-
dictable immediacy that gatekeepers can no longer reliably gate-keep.
"There used to be a rhythm to the day and to your schedule and to
your workflow," recalls Fluto Shinzawa, *the Boston Globe's* Bruins
beat writer. "Doesn't exist anymore."[160]

Sociologist Eric Klinenberg terms this phenomenon the "news cyclone" (playfully riffing off the "news cycle" concept of old): that
"erratic" and "unending" swirl driven by newer media competitors
that have "eliminated temporal borders in the news day, creating an
informational environment in which there is always breaking news
to produce."[161] Over half a century, we have seen a tremendous—
now almost instantaneous—compression of time from content captured to audience dissemination, consistently thwarting mechanisms
of journalistic (and subject) control.[162] Viral stories and images circulate with "exponentially greater speed and scope" given the networked culture that so defines our age.[163] (Some have even suggested
that "internet time," broadly construed, might be faster than "normal
human time," owing to Moore's Law, the hypothesis that computing
capacity doubles with regularity.[164])

From the vantage point of sports media professionals, the information abundance of today's communication environment simultaneously drives an acceleration of content through it. "News cyclone"
thus better represents the temporal framework within which to situate and think about their practices—the notion of a "cycle," after all,
implies predictable recurrence, which is not what journalists today
say they experience. Rather, their routines have been upended in non-
linear ways, befitting the violent and uncontrollable nature that the

word "cyclone" better implies. That temporal experience thus reflects the difference between information work in a mass communication environment and information work in today's new media ecology—a structural shift from predictable, parceled-out (top-down) dimensions to constant, relentless fluidity that seems to come at you from all angles. One eminent sociologist calls this experience "'timeless time,' whereby networked digital technologies create a random sequencing of social actions and events."[165] Metanarratives are that much harder to grasp—much less hold onto—amidst such information fragmentation, disorder, and speed.

Again "channeling" McLuhan, the medium itself bears some responsibility for the messaging here. Unlike a morning newspaper or prime-time network TV show, online sports content has no comparative restrictions on time or space; it can exist in potentially boundless form, digitally unshackled from former parameters like column inches and segment length. You can just keep scrolling through content, theoretically forever. The Web, as such, does not replicate the expectation of consistently allotted deadlines and limits of analog cultural production that had ossified over the course of a century. Moreover, as greater numbers of participants in sports communication have entered this space, relative to a generation ago, competitive pressure accelerates to post installments constantly.

And another weather-related term—"vortextuality"—captures the "whirlpool-like process wherein it becomes impossible for the media to talk about anything else, but some 'super-major events' or celebrities, that come to dominate headlines" for days or weeks at a time.[166] These scandals are welcomed, to some degree, as they become "grist for the media mill," which is ever hungry for content, and keep the cultural economy of sport humming along.[167] Fans' camera phones play a not-insignificant role here, making narrative control "infinitely more difficult" for player agents.[168] "Johnny Manziel—20 years ago—would have been able to hide," says David Canter, who represents other NFL players. "There might have been some rumors that he was having some issues, or he might have been an alcoholic . . . [but] you wouldn't have people tailing him, taking photos of him when he walks into a liquor store. . . . It's just amplified times 100."[169] This audience-generated content equally vexes journalists: "It used to be that reporters were competing with other people in the media. Now everybody is a reporter," explains *SportsCenter*'s Jemele Hill. "The person who shoots Johnny Manziel in a club, or in a fight, they're . . . your competition—the average person."[170]

Cyclically, the speed of information alters audience capacities for and expectations about on-demand content, which in turn, revamps production imperatives in gathering and disseminating it.[171] Everything spins faster now—in both the mechanical and mediated sense. This kind of frantic output has been aptly dubbed "churnalism"—the speeded-up manufacturing of processed information from reporters who are increasingly incapacitated to chase deep stories and must instead depend on PR subsidies.[172] "You might write a column more quickly than you would've before," notes *Sports Illustrated* senior writer Greg Bishop. "Before—you might have wanted a more definitive kind of take and now you want something to be up quicker because you know people are going to read it more immediately."[173] Michael Rosenberg, his colleague at *SI*, concurs. If he doesn't weigh in with a column on a breaking news story within a day or two, "Then, that's it. . . . It's just too late. That didn't used to be the case, but now it's just—boom! They want to know *now*."[174]

## FEEDING NEWSFEEDS

Within that networked media environment, there is also obviously greater concern given to creating "spreadable" content than in the broadcasting heyday.[175] This obligation can take a variety of forms in terms of sports media professionals and the institutions they work for.

The demand can be outsourced to individual workers; Tina Cervasio of Fox–New York, for instance, has been told to tease and promote upcoming segments through her Twitter account, appending the exact airtime "so it'll force someone to turn on a TV" and thus synergizing her networked self with corporate exigencies.[176] Following the lead of late night competitors like Jimmy Fallon, *SportsCenter* is now increasingly diced into segments that can more easily slingshot across the social media-scape—a reorientation toward building broadcast content for newsfeeds as much as channel surfers.[177] "It used to be that we would sit in a room at a production meeting in the morning and come up with content for our shows," explains one ESPN associate producer. "Now, it's become a lot of, 'Hey, did you see what someone tweeted that generated this reaction from this person that then resulted in this tweet from this other person?'"[178]

That production strategy is driven, in particular, by a common sense narrative about younger demographics circulating within the industry: specifically, needing to "break up the main meal into bite-size portions" for millennials.[179] "A network is not the way kids are watching TV today," Jeff Urban declares—a somewhat self-serving (though not unsubstantiated) conclusion, considering he co-founded an online start-up that aims to become "ESPN for kids" through co-created content as well "ubiquitous distribution" sans cable network infrastructure and overhead.[180] Bonnie Bernstein, ESPN reporter turned vice president of a similarly all-digital venture, Campus Insiders, further illustrates those "bite-size" tactics that her company seeks to refine. Even as, say, their college football playoff show is still airing "live" online, they have editors concurrently carving up a half-dozen segments into "digestible chunks" and pushing them out through a wide array of social feeds. Moreover, because "the research tells us that in our ADD society, people, when viewing digital content, zone out after two minutes or so," they've trimmed down the optimal video-on-demand segments from 5 minutes to 90 seconds so as to maximize the completion rates that please advertisers.[181] There is a certain raw supply-and-demand logic here: With more abundant media material to choose from in the digital world (but no more hours in the day to play with), content has to render itself more as snippets—textually, audio-visually, or otherwise—to better fit into people's lives.

And that anxiety—and, conversely, accompanying ambition—about the digital distribution of sports content is reaching a fever pitch.[182] Cable subscription peaked at 105 million American homes in 2011 and has teetered backward in the half-decade since; millennials represent a special source of angst, with more than one-third of 18-to-29-year-olds foregoing the delivery service.[183] Such statistics cue jitters and jockeying among the key stakeholders of sports—players, teams, leagues, marketers, and media alike—which can no longer count on the stable, orderly, and reliably profitable negotiation of conventional broadcast rights.[184] (This trend line is terrifying for ESPN, in particular.) For cultural producers accustomed to assuming generations of a "living room" target for their work, these trends force them to rethink and readjust to audiences' "anywhere, everywhere" expectations about content access.[185]

Raising the specter of fear are newspapers and pop music—fellow media industries that were emaciated, if not downright decimated by digitalization. When questions of copyright policy arise, the NBA is sometimes held up as one of the more forward-looking leagues, at least as far as accommodating and, more so, outright encouraging highlights and other dated content to circulate freely across social platforms, rather than pursuing cease-and-desist takedowns.[186] (On the other hand, as recently as 2015, the NFL and MLB engineered the suspension of Twitter accounts held by *Deadspin*, *Barstool Sports*, and *SBNation* for circulating user-created—albeit copyright-violating—GIFs and Vines.[187]) "Early on, we decided that content could not and should not be controlled," explains then-commissioner

David Stern. "That was going to be the nature of social media—that any attempt to wall in our content in some way would ultimately fail and would not really grasp the full opportunity presented by social media."[188] He elaborates why sports leagues should not follow the Hollywood model when it comes to guarding IP so jealously: "Understand that the nature of sports is one continuous reality show and if yesterday's game [has] a spectacular shot or sequence, it's really gone. And so, it's different than if you have a half-hour series or some other intellectual property. Our goal is to get people to watch the next episode and the next and the next. We're not really the same as every other intellectual property owner."

In other words, for Stern, the "last episode" matters much less in terms of direct monetization as compared to leveraging it toward attentiveness to the *next* one. That's not to underplay the anxiety, though, or overstate the confidence that yesterday's content will sell to tomorrow's "buyers," just as it always has. After decades of reliable growth, sports television viewership saw double-digit drops commence in 2016—from the NFL to the Summer Olympics to MLB to NASCAR.[189] Some suspected that the "atomization of entertainment" had finally arrived in sports in much the same way the internet had earlier "ransacked" the music album and newspaper business of their once-bundled products for singled-out song and article alternatives.[190] Younger audiences were seen "unbundling" sports in two ways, particularly: bailing on cable TV packages and consuming highlights via those chopped-up, social media formats. As one expert observer asks: "Why spend four hours on the couch when you can get on with your life and catch the most alluring moments in 60 seconds in line at Starbucks?"

For American sports, that cord-cutting—and perhaps the subsequent unbundling of the cable line-up, which digital delivery might well foretell—represents a clear and present danger to the established revenue model. Take, as but one example, the Texas Rangers, which were, at one point, averaging only 60,000 nightly viewers yet still collecting $115 million in fees from all 2.7 million Fox Sports Southwest subscribers; it is dubious that the ball club could recoup so princely a sum if channel purchasing went à la carte.[191] A whole lot of non-fans help pay for the privilege of keeping sports in *fans'* channel lineup. And because of that cable bundle, sports can generate lavish wealth for networks, advertisers, leagues, teams, and players up and down the supply chain.[192]

Clients like Adidas are closely watching how this uncertainty surrounding content delivery gets resolved and claim to be agnostic about their preferred platform—they'll go "wherever these teens and millennials are watching those live moments in sports," lugging their sponsorship dollars with them.[193] In turn, leagues like the NFL are proactively trying to bait digital competitors like Google and Facebook to contemplate rights bids down the line when current TV contracts expire—spinning the sales pitch, echoed earlier, that their product helped make carriers like ESPN huge in the first place and could do the same for some lucky Silicon Valley suitor.[194] Hawking its sample to a wide range of bidders, pro football first experimented with a Yahoo!-streamed regular season game in London; later lured a 10-game, one-year deal from Twitter for reportedly less than the highest offer (attracted by the potential for mobile and social synergies); and then awarded Amazon 10 games at $50 million (perhaps coveting those Prime customers who "over-index" with cable cord-cutters).[195]

Such seismic shifts are equally reconstituting what it means to be a sports media professional within that non-linear, multiplatform space. Not surprisingly, the overriding mandate—emblematic of the neoliberal ethos—seems to be: Do more, more flexibly, with less. A recent survey of newspaper editors and TV directors found that newsrooms increasingly needed jack-of-all-trade, convergence journalists to shoot, report, write, edit, blog, and post their storytelling, "aggressively—several times a day."[196] "The entire journalistic edict has changed," confirms ESPN alum Bonnie Bernstein. "Now the bosses are saying: tweet first, blog second, write your article third. So, there's not only an additional workload for journalists but there's this rush to be first," as the news cyclone swirls around them.[197] Journalism futurist Jeff Jarvis has a nice line distilling this pattern: "The process has become the product."[198]

As bitter irony, however, these elevated expectations about content output are happening concurrently with a downsizing of American newsrooms; not only is there more technological dexterity demanded, there are fewer hands to go around to help out in executing those goals and often "little or no remuneration" for the additional blog or podcast labor accomplished.[199] Thus, even those who have risen to the pinnacles of the profession—in print, say, filing for *Sports Illustrated* as a senior writer—can't help but lament what has befallen their industry. "It just sounds like the good times we missed the boat on by about 20 years," bemoans one; "I feel like I was the last generation having an excuse to get into journalism—like, one of the last years before you realize the whole institute is going to blow up," gripes another.[200] There is, however, some solace and relatively good fortune to be found: Even as American newspapers are flailing, sports—and, especially, pro football—remains a healthy, even flourishing beat. "It is a paradox. . . . I'm covering a sport that's gushing with money," puzzles *Los Angeles Times* columnist Chris Dufresne, "at a time when our resources are dwindling."[201] While other departments at the paper and other assignments on the sports desk might face the chopping block, he adds, a journalist who covers a "big click sport" like football can savor some serenity in being safer from those layoffs, for the time being at least.[202]

Moreover, Dufresne's use of the phrase "big click" is instructive here, as both individual and organizational practices contort to maximize web traffic—sometimes justifiably, sometimes embarrassingly—as part of a broader "BuzzFeed-ization" of American journalism. Yahoo! Sports' Marc Spears dissects the process of trying to boost the viral odds of his output:

> It's almost like putting some bait on a hook—there's so much stuff out there, but how could I get that fish to bite my hook? . . . Sometimes, I feel like I tweet something out to tease—I'll have a tweet about Ben Simmons where it basically says, 'Is Ben Simmons the next LeBron James?' When I did that, I'm sure there were people like, 'Huh? What? Next LeBron James? . . . Let me read this—who is this guy?' You've got to basically put something out there to get somebody to bite the hook.[203]

Indeed, this is why "click-bait" is so perfect a term—it articulates how technology is driving and rewarding norms of (often dubiously substantiated) sensationalism and provocation. At *Deadspin*, former editor-in-chief Tommy Craggs notes that they used a program called "SocialFlow" to optimize the ideal time over the course of a day on Twitter to post news, based upon headline keywords and trending hash-tags: "It was total carny bullshit, but . . . I want to game Facebook."[204] He later expands on how that BuzzFeed logic has also reshaped substance imperatives: "To the extent that there's any trick, it's, like, figuring out how to frame something so that it reflects well on the person sharing it. . . . What looks good for you to share on Twitter or Facebook? How does this [content] position you in your social circle?"

Such marching orders—reporting and writing to supply cultural capital within audience communities—are of a very different variety than journalism has historically abided by. It's still "news you can use"—just, instead, to troll for likes and comments and shares. And the naked visibility of readership popularity as the outcomes of that effort (i.e., most-read story tallies appearing on websites, not to mention data monitoring internal to organizations) etches itself, incentive-wise, into the reporter's mind. "What I find extremely disturbing is the obsession with self-promotion in the business—the 'how many hits,' 'how many followers,' 'how many this and that,'" gripes Filip Bondy of *The New York Daily News.* "We do get many proddings from up above about this—about how many hits we've had, views. This is the new obsession. And we have a whole department built around that. So, we do have to be conscious of promoting ourselves."[205]

That culture of self-aggrandizement is no doubt also a product of and response to the precariousness of contemporary media work—even at august institutions that once represented pillars of professional stability. Being popular and prolific on social media has specifically become a significant "deciding factor" in hiring sportscasters, anchors, and reporters, according to one Comcast SportsNet president; it also blurs the public and private boundaries of their "always 'switched on'" working lives and erodes the formality formerly expected of journalistic decorum.[206] Social media "enables you to develop your own brand without having to pay $5,000 or $10,000 a month for a publicist," explains Bonnie Bernstein—especially when limited on-air time constricts the ability to project oneself as a multidimensional *personality*, with interests above and beyond strictly sports (more on this in chapter 3).[207] Perhaps no platform is seen as more effective toward those ends than ESPN's long-running debate show, *Around the Horn*—"the Holy Grail for scribes looking to build their own brand."[208] The reason is simple: In an era of digital media abundance, opinionated content is increasingly thought to be the only way to be heard above the din.

## THE HOT-TAKE INDUSTRIAL COMPLEX

> There was a time in sports journalism when beat reporters, in particular, were asked and expected not to include their opinion in the product. I think that's almost the reverse today. . . . Because as we've gotten to a more instantaneous digital age in terms of the flow of information, everyone hears so much and makes up their mind about what has just occurred in front of them that they expect that. . . . There has been far more and more push on the part of editors and the part of beat writers to be far more opinionated in their journalism than this industry has ever allowed before.[209]

What Kevin Blackistone, *Washington Post* columnist, describes here might be called the "hot-take industrial complex"—or, a form of media output that confuses trolling for journalism. Over time, the U.S. news industry, broadly, has seen the gradual erosion of once-functional distinctions between reporting and commentary.[210] Simultaneously, sports television has wallowed in what one scholar calls "*confrontainment*, the packaging of confrontation as entertainment"—that staged spectacle of gladiatorial debate, with provocation and polarization as outright aim rather than enlightenment (in both the educational and Zen-calm sense of the word).[211] No institution is more responsible for and emblematic of this format shift than sports talk radio; a decade after WFAN pioneered the genre in the New York market in the late 1980s, 150 imitators had mushroomed nationwide.[212] Today, these set the tone for *all* sports media.

The program director at Philadelphia's WIP claims that sports talk's daily agenda is reactive and sensitive to fans' preferences (previously phone callers and now increasingly social media input), but such rhetoric glosses over the deliberate ways that conversational content is actively funneled and shaped.[213] At ESPN, for example, a group of news editors apparently circulates a "hot list" of stories, between six and ten times a day, which gives personnel a sense of "what they think we should be talking about."[214] Decision-making about which specific topics to engage is left to producers and talent, though of course, there is formula and routine there, too: "I always say a good sports radio topic for us is if you were to walk into a room filled with people . . . and loudly state your opinion [and] people would either want to tell you how full of shit you are or say, 'Finally, somebody said it the way that I would want to say it.'"[215] As for caller screening, despite having to often cull from "the bottom 5 percent of society," a successful show can nonetheless make use of a bad caller with a counterpoint that the host can "just crush" so as to "further enrage the fire of the argument."[216] This "lowest common denominator mentality," as one host put it, is built into production norms; such media is averse to subtlety and aims to rile, not reconcile, conflicting sides.[217] In sports, the format shift is annoying, if arguably harmless; applied to politics, it feels more democratically corrosive.

That approach has, over the course of two decades, migrated to television and taken deep root there. John Wildhack, ESPN executive vice president for programming and production, acknowledges that talk radio, the blogosphere, and other social media "have upped the ante" in terms of network strategy; *SportsCenter* anchor Linda Cohn pins it more so on Fox News' success, which ESPN "in a flattering way, copied."[218] She adds that, over the last decade, there have been increasing liberties afforded to straight news hosts who want to offer an opinion or reveal fandom allegiances—the kind of edgy asides that had earlier been verboten.[219] (Indeed, ESPN founder Bill Rasmussen reveals that Chris Berman was initially reprimanded for allowing his signature corny flair to betray "the old broadcast mentality" of stone-faced decorum.[220]) *Pardon the Interruption*, the debate show featuring Tony Kornheiser and Michael Wilbon, pioneered this TV format around the turn of the century, with *Around the*

*Horn* following in its wake.[221] Today, the daytime lineup is clogged with shout-fest panels, boxes-within-screen-boxes, each talking head trying to out-take the next. All of which has led to *Deadspin*'s Will Leitch to savage what he calls the "[Skip] Baylessing of ESPN":

> The key to ESPN's "coverage" of sports is that you Have a Reaction . . . After a while, no viewer could believe anything any analyst said anymore; their job seemed to be to disagree with whomever they were talking rather than to offer actual analysis or reasoned arguments. . . . The television became populated with people screaming opinions into the camera until it was time for another topic, which meant more opinions and more screaming. It didn't matter what position the "expert" took on an issue; what mattered was that it was in opposition to the person they were "debating" with, that it was forceful, loud, and quick.[222]

Leitch seems more or less correct in his inference of how the sausage gets made. Blackistone, a regular panelist on *Around the Horn*, explains while producers won't force a hot take onto participants, they do prefer and seek out the widest variety of hot takes conceivable: Call this a Miltonian sop to the marketplace of loudly stated ideas.[223] (Another columnist, however, counters that he was, in fact, handed "a packet of ready-made 'viewpoints'" to adopt for the show to help "create debate."[224]) "I think it's very difficult for our radio hosts, because we're always asking them to have strong opinions and what if they don't have a strong opinion on a topic? It's almost like you have to force a strong opinion—that's the only way you stand out, that's the only way that people keep listening to you," bemoans Dan Stanczyk, an associate producer at ESPN Radio. "The only way to keep them listening is to have crazier opinions and stronger opinions. Everything's getting pushed to the extremes."[225]

Moreover, that pressure to have a take (and, in the parlance of "Jungle" host Jim Rome, have it "not suck") seeps outward from talk radio or TV panel confines. Michael Rosenberg of *Sports Illustrated* feels the weight of it when he shows up to a game or event swarming with other media personnel and "now it's like I have to have something that other people don't have or say it in a way other people aren't saying it—you have to bring something different to the table to get noticed in the crowded marketplace."[226] This is, of course, not unrelated to the aforementioned trend of provocative click-bait—the broadcast and print equivalent of such social media feed gimmickry.[227]

The causes of this hot-take industrial complex merit further elaboration. Certainly, characteristics of today's information landscape—defined earlier in this chapter by its digital limitlessness and ensuing abundance—are most consequential in terms of reconfiguring opinion-driven production strategies. "There's just such an oversaturation of content now—an oversaturation of outlooks from which people can get their sports news—now the folks in the C-suites are figuring out, 'Well, what the heck do we need to do to differentiate ourselves?'" asks Bonnie Bernstein. "They're really trying to push the most opinionated folks up front because it's basically . . . 'Who's going to say something that's going to generate enough interest to go viral?' . . . And there is less emphasis on the nuts and bolts and more emphasis on the outrageous."[228]

At least one report from those C-suites confirms this logic. With the rise of mobile devices and online venues, "breaking" sports news arrives way too late for linear TV schedules, explains Norby Williamson, ESPN's executive vice president for production: "Now, it's incumbent upon [us] to take the next step of what's the interpretation of the news, [because] . . . news is everywhere, digitally, on-demand, at my fingertips." Indeed, he raises a fundamentally existential question for sports journalism: What *is* the point of scores-and-highlights programming in an age when a show like *SportsCenter* no longer has the monopoly on delivering those scores and highlights at an appointed time as it once did? One longitudinal content analysis of the show over the first decade of the 21st century finds a clear trend away from that traditional "information model" (e.g., simply reporting scores and hard news updates) to both more analysis (e.g., "more digestion of news items, more synthesis between related stories, more interactive components, more multimedia, more commentary, and more expert opinions") as well as more tabloid flourish (e.g., "more sensationalism, more drama, more popular culture stories").[229] *SportsCenter* has, in short, gone "out of bounds" and made peripheral contexts more central in order to maintain audience interest. Hence, too, the network's initiative to accentuate host personalities (e.g., where "each show has its own identity" like Scott Van Pelt's midnight witticisms or Michael Smith and Jemele Hill's pop culture–savant former 6 p.m. edition).[230]

The sports media executive arguably most identified with and indebted to this formatting shift is Jamie Horowitz, who, after producing shows like *First Take* at ESPN, became president at Fox Sports and announced he would remodel the entire network explicitly in the divisive, polarizing image of its corporate news cousin; this included canceling the nightly highlight show, firing 75 reporters, and loading up on charismatic blowhards like Bayless to run more opinion-driven studio shows.[231] "There seems to be an insatiable appetite for consumers to hear interesting, incisive takes on the day's news," Horowitz theorizes. "This is not dissimilar to what you're seeing in the news space."[232]

That professional norm resonates at the local level as much as the national: "I think a good sportscast should . . . spur some type of reaction: 'I hate that Lynch!' 'Did you hear what Lynch said last night? I can't stand it!'" jokes Boston-based sports anchor Mike Lynch.[233]

He adds later in the interview: "You have to find ways to differentiate. . . . I don't want a vanilla ice cream sportscast every night." It is, moreover, not just a broadcasting bias; the rich abundance and instantaneous availability of sports news equally impacts the self-conceit of print scribes. Chris Dufresne attributes his continuing livelihood to the production of hot takes: "What you used to be able to provide to people—that information—they already have. . . . The key to my survival is that I became strictly more of a columnist. It's my opinion more than my information that keeps me going."[234] The rise and appeal of the "listicle" format arguably also traces its genesis to the demands made by a cluttered information environment: cutting through the cacophonous news noise in crisp, bullet-point fashion.[235]

As noted before, abundance begets more abundance—those "exhausting" demands for overproduction placed upon media workers within this environment (for one freelancer, churning out 2,500 words daily across websites, blogs, podcasts, and print) rather *forces* one into hot takes rather than deep, nuanced reporting: "You find yourself, not *making* things up, but you find yourself saying things for the sake of saying things."[236] The industrial pressures here are simultaneous, from two streams earlier identified: a digital media landscape necessitating more output (because analogue parameters of time and space have been obliterated), while reporting access to sports' sources is also being squeezed (offering less assistance in subsidizing that output). Hence, the "solution"—churning out hot takes.

That also radicalizes the tone of digital discourse: "It's always about who has the louder, more strident viewpoint—there's not really a whole lot of room for reason and nuance on Twitter. You're trying to make yourself heard," explains Ben Shpigel, the *New York Times'* beat writer who covers the New York Jets. "People chiming in one after another trying to one up each other. . . . It's difficult to stomach sometimes."[237] Michael Rosenberg of *SI* similarly describes writing for a "mob mentality, where the same things get repeated over and that group shouts down everybody else."[238] Compared to the pre-digital era, with its glacial letters-to-the-editor turnaround times, the audience now feels so much "closer" and less anonymous to media workers and, in turn, the heat of its vitriol more scorching.[239]

That said, there is a central supply-side factor, which cannot be discounted, that also explains the hot-take industrial complex: Put simply, talk is cheap. Dave Revsine, the Big Ten Network's studio host, elaborates here on the basic economic advantageousness of opting for opinion-driven shows:

> They're easy to produce—I mean, all you need is a couple of guys with opinions. . . . Studio programming like that is very cheap, because you don't have to go out and have reporters gathering information; you don't have to have bureaus; you don't have to have producers in the field, the photographers in the field. It's just a simple matter of: "Here's what happened, here's what the Lions called on 4th and 3 last night. Do you think it was the dumbest play ever or the second dumbest?" And then people just go [off], right? . . . It's an easy way to fill time.[240]

The "cheap food" like this—as *Outside the Lines*' Kelly Naqi calls it—helps balance out the pricier items, which includes those exorbitant rights fees or, for that matter, her show, which she acknowledges is not a "ratings-getter," but rather a prestige program that "ESPN knows they have to throw some money at and just wave it goodbye."[241] (Moreover, it's not really even part of the branded identity of the network; as Naqi points out, when she visits the ESPN store on the Bristol campus, amidst all the *SportsCenter* and *Baseball Tonight* logoed gear, she jokingly asks her boss where the *Outside the Lines* merch is hiding.) But the trend nonetheless leaves her feeling "siloed" in an environment increasingly characterized by the noisy *PTI* model.

To be sure, there's also a demand-side logic that sports media professionals articulate to justify and rationalize the preponderance of debate-heavy content: an assumption that the audience wants to be inflamed as much as informed. Political communication research has, for example, long documented the selective exposure bias among partisans who hope to avoid information challenging prior assumptions and values.[242] This has no doubt buttressed cable channels like Fox and MSNBC that masquerade as "news" while delivering mostly debate. Similarly, defending his network's embrace of the hot-take industrial complex, ESPN executive John Wildhack suggests that, "In a sense, all we're doing with those shows is doing what fans do every day."[243]

Debate is, ironically, communal and inviting (unless, of course, you're constitutionally turned off by it): communication as feisty, give-and-take ritual rather than the chilly, disinterested transmission of incontrovertible information. It pursues not objective truth, but attention grabbing for its own sake and offers up tribal affirmation in exchange. All of which transforms the valence, and values, of the sports media professional—a shift triggered, in no small measure, by marching orders that come from the top. Thinking back on one *SportsCenter* segment they explicitly redesigned to stir up on-set debate, Mark Gross, an ESPN senior vice president, explains, "It would force our analyst to have an opinion, because I think there was a sense . . . maybe analysts need to have stronger opinions—maybe we were letting them off the hook a little bit. And these devices—'Take Your Pick,' 'Fact or Fiction'—were ways to force people to have an opinion and it has evolved from there."[244] The head of ESPN's audio division adds: "If you're not getting in trouble once in a while, you're not pushing things enough."[245] Such an admission bespeaks how today's media is, undoubtedly, trying to troll you.

Jemele Hill and Michael Smith, both of whom came up through the ranks of print media, like to post a bright-pink sticky note on their production rundown sheet as a reminder of that hot-take imperative: "WE R NOT A NEWSPAPER."[246] Ivan Maisel, the college football senior writer for ESPN, finds that he has been gradually "re-assigned" from summary stories filed from the weekend's games to more opinionated pieces, because the data analytics department "figured out that nobody reads the game stories anymore."[247] And, in turn, the metrics (and therefore revenues) at a site like *Bleacher Report* reward those who "write controversial articles that get a lot of hits and comments, but [don't] know how to break a story or even conduct an interview."[248]

Moreover, the hot-take industrial complex not only dictates *how* media professionals do their work differently, but also what they do it *about*. A practice of cultural production that is drawn toward divisiveness will naturally gravitate toward "lightning rod" stories, players, and teams that command the limelight, deserving or not.[249] In Boston (and no doubt elsewhere, too), the most grotesque indulgence of this habit has been Deflategate, the New England Patriots operatic pigskin-pressure scandal: "You can write the most absurd point of perspective column on [it] and that would get you huge viewership, huge readership, just because it's a hot-button topic," says *Globe* media reporter Chad Finn.[250] Nationally, that bias favors focusing on franchises that draw lovers and haters in equal measure, like the New York Yankees, Dallas Cowboys, or Los Angeles Lakers, and stars that cross over and become pop culture icons, even in the absence of professional talent, like quarterback Tim Tebow.[251] "It's almost like playing songs on the radio: You play the hit," ESPN Radio's Dan Stanczyk says. "People know who Justin Bieber is—they like his songs, so his songs are going to get played a lot more than . . . some no-name artist."[252]

ESPN executives try to refute the notion that they are pushing Tebow-style over-coverage onto audiences: "If people weren't watching when we're doing that topic—whatever that topic it may be—

we wouldn't be doing it," says one.[253] "We take our lead from the fans—we have no agenda that we're trying to get out there," says another.[254] Although this is an evasion and self-effacement of the media's agenda-setting power, it is not uncommon.[255] For as ESPN host Jemele Hill analogizes of Johnny Manziel's ability to grab attention (and thereby revenue): "[Athletes] who fit in that category . . . it's almost like pornography for networks. It's hard for us to resist that when the audience is clamoring for it. . . . It wasn't us pushing them, it was them pushing us. . . . What I do care about is that every time I talk about him, we get 75,000 more people watching the show."[256]

Increasingly, given the "challenges" that ESPN's business model faces (as parent CEO Bob Iger cautiously admitted), that is not an insignificant calculation.[257] Its problem is, broadly, a cable subscriber base and broadcast rights market veering in opposite, budget-busting directions: 13 million cord-cutters and basic-tier buyers had abandoned the network from its peak even as it was still nailed to lavish long-term league deals it may have overpaid for.[258] In 2015, 300 employees were laid off, followed by another 100 pink slips two years later to on-camera talent; some bearish analysts and Disney investors were even suggesting it unload the company—once the aforementioned "protector" of Mickey Mouse's solvency.[259] At the time of this writing, tumult was clearly afoot at the "Worldwide Leader."[260]

Overall, as demonstrated here, the world of American sports media is being "reformatted" in a dual sense. New technologies and social media are forcing institutions and organizations to rethink the format of their content from assumptions endemic to the mass communication era. That format is not strictly a product and effect of platforms alone, but equally the norms practiced there. On balance, the abundance of competing content across the digital landscape orients sports media companies (and, arguably, all news companies) toward faster and more provocative presentations of it. And one of the most significant competitors entering that space is sport itself: Those staging and participating in the events are now, more than ever, also staging and participating in their representation.

## WHO NEEDS SPORTS JOURNALISTS?

Looking ahead, there remains the distinct possibility that American sports journalism will be "dis-intermediated" altogether—with players, teams, and leagues taking full advantage of the ability to tell their own stories without having to bother with any press filter. This has some precedence over the years (and it's also being mirrored, currently, in that other competitive media context: politics). When Jackie Robinson retired, for example, he announced the news through a $50,000 paid announcement in *Look* magazine and, ever since the 1960s, NFL Films has been "perhaps the most effective propaganda organ in the history of corporate America," in the estimation of sports media scholar Travis Vogan.[261]

More recently, veteran CBS sportscaster Lesley Visser points to the rise of Nike advertising in the 1990s as the beginning of "when athletes realized they didn't need us. . . . They realized they could cut us out. . . . That they could present themselves the way they wanted to through their own writers at their own company."[262] Nevertheless, today's spike in social media accounts and other vested news sources does represent, according to one veteran scribe, "the biggest journalistic game-changer of our time."[263] *Boston Globe* media columnist Chad Finn connects the dots: "The savvier athletes and, I guess, franchises, teams as well, can sort of cut out the middle man and don't need the reporters to get their message out, to get their image out to help them build their personal brand. . . . [Later in the interview, he adds:] Conversely—I guess it's actually related to that—you have less access than you probably had certainly ten years, twenty years ago. . . . Now, they can have a fluff piece on Derek Jeter's

*Players' Tribune* website or something through their team or something through a team-operated television show."[264]

Indeed, these platforms herald a diminished role for the gatekeepers of old, whose monopoly on information—and the agenda-setting power that comes with it—has been comparatively dispersed and diminished.[265] Increasingly, players have recognized that they no longer need traditional channels to manage their "self-presentation"—channels in which players were long the lead actors in, but never the producers of the story.[266] For athletes at the highest echelons of wealth and celebrity (and therefore those already the most difficult to access), this redefines reporting practices by allowing *them* to directly break news on their own.[267]

The future, Pepsi senior director of sports marketing Kim McConnie forecasts, might well be, "With social media, with increased production capacity, [athletes] are becoming their own channel. . . . Maybe the most powerful way to do that in a couple years' time is actually through the LeBron Channel"—as much as, say, ESPN or Fox Sports.[268] Golden State Warriors superstar Stephen Curry is already ushering in such a future. He debuted a social media platform all his own called Slyce to better coordinate the chaotic cacophony of Twitter, not to mention cut out traditional journalists: "It's just kind of having control of your own voice," he explained, as opposed to "after games, when you're in front of the media [and] they're just asking questions that will just filter into stories that they've already written—they just need a quote or maybe stirring the pot in a direction that you don't want to go."[269]

Franchises, too, see the advantage in extricating the press—not only in terms of precluding any potentially unflattering representations, but also in hooking fans with the very (monetizable) exclusivity that they've deprived of those more negative interlocutors. "I used to live in mortal fear about what [*The Washington Post*] would write. Now, I don't care. I think that's something you need to internalize: that we're our own media company," Ted Leonsis, owner of the Washington Capitals, advised a sports business symposium at the start of this decade. "When someone goes to find out something about me or a team or a player and they go to Google and they type that in . . . I don't want *The Washington Post* to get the most clicks. I want the most clicks."[270]

Similarly, the Miami Dolphins, for example, converted more than three-quarters of their marketing budget to social media programming to achieve these branded content ambitions, distributing short online shows that offer "insider access" and "appear to have no marketing messages at all."[271] The video coordinators for a slew of college athletic departments are also increasingly migrating their own output from the university website to channels like Facebook Live— leveraging brief, behind-the-scenes footage like team meals and locker room moments (which are exempt from more formal broadcast rights).[272] The Jacksonville Jaguars' senior vice president of fan engagement explains the motive for this:

> Where teams can add real value to their fans is by . . . delivering content that other people just don't have access to. . . . There are things that they see and interact with and have conversations about that our beat writers [in the press] just don't. . . . For instance, if you look at the tone of some of the things that come out of the beat writers, there'd be no way that [Jaguars.com senior writer] John [Oehser] would take that tone. There's no way that it would be appropriate for him to be as snarky, say, as other folks might be. . . . For instance, the coach's speech after a game: There's a certain comfort level he has with our crew that—we are in there and there's a certain level of intimacy behind that . . . fans really appreciate. . . . And there are things that teams can deliver with a certain level of comfort that other outlets might not be able to.[273]

Needless to say, those other—more independent—outlets in the media would surely love to be able to be privy to such moments but would not necessarily take as reverential a tone as the team desires. Further to that end, this inventory of content, teams and leagues have gradually realized, is "an untapped revenue source" that fans or advertisers might be willing to acquire or subsidize.[274] Garry Howard recalls this trend beginning to unfold during his time as senior editor of the *Milwaukee Journal Sentinel* in the 1990s: the Green Bay Packers limiting, say, the "amount of interview sessions you could have . . . to protect their own intellectual property. . . . As you can see how they monetized it, the way it's monetized now, they were letting a whole lot of money go out the door."[275] Nearly two decades ago, then-commissioner Paul Tagliabue emphasized that the NFL should be fully "invested in the production and facilitation of media messages."[276] Now that assumption and ambition is widespread across leagues: "They've all turned into media companies—everybody is a content provider now," observes *SportsBusiness Journal*'s Terry Lefton, a truism fast approaching the point of cliché.[277]

Probably the best, or most troubling, example of these initiatives is *The Players' Tribune*, an athletes-authored news website created by former New York Yankees superstar Derek Jeter. Stories for the site are basically "monologues" dictated from players with some light Q-and-A from ghostwriters to orient the flow; there is minimal editing and final approval of any draft ultimately rests with the player.[278] One year into publishing, the *Tribune* had already boasted scoops ranging from Kobe Bryant's retirement to Kevin Durant's free agency decision to David Ortiz's rant against suspicion that he had used performance-enhancing drugs; upon receiving the *SportsBusiness Journal*'s "Sports Breakthrough of the Year" award in 2016, the *Tribune* president attributed its success to "the stories [being] just really compelling because [the players] have this place to share without worrying about their words getting twisted."[279] Jeter protests that the platform is not meant "to take away from sportswriters," but this is plainly disingenuous.[280]

According to Gary Hoenig, who had been the editorial director at *ESPN The Magazine* before joining the *Tribune* in a similar role, the project is, in fact, a direct response to an "atmosphere between fans and players poisoned by the media," thanks to sports reporters (apparently misguidedly) importing the same "adversarial relationship" that other journalists apply to their beats: "There's a longing here for the athlete to be able to get out of that silly scrum of people with microphones, when he's half-naked and has just completed a very difficult experience, win or lose, and communicate directly with the people that care about him."[281]

By bringing stars and fans closer together, there is less (and perhaps one day soon, no) space—physically or metaphorically—for the disintermediated journalist. To some degree, this is actually already well underway—as locker rooms are increasingly overrun with "friendly media" pseudo-reporters who make source relationships, professional responsibilities, and, frankly, elbow room in that scrum all the more vexing.[282] Reflecting on being outnumbered five to one by team media after a Thunder shoot-around, one *Oklahoman* reporter observed, "Any question that I ask that's perceived as threatening is going to look worse when these guys are asking softball questions."[283]

Moreover, there seems to be increasingly less time for those comparatively probing questions, as Howard points out: "They don't open the locker room until 15 minutes after [the game] and, in the meantime, the league is already getting their own quotes; they're putting out the quote sheets; they're putting out things that are basically taking the job away [and] your ability to be able to do it."[284] Couldn't teams eventually just cut out independent media access altogether? In Swindon, England, the professional soccer club there has done just that: prohibiting reporters, photographers, and broadcasters from interviewing any player, coach, or management figure, in favor of fan access through the in-house "journalist," with the ownership admitting, "at the end of the day, the local paper needs the football club more than the football club needs the local paper."[285] That notion—and policy—may prove prophetic.

"What's preventing them from doing that?" wonders Ben Shpigel, who covers the Jets for *The New York Times*. "I'm sure there's a segment of the population that would rather have that—where they're not compelled to go and read reporters who they might perceive as biased or who they feel don't treat their team fairly. They can just go ahead and click on the team site and, see, look, everything's hunky dory."[286] The teams are wielding that most valuable of advantages over the fourth estate—sourcing—which, in turn, transforms the roles for both to the point that, bizarrely, "every media outlet is competing with the teams that they cover" nowadays.[287]

All of which begs a concluding question: Who, ultimately, *needs* sports journalism? And, moreover, who needs sports journalism held to the same standards of excellence applied to coverage elsewhere? The noble ideals and myths (or, at least, kneejerk clichés) that inform journalistic ambition on other beats—objectivity, watchdogging power, comforting the afflicted and afflicting the comfortable—do not sound quite so applicable when extracted from more "serious" matters like politics, war, or business. And, yet, sport *is* big business, as a slew of statistics has already documented, and sport *does* have major political ramifications, as chapters 4 and 5 will show. Is it because sport is inextricable from the realm of entertainment—never to rise above its "toy department" diminutive status—that it should not be judged as such?[288]

Émile Durkheim's theory again offers a compelling contextualization for many of the practices, trends, and norms illustrated throughout this chapter. For if the team functions as totem for its followers—furnishing fellowship, projecting a source of enduring identity, and cultivating collective conscience and consciousness—it becomes possible to imagine objectivity as tangential, if not altogether less than idyllic. Totemic allegiance lends itself toward Bill Simmons–style, unambiguously partisan populism; totemic allegiance encourages and elicits "hot-take" reactions to the subject of that coverage. As a vessel for social unity, the sports totem, theoretically, invites any otherwise "independent" observer to want to become one with it—just as fans are equally drawn to that allure, rather than remaining autonomous from or critical of it. Tribes don't really need objectivity, because objectivity is anathema to tribal identity. Just ask any hardcore partisan nowadays.

To do sports journalism is, then, to do "public service" journalism in a very different sense: Its task is, partly, to help forge that collective consciousness as one of the custodians of the imagined totemic community. Sports, in that sense, are far from trivial. They "represent ideas about how the world works and what is important in life" (especially politically) as sports sociologist Jay Coakley contends. "[And] sports journalists are key players in these constitutive processes, because their representations of sports can influence the ideas and beliefs that people use to define and give meaning to themselves, their experiences, and the organizations of social worlds."[289]

None of this is to absolve sports organizations of criticism when they withhold access or complicit media organizations when they downplay blemishes to protect their financial interests. In a paradoxical way, as documented throughout this chapter, the sports media is both too antagonistic and not enough: inciting ever-hotter takes on "safe," often trivial, even asinine subjects while shying away from covering more serious issues like concussions, domestic violence, and so on (for fear of jeopardizing revenues). The faux controversies ginned up via debate panels veil the reality of often toothless reporting about that big picture: It is much ado about nothing—posturing entertainment obfuscating the absence of critical objectivity.

The story told in these pages has been one of industrial transformation, wherein technological change reshapes norms and, in turn, norms dictate technological strategy. Sports journalists have always occupied a precarious perch within the news media; the trends of late seem to suggest an enlargement of the definition of their profession. Whether it's boisterous fans clattering on social media or player, league, and team organizations slipping into content-producer roles, the "traditional" sports reporter is feeling his or her responsibilities and advantages pinched from all sides.[290] If sports journalism had an illustrious and idealistic tradition of distance, objectivity, and critique to draw upon and reference—as a defense against these encroaching forces—those professionals might not opt for churning out hot takes as the normative recourse. But it doesn't. And, apparently, the only way to survive in a news cyclone is to be louder than the next competitor shouting for audience attention.

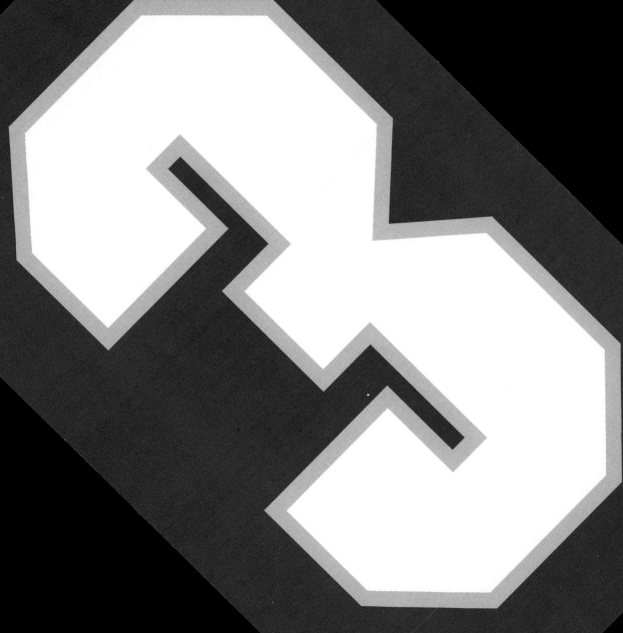

Basketball isn't my job. For me, my job begins the moment I walk off the floor. It's everything that surrounds the actual playing of the games. My job is being a product endorser.
—**Michael Jordan**, product endorser

# FEVER PITCH

## The Creeping Colonization of Commercialism

There are only four things that travel across borders: sports, music, violence, and sex. And it's difficult to find sponsors for violence and sex.
—**Juergen Lenz**, FIFA marketing agency executive

# O

NE COULD BE

# FORGIVEN FOR THINKING THAT

American sports in the 21st century function basically as a backdrop for commercial activity. Some see a "hyper-commodification," both quantitatively and qualitatively, the likes of which professional athletics have never before experienced: exploding revenues derived directly from the games themselves while related experiences and practices are co-opted off the field.[1] Sport may have once operated comparatively autonomously from profit-driven motives, but, today, it is hard to see it as "anything but an important arm of the global capitalist order," as one critic charges.[2]

This chapter offers a snapshot of that creeping colonization, where any space that can be sponsored and any cultural context that can be commercialized finds a corporation capitalizing. Along the way, to satisfy the demands of those media companies and marketers, the structure of the games themselves has become a malleable feature of the product that is packaged and sold. Simultaneously, the dynamics of product placement that have reshaped other forms of American pop culture equally emerge in this space—defining the parameters of possibility for media production and corrupting any ideals of independence for the professionals who labor there. We see this most clearly in the murky "native" advertising messages that aim to blend in and blur with the content that audiences actually *want* to watch.

Clearly, too, sports celebrity is integral to wringing capital from content and this chapter tracks the formula for the production of that human spectacle, focusing on the social media advances and aesthetic aspirations that determine digital strategy. Ironically, the yearning for identity and community that lures fans into worshipping at the altar of the sports totem becomes the very product that franchises are increasingly keen to exploit. Worse still, the corporate globalization model threatens to render those local loyalties superficial and superfluous. Whatever more "pure" values of play that might define sport (or once did) seem to be now, quite literally, negotiable. Brands want in from out of bounds: into the game content, into the human identity of performers, and into our social interactions as fan community. There is little to indicate this colonization will be resisted.

## PLANTING THE BRAND FLAG

An opening caveat: It is somewhat naïve to long for a bygone era when sports supposedly existed in a commercially undefiled form.[3] Beginning in the 1800s, modern sport and modern capitalism ascended in parallel, for all the practical reasons illuminated in this chapter and a few ideological ones, as well, that will be tackled in chapter 5.[4] Symbiotically, professional sport boosted sales for the sporting goods and athletic clothing industries in their nascent years.[5] It's easy to overlook, but every single NBA game is a long-form ad for Spalding; every MLB game, a pitch for Rawlings. By the 1930s, the advent of mass media—and U.S. sports' cooperative positioning within it—tantalized brands and multinational corporations keen to communicate with enormous audiences, even if their goods and services bore little connection to the athletic activity on display.[6] (Note here the particularly peculiar paradox of beer commercials' bacchanalia interrupting the display of highly disciplined bodies competing at peak physical form; the latter perhaps theoretically absolves the former on behalf of guilty consumers.[7]) Once baseball got over its haughty reservations that the World Series was "too ingrained in the nation's cultural heritage to be compromised by commercial sponsorship," Gillette shelled out $100,000 for exclusive patronage, spiking sales by a reported 350 percent.[8] Sport, moreover, not only proved expedient in selling *through* the media; it also literally *sold* the media, from the radio and TV sets necessary to hear and see games to the other network programming promotionally teased during them.[9]

Consultancies like IMG grew powerful brokering marriages with commercial suitors—particularly as sport became the largest annual recipient of those corporate sponsorship dollars, with some brands relying upon it exclusively for their marketing communication strategy.[10] Sans sport, Gatorade and Papa John's and State Farm don't have much of a voice to talk to us through; because of sport, we can't help but listen to them. And since naming rights "can't be DVR'ed," as one T-Mobile vice president who financed a $400 million eponymous arena phrased it, sponsors have fanned out across college bowl games, the English soccer league, and even team monikers themselves (e.g., the New York Red Bulls) to become inextricable from the field of focus for fans.[11] It is almost impossible to watch U.S. sports nowadays without an advertisement aggressively, annoyingly poking in the way. (Baseball radiocasts are, arguably, the most obnoxious offender on this point.)

Thus, even from this cursory historical review, it is clear that there is no uncluttered Edenic space of sport to be found in the rearview mirror, much as some nostalgists might like to assume; no Iowa cornfield baseball diamond bereft of garish signage, save in film fiction.

On the other hand, we also can't undersell the contemporary pursuit of patronage and the conversion of more spaces to satisfy those demands; according to one expert, this consumerist drive represents "the single most influential development" within sports culture since its emergence in the late 1800s.[12] It motivates the biggest and most powerful players in the game—and not just those with names like Jordan and Beckham. ESPN has been amusingly accused, by former host Keith Olbermann no less, of inheriting parent corporation Disney's "relentless, almost pathological . . . genetic disorder . . . . for marketing a product ten times every millisecond"; the NFL has likewise been likened to a "shark that will die if it doesn't keep moving and ripping little fish to shreds" to feed its coffers.[13] It is to the aggressions across those new frontiers that I now turn.

## REMAKING SPORT FOR OUR TIME

To maximize sport's economic potential, it has to be embellished, if not outright transfigured as "spectacle," so as to capture the interest of not just die-hard devotees (they'll always need their fix) but casual onlookers as well.[14] This impetus has given us the slinky cheerleader, the exploding scoreboard, the mugging mascot—all out-of-bounds gimmicks to better compete with alternatives in the entertainment marketplace.[15] Television has long wielded the greatest leverage—a "corrupting parasite," in the acid phrase of sports scholar Michael Real, "that latches onto the host body, sport, and draws life support from it while giving nothing back in return."[16] (Nothing—if you don't count some $20 billion in North American media rights.) Slavish for the attention and revenue that TV lavishes, sport prostrates itself before broadcast capital and accedes to changes in its format and appearance—above all, attempting to accentuate "maximum action in minimum space."[17] Even more so in the aftermath of the most recent global recession, as corporations scaled back some of their sponsorship subsidies, leagues became even more "proactive" and "incestual" in catering to those demands against the weight of tradition.[18]

The NFL is, as ever, the most apt archetype here. It owes its cultural dominance within the U.S. to that enduring deference, remaking its product as "televisable" as possible over the years.[19] "They fit the standards and specifications of television and football is tailor-made for it with the built-in mini-dramas. Americans need the cues to tell us when to watch," jokes Filip Bondy, columnist at *The New York Daily News*. "We don't like the soccer drama, when you don't know when the goal is going to come and we don't know when we can go to the refrigerator and get a beer."[20] Examples abound from other sports' efforts to placate broadcast needs. These have entailed extending the number of games played or events staged (for there is always more linear airtime to fill) and amplifying offensive opportunities and accelerating the pace of play (for that airtime seems to demand action movie-style narrative flow), while also simultaneously partitioning that pace within commercial-friendly halts (because someone needs to pay for all that "free" airtime).[21]

In basketball, for example, marketing necessities have mutated the game in a variety of ways that Dr. James Naismith might not recognize: the inclusion of those advertising break timeouts; a 24-second shot clock to induce more ball-handling initiative; a three-point line to juice scoring; and the opportunity for overtime to elongate the dramatic dénouement.[22] Elsewhere, the Super Bowl has been shifted to a nighttime kickoff; the outfield fence perimeters got shrunk at baseball parks while football's goal posts (and extra-point kicks) got pushed back; and the American League appointed a "designated hitter" position to beef up lineups.[23] Beyond the United States, cricket similarly remade itself to fit within TV entertainment norms and rugby pursued "faster" and "sexier" transformations of its own product.[24] On balance, "the longer the ball is in play, the more entertainment value for the fans," explains one Major League Soccer executive, who adds that they've run analyses to figure out how to increase that quality in a sport sometimes mocked by Americans for its feeble scoring.[25]

One might add another critical component for maximizing market share: the presence of parity, both within individual matches and across the duration of a season's entirety. "There isn't a major sport that doesn't come down to the last few minutes now. That's been by design and the way that they change the rules, the way that they change officiating [and] . . . salary caps . . . leagues have tried to create parity," explains sports marketing executive John Rowady. "It's all designed to carry the fan all the way to the end of the game, because they want the ratings. It's subtle, but if you look at them all, they're all ending tight. . . . There are fewer blowouts than there used to be."[26]

Sociologist Eric Leifer argues much the same, on a longer timeline, in his history of American team sports. Leagues have, since their earliest days, been preoccupied with spreading talent across the widest range of competitors so as to maintain annual attachment from fans, socially and financially, and shepherd them through as much of the season as possible.[27] Media executives equally depend on—and perhaps exert pressure toward—that outcome; anecdotally, the former president of Fox Sports recalled scrambling to find a "lucky seat" in the production compound and lighting candles from St. Patrick's Cathedral, all in the hopes of extending the playoff matchups his network was airing that were in danger of drama-deflating sweeps.[28] Even the arbiters adjudicating those games might themselves feel the unconscious weight of that bias: Research has shown that, all things being equal, baseball umpires tend to prolong at bats (and the micro-drama encapsulated therein) rather than issue a strikeout or walk call on close pitches.[29]

How, then, to theorize the relationship between temporal context and commercial pressures? On one hand, the accelerated pace of contemporary life within digital media-worlds would seem to impel those who manufacture and manage the sports spectacle to try to somehow keep up: "If you were to create an entertainment product today, from scratch, you would make it one hour or one hour and forty-five minutes," postulates A. J. Maestas, a sports marketing executive. "It [would] have a hard stop and a hard ending. . . . You would not make it as long as most of our sports are. Certainly, you wouldn't have it with an unknown end-time like baseball."[30]

Increasingly, those anxieties pervade industry leaders' discussions about and alterations made because of the millennial generation of fans—adapting their courtship to a demographic that's grown up browsing "digestible, short-form" clips rather than sitting through a multi-hour flow of "continuous content."[31] Nielsen ratings already bear out this panic, as one recent study found that for almost every major televised American sport, the median age for live games had ticked upward (though, on the plus side, that audience is graying at a slower pace than that of prime-time competitors).[32] One doomsday report from a prominent sports consultant points to a major decline in interest from young people—as self-identifying "avid fans" in this cohort have plummeted from half to just one-third over two decades.[33] Some think that eSports might be cannibalizing that traditional (physical) consumer sports market; another theory holds that millennials and Generation Z simply aren't consuming as much content overall—as their numbers should otherwise predict—through what *Ad Age* calls the "archaically inflexible linear TV model."[34] Whatever the reason, for the vice president of consumer connections at Anheuser-Busch, which wields some $360 million in sponsorship power: "This is the most fundamental, far-reaching philosophical debate the sports industry has today: how to shape the games and leagues in ways that will connect with an audience that is not as heavy consumers of traditional TV."[35]

Given its solemn reverence for tradition—its sepia-toned, Ken Burns slow-motion aesthetic; its fusty anti-spectacle scorn for showboating—probably no American sport bears this weight heavier than baseball. "Baseball, in general, has struggled in recent years to connect with the younger fan base," admits Mark Lev, managing director at Fenway Sports Management. Because of that, he stresses the importance of embedding their product in the fan's emotional memory at an early age and making it the connective tissue among families: "Creating some sort of a connection . . . is creating that identity that you hope is going to grow over that young person's lifetime."[36] Moreover, he adds, off-field spectacles in the form of virtual reality tents and roving mascots—not unlike the addition of cheerleaders and scoreboard programming for a generation of fans before—are seen as effective inducements for this fickle market.[37]

Will, however, the games themselves be fast enough to survive in an ADHD-addled media era? At a recent World Congress of Sports gathering, the worry over declining audiences in their teens and twenties was attributed by insider executives to these temporally anachronistic formats: "The reality is, and baseball is the perfect sport to pick on, people don't have four hours to watch 162 games. . . . Being able to push that game into a more consumable form becomes essential," noted Twitter's head of sports partnerships (no doubt a self-serving conclusion, too, for a platform that long specialized in 140-character brevity).[38] But Twitter's not alone in making this argument.

Media production prescriptions are being widely written for "short, sweet, to the point and on demand" as the kind of content a snippet-driven, second-screen environment demands and rewards.[39] Those that oversee their sports' formats are responding in turn, with almost every league and sports property contemplating rules changes to better compete in the modern media-scape—from baseball's pitch clock to tennis's "Fast4" truncated matches to 11-minute quarters in the NBA's preseason to FIFA's use of a spray can to streamline stalling before free kicks.[40] In the case of the NFL, where, on average, just 14 minutes of actual action balloons out to a 3-hour-plus run time, the "only surefire way" to shave minutes is—ironically—to siphon out the advertising breaks, which are the league's *raison d'être*.[41] All this pressure freights media producers like NESN's Russ Kenn, who was tasked with staging the spectacle for those increasingly antsy audiences:

> In the past, the concept was really, the ratings will be good if the team's good and it was sort of out of your control. . . . But as things evolved and as social media and people got more choices on the cable, yeah, we definitely programmed differently where we would do a lot more pieces, like at the end of an inning, say, "Coming up, we're going to ask Dustin Pedroia what crazy thing happened over the weekend for him"—that type of thing. We would be sort of judicious about it on the quarter hours, when the ratings would be marked, you know, for each fifteen-minute segment . . . is rated by Nielsen and all that. So, with an eye on the clock, if it's an hour forty-three or whatever, we would sort of save some of the teasable items that we would have and try to get the best ones at the fifteen-minute marks going into the break. . . . If the game has lulls, then you need to—that's where the work is, you need to entertain the audience with interesting things.[42]

The occupation of time, both figuratively and literally, ought to be considered not just in terms of how minutes and hours are managed but also how days, weeks, and months are parceled out.[43] ESPN founder Bill Rasmussen recalls from his early days at the network having conversations with college coaches, athletic directors, and conference commissioners who would enthusiastically consent to midnight time-slots if needed: "'Bill, we'll play at any time of the day or night if you would just televise our game,'" they'd say. "[And] they came and they started pleading, 'We'll move it and we'll do whatever you want to do.'" As he'd summarized earlier in our interview: "Basically, they would create an 'ESPN Day' [on campus for us]."[44] In the years since, ESPN has remained "both puppet-master and kingmaker," particularly in college football where—for the handsome rights fee it bestows—it meddles in both scheduling week-to-week matchups and adding brand-emblazoned bowl games to an already bloated postseason (e.g., the prestigious "Beef 'O' Brady's Bowl").[45]

Leagues and sports media are equally eager to "own" unclaimed time-slots, be they weekly or annual: Pro football saw an opening to colonize Thursday night's broadcast prime-time and ESPN hoped to hijack New Year's Eve as a "new sports holiday" for its college play-off games, much as Thanksgiving and Christmas have long been strategically synonymized with NFL and NBA programming.[46] Indeed, the "ready availability"—even "oversaturation"—of NFL content, that is thus watered down in quality, became one of the running theories to explain its softer ratings in recent seasons.[47] In many ways, that league is emblematic of an insatiable appetite to consume our cultural attention year-round (and a temporal microcosm of capital's constant craving of new market spaces): "One of the key challenges is from the Super Bowl to the start of football season the following year, there's a real, precipitous drop in the conversation around the NFL," notes Hussain Naqi, senior vice president for fan engagement with the Jacksonville Jaguars. "So one of the challenges we have is to try and pull on that conversation—do things that make the sport still relevant."[48] The April player draft—and the hype machine that envelops it as the "centerpiece of the NFL's plan for full-calendar domination"—embodies that "off-season creep" of empty pseudo-event spectacle.[49] Even, as *SportsBusiness Journal* media reporter John Ourand jokes, "You can't think of less compelling television than a bunch of men sitting around and deciding that they want somebody to get to play on their team."[50]

## THIS SECTION BROUGHT TO YOU BY

More than two decades ago, pop culture scholar Matthew McAllister presciently observed: "Advertising is . . . geographically imperialistic, looking for new territories it has not yet conquered."[51] In the years since, that military metaphor has proven ever more apt, though *guerrilla* warfare now better captures the ambitions and executions of today's marketers as opposed to the conventional conquests of the colonial era.[52] An array of covert and outsourced advertising campaigns—optimized for 21st-century media content, social patterns, and digital platforms—have multiplied, as brand messages creep ever deeper into the landscape of our lives. These advance across a wide range of fronts in the battle for human attention: from the product placement that seeks to be subtle and seamless as it is stitched into pop culture to the micro-celebrity, buzz-agent bloggers, tweeters, and Instagrammers who crowd-source promotional messages in the hopes of sparking grassroots viral enthusiasm.

Guerrilla marketing's creative license is remarkable not only in terms of content but, more so, context: expansively reconfiguring the space traditionally partitioned for commercial petition, and in turn, reorienting the media industries and the autonomy of the creative producers who labor within them. Theoretically, as I argued in my first book, these tactics and techniques represent a form of "invisible" governance, in the Foucauldian sense: accommodating yet channeling participatory agency; self-effacing advertisers' own authority through disinterested spaces; liberating the brand-text as a more flexible form for meaning; and democratizing in favor of decentralized collaboration. By design, we're not supposed to notice guerrilla marketing—at least, not obviously *as* "marketing." It is, above all, advertising that tries not to seem like advertising. And it is paradoxically more pervasive and less apparent than ever before.

In many ways, the same tectonic forces and industrial demands that generate guerrilla marketing in mediated culture *beyond* the American sports world are also responsible for experimentation and efforts *within* it: Here, I refer to the development of ad-zapping tools, the fragmentation of markets, the escalation of competing commercial clutter, and the default disbelief of audiences. The empowered consumer—and all of her assorted technological and psychological means of advertising avoidance—represents the foremost specter frightening marketers into "native" alternatives.[53] "Because everybody has a remote control and because more people DVR television programs . . . advertisers have figured out that perhaps the best way to get their product noticed is to have it attached to the action itself—not a break between the action," explains NBC's Bob Costas. "You can't turn away during something that's not strictly a commercial break."[54] Indeed, the imperviousness of content to eyeball evasion is its central allure: If you're here for the show, why not make the show commerce?

This, in turn, overlaps with U.S. media economics trends and attendant business imperatives. As *Los Angeles Times* sports columnist Chris Dufresne says of the wrap-around front-page advertisements that now borrow his publication's masthead logo: "These are concessions that we've had to make . . . Something that would have been unthinkable twenty years ago is now something we have to do . . . to keep up with gushing revenue losses."[55] On the flip side, former Anheuser-Busch vice president Brad Brown says there has been evolving concern, among advertisers, that sports expenditures in all the same places (e.g., stadia signage, commercial breaks), year after year, has turned it into forgettable "wallpaper."[56]

To better arouse attentiveness, advertisers think that "they can create a greater emotional connection to their product if they make that leap from the pod execution [i.e., commercial break] into the content" itself, notes ESPN executive Norby Williamson.[57] Hence, the insight of the "imperialistic" metaphor as a way of seeing this colonization of unspoiled spaces, this planting of brand flags on hitherto virgin editorial territory. Given profit pressures, networks and media companies seem more than willing to proffer inventory; in 2017, for example, Fox rolled out six-second, split-screen (comparatively unskippable) commercials during pitching mound visits and offensive huddle opportunities that were priced at half-a-million bucks a pop.[58] Gary Hoenig, who ran *ESPN The Magazine* before joining *The Players' Tribune* in a similar role, outlines the give-and-take here:

> The fact that we are so cowardly . . . about asking customers to pay for what we give them has created this environment where advertisers feel that they have the right to pretty much shove you [the journalist] right out of the way and get their message to your viewers or readers or whoever the hell they are . . . They want cover flaps, which they're now getting. They wanted sponsored content, which they knew they would be getting on *SportsCenter*, so why couldn't the "Bud Light Hot Seat" appear in *ESPN The Magazine?* . . . They'd say, "Come on, everybody knows there's no big deal—you're not selling journalism here. The 'Bud Light Hot Seat' is about an interview with an athlete—so what?! What's the difference?" I'm not even sure they're not right. . . . If you didn't do it, someone else would.[59]

Moreover, access itself to those content subsidies is now seen as a potential revenue stream. ABC-Boston sports anchor Mike Lynch reports that exclusive coach and player interview shows are increasingly part of an explicit financial bargain, such that if New England Patriots coach (and troglodyte mumbler) Bill Belichick takes questions after a game, that content has to be embargoed until the affiliate that owns *5th Quarter* rights airs it: "Everything appears to be for sale. . . . I don't want to say you sometimes have to buy your way into an interview, but it certainly has been a [growing] fence" around it.[60] Teams and leagues similarly seem ever more eager to affix a partner logo to any and all affiliated contexts one can conjure—right down to the "official" waste management company that disposes of effluvia at venue events.[61] "[Advertisers] want to be anywhere there's an eyeball," says Big Ten Network studio host Dave Revsine. "They're not going to say, 'Scandal of the Day brought to you by,' but . . . anything else is fair game."[62] Indeed, I queried former NBA commissioner David Stern on precisely that point: Was there any line that he could envision being drawn that would place something off-limits to a potential commercial patron? It took him a few seconds to respond—as though I'd asked him if he'd want to leave his wallet, full of money, on a Central Park bench. "I guess we could [say] sponsor tattoos," he eventually concluded. "I think we've drawn the limit at [putting ads on] the body of our athletes."[63]

That hyper-commodification was not always so ubiquitous and ridiculous. Admittedly, there have been traces of native advertising going back to the early days of ESPN, when, say, the orange broadcast set and anchor jackets matched the colors of Getty Oil, the network's majority stakeholder, and the first live game featured a slow-pitch softball matchup between the Milwaukee Schlitzes and Kentucky Bourbons (to the apparent consternation of sponsor Anheuser-Busch).[64] But in the 30 years since, such integration efforts have escalated exponentially.[65] Former *SportsCenter* anchor Revsine recalls the paradigm-altering moment, sometime around the turn of the century, when Budweiser breached the advertising break "firewall" and got mentioned and incorporated as part of a segment package: "I remember thinking as it was explained to us in the show meeting that day—I'm like, 'Whoa, the world's changing here.' Like, that's a pretty big deal," he says. "There's been, like, this trickle and they keep kind of pushing the bar of what's acceptable, what fans are willing to take until they say, 'This is just too much.'"[66]

What, however, is too much? If the history of advertising has shown anything, it is that yesterday's saturation is tomorrow's status quo: There are always new contexts to conquer, especially when the old ones seem overstuffed and ineffective. Today, examples of that "trickle" are so manifold—and the levee that is editorial restraint so breached—it is hard not to view sports media as a commercial gusher. ESPN analyst Kirk Herbstreit admits that his show, *College GameDay* ("built by The Home Depot"), has basically become a "48-hour infomercial" for the hosting school.[67] When daily fantasy flooded network coffers with more than $200 million in revenue at the start of the 2015 NFL season, their "ad messages" began popping up not only as 30-second spots but equally ingrained as experts' in-show branded recommendations for lineup settings (e.g., "Draft Kings presents").[68] One scholar's study of *SportsCenter* episodes over time confirmed a dramatic upsurge in product placement and synergistic corporate messages.[69] All of this is, again, driven by advertisers' and media companies' collective sense that the digital abundance at one's smartphone or tablet fingertips—ever at the ready during commercial breaks, when fans' consciousness drifts away from the delay in action—makes the "in-game stuff all the more valuable" and forces sales staff and production personnel to "integrate it more," says NESN's Russ Kenn.[70]

Indeed, the more focally located, the better—either visually or conceptually. This makes, for Kenn's sport, baseball, the pitch zone highly attractive for its premium visibility and competitive centrality. Better still for buyers, he says, would be a brand-backed narrative or anecdote to go along with the game: "So, sure, they would read— 'Here's a story brought to you by Twisted Tea,' but then [Red Sox announcers] Don [Orsillo] and Jerry [Remy] would continue to talk about the story throughout the half-inning. . . . The more embedded into the content it is, it doesn't seem as invasive as something hitting you over the head." The "fan camera" segment, he adds, is another example of content they probably wouldn't even bother with, were it not for sponsor demands. (After all, nothing casts a happy halo for a brand like crowd cutaways to adorable children in the stands who are, in effect, doing the work of selling the logo overlaid on-screen.) Morry Levine, the managing sports editor at Kenn's crosstown rival, CSN–New England, reports much the same: "Every single sales meeting I've been in used to be, 'We just wanted to let you know we sold Town Fair Tire for blah-blah-blah and there's going to be a billboard coming into your second segment or whatever.' Now the meetings are: 'We want to sell to Town Fair Tire—how can we build a segment around it?' Nobody wants to buy [commercial break] time . . . unless it's part of a segment in a show where you're the full-title sponsor. . . . That never used to happen. That is everywhere [now]—it's almost suffocating, truthfully."[71]

That invasion and influence is hardly unique to television, even if it is probably the U.S. medium most visibly infested and most willing to accommodate. Garry Howard recalls from his days at the *Milwaukee Journal Sentinel*—an era well predating what has become the BuzzFeed editorial-entrepreneurial model for financing Web journalism—"creating revenue by the stories we made," in that they would conceptualize standalone projects and sections with sponsors in mind.[72] More recently, *Sports Illustrated* set a record among properties owned by Time Inc. for featuring the biggest magazine cover-wrap ever—16 pages of DirecTV advertorial based upon the brand's "Don't Be Like This" campaign theme and made to look indistinguishable from the NFL preview issue contained therein.[73]

If all these integrations seem like they might sap the integrity of the editorial side, it's because that credibility is precisely what advertisers are paying to own. Then–*Deadspin* head Tommy Craggs says he recoiled when he saw a State Farm–backed pseudo-story about NBA star Chris Paul embedded, "natively," amidst his editorial content: "They had good writers who know how to write in the [parent company] *Gawker* voice and that was part of the issue—that they were too good . . . The whole thing was done in the grammar of a breaking news story." He sent a "huffy e-mail" to the sales side, carping that "I can live with these when they're not designed to trick people . . . but this seemed like too much. . . . The whole point of it was that it looked like a news story. I was like, 'We've got to change that headline.'" But ultimately, he says, "I kind of made my peace with that, because as much as I hate it, this was the way things were going and, in the long run, it's better for the company that we have good relationships with places like State Farm."[74]

For the professional journalist adapting to today's commercial media environment, native advertisers *of course* want their content to look like news rather than protrude as an external addendum to it; that's what audiences are there for, after all. These same shifty schemes have been seen across American pop culture over the years from detergent companies financing early soap operas to Reese's Pieces landing in E.T.'s outstretched hand to brands buying off hip-hop lyrics to the U.S. military creating an entire video game for recruitment goals.[75] Sports media's uncertain limbo—floating somewhere between journalism and entertainment—makes it the most readily compliant of all the news sections. And when brands approach leagues, becoming "endemic" to the action seems just as much the ideal in sports as it is in scripted entertainment, even if the structure of sport as a popular text makes integration opportunities somewhat less accommodating and abundant than with, say, a sitcom or action movie. "The holy grail is, as a brand, how can you authentically integrate yourself into the game itself, without being over the top," explains David Wright, a former marketing executive with Major League Soccer. "As properties think forward and the pressures to run a profitable business continue to increase, you're going to see more and more properties push that envelope."[76]

"Authenticity"—not to mention its inverse, being "over the top"—is, of course, in the eye of beholder. (It is also a term that advertising professionals cannot go five minutes without invoking.) To get "as close to the action as possible," as one sports advertising executive puts it, typically means stationing the product on the sidelines or in dugouts, given that the instrumental purity of gameplay precludes the use of non-relevant branded products diegetically.[77] In other words, Ford can't pay to have a base runner steal second in one of its vehicles—as it can ask of, say, *Fast and Furious* screenwriters—although the NBA did manage to get Blake Griffin to jump over a Kia Optima, the official car brand of the league, in its 2011 All-Star Game dunk contest.[78] There is apparently no "instrumental purity" compromised in a competitive event that is created expressly and exclusively for performative spectacle.

Nonetheless, as John Rowady, president of a sports marketing agency, notes, "Non-endemic advertisers [like Ford] want to become endemic; they want to be a fixture in the game play. . . . That's what fans gravitate toward—that becomes part of their tribe and if you can enter their tribe, you are going to get the reward of them looking at you."[79] He cites what might be the oldest—and certainly most conspicuous—example of this success in Gatorade, a product that positioned itself, enviably, as essential to both peak gameplay and the rituals that accompany success; Microsoft tablets, Apple iPads, and Bose headsets in the NFL and MLB also represent notable "product placements" in the sense that they fit naturally within "scripted" actions and needs from the field of play.[80] And similar to the Gatorade victory bath in football, the NCAA's championship tradition of trimming the basketball net furnished a high-visibility integration opportunity (and favorable emotional context) for the Werner ladder company: "No photographer actually means to take a picture of the ladder, but they can't help it," *SportsBusiness Journal* reported of the placement. "The beauty is in the authenticity of the ladders. You can't

make that up."[81] An environment in which ladder "authenticity"—
rather than, say, ladder *functionality*—is openly contemplated is already pretty well through the postmodern looking glass.

Such integrations are, however, still sidelined in a marginal time or
space vis-à-vis the content of play itself; much more ideal for a brand
is to become inseparable from the action. Among American sports,
NASCAR best represents this inextricability; those fans are, in turn,
most loyal to their racers' patrons, to the point that, some research
has found, they were also inclined to *dislike* opposing sponsors "simply for helping underwrite drivers they disliked."[82] By contrast, for
years, the uniforms of the major professional sports leagues in the
U.S. had been uniquely "clean" relative to soccer clubs abroad in
terms of jersey advertisements (with the continuous gameplay—and
therefore lack of commercial time-outs—necessitating kit logos).[83]

Eager to tap into an estimated $150 million annual revenue
source—and "not satisfied selling title sponsorship to the Rising Stars
game (BBVA Compass), Inside the NBA (Kia), the D-League All-Star
Game (Kumho Tire), All-Star Saturday Night (State Farm), the Skills
Challenge (Taco Bell), the Three-Point Contest (Foot Locker), the
Slam Dunk contest (Verizon), and NBA Tip-Off (AutoTrader)"—the
NBA was the first to breach that tradition by slapping a Kia patch on
All-Star Game jerseys before subsequently opening up any team's regular season garb to such advertising.[84] This peaked with a $20 mil-
lion deal from an electronics company to plant its name on Golden
State Warriors gear, as consultants egged on the NHL to consider
following Europe's lead and exploit the "low hanging fruit" that is a
player's helmet space for corporate iconography.[85] "If there's a blank
space," concludes one marketing executive at Allstate, "someone's
going to figure out how to sell it."[86]

The NBA also rebranded its minor league (formerly known as
the "D-League") the "G-League," as paid for by Gatorade—the first
deal of its sort among the U.S. big four—as the sports drink got

to plunk its logo on balls, jerseys, and signage; synergize research (i.e., product testing) at its Gatorade Sports Science Institute; and collaborate on behind-the-scenes branded video content featuring players.[87] Some suspect an auction for a championship series sponsorship (e.g., "The State Farm Finals") cannot far behind. Almost perfectly befitting that geographically imperialist ethos of contemporary advertising—and with a tin ear for drawing politically incorrect 19th-century analogies—NBA commissioner Adam Silver boasted that the branded uniform initiative was part of the "manifest destiny of sports" to move toward more commercial opportunities of just this sort.[88] Jersey ads are, in particular, an emblematic—if unstated—exploitation of totemic power, in the sense that brands seek to cozy up, as closely as possible, to the copyrighted symbol that retains such a powerful emotional hold on identity and community.

Much as has been seen in other genres of American pop culture, advertising integration in sports media harbors "guerrilla" ambitions; that is, by strategizing subtle appeals engaging consumers outside clearly circumscribed commercial contexts, this advertising tries to camouflage itself in unexpected media spaces and cultural forms.[89] "What ESPN has done—and not only ESPN but all of the sports channels and news channels and so on—is they try to blend it as much as they can with the program," confirms network founder Bill Rasmussen.[90] For example, Tas Melas of NBA TV's *The Starters* reports being asked to come up with daily fantasy segment content for a sponsor in a way that "blends into our sensibility and our tone" (i.e., casual, irreverent) rather than stick out as a stilted formal message; syndicated radio host Doug Stewart likewise says that advertisers ask for his sponsored reads "to seem real natural in the conversation. It seems like ads that you just casually have a conversation about the product—they work a lot better."[91]

This is much the same logic of "naturalizing" that which is commercially contrived as seen in the rise of buzz marketing and social media schemes over the past two decades; advertisers covet influencers for that influence and want to cozy up and blend into it.[92] The economics of sports media reflect this, with premium rates being charged for these sort of live reads that, brands assume, listeners and viewers won't switch off or tune out: "Our hosts and our content—that's what we are, that's what we have. That is our most valuable asset and for our sponsors to associate with that content is the most valuable thing they can have," explains Spike Eskin, program director at WIP Philadelphia.[93]

It is not only journalists and pundits, though, who are targeted for conversational conscription; increasingly, athletes view interviews and press conferences as platforms to work in mentions and uses of partner products.[94] Teams have long leveraged the latter in terms of podium backdrops being sold out for sponsor designs (i.e., intertwined with team totems); recently, a more subtle—and effectively guerrilla—variation has found athletes touring on "raising awareness" junkets on behalf of pharmaceutical backers who stand to benefit from media coverage of a particular health condition or problem.[95] Probably the most spectacular example of these tactics came when Super Bowl victor Peyton Manning—defying Disneyland tradition—gifted Anheuser-Busch some $14 million worth of free media exposure with two post-game brand mentions, including the bizarre and seemingly untenable claim that "what's weighing on my mind is how soon I can get a Bud Light in my mouth" (and which arrived after a conspicuous pre-game Gatorade guzzle and a post-game embrace with the founder of Papa John's, other partners in his portfolio).[96] Wayne from *Wayne's World* could have scarcely been more obvious in accommodating the product placement.

Indeed, the ham-handed nature of that integration suggests that brands might wish to align themselves in more conceptually congruent (or, at least, subtle) ways. Mark Gross, an ESPN senior vice president, explains how that has impacted segment production at the network: "Taglines have turned into a big deal over the years: 'How can we make the sponsor tagline work with the content?' That's what we hear a lot of and, 'How does this play into this sport [or] . . . player [or] . . . play?' . . . [With] General Motors . . . it's, like . . . how do we make 'the smoothest drive' for some form of basketball sponsorship or hockey sponsorship? We roll out a highlight of 'the smoothest drive' of the night."[97]

Examples of this effort to marry brand identity with content texture within sports and sports media are everywhere: from Blue Cross Blue Shield sponsoring an injury report to another health care provider paying to promote walking as healthy lifestyle with every "branded base on balls" to DraftKings installing an outfield wall billboard with fantasy stats to Microsoft furnishing the "Big Data" breakdown of Major League Soccer (hailed, fittingly, as "an authentic way to integrate Microsoft into that message without being completely in your face").[98] Seemingly every category of commercial product—however tangential—can find a willing patron; the Baltimore Orioles recently brokered, for example, the first ever official olive oil sponsorship deal, complete with a "Now We're Cookin'" animated scoreboard feature cued up for big innings.[99]

Increasingly, as with other forms of pop culture, the strategy is to not simply fit the brand into the existing form, but to own the form in full so as to make *it* fit the brand's needs and desires. Or, put differently: "Sponsors do not want to be part of the event; they want to *be* the event."[100] This was more or less borne out in my conversations with buyers and sellers. David Wright, then–senior vice president of global sponsorship for Major League Soccer, notes a shift among clients like Anheuser-Busch away from "slapping a static logo on the outfield wall and paying millions of dollars" to be "a mile wide and an inch deep" and toward "going really deep and owning that space and . . . surrounding that property rather in a way that drove your business forward."[101] This "content imperative"—along with those aforementioned vexing issues of delivery platform—is radically re-shaping sports as every sponsor fancies itself a content creator and every property pursues media company ambitions; as *SportsBusiness Journal*'s Terry Lefton summarizes, "If the biggest question facing the sports industry is how it transforms from a business based on TV rights to one based on new forms of media consumption, then the second-biggest industry question is how its supporting sponsorship industry changes with it."[102]

Answers are already emerging. Lia Stierwalt, senior director of global communication and media for Adidas, emphasizes, "For us, we never want to sponsor content or be an external partner looking in. . . . There has been an evolution in our advertising strategy to go beyond just your traditional 30-second spot." She cites, as the best example of this kind of initiative, Adidas's episodic, documentary-style mini-series released online that chronicled (one of) NBA star Derrick Rose's injury comebacks.[103] "HBO wanted to cover his story and ESPN wanted to cover his story, but he didn't want a media partner telling his story so he came to us," she reports, echoing the themes of dis-intermediation from the last chapter. "It was in full collaboration with Derrick Rose and his family—so we were partners in creating that content."[104]

Other examples of this kind of athletic "advertainment" strategy abound. The NHL's Nashville Predators launched an online show called *Beneath the Ice* (featuring co-sponsor Nissan integrations laced throughout) that mimics the behind-the-scenes *verité* of HBO's *Hard Knocks*.[105] Attempting to win over apathetic millennials to golf, Callaway, in conjunction with Vice Sports, produced a 10-minute film of the rapper Scarface testing out clubs at a Southern California course.[106] NASCAR has partnered with top Hollywood producers to roll out scripted dramas and reality series that feature race car–driving characters and the NFL was fully enmeshed in the production of the 110-minute long-form advertisement *Draft Day*.[107] Its

Saturday morning branded-content cartoon show, *NFL Rush Zone*, represents, as one league senior vice president puts it, how "we've been laser-focused for the last 5 years trying to connect kids to the NFL."[108]

Does editorial or artistic integrity matter? Among interviewees' recollections and experiences, there seems but a modicum of resistance to this commercial intrusion. One *SI* writer invoked the scandal surrounding the *Los Angeles Times*' collusion with the Staples Center, when it ran a special quasi-advertorial magazine section in the paper and shared profits from it with the arena, but those norms seem quaint in the "native" partnership digital era.[109] One broadcast host recalled a Red Bull–branded, color-coded "red zone" portion of the football field that was pulled after a few games on his network due to the unwatchable obtrusiveness.[110] Another veteran anchor for a local network affiliate referenced a "Nissan Play-of-the-Week" feature he read on air once, before his news director requested that they scrap the feature ("I said that's great with me—I'm uncomfortable saying it").[111] Despite getting constantly peppered by interviewees and sources to name check athletes' brand affiliates into copy, *Sports Illustrated* senior writer Greg Bishop says he maintains a blanket policy against any such offers of access in exchange for advertorial mention.[112] And *Deadspin* editor Tommy Craggs actually resigned in protest of an alleged breach of the editorial-business firewall.[113]

More common, though, seems to be a weary resignation to and rationalization of those ever-advancing corporate overlords: "I have read ads on the podcast before—I'm not sure my editors wanted me to do it," ESPN's college football senior writer Ivan Maisel says with a shrug. "You know, there's always a groping about to figure out where the line is between church and state, but I think the listener is smart enough to figure out that you're just running an ad, you know?"[114] In fact, the commercial clutter that so saturates contemporary sports media increasingly represents an impediment to any narrative or content-driven flow: "To be perfectly honest, it's something you have to navigate around. . . . It does get in the way of what would be the normal rhythm of a broadcast," NBC's Bob Costas acknowledges of the ad-reads that clog up any "nice, easy flow" back from a (formal) commercial break between innings.[115]

In order to meet the challenge of fitting in the "upwards of forty- or fifty-plus" sponsored moments throughout every Red Sox broadcast—and preclude them from chewing up time during a close ninth—NESN coordinating producer Russ Kenn tried to map out and frontload them early in every game.[116] In another case, during an appearance on *Around the Horn*, ESPN's Jemele Hill actually recalled a negative aside about McDonald's being bleeped out in postproduction: "It was one of those realizations of, like, I could easily in a column, when I was at the [*Orlando*] *Sentinel*, just say that I hate McDonald's Chicken McNuggets. I say that on TV now and they might decide, 'Hey, guess what? We were going to advertise on your show—now we're not.'"[117] And this increasingly impedes development of content in the first place, as Fox–New York sports reporter Tina Cervasio details:

There's definitely times where you do a sponsored report that's promoting an area of the ballpark that has nothing to do with anything but that. Sometimes, as a journalist, you're like, "Really? I have to do this hit?" But it's part of your job and that's who you're working for and you learn to accept it. . . . You can't get all journalistic and say, "I'm not doing this, because it's fluff." That's what you have to do. . . . [Later in the interview, she adds:] Sometimes you'll want to do a segment and [producers are] like, "Well, get a sponsor—it helps." . . . You also find yourself learning a little bit more about sales and what fits and if that advertising fits the demographic and their audience. That doesn't bother me, by any means—as long as I can get the story across. Or if it's a really cool interview and it's sponsored, great, that's money for the network.[118]

The irony, of course, is that the obviousness of all this abundant branded content being squeezed in only accelerates aspirations toward its textual inverse: invisibility. All of which seems to have created, from the vantage point of professionals working within sports media, a feeling that commercial integration has spiraled out of control. Maisel lays out an apt analogy here: "What started out to be a seamless and subtle advertising method to not get in the way has overwhelmed the content. You know, I mean, you put a quarter teaspoon of red pepper in chili, it's really good—you put four tablespoons, you've created tear gas."[119]

## PRODUCING CELEBRITY CAPITAL

For the players, their primary employer is not only the team. . . . The team is on their side when on a court or a field, but the team can trade them. . . . [James Harden] gets paid more by Adidas than the Rockets and Adidas is not going to trade him back to Nike. . . . Adidas will not complain that he's not practicing or playing defense. Their devotion to him is going to be complete. All they're going to care about is selling his brand. . . . Look at LeBron. . . . LeBron's been more loyal to Nike than he's been to any of his teams.[120]

The cynicism that *Sports Illustrated* senior writer Michael Rosenberg underscores here points toward a second category of commercial colonization: branded athletic celebrity. Sports stardom seems increasingly unique in the postmodern firmament. Fame used to be thought of as more celebratory of democratic capitalism—that is, a meritocratic space where people were free to become well known by dint of skill and pluck.[121] Over the course of several decades, as reality TV inundated the American celebrity landscape with "human pseudo-events"—those who are well-known, tautologically, for being well-known—the Kardashians and their "effort-less" ilk would seem to repudiate that theory of stardom as something "earned."[122]

Sport, on the other hand, still mostly foregrounds personal achievement as the rationale for our reverence, perhaps given the visible crucible of physical toil necessitated.[123] "In true neo-liberal fashion," one scholarly analysis proposes, "the ascent to sport celebrityhood is habitually reduced to individual qualities such as innate talent, dedication, and good fortune, thus positioning the sport star as a deserved benefactor of his/her devotion to succeed."[124] (Chapter 5 will further tackle the pernicious inequality implications of this myth.) For now, though, we might note that if a celebrity is a *product* of capital accumulation, he or she also obviously *produces* capital for aligned entities (and, peeling back the curtain further, *is produced* him- or herself by an elaborate media apparatus). The historical precedence for this economic logic runs deep—it is, indeed, more than a century old, stretching back to the beginnings of the motion picture industry and the Hollywood star system. Film studios would seize upon hot young talent and scaffold out appealing personas through well-oiled publicity machines, assuming that identification with and attachment to beloved celebrities could lure audiences into theaters; these dependable fan bases helped the industry cope with the inherent risk of producing expensive cultural texts like movies.[125]

Sport has been no less immune to these market imperatives and promotional recourses, with athlete celebrities playing a critical role in building audiences across each successive media era from newspapers to broadcasting to digital; television, in particular, needing reliable viewership to show up on couches at the appointed times, devotes much of its work to introducing appealing stars and facilitating fan affinity for their fates.[126] "Is [that] any different than a big name actor being in a movie?" asks David Wright, former MLS sponsorship head. "That's going to grab your attention . . . You're drawn to familiarity, so if you recognize players, particularly the more high-profile the player is, there's that element of awe and that element of—man, I wish I had that or that element of the lifestyle that the player lives."[127]

Since the early days of modern sport, the American mass media have proven essential to symbiotically constructing that image that went beyond mere box score stats and, thus, creating celebrity capital for athletes; newspapers and newsreels helped define and disseminate the profiles of those like Red Grange and Babe Ruth as icons for aspiration.[128] Simultaneously, television helped catapult athletic stars beyond the confines of sport and into the wider stratosphere of pop culture, not least due to the increasing primacy of facial appeal as a marketing mandate.[129] The NBA has been the biggest beneficiary of these trends, thanks to its sartorial dictates; that is, a player's visage and expressiveness is unconstrained by hat or helmet and therefore more promotion-friendly as a human "product" in the attention economy. "They play in their underwear and you are much closer to them as a fan than any other sport," observes Terry Lefton, *SportsBusiness Journal*'s marketing reporter. "It's easier to imagine being like Mike than it is being like someone wearing a lot of armor."[130]

The successful industrial production of—and ensuing receptiveness to—athletic celebrity benefits almost every institution in the supply chain that is the sports media complex. For teams, sports stars serve much the same economic "insurance" policy that, say, Tom Cruise furnishes his own film franchises: bankable attraction. As one sports marketing executive notes of the imperative to find a "face" of the franchise: "It's so hard to maintain casual fans when they don't really know who to identify with."[131] Despite those helmets and armor, the NFL is no less beholden to and dependent upon that "minting [of] stars, whose storylines [fans] can follow week to week, like episodes of a favorite scripted show"; in 2016, for example, the few regular season games that outdrew the previous year's audience had some of the most famous players involved.[132] More broadly, entire leagues—particularly for new and ascending sports—also need attractive personas to stake their institutional identity upon; ideally, "a superstar who embodied the essence of that sport," as Mark McCormack, IMG founder, often advocated.[133]

Perhaps the most emblematic execution of this strategy in recent memory was Major League Soccer landing global icon David Beckham in the winter years of his career. This "watershed moment," former executive David Wright recalls, immediately burnished the entire league's credibility and kick-started a virtuous and profitable cycle of audience interest, TV ratings, live attendance, sponsorship dollars, and other soccer stars gravitating to the U.S.: "The fact that, arguably, the most recognizable athlete on the planet at the time was choosing to ply his trade in MLS was a really powerful statement. . . . Hundreds, if not billions of people . . . knew he played in Major League Soccer . . . That in and of itself had tremendous value just from a marketability standpoint."[134]

That need to cultivate celebrity capital persists at the forefront of MLS's efforts to grow within the U.S. sports marketplace; recent policy changes include allowing cameras in the locker room before games and in huddles during play and affixing microphones to coaches so as to enlarge performer identities and amplify ratings.[135] "We share the same view with the league that we have a responsibility to 'star build' and to make the players part of a bigger conversation that goes beyond the play on the field but into who they are," says Amy Rosenfeld, ESPN's executive producer for soccer. "If we can personalize these guys a little more, that may expand our reach and help get an audience beyond that soccer-centric viewer."[136]

Finally, as with Paramount, MGM, and other Hollywood studios, sports media and professionals alike have a vested stake in inflating and being carried upward by rising athletic stars. They remain the choicest click-bait for headline schemes: "Obviously, if you write Curry, if you write LeBron, if you write Kobe, you're going to get hits. It doesn't hurt to write about them as much as possible," explains Marc Spears of Yahoo! Sports. "I'm giving the people what they like. They like Kobe, they like the Lakers, so until they stop reading about them, I'm going to give what they like."[137] This is no less true for ESPN, which has been criticized for cultivating "a sycophantic celebrity culture" that builds "athletes into superheroes," not unlike its parent company Disney betting on blockbusters to shore up shareholder value.[138]

Athletic celebrity also buoys corporate brands—endemic and otherwise—seeking lucrative alignment opportunities. Horst Dassler, Adidas founder, might have been the earliest executive to calculate and capitalize on this, recognizing that the best way to sell shoes was to have top athletes sport them and thus securing sponsorship of national teams.[139] More recently, as sports marketing executive A. J. Maestas points out, Nike—a virtual non-entity in the golf business prior to signing Tiger Woods—rode his success to the top of that retail category: "People aspire to that athlete, they're in love with that team—and that loyalty transfers. It's crazy, it's irrational—and that's the whole definition of fanatic, right?"[140]

Indeed, recall from chapter 1, there is a fundamental irrationality underpinning the attachments forged between consumers and their idols, be they individual or team—an affective value that sport is becoming ever more adept at evoking, manipulating, and harvesting. In turn, players have become conscious of and savvy about their relationship with and, furthermore, identity *as* brands—evinced by the unsentimental Michael Jordan quip that opened the chapter. Jordan was both the trailblazer and still-reigning champion of being Athlete Inc.—"an embodied fusion of sporting mastery and commercial maximization," which boosted his own standing along with that of the Chicago Bulls, the NBA, and Nike in a circuit of mutually profitable promotion.[141] More brazenly putting the retail cart before the on-court horse, point guard Lonzo Ball debuted a $500 signature sneaker (the "Big Baller Brand") prior to ever playing his first Los Angeles Lakers game; his father defended that price as "missing the point" with Baudrillardian blasé: "The point, he said, is that the shoe is symbolic. According to Ball, 'Symbolic as he's [Lonzo] the first one ever to come in here [the NBA] without ever playing a game and have his own brand.'"[142]

Veteran agent Leigh Steinberg suggests, through an example, that this individual self-promotion can sometimes collide with league-level schemes and contexts:

> The NFL puts a lot of pressure on players to be at the draft. They sell it as an event—it's now become a four-day event. They rely on the fact that all the top players will be there to promote new draft ratings to drive all sorts of promotions. [In 2015, top picks] Marcus Mariota and Jameis Winston didn't come . . . It's generally understood they were paid a large amount of money—it's rumored to be $250,000—to stay at home and wear Beats headphones while they were being drafted [as opposed to those of official league partner Bose].[143]

If, therefore, fame can be conceptualized as a cultural product— one that is inextricably woven into commercial opportunities and constraints—what might be the "institutional structures, production practices, [and] representational conventions" that inform and define the image-making industry of sport celebrity in the digital age?[144] For global sports agencies like Octagon and IMG, manufacturing that celebrity has become a "highly systematized, almost McDonaldized . . . process"—and even agencies like William Morris and CAA, which historically catered to a wider realm of entertainment properties and clients, have reportedly gone "all in" on sports.[145] Young stars are typically packaged through a journalistic narrative frame (and, twinned, commercial messaging) that emphasizes a fairly predictable set of traits: vivacity, raw talent, and the looming weight of high expectations.[146] Bob Dorfman, executive creative director at Baker Street Advertising, further condenses the formula for celebrity production—that is, what is sought out from the athlete and what is accentuated as that athlete is fashioned into commercial spectacle—to an alliterative aphorism:

> I call it the "five P's," which is: performance, which is obviously on the field; personality, which is how you carry yourself off the field, how you are in front of the camera; purity, which is, again, more off-the-field stuff, how clean you are and how scandal-free you are; poignancy, which is backstory, if you've got a good backstory, if it's a rags-to-riches story, if there's something in your past that you've overcome, those kind of things help; and last one is perseverance, which is, you have to really want to be a marketable guy.[147]

It is instructive (and perhaps self-serving) that only one of Dorfman's five categories actually has anything to do with that which happens in the game itself—the rest representing out-of-bounds opportunities and contexts for spectacle-makers to involve themselves and bill for services. And, yet, Kim McConnie, senior director for sports marketing at Pepsi, echoes the notion that appearance might matter as much as accomplishments when it comes to star assembly: "When we look at someone who's going to be a brand ambassador, [we ask] . . . , 'Do they have a lifestyle and personality that fits what the brand is about as well?' Then, obviously, having on-court performance or on-field performance, but not always."[148] This is the essence of branding, really: overwhelming substance and function with style and performance as the crucible of and motivation for economic activity. Phil Knight's insight was in recognizing and exploiting this postmodern transformation—that his sneakers were made "to be displayed rather than just worn," a commodity whose "value lay less in what they were, more in who was wearing them" (namely, Jordan).[149]

Leagues also recognize the importance of crafting off-field identity for their stars so as to snare spectator interest. WNBA president Lisa Borders calls this her league's "biggest area of opportunity" (which is also PR spin for "present deficiency"): "It is marketing our players as individual players. There are many dimensions to their personalities beyond the court. People follow not just a league but follow people. . . . We have players who we haven't introduced to sponsors and the public and perhaps not elevated what they do beyond the court. We have focused on what they do as team players and we have promoted their statistics and their athleticism."[150]

Some of the techniques for achieving this are fairly obvious. Dorfman notes the need to "play up" and ensure the visibility of charitable service and visiting hospitals and such (i.e., "the good stuff—they're not just beating their wives and drinking in clubs and making it rain").[151] The narrative focus within sports media on covering player lifestyles, à la *Entertainment Tonight*, also helps manufacture and manage those off-field impressions.[152] Some players take this upon themselves, as seen most elaborately in the case of Chad Johnson, the Cincinnati Bengals wideout who changed his name to "Ochocinco," staged flamboyant touchdown dances, formed his own "news network" Twitter handle, and competed on *Dancing with the Stars*.[153] "I no longer play football," Ochocinco emblematically declared amidst his fifth season, "I'm an entertainer."

Similarly, when a former Fox Sports vice chairman was brought in to jazz up content and juice ratings at the Tennis Channel, he advised running features on pop culture tastes and media preferences (e.g., favorite movies, music) to better personalize the sport's up-and-coming stars: "There's a tendency when you do that, there are people in the audience who are going to say, 'Hey. He likes the same television show that I like.' In a small way, there's a connection."[154] The NHL has similarly redoubled its efforts to accentuate player personalities, as explained by its chief content officer (itself a relatively new C-suite portfolio): "We want our fans to get to know the players even better, and some of that has to be in fun situations. Sometimes it's those little moments where someone says, 'Hey, I didn't realize that guy had that great smile or that sense of humor' that makes them a fan.'"[155] (For a league whose labor force often struggles to maintain dental normalcy, the "great smile" gambit might be challenging.)

To be sure, these calculations are hardly novel; embedding sports celebrity in the fabric of American pop culture is a tactic that former commissioner David Stern pursued as a way of "legitimizing" the NBA and its stars back in the 1980s and 1990s: "We worked very hard to get our players on places like everything from *The Tonight Show*, Arsenio Hall, the David Letterman show. You name it, we were there and then you started seeing our players appearing in bit parts in *Seinfeld* or things like that. We worked very hard just to make our game and our players as mainstream as we possibly could and fighting off certain perceptions however we dealt with them— that the sport was too black, that the players used too many drugs, that their salaries . . . were too high."[156]

Stern also, rather inadvertently, fostered the biggest aesthetic transformation of professional athletes when, in 2005 following a vicious brawl among players and fans at a game in Detroit, he instituted a dress code that forbade hip-hop couture (e.g., do-rags, gaudy jewelry) in favor of more "professional" attire. "Why did NBA commissioner David Stern feel compelled to implement [that]?" scoffs ESPN's Jemele Hill. "It's because Stern wanted the league to remain appealing to mainstream fans. Translation: He wants white America to feel comfortable watching his product."[157]

Although unquestionably policing a racially specific style and drawing rebuke from stars like Allen Iverson, other players recognized an opportunity to further expand their brand share through sartorial expression. High fashion followed. "I think eventually guys felt more into being *GQ* than being hip-hop," says NBA writer Marc Spears of Yahoo! Sports. "Once they had started becoming more business-like, becoming more professional in their dress, so to speak, it seemed like doors were opening for them that you hadn't seen before."[158] Stern adds: "We told the guys they had to wear shoes and a shirt with a collar, but—maybe it was a trigger point, a catalyst for them to realize—as I realized, of course—if I had bodies like theirs, I would dress myself up the way they do. They're handsome, well-built guys. And they went well beyond the dress code."[159]

David Beckham has similarly been called the quintessential "postmodern star"—someone who represents the triumph of style at the expense of substance and has licensed his image across a wide range of commercial contexts.[160] Appearance plainly matters, even in an arena of "democratic capitalist" fame where the scoreboard doesn't give out points for form. The attractiveness of certain stars—Beckham, Jordan, Derek Jeter, Tom Brady—obviously amplifies their marketability. So, too, does distinctiveness: "It can be so shallow sometimes," says *Sports Illustrated*'s Michael Rosenberg. "If [James Harden] doesn't have a beard, how much money does Adidas give him? That's a great question that I can guarantee it's less. He just a guy in Houston."[161] Over the last generation, that metrosexual evolution of athletes' fashion from baggy to tailored, not to mention many hiring stylists ("that will monitor everything that they do off the court") and showing up at runway shows suggests that there is now a more manicured set of practices that go into "building the brand."[162]

Oklahoma City Thunder point guard Russell Westbrook perhaps most embodies this shift and mentality. In a profile for *Adweek* (clad on the cover in a tight-fitting, buttoned-to-the-neck leather shirt), he declares, "I don't want to be seen as just a basketball guy. . . . I think of basketball as just a great platform for me to jump off into different things."[163] Such "things" have included brand collaborations, co-designs, and line extensions into cologne, jewelry, eyeglass frames, croco-print luggage, and snakeskin slippers, many of which retail at Barneys stores. An aesthete who draws inspiration from women's clothing and the interior décor of hotels he has visited, he also helped develop the first lifestyle shoe within the Jordan brand ("The Westbrook Zero"), which, he hopes, will "compete with Gucci, Prada" and other luxury shoes.[164] Admitting that he takes nearly an hour to get ready—and often three outfit changes, along with a texted photo to his mother to get her opinion—Westbrook is part of a generation of player-dandies who have turned the arena-arrival tunnel walk and post-game podium appearance into "red-carpet event[s]": *Queer Eye for the Point Guard.* Pepsi marketing executive Kim McConnie explains all this persnickety couture curation is partly why they signed him to their Mountain Dew sub-brand:

> Our association with Russell is not about what's on the court. If you have a look at the advertising and what we've done with Russell Westbrook, it's all about celebrating the lifestyle of basketball which exists so much so off the court: What are these players doing outside of the court? What are they wearing? They're becoming fashion icons. What are they listening to? That's really what we've tapped into there . . . No one's going to drink Pepsi when they're playing sport, but that's not what we want either—how do we make sure that we're recognizing the player holistically and finding those moments? That's more relevant.[165]

Not surprisingly, social media has become indispensable for packaging those moments. Much as we saw of these platforms helping athletes dis-intermediate traditional journalists, so, too, have they become intrinsic to and inextricable from personal brand building.[166] "Athletes have been able to create their own persona independent of any other vehicle other than themselves," laments Chris Dufresne of *the Los Angeles Times*. "They've become almost like independent contractors where they used to be—your celebrity, your stardom, may have been tied 20 or 30 years ago, to what team drafted you. If you were drafted by a crummy team that was in a small market, then you weren't going to get as much attention." Nowadays, though, "you can kind of create your own empire independent of your circumstance."[167] Russell Westbrook—playing in the infinitesimal media market that is central Oklahoma but nonetheless peddling luxury goods to cosmopolitan consumers nationwide—embodies this comparative irrelevance of geographic placement. And to achieve those entrepreneurial aims, more athletes and sports figures are putting their agents' and managers' contact information directly into their Twitter page bios.[168]

Brands, for that matter, increasingly reward and sometimes even demand that endorsees engage online in prolific and savvy ways. Sponsorship deals now feature social media clauses; Dunkin' Donuts, for example, reportedly won't even consider an athlete without "a proven track record of engaging . . . posts."[169] One veteran agent reports having to adjust to a whole "new quantification system" for categorizing his clients based upon their followers across Instagram, Facebook, LinkedIn, Snapchat, and the like when evaluating and touting their ability to move product.[170] Simultaneously, a scrappy micro-industry has sprung up to try to finance product placements in these digital confines much like their analog antecedents.[171] For example, golfer Rory McIlroy's Twitter postings on behalf of Bose were reportedly worth more than $7 million; swimmer Michael Phelps did almost $300,000 of social media work for Under Armour; and LeBron James netted nearly $150,000 for Kia integrations.[172]

Similar to the efforts discussed earlier where brands seek to blend themselves subtly into more objective sports media content, social media marketing also tries not to come off as commercially "intentional." Take the comments of one executive at a celebrity content marketing firm on a McDonald's "branded storytelling" social deal inked with running back DeAngelo Williams: "It's a very collaborative piece with him. . . . He wanted to make it an authentic process so it wasn't so sales-y. . . . He talks about how he eats pancakes in his own funky way, so fans feel like they are having breakfast with DeAngelo. So it is not as much in-your-face as normal ads."[173] In other cases, brands are looking to repurpose some of the video content that emerges from the social feeds of their stars, drawn to the "[un]scripted" persuasive power that those clips might retain.[174] "[Athletes are] already putting all of this content of their own out into the world, so what we will do, thanks to social, is use that to make our ads," says Jason Norcross, executive creative director at 72 and Sunny.[175] One start-up even offers personalized social media postings from athletes, the digital equivalent of an autographed trading card message; for $50 fans can purchase a birthday or congratulatory online message from their favorite sports stars to show up on Facebook or Twitter.[176]

The end goal here is, of course, producing and projecting celebrity characters to secure "para-social relationships" with fans. This term refers to a curious, albeit widespread psychological state of imagined connection (and subsequent market value) that seems much more plausible and practicable given the technological advances of the last decade.[177] Moreover, in order to justify the meritocratic foundation of their sports celebrity, establishing (or, at least, simulating) intimate familiarity and everyday accessibility becomes especially critical. The public must be reminded of sports stars' earthbound roots even as they soar through the stratosphere of success and fame: "Whilst being extraordinary they are also ordinary—

like the rest of us, they have parents, partners, and children, whose admiration will be part of the prize. . . . They did not get where they are through unfair advantage."[178] The more astronomical the salary, the more remote the athlete might seem; the media infrastructure of celebrity now has to help humanize and authenticate the same star it boosted to such great heights. Thus, producing a commercial of LeBron James running around with children in his neighborhood—and making it seem like his "life is an open book," as Norcross sought—not only stages his "approachab[ility]," but, more so, anchors his otherworldliness in a context that provides faith in both the brand and in the capitalist system he hath ascended.[179] Ironically, it makes him worthy of our worship.

## THE VALUE OF TOTEMIC FELLOWSHIP

It is through consumer goods that the "fan" can increase their knowledge, and more importantly, display their commitment through conversation and the consumer goods they own and display, which allows them to . . . feel increasingly integrated within their chosen supporter community. For crucially, this is what the contemporary sport venue sells. In an increasingly unsafe, insecure and individualized world, the contemporary sport venue provides a sense of community and belonging—be it a community you can buy into with limited knowledge and commitment once a week or a much deeper sense of belonging and commitment, the consumer goods exist for you to achieve this.[180]

As chapter 1 argued, the affective power of the sports totem resides in its capacity to grant identity and cohere community; this is also, as the above passage suggests, the most valuable commodity that a team can produce and sell. Indeed, sport is probably unsurpassed among contemporary cultural spaces where transcendent social experience can be leveraged and exploited to generate massive returns on capital investment.[181] Roone Arledge, the pioneering ABC producer whose designs for *Monday Night Football* helped establish the aesthetic template for all TV sports, understood this well: to seduce sponsors, he knew that he had to first hook viewers emotionally in his broadcast, which meant shifting the focus of coverage away from the game, exclusively, and onto the audience community, with whom fans at home could identify.[182] For sports media, then, the audience has always partly been the *product*—and not just in an advertiser-exchange sense: Fellow fans are sold to each other as the inventory for fellowship and the reason for caring.

Corporate sponsors have similarly wised up to this ambition: "The brands with the big money, that spend all this money in sport, don't really need awareness anymore," reports A. J. Maestas, a sports marketing executive who has brokered some of those pursuits. "They're looking—the big spenders in particular—are looking to deepen their relationship with consumers and have a more emotional or loyal relationship."[183] One example of this effort to "tell shareable, touching stories" that "are not promotional in nature," but rather "a means to effectively shape the way people perceive their identity," as one digital director puts it, was his firm's campaign for Tide that featured a heartstrings-tugging "homecoming and reconciliation" video about quarterback Brett Favre's return to Lambeau Field for the retirement of his jersey. Posted to Favre's Facebook page, it earned 24,000 shares, while allegedly "help[ing] fans reconnect with a star they wanted to love again."[184]

The activities of fan cultures are therefore, both by default and by design, mostly consumer-oriented.[185] Framing this in Durkheimian terms, to be identified as a member of the totemic tribe requires performing a series of commercial acts that communicate those "essential coordinates of the self" outwardly.[186] And because such consumption underpins our "identity performance," the more merch we buy, the closer we show ourselves, in public, to be linked to that sacred social center.[187] This explains the appeal of getting decked out in logoed team goods from head to toe: It declares righteous allegiance to a (commodified) form of faith. "We are true fans only if we successfully keep up with the items that teams and professional leagues churn out," concludes one scholar. "Instead of showing loyalty to the team by supporting the players, fans show loyalty by buying the latest shirts and hats."[188] In turn, sports institutions have realized that "fan equity" is what remains on the balance sheets once all other revenues and liabilities are factored out and seek to "harvest this affectivity" toward commercial ends by providing ample and ever-evolving opportunities to embed that identity in the copyrighted property that affords collective connectivity.[189]

Such opportunism arrives at birth: The Washington Capitals started giving out free (branded) onesies and bibs to newborns at various DC-area hospitals, encouraging parents to "share photos of their newborn by using the #CapsPlayoffBaby hashtag on social media."[190] And it continues unto death: At West Ham United's new stadium, fans can purchase "personalised message stones in the different legends' sections so that your name can be immortalised alongside theirs."[191] (Recall the prophecy from chapter 1: As long as the totem survives, so do we.) Mark Lev, who runs a sports marketing firm, explains the logic of that lucrative attachment: "It's a religious experience for some fans and because they're so connected and interested in everything about this passion that they have because of their identity . . . it's that passion and that affinity that you leverage and that you connect sponsors to."[192]

Selling back to fans the very energy that they generate? Some theorize that this is, abstractly, the point of all successful branding: to elicit action and affect among enthusiasts on behalf of corporate copyrights; to provide, as one scholar puts it, "an environment, an ambience, which anticipates and programs the agency of consumers," so as to produce "ethical surplus—a social relation, a shared meaning, an emotional investment that was not there before."[193] Probably even more so than with Harley riders or Apple fanatics, sports fans see themselves as "extensions of the team," which makes their culture the pinnacle of brand productivity.[194]

The most conspicuous (or, at least, loudest) example of co-opting fans' free labor in this vein might be the Seattle Seahawks' "12th Man" tradition (i.e., fans as a complementary force to the 11 players allowed on the field).[195] Deliberately designing CenturyLink Field's structural acoustics to maximize the "sonic labor" of spectators, that output then becomes an "exploitable . . . . commercial resource" that gets cleverly marketed *back* to ticket-buyers as one of the primary reasons for attending games—and winds up selling no small number of #12 jerseys along the way.[196] "Their '12th Man' organization is not like some, 'I pay to be a member of the club and then I get discounted tickets back from it,'" notes A. J. Maestas. "The '12th Man' club means that I am a member of this community and I help the Seahawks win."[197] Such delusions of impactful unity have been similarly indulged to valuable ends elsewhere across the sports landscape: After winning their first championship, the Miami Heat gave out replica trophies to season ticket holders at a private event that were meant to explicitly imply, "You were a part of this championship."[198] (When the team finished 23 games back and out of the playoffs in 2015, we can assume that the same fans were not issued pink slips.)

Social media is again essential, setting the stage for and initiating the activation of that free labor. It is assumed that, through Facebook, Twitter, Instagram, and Pinterest, fans' interactivity might "help [them] feel as though they are part of a larger group"—as when the team solicits fans to post content and images of themselves in licensed apparel in social settings, be they directly game-related (e.g., tailgating and in the stands) or otherwise incidental (e.g., themed weddings, home décor, and other "personal affects such as team-related tattoos and manicures").[199] In turn, within these spaces, the team—a branded, corporate entity fixated on revenue diversification—can affect the sheen of "authenticity" and a pretense of "disinterested" objectivity about its own instrumentality of profit-purpose; the totem exists for identity and community, we are meant to believe, not for the cash registers ringing in our ears.[200] Thus, social media gets hyped not merely as a promotional tool, but as the "space for a brand or organization to be *real*, just as its consumers or fans are," "relatable," and acting with a "heightened degree of earnestness and truthfulness."[201] All of this is, of course, both total bullshit and often genuinely experienced; the former need not preclude the latter. As a Chargers fan, I certainly buy into it, even as I know I'm being conned.

"That's really the ultimate principle that we operate on: that if you're glued to your TV and you're a huge Cowboys fan and you see that the Cowboys drink Pepsi, and they're a fan of Pepsi, then you feel more positively predisposed to Pepsi," diagrams Kim McConnie, senior director of sports marketing for the soft drink company.[202] Simplistic, irrational, and even mindless as that "logic" may sound (recall here the arguments of chapter 1), the fulcrum for that transference of allegiance is the totem. As such, it is, in the words of another business executive, "the single biggest, most valuable asset that a sports property has to deliver," because it is the repository for all that latent emotional and social energy.[203]

How else to explain the 4 percent sales bump in 2015 for Bud Light in markets where the cans suddenly started featuring the local NFL team's logo embedded in the aluminum design?[204] As the campaign rolled out to the whole league, the brewer hoped, amusingly, that the cans might "become another way for NFL teams to fly their club's flag, like wearing a favorite team's jersey." As with crucifixes (and Chargers' caps, for that matter), so, too, through Anheuser-Busch, the (unstated) corporate theory runs, human social identity and fellowship might somehow be forged.[205]

Ultimately, the goal—however far-fetched it may sound—is to convince fans to care more about the means in the stands than the ends on the field; that is, to be so bound to allegiance itself (as a source of identity and a space for community) that totemic worship is worth more than individual game or even season-long outcomes. As the executive vice president of business operations for the San Francisco Giants explains, "We want to make the connection between our organization and our fans so tight that, if we have a rough year, they're going to stick with us. They're not with us because of wins and losses; they're with us because we're the brand they want to be connected with."[206] Sometimes, this takes (see: Cubs, Chicago); often it doesn't (see: those "fair-weather" fans in Miami, Phoenix, and, yes, San Diego).

At a time when community can feel in short supply, that is an enticing, perhaps even unrivaled product to stock and sell. Sport slings it about as well as any purveyor, marketing not just the games themselves but also, as sports culture scholars Richard Gruneau and David Whitson discern, "the prospect of belonging to the community of team supporters . . . even if 'community' here [takes] on a meaning more akin to shared brand allegiance."[207] This is also what the literature on "brand communities" and "tribal marketing" revolves around.[208] The trademarked logo aims to be an amulet against anomie; a fortification of fellowship amidst fragmentation. To that end, an op-ed in *SportsBusiness Journal* reimagines Maslow's hierarchy of needs—that psychological theory which holds humans are driven by motives ranging, pyramid-like, from physically basic to more cosmologically abstract—through the lens of sports consumption and fandom, concluding that it is critical for business interests to cultivate "love, belonging, and community" and "self-actualization" through the team:

> The relationship can evolve to the point where the ticket-plan holder feels part of the organization and belongs to something bigger than himself/herself. . . . They refer to the team as "we," "us," and "our" regardless of wins/losses because they have identified with the team and become part of a community that belongs to each other and the team. . . . The love of the team has reached a point when benefits, recognition, team performance, accomplishment, etc., are almost irrelevant with regard to extending the relationship. The relationship continues because it has become an important part of the fabric of fans' lives, a behavior that has become part of their lifestyle, and in many cases how they define who they are and what is important to them.[209]

This also requires reframing and reemphasizing apparel and accessories as the means by which new fans are socialized into that community and old fans reaffirm their commitment; unknowingly echoing Durkheim, another article in a sports marketing journal concludes, "Tribal groups are constantly on the lookout for anything that can support or facilitate their communion—e.g., a site, an emblem, the support of a ritual of integration or of recognition."[210] The savvier teams and leagues are packaging precisely that.[211] This makes articulations of a "tradition of 'community'" often inseparable from "traditions of commercial spectacle"—and while, again, the latter does not invalidate the former (that affect is often true, real, and felt), it also clearly enriches stakeholders because of it.[212] Another op-ed in *SportsBusiness Journal* about Real Madrid supposedly caring "as much about bringing joy to the community and spreading and sharing the community's positive values . . . as they do winning championships" reads even more like a TED Talk translation of *The Elementary Forms of Religious Life*:

> It is impossible to tell where the fan's identity and life as a Madridista and the club's identity and purpose start and stop. . . . [A] Madridista benefits from the community with new friendships, a sense of belonging, shared experiences, recognition, and increased self-esteem. . . . Since Real Madrid's community values are inclusive and universal, the community itself grows globally, which leads to worldwide sponsors spending big money for association with and access to the Real Madrid community, as well as television broadcasters paying lots of money to distribute the game to the large, passionate global audience. . . . Real Madrid isn't just providing a soccer game; they are providing a larger experience or entertainment that draws in a community member to actively participate, for a memorable sensation.[213]

Slogans are one way to conceptualize community through marketed form. Liverpool FC's "You'll never walk alone" anthem and crest motto is a superb example of putting into words the totemic allure that sports allegiance affords amidst a world of postmodern anonymity. Nike's most lavish football marketing campaign in half a decade pegged itself to "the importance of an NFL jersey as a social and cultural totem" with the tagline "Who You With."[214] Former NBA commissioner David Stern notes that inclusivity has also informed a generation of his league's taglines (e.g., "Join In").[215] And discussing his agency's work on the "+ Together We're Giant" campaign for San Francisco's baseball team, advertising executive Bob Dorfman explains how to situate that loyalty within profit-friendly expressions:

The idea is that the fans are the 10th man. The fans are as much a part of the team's success as the team is, as the players are—their being there contributes to the enthusiasm, the emotion. It makes the players play better. That's something we've always tried to establish . . . Your enthusiasm; your fandom; your wearing panda hats or giraffe outfits or painting your face orange, black, and orange; wearing the team colors—all that stuff contributes to the success of the team. . . . [Later in the interview, he adds:] Pretty much everything we do, in one way or another, has the fans involved in it. Whether it's visual representation—some spots we're working on now really are featuring fans more than the players, in a sense. . . . It's all . . . about the "we-ness" of everything.[216]

It is not only slogans and commercials, though, which seek to cement that sense of shared social identity; physical spaces also cultivate community by enabling and encouraging bodily ritual to take place. The Seahawks' CenturyLink stadium, discussed earlier for its advantageous properties in channeling noise labor, was specifically designed to foster that bygone experience of interdependence in an otherwise "deterritorialized" era of "postcapitalist placelessness."[217] The Milwaukee Bucks attempted to launch an audition-evaluated "super fan" section, evocative of the traditions of rabid soccer devotees in Europe who "make going to the game an experience"—*the* experience, I would suggest—and whose enthusiasm might be co-opted into merchandise markets.[218] "One of the stickiest factors for people being loyal to attending and passionate about a team is the tailgating experience, because it takes it outside of just the football experience and makes it a community affair. It's a barbecue; it's family time; it's a tradition with my old friends from college, at a university, or my buddies at work," one sports marketing executive points out. "It's about community; it's about loyalty; it's about connectivity."[219]

There is an architectural upshot to these schemes as well. The communal focus is literally reshaping the structure of team venues from Sacramento to Minneapolis to Denver to Atlanta, as seen in the trend toward ripping out cheap seats in favor of standing-room-only social areas in which to mingle and graze; this has been especially driven by assumptions about how the younger generation of fans prefer "a shared experience instead of the game itself being the center of attention."[220] Given a competitive entertainment marketplace, excellent home viewing alternatives, and the "experience economy" appeal, these spaces can be sold at a healthy premium, as the Minnesota Vikings discovered with their successful "Club Purple": "It's not just sitting and watching the game anymore. It's interacting with other people," explains one Vikings vice president. "It's becoming a community in and of itself. People aren't confined to a traditional club seat. They can wander around in their own space and see another couch owner and interact with them." One senior vice president of planning and development for an MLB franchise calls this change in behavior and building "one of the biggest issues she's seen in her career designing ballparks."[221] Elsewhere, NASCAR has contemplated redirecting track noise to make races just a bit quieter and therefore more conducive for fans—especially millennials—to talk to one another.[222]

As Rich Luker, a consultant who studies sports trends and advises leagues, argues: "Make your strategies around how your sport enhances the opportunities and quality of experience with family and friends. Make the fan experience about a better way to be with family and friends, not just about the sport."[223] Similarly, for FanDuel and DraftKings, the purported key to winning over "casual fans" to daily fantasy sports—and thus feeding their revenues—is "replicating the camaraderie and friendly competition" that already drives workplace and family leagues.[224] In sum, fellowship is a valuable feeling (and, literally, a lucrative commodity) in a fragmented age.

But how does one manufacture that fellowship in the absence of history and success?[225] It seems easy enough to co-opt community and merchandise identity if one is CMO of, say, the New York Yankees or Green Bay Packers—tougher if you're an expansion franchise in Tampa or Vegas. How, in other words, to sell a totem from scratch? The Jacksonville Jaguars present a compelling case study that draws together several of the aforementioned strands, not least because it is a youthful franchise lacking many traditions (like, for instance, winning) in a city plagued by a high population turnover. "We started doing things like introducing traditions that we didn't have before," explains Hussain Naqi, the team's senior vice president for fan engagement.[226] These have included "The Prowl," where players pass through a gauntlet of fans en route to taking the field, and a bell-ringing by honored members of the military to mark the start of the fourth quarter.

"You try to seed [these] and you hope that it becomes organic and you hope that it becomes something that fans take to," Naqi notes. "Drawing people to a game and having people stay for longer with traditions to bring them along the way are really, really important. The Red Sox could be getting blown out, but people will stick around for the [eighth] inning." (Neil Diamond sing-alongs have that effervescent effect, apparently.) But building amenities that accentuate the social setting don't hurt either: A recent stadium renovation added two pools and 16 cabanas to a "party deck" beyond the end zone, as well as stadium-wide Wi-Fi and a fantasy sports "fan cave." The vibe itself, in other words, might eventually become the draw: "People are just up there [in the pool] having a good time, listening to music, dancing, enjoying themselves and half of them can't see the fields, because of the depth . . . They're just there for the atmosphere." In sum, what's out of bounds, socially, increasingly matters most financially.

## THINK GLOBALLY, NOT LOCALLY

As with any other industry operating under market imperatives, it is ownership—not producers (i.e., players), much less consumers (i.e., fans)—that most determine the terms, conditions, and extent of the American sports spectacle and, as has remained true for decades, "their loyalty to their capital will always surpass their loyalty to the team."[227] These commercial patrons exert an "agenda setting power" in their capacity to decide which culture exists and which doesn't through their finicky financing.[228] Over the course of a century, the integration of sports into commodity culture has refashioned how we are supposed to relate to our favorite teams and players—shifting attachment to institutions once deeply symbolic of specific communities to more corporate, delocalized contexts.[229]

This necessity manifests itself in all kinds of ways, as shown throughout the chapter. In the UK, for example, in pursuit of fancier (and, thus, more lucrative) audiences, soccer clubs have redesigned seating to price out and preclude the working stiff—exorcising the "jumping, swaying, and communal celebration" that, in the past, generated tribal-style "ecstatic solidarity" among those less privileged fans in standing-room-only sections.[230] For U.S. leagues, given the fact that securing a broadcast or cable contract has become the paramount financial objective, those live spectators are, anyhow, nothing more than exploitable "extras" on a TV show set.[231] Simultaneously, team ownership has displaced more affordable seating in pursuit of maximizing money made off of corporate quarters.[232] Such cynicism is merited even as (and perhaps because of) many teams' strategically invoking an old-timey atmosphere—think here of the Camden Yards–ification of American baseball stadia.[233] Nostalgia is not only an expression of longing for lost community; it is also a way of obfuscating the naked greed that triggers it in the first place.[234]

That greed that drives the sports spectacle—and the way in which it disregards local totemic attachments—is cast in particularly stark relief when thinking about the global ambitions of sports leagues, franchises, and players. Since the 1990s, expert observers have forecast a "fundamental reorganization" of big-time sports in response to the foreign markets that beckon.[235] Not unlike Coca-Cola, sports leagues that sense their domestic potential has "peaked" or "tapped" out must naturally look elsewhere for revenue growth (and rumors of an NFL franchise in London have been the loudest).[236]

The NBA has been at the forefront of this "indigenizing" effort—opening offices abroad, playing preseason games in destinations ranging from Beijing to Berlin to Istanbul, and fielding dozens of players from around the world.[237] "We always thought the way you built up and satisfied your fans was to show that you were coming into their time zone. It was a sign of respect—together with television, together with encouraging the athletic shoe and apparel companies to do things on the ground, so to speak, together with making our goods available with licensed merchandise," explains former commissioner David Stern. "You know, we were, like, planting little flags so we could convince the local media."[238]

Certain players themselves became the human vessels for executing those corporate stratagems; this has been termed the "Nowitzki effect," whereby a local boy vaults a particular sport's popularity beyond the margins in his home country by fusing national pride to capital outcomes.[239] Yao Ming might be an even better example here, as the individual who singularly helped the NBA muscle its way into the hearts and minds of a 1.4-billion-person-strong consumer marketplace. "We bridged two countries so that the Chinese could see the U.S. and the U.S. could see a bit of China through Yao," adds Stern. "The most important aspect of it was that we began to get youngsters growing up watching our games and to they extent they can watch—a young French man can watch Tony Parker or an Argentinian can watch Manu Ginobili . . . It was a perpetual motion machine."

A perpetual motion machine of *profit*, Stern might have added. And the reality is that the local is, in fact, a direct impediment to the global. Take, in closing, the following "modest proposal" from one scholar who has studied this issue:

> The major stumbling block to cultivating international publics, however, is the attachment of teams to cities. . . . Local loyalties have become a hindrance to the cultivation of broader publics. . . . Teams must detach from locales altogether and set out to captivate viewers on an international scale. . . . Multinational corporations are ideal for this purpose, and in many ways stand in need of clear identities much as cities and networks once did. . . . Were major league teams to attach directly to multinationals, they would confer identities to the names of these corporations that would make them more a part of the landscapes they alter and provide some security for them in a tumultuous world. . . . The lack of locale is the key virtue of multinationals. . . . Teams would be freed of home locations, and home crowds would be freed of seeing the league entirely through the lens of a single team.[240]

Such a prescription, unfortunately, goes against everything the sports totem stands for and, in turn, provides to believers: tribal rootedness, enduring identity, communal authenticity. It addresses fans as "free-floating consumers rather than as customers with assumed loyalties."[241] It confirms how the durable regionalism once entrenched in sports culture has been displaced by marketing in favor of more gossamer connections forged through mere "stuff" (i.e., media and merchandise).[242] And, by demonstrating the traitorous mobility of franchises and their roving capital concerns—in contrast to that rootedness of human community—fans are thus "disabused . . . of any illusions that they might have harboured that their team 'belonged' to them," as that discourse of belonging is offered up to a new, often broader, and almost always richer set of consumer constituents.[243] In short, the global sports market seems "inimical" to the needs of traditional fans and prioritizes profit over history, culture, or sociality.[244] This might buy owners and teams a wider set of potential allegiances. But the prospect that we should one day pull for truly placeless, commercially homogenous, corporate team icons, à la the "Toyota Tigers" or "Nike Panthers," refutes the very basis for that fellowship.[245] Such aims would certainly make commercial dollars, but they would make little cultural sense.

> I believe in . . . rough, manly sports. I do not feel any particular sympathy for the person who gets battered about a good deal so long as it is not fatal.
> —**Theodore Roosevelt,**
> U.S. president

# MAN UP

## The Gendered Anxieties of Sports Production

> I always felt I had to prove that I know what I'm talking about when it comes to sports and that I have opinions. . . . There will always be men who don't want women involved in knowing and let alone talking sports to them. They like it the other way around.
> —**Linda Cohn,**
> *SportsCenter* anchor

# GENDER POLITICS

# HAVE NEVER BEEN ALL THAT

subtle in sports. Back in the medieval era, folk games represented and expressed a set of unambiguously "*macho* values" that, in turn, upheld patriarchal practices off the pitch.[1] By the time America's first professional sports league arrived in the 1800s, belligerents like Ty Cobb would cast baseball as "a red-blooded sport for red-blooded men"—treating the diamond as crucible for proving one's masculinity on a public stage.[2] For millennia, really, sport has both defined and validated male identity; this is so pervasive and commonsense that it's an almost invisible form of political power.[3]

This chapter seeks to unravel the construction and adaptation of that power by examining interviewees' practices and perspectives within the shifting dynamics of gender roles and masculine authority. I begin by cataloguing all the ways in which men's identity has been tethered to sports for status, socialization, and supremacy, before turning to how coverage of violence by and against the male body—long a source of pleasure, swagger, and nobility—is now more of an ethical struggle, especially in professional football. The second part of the chapter focuses on the experiences of women in

American sports culture: the still-belittling space relegated to and acute pressure reported by female journalists who must be seen (as attractive) but not heard (as opinionated); the self-fulfilling logic that marginalizes women's athletics as "unprofitable" in their struggle for symbolic equality; and the patronizing pursuit of female audiences through superficial consumption schemes. Finally, the chapter concludes by situating a new generation of sports culture "heroics"— more data-driven than brawny in the wake of fantasy gaming and *Moneyball*—against the economic crisis of masculine labor identity and the enduring morality of blue-collar work. Men may not have met their "end," as one popular recent book foretold, but the anxieties charted throughout this chapter do showcase a waning of traditional professional roles and norms and a transformation of their relationship to the means of production—both on the field and off.

## MAKING MANHOOD

Some say that sport fills the void of manhood initiation rites that structured ancient tribal life but are otherwise lacking in contemporary society.[4] For boys negotiating awkward adolescence, sport can shroud supposedly feminine feelings of vulnerability. Take this confession of one young man: "Fandom protected me from being labeled a weakling and a coward, particularly by my brothers . . . and later attempting to fashion myself into an athlete, [it] also served as a kind of inoculation against the more elemental fear that I was insufficiently masculine."[5] To play like a "big baller" is to strut like a big *ball*-er, that deeply unsubtle conflation of game-time prowess and well-endowed virility. Woe to the klutz, though; for athletic deficiency traditionally telegraphed masculine inadequacy.[6] Coaches sometimes view such "masculine insecurities" as leverage through which to manipulate their players and maximize performance.[7] The University of Iowa, for example, painted their visiting football locker rooms pink, apparently hoping to emasculate opponents through interior décor intimidation.[8]

In that, sport offers men a durable system for accruing status and amassing alternative forms of capital. This process begins early—studies show that sport remains the single biggest factor in terms of gaining (or losing) prestige among fellow boys.[9] It continues on into adulthood, where sports become the preeminent form of bonding among men, no matter what their social or educational background.[10] The statistical information that now saturates sports—a curiously wonkish trend taken up later in this chapter—may further furnish fodder for that male "cultural capital," as grasping and recalling arcane data about on-field performance offers men a convoluted means of displaying devotion and engaging in meta-competition with other fans.[11]

Indeed, the negotiation of that masculine identity through sports culture is more mediated than ever. Newspaper sports pages have long offered men a "socially sanctioned gossip sheet," unusually evocative of the lifestyle and society sections that they run adjacent to (even as those are conversely circumscribed as feminine content).[12] With the ascendance of sports talk radio over the last quarter-century—and its loud, brash opinion-mongering—American men gravitated toward the alpha-male hosts who could affirm (or revoke) the performance of their masculinity as callers.[13] On television, producers honed a "sports manhood formula" that condenses and amplifies interlocking themes about the male essence: strength, aggressiveness, bodily sacrifice, and so on.[14]

I caught a bit of this in the comments of Russ Kenn, the coordinating producer for NESN's Red Sox game-casts, who recalls assembling one opening montage ode to veteran catcher Jason Varitek with Teddy Roosevelt's "Man in the Arena" speech overlaid: "We were certainly aware of that storyline and aware of how attractive that was to viewers. . . . That kind of toughness and macho certainly was a part of what we did and, again, it's a compelling storyline that, you know, if the pieces fit, that's definitely the vehicle that we used."[15] From the vantage point of most media professionals, however, macho toughness is not contrived as spectacle but discovered authentically; the evidence from my interviewees—or, I suppose, lack thereof—suggests that "manliness" seems fundamentally unremarkable to them as a quality of veneration.

Big picture, that also makes it increasingly unique. Ours is a more dynamic gender world than generations prior and sport might just represent the last large-scale institution of American culture where men and women are still legitimately, acceptably "segregated"—thus buttressing a "male preserve" more receptive to boys and men and more celebratory of the values and skills aligned with traditional masculinity.[16] For young amateurs, locker rooms and dugouts offer a "rehearsal" space for that insular experience; when fantasies of going pro have receded into the twilight of memory, sports bars stage similar "refuge" from the presence of females.[17] Noting how she's reported from Super Bowl parking lots for the better part of four decades and can count precisely zero tailgates that she's ever seen comprised of only women, sportscaster Lesley Visser concludes, "I think sports and Wall Street were the last areas that men were going to give up."[18]

Ironically, though, sport simultaneously provides a space for men to act in stereotypically feminine ways, accommodating emotional urges and facilitating social bonding; totemically, it invites allegations of acting "girly." Spectatorship gives men license to "open up" with fellow fans; athletes' reluctance to let go of career aspirations may well stem partly from the affection for male teammates that society thwarts otherwise.[19] "It's a structured life and it's a life also that has them surrounded psychologically by a band of brothers," explains player agent Leigh Steinberg. "There's a code and an honor and rapport and camaraderie that's really nurturing. It may not look nurturing—the language may not be touchy-feely—but it's that."[20] The relationship that most embodies—and is perhaps dependent upon—that covert intimacy is, of course, fathers-and-sons, for sport gives them a vehicle for expressing and experiencing tenderness in the absence of sanctioned language and amidst sometimes stunted relationships and emotional or physical distance.[21]

Yet all that homosocial yearning seems equally freighted with homophobic panic: To love a fellow fan (through the totem, of course) is, for many men, to invite discomfiting suspicions and accusations of gayness. Some have cleverly theorized, then, that the violence of sport, especially in football, offers the overt "camouflage" of machoness beneath which men can engage *agape* without fear of shame.[22] Yet the "challenge" nonetheless remains that sport is still the rare cultural space where straight men regularly gaze upon and obsess over other men's bodies; it is, indeed, not incidental but elemental to the experience of fandom.[23] To avoid, then, being "tarred" as homosexual and to affirm a fan's "mandatory" straight status, spectacle sweeteners like the *Sports Illustrated* swimsuit issue and comely cheerleaders undulating on the sidelines help "legitimize" any unintended erotic appeal and errant erections.[24] Put more simply, female boobs compensate for the abundance of male butts—"no homo"–style, in the kneejerk parlance of phobic bros.

Within scholarly theory, these cultural practices and popular representations are pretty much taken for granted as "hegemonic masculinity."[25] This fancy phrase defines the traditional American male ideal, athletic or otherwise: he who is "stoic, self-reliant . . . rugged, strictly heterosexual, and void of complaint."[26] Hegemonic masculinity venerates and rewards a specific set of gendered values like "physical strength, competitiveness, success, active agency, aggression/violence, and power," through countless, diffused sports culture forms, as sports sociologist Michael Messner has collated.[27] One study of children's soccer found, for example, that boys' team names are far more likely to imply power (e.g., "Shooting Stars," "Killer Whales") than their female counterparts, which tend to sound adorable or weak (e.g., "Blue Butterflies," "Beanie Babes," "Purple Grapes").[28] Occasionally, hegemonic masculinity has to be explicitly taught, as when a college rowing coach told future sportswriter Robert Lipsyte that boys on campus in the 1960s could be dichotomized into "jocks" and "pukes": the former admired for being "brave, manly, ambitious, focused, patriotic, and goal-driven," the latter suffering from being "woolly, distractible, girlish" hippies.[29]

There was perhaps no fitter paragon of this manly-man ideal in recent professional sports memory than Hall of Famer Nolan Ryan. Between his ferocious fastball, his Calvinist work ethic, his husband-as-breadwinner role, his Clint Eastwood offseason cowboy pose, and his taking–Robin Ventura–to-the-woodshed moment, the pitcher perfected a performance of mediated masculinity as few others have.[30] Sometimes, though, it's as much an archetype as it is an emblematic individual like Ryan. In professional football, for example, one of the more clichéd rituals along these lines is the "no-nonsense" head coach who takes over as the "new sheriff in town," ready to whip the troops into shape and dispense the heavy-handed discipline so sorely needed to get the team on a winning track.[31]

Sports-themed advertisements offer their own instructive portraits of hegemonic masculinity. One study from the 1980s of men depicted in beer commercials (a chief subsidizer of sports content) found mostly physical laborers in outdoor settings.[32] More recently, a less desirable vision of manhood seems to fill the interstitial spaces of sports media. As broadcasts cut away from the virile, sculpted bodies on field, drug makers incite anxiety about erectile dysfunction and beer makers exhort those of insufficiently masculine fashion choices to "man up," while fans come off as shirtless "screaming lunatics" and losers.[33]

For some feminist critics, the gendered aggression on display in sports culture links to other "antisocial" political tendencies that will be exhumed in the next chapter (specifically, hawkish militarism and neoliberal economic thought).[34] The power which is embodied *within* sport naturalizes a message about "male superiority and female frailty and dependence" that is then transported to legitimize patriarchal domination of *non*-sports arenas of human life.[35] In other words, gender-wise, the game is rigged: Sports are both inextricably intertwined with male culture and often predicated upon physical might—specifically, upper-body strength—all of which adds up to a kind of "biologically determined supremacy."[36] One might shorthand this as the "ideology" of muscles. And violence is an essential part of that ideology: "The power of men in any society is reinforced to the extent that important institutions in that society sanction and indeed celebrate the use of force," sport scholars Richard Gruneau and David Whitson conclude.[37] What, then, is the status of sports-sanctioned violence today? And what can it tell us about the evolution of hegemonic masculinity?

## THE PLEASURE OF PAIN

Although an armchair view of our mediated reality would seem to belie it—what with grisly ISIS beheading videos, footage of school-shooter carnage, and so on—the world is actually, on balance, a much safer, tamer place than it used to be. Between the sensationalist news norm that dictates, "if it bleeds, it leads," and the mental tendency to recall and fixate on calamities rather than calm, we often overlook macro-global trend lines from domestic abuse to genocide to war casualties.[38] Donald Trump's fear-mongering aside, American cities, in particular, have shown a dramatic drop in crime and violence over the last three decades. Without question, there remain clear, tragic hotspots of suffering pockmarked around the world (e.g., Syria, North Korea, Chicago), but—taking the long view, that is, over several centuries—life seems less nasty, brutish, and short since Thomas Hobbes first took stock of it. "Part of it was, we lived in a culture then in which people died in random and awful ways all the time, right?" says Big Ten Network studio host Dave Revsine, who authored a book on the vicious years of early college football.[39] "Some guy gets sucked into a piece of heavy machinery at the factory or a farming accident. It was just kind of part of life. I think we looked at death—they looked at death—on the athletic fields as part of life then."[40]

Indeed, as chronicled by social theorists Norbert Elias and Eric Dunning, there has been, since the Middle Ages, a broadly "civilizing" instinct that has taken root in lived culture: animalistic urges tamped down beneath the threshold of consciousness rather than indulged as destructive impulse; self-control and manners increasingly governing public conduct and social interaction; and people taking less overt pleasure in watching acts of bloodlust and the suffering of others.[41] Sport, in turn, succumbed to these same sympathies and became more sensitive to its own savagery. Much as the ancient and medieval world was a more dangerous place, so, too, were the fields of play, as sports like boxing and wrestling allowed far more gore (and even disembowelment was not an uncommon fate).[42] Our contemporary aversion to an injury like Joe Theismann's shows just how starkly that squeamishness has evolved.

However, according to Elias, that restraint of passion still needs a cathartic outlet—a chance to satisfy and purge "strong feelings, of strong antipathies towards and dislike of people, let alone of hot anger, wild hatred or the urge to hit someone over the head."[43] We perhaps seek, in our leisure time, to scratch some primal itch for exuberance, tribalism, and barbarity that everyday life has (thank-fully) otherwise deprived us of; sport can liberate those tensions and restore mental equanimity by exhausting us of potential depravity.[44] Because Chargers defensive end Joey Bosa can lay an opponent out in the open field, I supposedly feel less crazed to do so myself—or so goes the Freudian theory of sublimation.

Sport is, therefore, often the only space in many "civilized" so-cieties where such bellicosity is not only tolerated, it's celebrated.[45] Studies of hooligan culture have similarly demonstrated that fan pleasure derives partly from the participatory expression of violent machismo; in blue-collar British neighborhoods, especially, football-related brawling offers "a central source of meaning and gratification in life" and confers prestige on men who can hold their own amidst the scrum in the streets.[46] Such men, we might suspect, can no longer rely on other sources of social prestige as their fathers might have.

What, then, are we to make of American football? As one of the nation's dominant forms of popular culture, it would not seem to comport obediently with the notion that humankind has slaked its bloodlust. When a new head coach seizes power like, say, the Miami Dolphins' Don Campbell in 2015 and kicks things off with the con-troversial "Oklahoma Drill" (a full-speed collision between blocker, tackler, and ballcarrier) because he wants to see his guys "violently compete," mainstream sports norms and media narratives usually swoon: It is a supposedly "welcome philosophical change" for a los-ing franchise.[47] Brutal punishment is seen and sold, stoically, as the only solution for success.

Some have further theorized that the football helmet itself is not just a form of protection, but also actually, conversely, a means of dehumanization—the mask to better shield one's opponents from eliciting any (girly) empathy rather than meting out the proscribed violence that must be done to them.[48] Thus, football, according to philosopher Michael Novak, mocks the pretense of an enlightened modern era (i.e., that violence has, can, will, or should be "exorcised from human life"); rather, the sport harkens back to man's "most ancient ancestors," those who had to resort to raw physical force to demonstrate prowess and secure survival.[49] It is also, of course, another means of marking masculinity, given that men being "built for violence and death"—as opposed to birth, women's traditional purview and purported purpose—is a central "organizing principle" of the gender order, especially as other "anchors" of identity slip away from them.[50] (More on this later in the chapter.)

For players themselves, there is something powerful in the lurid allure of getting jacked up on the gridiron. "It's intoxicating, it's a drug, a drug that gives you the most incredible feeling there is," former San Francisco 49er linebacker Chris Borland says of the "euphoric high" of his playing collisions. "Outside of sexual intercourse, there's probably nothing like it."[51] Former defensive end turned TV host Michael Strahan similarly gushes, "It's the most perfect feeling in the world to know that you've hit a guy just right, that you've maximized the physical pain he can feel. . . . You feel the life just go out of him. You've taken all this man's energy and just dominated him."[52] NFL agent David Canter, who played at the college level, evokes this contradictory experience of violence's tranquility in even more Zen-like terms:

> I've often said the one thing I miss more than anything in football is there's a very, very, very micro-millisecond—I don't know if it's measurable—when you get tackled or you make a tackle, that everything goes black. It's very difficult to express in words. . . . There's a peacefulness and it's almost like you're dead. It's so fast that it doesn't really exist. Does that make sense? The world is silent—your brain basically shuts off for that fraction. I imagine it's a micro-concussion. Maybe I shouldn't worship that as much as I did when I was younger, but it was just this incredible experience. And then,

obviously, the pain comes and you got hit, the whistle, and the noise, and the huddle. I think all of that is part of the religion of pro football.[53]

Religion is, once more, an apt analogy here, for there is no human institution more practiced than faith in ideologically justifying pain as productive and somehow even moral. Marxist critic Jean-Marie Brohm terms this the "body-fascism" of sports culture, where media and fans alike valorize breaking through the "pain barrier, of going to the limits of endurance, of being drunk with 'animal' fatigue and of getting a kick out of bruises, knocks, and injuries."[54] It is, for him, a kind of "sado-masochistic" obsession with remorseless self-discipline that, in turn, naturalizes non-sport forms of and conditions for torture as noble, necessary—heck, even entertaining.[55] Sport's meritocracy myth, which will be debunked further in the next chapter, is centrally premised upon normalizing this notion that without the probity of pain, there can be no jubilee of gain.[56]

The body is thus an instrument in this rationalization—a machine, a project—the object of which is to alienate the player from his own feelings of tenderness, or at least neutralize them via cortisone shots.[57] Football announcers legitimize this violence with their homilies of adoration for those who can suck it up and work through that pain; an NFLer demonstrates his "bona fide[s]" by subjecting his body to the routine risk of destruction.[58] Such is the cruel paradox of sport: Participation almost guarantees eventual injury, yet the culture simultaneously celebrates only those healthy competitors who survive that winnowing.[59] And those survivors dare not call it "luck," lest the meritocracy of an intense training regimen lose its luster. Tom Brady's ability to defy the cruel and inevitable gravity of aging gets sold, literally, as *The TB12 Method*: body-as-temple rather than fate-as-capricious. Yet few other professional settings (save for the military, of course) can compete with sport in terms of this routine anticipation of workplace hazards and the likelihood of getting clocked before clocking out.

Somewhat grotesquely, in fact—in the existential sense of rational self-preservation—the threat of injury is actually *essential* to accomplishment: as an abiding source of risk, an obstacle to overcome, a "masculine badge of pride to prove how much pain you could take, even if it's at the expense of your personal health," as ESPN's Jemele Hill observes.[60] The NFL, in particular, cultivates that macho mentality where "being soft" is an infinitely worse transgression than "being crazy, crude, or barbaric."[61] And, as Hill adds, this is usually coded in unambiguously gendered putdowns: "If a man isn't performing, you know what he's called—usually something effeminate, something related to a woman. A young boy is taught early on, 'You can be anything, but don't be like a woman.' . . . You can't continue to reinforce that and then be shocked once they get older, that they don't respect women."

Yet those early sports experiences teach boys to affect a façade of invulnerability, so as to not to betray fear or weakness in the heat of battle.[62] One sociologist's study of male bonding in locker rooms found an overwhelming pressure to avoid any appearance of empathy or helplessness.[63] Such a transgression was actually deployed as humorous fodder for one TV ad for the San Francisco Giants that cast several as actors in a campy Spanish-language soap opera ("Mi Amor") and scripted catcher Buster Posey shedding showy tears for the beauty of baseball: "Some players might not be willing to do that—again, you're telling him that this is just a big goof and we're spoofing something," explains Bob Dorfman, a creative director who worked on the spot.[64] For as Tom Hanks famously ordained in *A League of Their Own*, there's no crying in baseball.

This swaggering willingness to withstand pain is intertwined with those other imperatives to play hurt and sacrifice one's body for the good of the game. "In the pool of testosterone in which the NFL is steeped, valorizing players who can play with and through injuries is a part of the game, right?" observes *Around the Horn* panelist Kevin Blackistone, recalling tales told fondly of gridiron heroes soldiering through broken legs, fingers, and ribs. "The entire concussion issue is far, far more difficult to get a handle on because the players have been inculcated their entire lives with this idea that the pain and injury that you can play through somehow underscores how masculine you are."[65]

To be certain, it's not just cultural compulsion; there are also powerful economic incentives to get back in the game, not least in a sport like football where pro careers average a mere three-and-a-half years.[66] Former Ohio State star Maurice Clarett admits that "[guys] often tolerate the trauma for the paycheck"—especially those who shuffled through college without ever contemplating a backup plan.[67] Theoretically, were there to be a severe decline in youth participation among well-to-do and middle-class families (as the trend lines augur), the future supply of football bodies would have to be extracted even more from those of "poorer backgrounds," as one NFL executive concedes.[68]

All sports laborers—but NFLers in particular—therefore fall victim to an "occupational trap" conundrum: knowing that their career choice will likely entail permanent physical disrepair, yet equally cognizant that their body-as-commodity operates within an "industry largely intolerant to injury."[69] In other words, sport somewhat expects that you'll eventually go down and that you'll be swapped out, unsentimentally, for seemingly interchangeable "parts" when you do. (No coach is more defined by this cold-eyed unsentimentality than, arguably, the greatest: Bill Belichick.) The biggest hurdle for the lawyer representing concussed ex-players against the NFL (a case that eventually settled and could cost the league upward of $1.4 billion) was apparently getting retirees to overcome their attachment to those masculine mythologies.[70] NFL veterans who cope with a lifetime of pain (e.g., "arthritis, failing knees and ankles, hip and back pain, severe headaches, dizziness, and memory loss") minimize, trivialize, or write it off as an inevitable and shared burden to bear—a "no regrets" mentality further fortifying masculine norms.[71] They did what they "had" to do.

"The players' mindset—their psychology—which has been built up over years of coaching and playing really has them in collusion with the teams and ownership and management of the league when it comes to concussions," notes Blackistone. "They've been reared in this, so unless somebody else looks out for them, it's really hard for them to look out for themselves." He adds that the head of the NFL players union has tried to disabuse his membership of evoking "gladiator" language and ambitions: "When guys use that term [gladiator], they don't realize that they're talking about a group of people who were literally slaves or somehow marginalized . . . And that their performances at the Roman Coliseum were simply to entertain the other classes of Roman society, which had absolutely no interest in their welfare . . . The NFLPA doesn't want players to be a gladiator class."[72]

This, however, invites the daunting task of getting a generation of young men to unlearn certain masculine "truths" about hardened self-sacrifice. Sports agent Leigh Steinberg articulates this inversion of gameplay priorities and self-preservation: "Athletes have set norms about health and injury that are at odds with the entire rest of society. You know: Real men ignore pain; real men don't want to be left out of the starting lineup. . . . They're surrounded by people who feel exactly the same way."[73] Indeed, an anonymous survey found that 85 percent of pros would try to play in the Super Bowl even if they knew they had a concussion.[74] Such is the product of a lifetime of deprogramming humanity: "Dehumanizing sounds so extreme," admits former 49er Chris Borland, "but when you're fighting for a football at the bottom of a pile, it *is* kind of dehumanizing."[75]

## WHEN MEN CAN'T WALK AWAY

The narrative of masculine nobility in the endurance of physical suffering is, of course, not only something that spreads organically among coaches and players. It is equally a narrative that the media has built up over decades of representation—though it seems, to my interviewees in the sports press, to be as instinctively reactive as it is consciously constructed. When talking through the "man up" ideal and gendered cliché of bodily sacrifice, WIP Philadelphia program director Spike Eskin stammers a bit—not something a talk radio guy is prone to do: "It's not an easy thing to vocalize—to say, 'Hey, I understand that he's hurt and he shouldn't play.' . . . I guess I don't know what my talking point would be in that respect."[76] On the other hand, says Dave Revsine, studio host for the Big Ten Network, a gutsy, bleeding-ankle playoff performance like that of Boston Red Sox pitcher Curt Schilling will always elicit hushed reverence.[77] Fluto Shinzawa, the *Boston Globe* beat writer who covers the Bruins, is also drawn to chronicle such carnage with admiration, as when Patrice Bergeron played through a "car crash" victim's worth of collapsed lung, torn rib cartilage, and dislocated shoulder: "Maybe that's not the smart thing for them to do, but it's the reality—that's the nature of hockey. . . . That's the culture. Yeah, maybe we're feeding into it as the media, but that's the reality."[78] It is an admission of representational ambivalence—"reality" but also "media-fed"—and neither the performer nor the recorder has, historically, much contested the template of that cultural pressure. That may, however, be changing.

For media depictions are never static, nor those doing the depicting pure automatons of pre-programmed gendered norms. A culture of callous indifference to and misty admiration for that bodily suffering as properly manly seems to be (very) slowly evolving toward more "enlightened" ends. Concussions, as the preceding pages have hinted, offer an ongoing health scandal against which to situate these shifting dynamics of how the male body and character is idealized—it's also, as general counsel to the Cleveland Browns put it, "a cultural IED . . . exploding in the middle of the business of the NFL."[79] When PBS's award-winning *Frontline* episode "League of Denial" aired (and was subsequently published as a book, along with the Will Smith film treatment in *Concussion*), it brought this simmering issue to the forefront; yet the attention also, perhaps unintentionally, began to reframe how we see NFL players, holistically, as "victims of"—as much as perpetrators and participants in—an exploitative system of violent hegemonic masculinity.[80]

Sports media institutions like ESPN—which, as noted earlier, withdrew from the "League of Denial" project, potentially at the behest of the NFL—suddenly had to rethink the packaging of pain as pleasure: its "Jacked Up" recurring segment that spliced together neck-snapping, spleen-splitting hits; its *Monday Night Football* opening credits montage where the two teams' helmets collide and explode in a crackle of kinetic lightning. (For the former, the postproduction placement of a gun-scope crosshair graphic over the impending victim's torso had only further militarized the footage.[81]) Such tropes now looked less thrilling and more ghastly, especially when confronted with the CTE-addled brains and broken bodies of those like Pittsburgh Steelers retiree Mike Webster, who had to duct tape his cracked feet together and superglue his teeth to stay in.[82] What once seemed noble now seems barbaric.

My interviewees reflected on this newfound sensitivity in ways that clearly contrast the classic callousness expected of hegemonic masculinity. "I think you can't really watch these guys without thinking, you know, what's going to happen to them later and how they might be impacted by stuff. I think that death looms over everything," says Greg Bishop, a senior writer for *Sports Illustrated*. "A big hit, definitely—you would look at maybe something you would have celebrated before, you don't celebrate as much now."[83] Television personnel are arguably even more responsible for having glamorized that violence—with some now seemingly chastened by the carnage. "My antenna's up—put it that way. Much more than it was years ago. You'd see a great hit and you'd say, 'Oh, wow! He laid him out! He knocked him cold!' And you'd be jumping up and down or your voice would sound excite[d]," recalls ABC-Boston sports anchor Mike Lynch. "Now, when I see that happen, I go [he inhales, catching his breath dramatically]—'Oh, my goodness. I hope he's all right. I hope he's going to get up.' I don't revel in the big hit like I used to."[84] Dave Revsine, an alumnus of *SportsCenter*, similarly recalls scaling back his enthusiasm and the show spiking segments like "Laying the Wood"; others have noticed less slapstick-style, NFL-follies televisual treatment of obviously concussed players stumbling around, "going to the wrong huddle" and such.[85]

There is even some evidence of media professionals being internally torn and feeling guilty about their complicity in covering the sport. "I've always felt that football—for all of its great athleticism and its excitement and drama and shared experience—it was always apparent to me . . . that there was something within the sport that needlessly celebrated violence for its own sake. And I was never fully comfortable with that," says Bob Costas, who nonetheless derives a not-insignificant part of his salary from NBC's Nielsen-dominating, money-printing *Sunday Night Football* franchise.[86] Chris Dufresne, who has covered football at the college level as a columnist for the *Los Angeles Times,* concurs: "The collisions, the violence— every week, you hold your breath hoping that somebody isn't paralyzed. . . . I'm sharing the guilt of, 'Why am I covering this or why I am interested in a sport where this could happen?'"[87]

The answer, of course, is money—or "blood money," as ESPN columnist Rick Reilly castigates the NFL's concussion settlement—one that "doesn't assuage [his] small sense of shame" for having made a living off of men who paid for that entertainment with their bodies and even lives.[88] Just as it was noted earlier that players might feel "golden handcuffed" to their physical fate in violent sports, so, too, are journalists loathe to walk away from the biggest beat in the most popular news section. "I'm conflicted about [football]—I don't enjoy it as much for a variety of reasons," admits Michael Rosenberg, another senior writer for *Sports Illustrated*. "At a time [of] . . . financial stresses on the [news] industry and needing to get noticed and all that, it's not a smart career decision for me to say, 'I'm not going to live off of football.'"[89]

By 2017, sports broadcasting saw its first high-profile resignation—48-year-old Ed Cunningham, ESPN college football analyst for two decades—specifically because of his "growing discomfort" with players' brain trauma.[90] Likewise, Morry Levine, managing sports editor at CSN–New England, feels like he's in the minority in questioning the message sent to kids by hyping a "barbaric sport" like football: "I feel like a lot of people are afraid to take that stance, because the NFL is such a huge moneymaker and it brings in so much money to everywhere—including this place with our Patriots coverage—that you start to go against it in any way and, then, who knows?"[91]

Even at (and perhaps because of) its height, in terms of national popularity and lavish finances, the fate of football was being widely pondered. Ivan Maisel, a college football senior writer for ESPN, muses whether football today is what boxing was in the 1960s: a once-dominant American pastime whose "violence and greed"—"two of football's leading qualities these days," he quips—turned audiences enough off to sideline it from cultural centrality.[92] Others wonder if football could be hemmed in by lower Pop Warner participation rates and an unusual spate of early professional retirements. Levine, for example, refused to allow his son to play in high school and the backlash made clear the gendered transgression:

"I'm like, 'Why do you want to play football?' He goes, 'That's what tough guys do.'"[93]

Levine's not alone; youth football has declined by almost 20 percent in the past decade and one Bloomberg poll found that half of all Americans wouldn't want their sons to take up the sport.[94] (That figure skewed upward, tellingly, by class: Among affluent, college-educated households, the reticence is even higher.) In response, the league has redoubled its PR efforts to market itself as guardians of a child-friendly product; in one overplayed PSA, Tom Brady delivers a chipper retort about safety improvements to the anxious mother of one such "little guy" (played by a glowering Ray Lewis).[95] Needing to "get to kids as early as possible"—especially as peak ratings falter—the NFL also rolled out a cloying "Football Is Family" campaign (stitching together user-submitted videos of fans and their kin, totemically declaring why they love the game); held "Moms Football Safety Clinics"; and designed an elementary school curriculum that encourages students to hypothesize the winners of games and then, in its words, "watch the game at home, with their families, to see if their hypotheses were right!"[96] Another strategy included restricting players from speaking with the news media if they were suspected or confirmed to have suffered a concussion.[97]

By mid-decade, the uptick in those players prematurely walking away from the game had attracted media notice—four times as many of those under 30 had retired as compared to five years earlier, a list that included stars like Calvin Johnson, Jerod Mayo, and Marshawn Lynch.[98] Most conspicuous was Borland, a 24-year-old who read *League of Denial* over the last month of his final season, furtively, for fear of being seen in the locker room with a copy of the book.[99] Borland understood, of course, that his decision would inevitably make a "shocking" statement about prioritizing one's health over a career as a professional athlete, but it also generated much macho backlash from players who both publicly and anonymously questioned the fire in his belly.[100] Borland's father, on the other hand, expressed only relief: "During the course of a 16-game season, everybody in the end is injured," he said. "It's almost as if pieces just get broken off, and you give up pieces or an appendage every year."[101]

Most athletes, though, never actually *choose* to walk away as Borland did. The singular, all-encompassing focus demanded to reach the professional ranks leaves little energy—mental or physical—to devote to "plan B," if or when one can no longer ball. And because sports demand of athletes a "field of consciousness" so total and enveloping, some have likened exiting that bubble to the experience of felons freed from prison or soldiers discharged from the military.[102] Official retirements capture media attention because they are relatively rare, particularly in the NFL; more often, a livelihood is simply cut short, unceremoniously, by injury in the course of normal play or, worse still, when a training camp roster gets posted.[103] "I have never met an athlete who willingly retired from sports," declares player agent Leigh Steinberg, a multi-decade veteran in the business. "They're too old; no one wants them; they're too injured—it's an extremely difficult concept [for them to handle]."[104]

That identity crisis of masculine self-worth is all the more acute, because it arrives at an age when men in other careers are just beginning to hit their professional stride.[105] Moreover, these former athletes are often confronted with an array of life troubles: weight gain, marital woes, public embarrassment, and—sometimes, more tragically—bankruptcy, criminal activity, and suicide.[106] "It is absolutely brutal . . . You have a guy that's played for years in the NFL and—for whatever reason—nobody wants him anymore. It's really, literally, jumping off a cliff drop-off," explains David Canter, who represents a number of league players. "A lot of guys are left in a haze for a good twelve to twenty-four months. . . . There's still a lot of guys that are in the gym right now working out, hoping for a

call that's never going to come, hanging on to a thread of hope."[107]
Another agent, David Cornwell, similarly embellishes the abyss that
stares back in that moment: "Imagine dying but still being alive."[108]
The loss is not merely occupational; it is existential in a profoundly
gendered way, given the context and conditions.

It is, moreover, exacerbated by a reluctance to seek therapeutic
help; just as sports culture encourages the cocky posture of physical
invulnerability, it also cultivates a mentality of *mental* invulnerability. For the rare athlete like wide receiver Brandon Marshall to open
up about his struggles with depression, "[he] might as well have said
[he] wears a pink thong underneath [his] uniform," quips *Nation*
sports editor Dave Zirin.[109] Indeed, Marshall himself reflects, "If
someone had said mental health to me, the first thing that came to
mind was mental toughness, masking pain, hiding, keeping it in . . .
that's what was embedded in me since I was a kid. You know, never
show a sign of weakness."[110]

As another anecdote of this mindset, the agent Canter reports hiring, on retainer, a full-time psychotherapist from the veteran's administration who specializes in PTSD to offer free, confidential
assistance to his clients (i.e., he gets invoiced for any sessions used
but the specific player remains anonymous to him); his records show
only a tiny fraction of them have ever taken up this offer. "To make
it to the NFL, you have to be crazy tough and play through injuries
and play through pain and do things to your body that most normal
people probably couldn't ever imagine. Just getting out of bed a lot
of times is tough for guys. Does that make them more resistant to
psychological help? I would say, yeah," he concludes, adding later in
the interview: "There's an uncomfortableness that they think if they
ask for help, or if they open up, they'll be perceived weaker and it'll
hurt them."[111]

Gendered anxiety around perceived weakness was also at the core
of the "Bullygate" scandal that rocked the NFL in 2013, when three

Miami Dolphins brutally harassed teammate Jonathan Martin with homophobic and sexist slights.[112] Fellow lineman Richie Incognito logged various infractions in a notebook warranting fines for Martin being a "pussy"; the line coach brought in a male blow-up sex doll for Martin; and Martin was regularly slandered as a "cunt," "bitch," and "faggot," accompanied by vile rape threats against his sister.[113] Martin, an unsuitably sensitive soul, abruptly left the team in the wake of this hazing, citing emotional distress; in text messages to friends, he acknowledged a very un-NFL-like (and therefore "unmasculine") vulnerability: "I'm a push over. . . . I avoid confrontation whenever I can. . . . I mostly blame the soft schools I went to, which fostered within me a feeling that I'm a huge pussy, as I never got into fights. I used to get verbally bullied every day . . . I would never fight back."[114] In another text to his mother, he implies that sports culture can disfigure a man's potential for empathy in demanding that performance of bravado: "Sometimes I very badly want to quit football, as I feel like it has 'forced me' to act a certain way."

For his part, Incognito did not disavow Martin's suggestion that sports norms bear some of the responsibility for their aggressive excess: "All this stuff coming out . . . it speaks to the culture of our locker room. It speaks to the culture of our closeness. It speaks to the culture of our brotherhood. The racism, the bad words . . . that's what I regret most, but that is a product of the environment, and that's something we use all the time."[115] In other words, hegemonic masculinity is *productive* and bonding is *solidified* through the enforcement of it; homophobia, sexism, and obscenity are but the collateral cost of achieving that camaraderie. And, frankly, Incognito was hardly out of line; bullying is, in a sense, how you keep your job in the NFL, for players will tolerate almost any expression of belligerence if it gives them or their team an edge on the field.[116] Such behavior is, above all, totally *normal*.

To even look askance at any of these gendered norms within sports culture is, for a critic—especially a male one—to seem like a "pussy" as well. The debate over football, like so many other facets of mediated life in America today, has found itself in the crosshairs of culture war politics. The right seems to resist any semblance of compassion weakening a proud institution of hegemonic masculinity. Former drug czar Bill Bennett sees the game being "chipped away at"; GOP strategist Stuart Stevens thinks "any attempts to make football a safe family sport, sort of a low level of volleyball, are absurd"; Utah Republican Jason Chaffetz chafes at the "politically correct wimps" turning it into "flag football"; and right-wing radio host Laura Ingraham sneers at those who'd (apparently) rather "walk around with bubble wrap" and watch "aquatic dance" instead.[117]

To these conservatives, sportswriter Bryan Curtis surmises, football is "being dogpiled by nanny-staters, media elites, P.C. dogmatists, trial lawyers, union organizers, and . . . those who would make us a softer, wussier people."[118] (To this list, I might wryly add "pointy-headed professors.") Lefty scribe Dave Zirin also marvels that the concussion issue has been somehow turned into a "red state–blue state" issue: "Like, if you're a tough right-winger, you don't buy any of this 'football is dangerous' shit, because it's really about keeping America weak and raising men who are not real men."[119] To even question the unreconstructed perpetuation of violence in boxing, hockey, and football—as columnist Filip Bondy has often done in the pages of *The New York Daily News*—is to invite vicious blowback for feminizing a proud masculine heirloom: "Oh, yeah, absolutely: 'You've never played sports in your life, Bondy—you wimp, you faggot.' That kind of stuff. Yeah, we get that all the time; that's standard stuff."[120]

Anxieties, thus, abound: from those media members who fret about the misbegotten "blood money" earned off of battered bodies to conservatism's angst that one of the pillars of micro-political power (i.e., masculine muscularity) might crumble if we're allowed to feel players' pain. The sports "product," they fear, is being feminized for better or worse. And, yet, from the vantage point of female media professionals, athletes, and fans who help co-create that product, such fears seem overblown and hegemonic masculinity as persistent and toxic as ever. I turn now to their experiences.

## THE APPEARANCE OF FEMALE CREDIBILITY

"I still get tweets to go back in the kitchen. It's unbelievable . . . They're worried about color of hair and how a woman looks. I'm going to be honest—and a lot of women will say it—if I was as fat and bald as [some male sportscasters], I would not have that job . . . These could be credible women—Emmy-award-winning reporters— but, you reach a certain age, and instead of saying, 'We have to give you a pay cut,' they just let you go and go to somebody younger and cheaper."[121]

If sports culture has long incubated that hegemonic masculinity, it has also been, in equal measure, an inhospitable environment for female participants. The sentiments above of Tina Cervasio, a sports reporter for Fox's New York affiliate, hardly seem unique, qualitatively speaking. A variety of statistics, however, illustrates just how vast that quantitative chasm is in terms of professional media opportunities: 95 percent of sports anchors are male; 99.5 percent of sports commentators are male; and 91 percent of sports page editors are male.[122] There had been just two female, full-time, sports talk radio hosts on ESPN in the 21st century before 2014, when an all-female sports panel show debuted—though the network hosts were quick to caveat: "It's not intended to be a women's sports TV show. . . . Will we discuss social issues and women's issues? Certainly when warranted, but that's not the sole focus of the show."[123] *The New York Times* devoted a whole article—by a rare female sports columnist, no less—to marveling that, in 2017, a female broadcaster was offered the chance to call men's NCAA tournament games for the first time in two decades; when asked why that staffing took so long, the chairman of CBS Sports shrugged, nonchalantly offering: "I don't really know . . . except probably it was easy to keep assigning the cast of regulars to the tournament. It just wasn't on our radar screen."[124] So goes the unconscious inertia of often-immovable status quos.

Lesley Visser, a reporter whose career has spanned five decades across multiple platforms and employers, was part of the first generation to try to break through that glass ceiling; her experience is instructive. She recalls, from her early days with *the Boston Globe*, violating a credentialing rule that stipulated, "No women or children in the press box."[125] Pioneers like Visser recognized, in particular, the need to breach the locker room seal, where the best stories emerged (and, in turn, the context ratified one's own journalistic authority).[126] In one particularly galling instance, the head coach of the University of Houston football team physically impeded her entrance, bellowing, with Archie Bunker brio, "I don't give a damn about no Equal Rights Amendment! I ain't having a woman in my locker room."[127] Why the resistance? One feminist theorist posits that locker rooms are, above all, "shrines to masculine might" and that, historically, the appearance of women has only been tolerated there as scantily clad, titillating pinups; by entering, the female journalist imperils that sacred exclusivity so essential to male bonding and "presents a threat unless the men can successfully sexualize her—asking her for dates, showing her their penises, commenting on her physical attractiveness—all of which they do."[128]

It is, of course, not only Neanderthal jocks sexualizing the intrepid female newshound, perhaps most notoriously in the 1990 harassment case of the *Boston Herald*'s Lisa Olson; fans and bosses alike eroticize the media talent (or, alternately, castigate her for failings on that front). Unsurprisingly, given its capacity to arouse trolling across all arenas of life—up to and including the Oval Office— Twitter has been at the forefront of that ugliness: "I've gotten tweets that the only reason I have a job is because of my looks; I've also gotten plenty more tweets that, you know, I'm an unattractive reporter who shouldn't be on television," notes Kim Jones of the NFL Network.[129] Kelly Naqi of ESPN's *Outside the Lines* says that when she broke some of the Deflategate scandal, the backlash was similarly sexually vile: "People were saying the most—like, 'die, you ugly whore'—and all this stuff."[130] In 2016, an award-winning PSA ("#MoreThanMean") called attention to this nastiness: It featured male fans reading real tweets—to their increasing discomfort—to sportswriters Julie DiCaro and Sarah Spain.[131] These included: "I hope you get raped again"; "one of the players should beat you to death with their hockey stick like the whore you are"; and "this is why we don't hire any females unless we need our cocks sucked or our food cooked."

Sometimes that routine harassment rises to the level of lawsuit-worthy threat, as when sportscaster Erin Andrews was stalked and taped in the nude through a hotel peephole; her female counterparts report regularly taking additional precautions like whispering their names when checking in, avoiding elevators full of leering male eyes, opting for private transportation, and avoiding crowds after games.[132] At the organizational level, ESPN has been accused of fostering a "locker-room mentality" "boy's club" where numerous cases of sexual harassment trickled up to management over the years—a problem that one former network head weirdly chalked up to Bristol's remote location: "It's one hundred miles from real civilization, and you got the kind of testosterone, jock mentality, frat house approach that's pretty much a recipe for stupid decisions being made."[133]

In the aftermath of the Harvey Weinstein scandal, as the #MeToo movement shamed sexual predators across Hollywood, the news media, and American politics, such harassment issues were seen by top executives as a "ticking time bomb in the male-dominated sports world—especially in its various sales departments and TV production trucks, which . . . have been the focus of rumors for years."[134] Following allegations, Fox Sports dispatched former president Jamie Horowitz (coincidentally, broadcasting's biggest advocate for the hot-take strategic shift) and Jerry Richardson announced he would sell his Carolina Panthers franchise after similar reports of misconduct. *Sports Illustrated* broke an investigative exposé of the "real life *Animal House*" that is the Dallas Mavericks organization, where a corporate culture apparently tolerated public fondling and crude propositions (by its team president), domestic assault, and intimidation from the staff fielding those complaints.[135] The NFL Network suspended several on-camera personnel (including Hall of Famer Marshall Faulk) for, variously, inquiring about a staffer's erotic proclivities, groping her breasts, sending her video of shower masturbation, propositioning a bathroom hookup, gifting a Christmas season sex toy, and stroking disrobed genitals in front of her; one executive reportedly told her she was "put on earth to pleasure me."[136]

A sexual harassment complaint filed against ESPN in 2017 similarly revived the network's reputation for harboring "a toxic environment" where "men make unwanted sexual and romantic advances under the guise of networking or mentoring, and 'mark' women as their own by spreading false rumors about sexual relationships"; given the lack of good gigs for female applicants, one anchor there even went through with her scheduled on-air broadcast, midway through a miscarriage, to demonstrate her toughness and commitment.[137] (These accusations reemerged around the same time ESPN had partnered for a show with Barstool Sports, a tawdry lifestyle site utopic for college bros, its rep meriting cancellation after just one episode.)

According to another published report, *Monday Night Football* sideline reporter Melissa Stark was asked by a top executive to wear "tight shirts and sweaters" that "accentuate her figure," which she accommodated; more recently, an insider I interviewed at another major sports network (anonymously) reports that the head of on-camera talent there was fired for telling women to "glam it up, to wear tight clothes, to show cleavage, to wear high heels."[138] Doris Burke, the first female analyst to call national NBA games, full-time, "softened her look"—from pantsuits and hair clipped back, which she assumed would "demonstrate her professionalism," to skirts and hair teased down—after her producer explained, in a "sobering pep talk," the lack of assignments she was finding at ESPN: "This is a visual medium, whether you want to accept that or not. And though it goes against every fiber of your being to be evaluated for anything other than what you say, the bottom line is you are."[139]

That logic articulated by Burke's boss need not be so explicit; such pressure, after all, gets quickly internalized by women in the sports media. "I would love to say that I hope people are only caring about what I'm saying and not how I look, but, absolutely— that's part of it," admits Sarah Kustok, the Brooklyn Nets reporter for the YES Network. "There's always a judgment, [like], 'Oh, well, she's not that cute.' . . . I think there's always, in some way, shape, or form, an extra layer of judgment on appearance."[140] ESPN anchor Linda Cohn, a veteran of the business for three decades, acknowledges that little has improved in that time; as she laments in her memoir, "Why do I always have the feeling that when my looks finally go, then so will my career? Why did I feel it necessary to mention . . . that I'm a size 4?"[141]

If the female sports media professional feels an acute pressure to be "cute," she also seems to bear the simultaneous (and, no doubt, related) weight of having her authority perpetually questioned. This makes for a contradictory double bind: being expected to look good, but—by virtue of looking good—that casting one's credibility in question. Jemele Hill, former *SportsCenter* anchor, is worth quoting at length on this front:

> The truth is that I can make an honest mistake about a statistic, or get a player's name wrong, or mispronounce something and the immediate reaction from a still-too-large segment of the public is going to be, "That's why women shouldn't talk sports." Even though most guys that are in [my] position probably would make a similar mistake, but it's never going to be about their competence. It's never going to be about their gender, where it will be for me. I think what you find for yourself is you're kind of up against and in this imaginary proving ground where you feel like, over and over, you have to prove what you're not, as opposed to what you are. . . . As a woman—and especially a woman of color— you're going to have to get used to the fact that you're going to be doubted; that people are going to think you're not credible; they're going to think you're sleeping with the players; that you're in it just to find a husband. You have to deal with all of that. You have to, unfortunately, have a really thick skin; otherwise you'll lose confidence in yourself.[142]

Because of that added scrutiny—that "closer eye, closer ear for what you're saying"—YES Network's Sarah Kustok feels compelled to have to "make sure you're at a step higher, doing more research, or extra work," so that critics don't fall back on the prevailing stereotype that women don't (or, more insidiously, shouldn't) "get" sports.[143] Thus, the female sports media professional still suffers from what was once famously phrased as the soft bigotry of low expectations: "My best compliment is not, like, 'Oh, wow—you look great,' or this or that," says ESPN's Linda Cohn. "The best compliment that I get is, 'Wow, I never—I'd shut off when I've seen women in the past in sports. This never happened with you.' . . . That's what you always strive for."[144] In yet another recent example of such slights, quarterback Cam Newton's bemused reaction to a female newspaper reporter's nuanced playbook question (that "it's funny to hear a female talk about [wide receiver] routes") bespoke such offhand sexism; it also earned him the loss of a yogurt brand sponsor.[145]

Sports journalism scholars Marie Hardin and Stacie Shain confirm from their research the persistence of this fragmented, "double bind" existence that female professionals must endure—struggling to reconcile their expected identities as women with the ability to "meet male standards, disguised as journalistic values" like detachment, aggressiveness, and being thick-skinned; a majority of these women report feeling they're not "taken as seriously" as their male counterparts.[146] "Ultimately," the authors conclude, "their ability to do a job like a man is what matters in the workplace."[147] For female broadcasters, in particular, that also means *sounding* like a man. In the *Monday Night Football* booth for the first time as a female play-by-play announcer, Beth Mowins was "greeted" on Twitter with a resounding and familiar chorus of critique that harped on her apparent shrillness; as veteran reporter Andrea Kremer discerned, "I have no doubt that 'hating the sound of her voice' is code for 'I hate that there was a woman announcing football.'"[148]

Notably, even as more females do filter into roles in the sports media and the hot-take industrial complex necessitates more opinion-oriented content to fill time, we find few, if any, women allowed to play provocateur. Again, ESPN's Hill offers insight into the industry's conventional wisdom on this front: "There's this prevailing stereotype that the dominant male audience doesn't want to see shows where the content—and the opinion content in particular—is driven by a woman."[149] Some chalk up this paucity of punditry from female voices to the perceived "fact" that audiences expect the analyst role to be played by a former player; Bonnie Bernstein, for one, remains adamant about this: "I firmly believe that you should not be an analyst. . . . unless [you] played the game or [you] coached the game."[150] This, of course, might explain the absence of color commentary and columns purveyed by females about football, but wouldn't seem to hold explanatory value for, say, basketball or baseball. More likely, I would submit, the opinionization trend is circumscribed by those same gendered anxieties, especially in a genre already steeped in traditions of hegemonic masculinity; it is unseemly for a woman socialized into "rapport talk," linguistically speaking, to be shouting hot takes at her sports panel counterparts.[151] Mansplaining, on the other hand, already comes "naturally" to one of the sexes.

Because of these limitations on professional license, when one pictures a woman working in sports media, the first role that springs to mind, historically, is that of a field-level reporter; women have been literally and figuratively "sidelined" in this sense. That's not to discount the luster or value in this particular journalistic capacity, but it does still represent a kind of gender "ghetto" in terms of the variety of roles a young female reporter might aspire toward. Visser, who has the veteran vantage point from which to appreciate progress (and regret regression), sees surprisingly little advancement since her early days in the business: "I go to the NFC Championship, and I'm telling you that in the press box there are maybe three women out of 2,000 credentials. I think we're at the same percentage as in the 1980s. There was a little burst, and it kind of went away. It didn't go forth and multiply."[152] Tina Cervasio shares that same lonely bafflement, noting that, of dozens of media members covering NBA or MLS events, she is often the only woman on hand.[153] The sports newsroom may have been "desegregated," but it has not yet been "integrated" and the distinction matters, given that informal norms guide social roles as much as official policy.[154] As Cohn posits,

The blame is on those who hire, which are usually men, because it's the safe way to go. And I put "safe" in quotations. Because a lot of men don't want to take a shot at—or working to perhaps develop a talent that could be female to do something else. . . . Because there aren't really a lot of women at big sports networks that are in managerial positions as opposed to pleasing the man that hired them to that managerial position. . . . [The sideline reporter's] still an easy, fallback way to put just another face up there and keep that stereotype alive, to just have the typical question that no sports fan even wants to hear or needs to hear when they can get that information from anyone in the booth.[155]

Acknowledging the dearth of female talent in the ESPN radio lineup, the executive overseeing that audio content framed it as a "market issue," related to the need to better serve female sports fans— the unstated assumption apparently being that more women on the sports talk dial could hardly increase *male* listenership.[156] As ESPN's Jemele Hill puts it, "[Television's] a copycat industry. There are very few TV networks or producers that want to do things for the first time. Everybody wants to make sure it works first before they try it. If they don't see it, they're not compelled to try it."[157] Although broadcast formats are the most visible media for this disparity, the problem equally extends to written genres as well; Garry Howard, whose long career included serving as editor-in-chief of *The Sporting News*, admits that the lack of women sportswriters had to do with lack of recruitment by news organizations (he adds that, upon assigning a female scribe to the Marquette University men's basketball beat, the head coach there was peeved by the perceived slight).[158] "It's different generations, different mindsets, and there are certain places where it's still the good ole' boys club," says Cervasio of Fox–New York.[159] Until those structures change, the ratios of those representing sport will likely not either.

## SELLING SPORTSWOMEN

Invariably, many of these patterns and problems persist for those women on the field of play. Here, too, the statistics calculating coverage disparities are as instructive as they are dispiriting. One longitudinal study that has tracked sports news for three decades finds little improvement as the majority of media representations focus, not surprisingly, on football, basketball, and baseball played by men at the professional and collegiate level; specifically, local network affiliates spend about 3 percent of their time on women's sports, with *SportsCenter* allocating only 2 percent.[160] Virtually every single study of sports media over the years—irrespective of platform format or game genre—has found female athletics "vastly underrepresented" compared to men's.[161]

The Olympics have been a particularly convenient context for comparison given the binary structure of participation; even the 1996 Games, which were touted by NBC as "The Olympics of the Woman," saw massively more airtime for men's team events while female athletes engaged in "power or hard physical contact" sports (i.e., these most acutely violating the norms of hegemonic masculinity) were almost totally ignored.[162] These same patterns have held true, historically, for print content: 90 percent of articles in *Sports Illustrated* between the 1950s and 1980s focused on men.[163] (The coverage is not much better abroad: A mere 3 percent of British newspaper articles focus on women's sports.[164]) Indeed, it was not until the 1990s that women's sports began receiving— barely—more attention than sports involving horses and dogs; emblematically, Serena Williams's selection as *SI*'s "Sportsperson of the Year" in 2015 ignited a debate among some media and fans that preferred the Triple Crown–winning thoroughbred American Pharaoh (which, some noted, was not actually, technically, even a sports-*person*).[165]

The WNBA is widely seen as the most successful female professional sports league America has ever supported, but nonetheless staggered into its 20th-anniversary season coming off the weakest attendance figures in its history, with double-digit drops in TV viewership; the $25 million in broadcast rights fees it receives from ESPN is dwarfed by the $2.6 billion payout to its men's league counterpart.[166] Compensation and employment is indeed revealing, especially among contrasting college sports. One study finds that male student-athletes average $600 more in scholarship aid, coaches of male teams average $190,000 more in salary, and men's teams average $270,000 more in recruiting than their female equivalents; operating budgets for men's basketball tend to be more than 10 times greater than those for women's basketball at the same institutions (relative to the comparative parity in a sport like, say, soccer).[167]

In 2016, several stars from the U.S. women's soccer team filed a wage discrimination lawsuit, claiming that—despite bringing in $20 million more in revenue than the men's team—they were still paid a quarter of their counterparts' earnings.[168] (World Cup prize money was itself unequally distributed: $575 million for men versus $15 million for women.[169]) Out of 345 Division I college athletic directors, less than 10 percent of programs are run by women, with even fewer atop big-time football schools (e.g., one was told she "never played football, so how could [she] possibly understand?"); similarly, nearly half of sports federations in the European Union have no women on their governing boards.[170] And a national survey by Pew found that 54 percent of Americans believe that a man "would do a better job" leading a professional sports team (as opposed to just 8 percent who would rather back a woman for that role).[171]

If this litany of quantitative measurements of America's treatment of female athletes fails to signal much progress toward gender equality, neither do more qualitative assessments. Sports media scholar Toni Bruce distills several fundamental "rules" of coverage when it comes to women's games: gender marking (e.g., calling it the "WNBA," which implies the male equivalent is the norm); traditional feminization (emphasizing emotional and physical weaknesses relative to men); and infantilzation (representing women as girls and therefore less of a symbolic threat to masculine power).[172]

Just as female sports media professionals face frequent sexualization of their appearance, so, too, do many female players—a phenomenon summarized as the "Anna Kournikova syndrome," whereby a conventionally attractive athlete ascends to the heights of popularity and marketability, without the talent to justify all the attention and therefore in a way no male star could conceivably achieve.[173] For example, Filip Bondy says that the story on a female athlete he wrote that drew, by far, the heaviest Web traffic ever was about Anna Sidorova, an Olympic curler who had posed in negligée and became Russia's "most popular" sportswoman.[174] The accompanying photo, featuring said curler seductively bent over the ice in a risqué outfit, embodies what has been called the "humorous sexualization" of female athletes: portraying them as simultaneously titillating and unserious.[175] Market "logic" drives this to some degree; as John Rowady, president of a sports consulting firm, explains, "The female athletes' fan base are still primarily men. [They're] not afraid to approach their sexuality about that—whereas with men [athletes], it's really about their athletic ability."[176]

Some have theorized that sportswomen *have* to cozy up to the heterosexual male gaze in erotic ways, so as to stave off the stereotypical presumption of being "not just a tomboy but a lesbian."[177] Moreover, the media production apparatus tends to privilege women who *do* fulfill those traditional "straight" roles. When the WNBA launched, its players were foregrounded in marketing materials as, alternately, hot models and loving mothers.[178] Two decades later, the WNBA's 2016 marketing campaign, "Watch Me Work," was also designed, according to one league executive, to capture "women who wear a lot of different hats—teammates, colleagues, mothers, role models."[179] One wonders whether the media would ever foreground NBA players as "fathers" in this same fashion.[180]

Almost as pernicious, in terms of audience-building, has been the persistent contrast between the hype and glitz accorded to men's athletics versus the "dull, matter-of-fact" style that usually delivers women's.[181] If the former gets dressed up like dessert, the latter tastes tends to taste like broccoli. This is apparent in the graphics packages appended to men's sports coverage and the volume and embellishment that commentators indulge; the production values for women's sports, on the other hand, often convey all the "flash and allure of neighborhood pickup games."[182] Even conference-affiliated channels like the Big Ten Network, which ostensibly herald a parity of coverage for men's and women's contests, almost never preface the latter with any kind of studio programming buildup: "I mean, almost none, because there's just not the interest, right?" laments one anchor there.[183]

Here he hits upon the circular logic that bedevils women's sports coverage (and, for that matter, media industries more broadly): Resources help generate ratings, which, in turn, wind up justifying the use of those resources. Or, put differently, how the sports media markets and covers female athletics—both quantitatively and qualitatively—winds up partly determining how much fan interest they are able to stir up; in the apparent absence of that interest, it becomes easier to starve the content of that structure. Commercialized sport thus systematically devalues women's worth: It sees little value and therefore finds little profit (and, cyclically, vice versa). Networks might claim to be responding to "market forces," as they often do, but they've hardly been "promoting and producing" programming that can compete effectively for attention within that cluttered marketplace.[184] "When you have generations and generations of figurative and literal capital being invested in men's sports, while completely marginalizing or punishing women," women's sports scholar Mary Jo Kane concludes, "why would you think it would be an equal comparison?"[185]

When I ask John Wildhack, the executive vice president for programming and production at ESPN, about that disparity in hours devoted to women versus men's sports, he replies, as expected: "What any media entity—whether it's a sports organization or whether it's a news organization—is you tend to focus the majority of your coverage on the topics that are most interesting to your viewers, right? For the widest viewership, widest audience online, widest readership."[186] In other words, the network is, like other sports media institutions, basically amoral on questions of gender equality; its obligation—and, frankly, fiduciary responsibility to Disney shareholders—is to simply give the audience what it (thinks it) wants. Rarely will you ever hear a media professional or executive acknowledge that he or she plays a role in *training* audiences to want certain content rather than others—outside of the marketing department, of course. These claims of responsiveness to audience interest are, then, a means of gatekeepers rationalizing decisions made, ex post facto, that maintain gender hegemonies through a pretext of "neutrality."[187]

But outlay matters. After all, the sports section, probably as much as any journalistic beat, is *especially* equipped to shape the "status quo" and "create interest"—rather than simply reflecting it.[188] "I spent hundreds of thousands of dollars [assigning reporters to travel] with the men's teams," Garry Howard recalls from his days running the sports page at the Milwaukee daily newspaper. "Women's basketball—we never traveled on the road with them unless they made, like, championship runs. And, unfortunately, it was, like, that's how much money was left, so they were between a rock and a hard place." Moreover, he says he knew that pushing women's sports content into the paper "wasn't always easy to do, considering that most people were buying us to get information on [men's sports]."[189] In general, newspaper editors harbor terrific confidence in their own ability to meet reader needs, but rarely use actual audience research to inform those content decisions; rather, these gatekeepers tend to rely upon "intuition, anecdotal evidence, what has been done in the past, and taken for granted beliefs about what the public want."[190] Such "intuition" becomes prejudicial when coupled with beliefs about women athletes and sports—like their "lesser quality"—that would serve to legitimize exclusion.[191]

As Mike Lynch, ABC-Boston sports anchor, summarizes, "They call it *broad*-casting for a reason, as opposed to *narrow*-casting. I think the audience is limited for women's sports on a regular basis. . . . I just don't think the excitement level in the games matches the excitement level of the men's sports, professional sports—except for major events."[192] Again, though, "excitement level" isn't some naturally occurring phenomena; it is also, equally, something that can get ginned up. That the media's agenda rarely prioritizes and encompasses women's sports helps naturalize the "logic" of ignoring it in a self-fulfilling way; it becomes common sense. "I try to make the judgment based on what I feel from people—what do they want to talk about—and I have never felt a rush of, 'Boy, we really need to talk about Serena Williams winning a grand slam on Sunday,'" says Spike Eskin, the sports talk radio program director at WIP Philadelphia.[193]

Others question whether any amount of time or promotional effort can overcome fundamental physical distinctions and their contrasting impact on the media product; take basketball, for example, where female athletes have arguably made some of their greatest gains. "Men, collectively, are never going to watch women play basketball, because they play below the rim. It's not exciting and men do have a superiority complex where they say, 'Hey I'm more athletic than them,'" theorizes Dan Stanczyk, a radio producer for ESPN.[194] (Incidentally, there was discussion in the WNBA's early years about lowering the rim precisely to cultivate a more action-packed tele-visual product.[195]) This, in turn, translates to market opportunities. When the agent for three-time WNBA MVP Lisa Leslie approached Nike about doing a signature shoe for his client, "The guys at Nike told me, 'We love her, but nobody is buying shoes because Lisa Leslie is wearing them. They are buying them because Michael Jordan is wearing them.'"[196]

Production and promotion of women's sports has thus long faced an uphill battle against the fortress of hegemonic masculinity. "We had to educate an entire generation of women and men that women's basketball was a great sport with everything but the dunking," says longtime NBA commissioner David Stern. "It will prevail, without question, as more and more women are drawn to the sport and more and more girls understand that it's great to sweat."[197] Stern's phrasing inadvertently bespeaks the fundamental "transgression" that all female athletes represent and, thus, the quasi-Victorian boundaries they must overcome. (Brazil, for example, still had a law on the books as recently as the mid-1970s that women couldn't participate in sports that were "incompatible with their natural [feminine and reproductive] condition."[198]) A woman running, one critic observes, is committing a subversive "feminist act"—her strength "a threat, a harbinger of the demise of men, masculinity, or male privilege."[199] This is not to sell short the strides made since Title IX was passed, but rather to spotlight media and marketing's continued confinement of those strides, due to economic obligations and self-fulfilling constraints.[200]

Some have thought that the transition of sports media—from being curbed by linear broadcasting spectrum to the limitless digital landscape—could create new opportunities for more exposure, but any such revolution, it seems, still needs to be televised; for most "lower-tier sports" (which women's still finds itself pigeonholed as), "the hierarchy of sports funding, facilities, and overall attention" has changed little.[201] Others maintain "liberal feminist" hopes that more women being employed in sports media could yet prove instrumental in female athletes being depicted more often and more respectfully; there is, however, scant evidence of either trend tracking positively, not least because volunteering to cover women's sports is hardly a path to professional advancement.[202] In sum, sports media still harbor the vibe of a "'mediated man cave'—a place set up by men for men to celebrate men's sensational athletic achievements."[203]

From a marketplace perspective, this would seem to ignore a huge potential demographic share. Yet it turns out that the experience of the female sports *fan* is not all that different (and certainly no more reverential) than that of the female journalist or female athlete—at least as conceptualized and articulated by the cultural producers who come courting her. This is driven, as with so many other facets of sport analyzed throughout this book, by overriding commercial demands: "[Sport] still is—in terms of advertising—largely a device to get an 18-to-49-year-old male. That's what it's about. That's why they're in business. That's what they're selling," explains Terry Lefton, the marketing reporter for *SportsBusiness Journal*. "If you wanted to reach women—yeah, there are some women there, but if you want to reach a high concentration of women . . . wouldn't you go to something in daytime TV [or] . . . reality shows?"[204]

This niche segregation has long been the intent. Women's sports programming rarely received plum time-slots in ESPN's early days, as the network instead chased a more lucrative male market on behalf of advertisers (i.e., seeking out "the right kind of people," as one study puts it); these efforts confirmed which audiences were valued most—both financially and socially—and informed what content would get produced for them and what would be ignored.[205] Today more than ever, the attention of that young male consumer is, in equal measure, rapaciously prized and frustratingly flitting;

sports, however, have had a unique ability to loyally lure those eva-sive eyeballs.[206]

Corporate patronage has followed, which could care less about issues of gender parity either on the screen or on the couch: "If there was one single reason that brands flock to sports, they would all say—I mean, 99 percent of the educated buyers and smart marketers—would say the eighteen-to-thirty-four-year-old male. It's the most attractive historically—even today, believe it or not—the most attractive audience to capture for lifetime customer values, spending power, and the most difficult to reach," A. J. Maestas, CEO of a sports market research firm, summarizes.[207] ESPN loves to boast about its success in this regard; its head of research notes that, at one point, men had identified it as their favorite channel for 14 years in a row.[208]

That said, where there's demographic saturation, commer-cial logic demands that vested parties scour for new buyers. The espnW initiative—a dedicated sub-site along with various branded programming—has represented one strategy to "get people into the bigger tent" of ESPN, according to one network executive.[209] That matches the evolving enlightenment within the sports media pro-duction complex that it's "economically and otherwise senseless to alienate" half your potential audience; tactics to win over female consumers have included playing up the sex appeal of male ath-letes, explaining game details to the fan dilettante, and—though this chapter has shown there to be mostly a failure of will thus far—improving the quality of women's sports coverage and quantity of female sportscasters.[210]

Another tactic to woo women as sports consumers is to package the product or experience as feminist fantasy: that is, to be a sport-ing female (game for either athletic participation or fandom in the stands) is spun, by some stakeholders, as a demonstration of gender empowerment. The commercial seed of this idea was planted in the mid-1990s, when tapping market share meant promoting some hazy, generically progressive sense of sports culture values.[211] Nike perfected the pitch, aggressively targeting female consumers by selling sneakers and apparel through a commodity-based, neoliberal rendition of feminist headway; their ads featured adorable young girls beseeching, "if you let me play," as the key to unlocking a variety of pro-social life outcomes and underscoring sports' longer-standing mythology about individual initiative.[212]

More recently, Under Armour has inherited and engineered much the same ethos, as seen in its "I WILL WHAT I WANT" campaign, whereby its ad agency was apparently "tasked with creating an empowering and beautiful space for [its] Women's brand to grow" by speaking to "women who do not wait for permission, advice or affirmation from others in order to go after what they want."[213] (The intended *Lean In* allusion is obvious, I know, but pause and take note here of how unseemly it would be to conjure a campaign in which UA's other endorsers like Tom Brady or Stephen Curry explicitly spoke to a masculine ambition to "not wait for permission" in pursuit of their goals.) Sports media has adopted some of these talking points as well, as when one NBC executive explicitly framed his network's "girl power" promotion of the U.S. women's Olympic team thus: "We want to have this be a story of women's empowerment."[214] (The NFL has had to do its own PR-related image repair with female fans—not only for the purpose of demographic profit, but to put a shine on an ugly spate of domestic violence crises.[215])

Thus, "appealing" to female fans often looks and sounds somewhat indistinguishable from "pandering" to them. Again, take the further comments of that NBC sports marketing chief: "The people who watch the Olympics are not particularly sports fans. More women watch the games than men and, for the women, they're less interested in the result and more interested in the journey. It's sort of like the ultimate reality show and mini-series wrapped into one."[216] The conventional wisdom within sports media consequently seems to hold that, in order to win over women to sports content, one must do more "storytelling" around the games and "much less x's and o's"—that they either can't or don't want to engage with the more technical details of competition.[217]

Other initiatives have betrayed this patronizing professional logic over the years. NHL teams have offered "Hockey in High Heels" seminars to explain the game's rules and allow women attending to test out the equipment and practice shooting motions; the CBC similarly stooped with a (regrettably named) "While the Men Watch" simulcast of the Stanley Cup Finals that offered alternative "female-centered" game narration where the hosts "engage in girl talk" including "celebrity gossip" throughout the match-up.[218] Elsewhere, the NFL's courtship of female audiences has included "sorority reunion"-style fan clubs, fashion lounges (offering team-theme makeup tutorials and "fanicure" nail patterns), and "pink-washing" the game landscape to raise awareness of breast cancer.[219] Among individual teams, the Tampa Bay Buccaneers, for example, launched "RED," a "brand new women's movement that will re-invent the female fan experience"; said "re-invention" website included sub-pages dedicated to parsing such esoteric quandaries as "What does the term 'play clock' mean?" and posted explainer videos where the starting running back reveals, "My job is to run the ball and score touchdowns."[220]

More so than these ham-fisted attempts at gameplay explication, the energy devoted to courting women fans is spent mainly on merchandising design and consumer interpellation. The NFL deployed a dedicated women's website that, while mostly pushing merchandise, also featured "tailgating-at-home" recipe tips and made "it easy for families and people hosting parties, and certainly women are largely driving that in the home."[221] The NFL's apparel director notes that, as the female fan base has grown in recent years, "We weren't giving them the best outlet to express their fandom."[222] Historically, female fan attire has been a production afterthought—what industry insiders refer to as the "pink it and shrink it" model that captures the narrow scope of marketing imagination of yesteryear.[223] Tina Cervasio recoils at the notion that sports need to be packaged differently—and somehow more superficially—for female audiences: "That's assuming the female thinks differently. I don't think so. Like, I hated the pink hat movement—wear your team colors. Why does it have to be pink? . . . That offends the very knowledgeable female sports fans."[224]

The problem, of course, is that "authentic" sportswomen jeopardize "the hallowed fraternizing element" of men's sports culture and "disrupt" the retrograde gender power balance maintained therein.[225] That disruption is witnessed across a variety of fronts chronicled in these pages—from female journalists "taking" media jobs to female athletes "taking" airtime to female audiences "taking" couch space. The anxiety that ensues derives mostly from a historical presumption that those contexts somehow "belonged" to men in the first place. As it turns out, the final section of the chapter will argue, these transformations and grievances within sports culture are but a microcosm of and metaphor for men's wider relationship to industrial production.

## RETHINKING THE MASCULINE BODY OF WORK

"The life of man in America or in any of the industrialized countries today, laboring on the farm, in the factory, in the office, is not the natural life of man. He is still an animal formed for battle and conquest, for blows and strokes and swiftness, for triumph and applause. But let him join the crowd around the diamond, the gridiron, the tennis court or the ring. . . . Let him identify with his favorite fighter, player or team. . . . He will achieve exaltation, vicarious but real."[226]

If history doesn't repeat itself, as the old saying goes, but rather "rhymes," there is something familiar about these gendered anxieties that freight the contemporary sports moment—echoes of a hundred years prior, even. For at the turn of the 20th century—not long before the above observation was drawn—masculinity found itself in similar crisis in American culture. Then, as now, traditions of labor aspiration and the intertwined social norms were fast unraveling. An agrarian age was winding down, subsumed by the new industrial world, with different roles offered and demands made upon the bodies and livelihoods of men. As machines replaced what had previously been accomplished by brawny dint, fears of "physical degeneracy" and "national virility" became widespread—a perceived atrophy of not just muscles, but the visible, physical index of masculine social and cultural power.[227]

Simultaneously, the demise of the wild western edge of the American continent was greeted with alarm, accelerating anxieties that the new urban orientation and lifestyle—lacking the "rigors of physical labor, frontier dangers, and warfare measures of manhood"—might somehow feminize society as a whole.[228] Employment, too, felt suddenly more precarious—unlike the noble and independent yeoman tilling his family farm, breadwinning was now scavenged in cramped factories and dependent upon lordly owners.[229] As the political and civic gains of first wave feminism solidified, some of the old pillars of patriarchy were simultaneously crumbling.[230] Modern man—of 1900, that is—seemed suspiciously soft when compared to his hardy forefathers.

Against this backdrop of angst, organized sport emerged to help validate masculine identity, through its symbolic "proof" of gender superiority, proffering a sphere insulated from the alleged feminization of everyday life.[231] It carved out a fresh-air escape hatch from the iron cage of powerless, bureaucratized work-experience—a space where heroes still modeled "the pioneer traits of physical skill, toughness, and daring," and sports like boxing recalled, tantalizingly, a simpler era where pure muscle and raw effort foretold survival destiny.[232] Hockey was similarly ratified as "a man's game," given that it became one of the last arenas of labor and competition where "hardness and overt physical intimation" still counted for something—a preserve that much more crucial in a changing world where less physical (and decidedly less rural) jobs destabilized men's sense of control over their own fate.[233]

Amidst increasingly suffocating cities, with no frontier to offer either psychological respite or physical flight, sport afforded "a new safety valve for a congested America."[234] Baseball expressed this solution especially aesthetically; its agrarian texture and attendant pastoral nostalgia, at a time when the means of production were changing so dramatically, implicitly critiqued what industrialization and urbanization had done to the modern world and, by extension, modern man.[235] In that, there is an ironic note of history: Even in the "good old days" of the late 1800s, when it was born, baseball already felt wistful and backward-looking.

What emerges, then, from this brief historical summary is the enduring notion that men have primarily defined their identity—and therefore existential value—through their labor in public spaces (as opposed to the confines of the home, where women have less visibly and remuneratively toiled for ages).[236] Not all forms of labor equally uphold the ideals and necessities of that hegemonic masculinity; physical labor is, of course, privileged as more admirable than, say, emotional or intellectual, where women can compete with greater parity and less biological slight. Sport thus "performs" that function of discrimination on behalf of men.

It also fetishizes the productive body: Backbreaking labor is romanticized; backbreaking labor is moral. A favorite American sports media cliché, especially in football, is that of the workaholic coach sleeping in his office. Even at the New England Patriots' 2017 Super Bowl parade rally—their fifth under Bill Belichick, with no other foes left to vanquish—the crowd exuberantly broke out in the team's signature "Do! Your! Job!" chant, adding a new one that equally exalts grueling commitment: "No! Days! Off!" It might seem puzzling why workers—albeit on lunch break and in their fan garb—would so mimic the rhetoric of heartless employers, were it not a central ethos animating the Protestant sports ethic. "Belichick views players as commodities, moving parts in a system, and doesn't seem to get attached to them," one former NFLer writes (apparently admiringly) of the Patriots' unsentimental, neoliberal willingness to cut, trade, or bench stars and veterans, regardless of their loyal service. "I love this. Pressure, when applied properly, makes us perform at a higher level."[237]

Indeed, few cultural forms besides sports more aptly "embody" philosopher Michel Foucault's notion of biopower: the way that a regime can structure and discipline the physicality of human experience, both placing restraints upon and, more critically, enabling the movement of bodies for maximum efficiency, until these coordinates are simply internalized and voluntarily obeyed.[238] At various moments in history, this asceticism even came tinged with theological logic—the athletes of ancient Greece found that moral character was formed through self-denial and the Puritans portrayed purification in punishment and salvaged spiritual value from suffering (themes that Nike advertising would later absorb and commercialize, propagating itself as "secular religion" while preaching body-as-temple).[239]

Within sport, as in industrial capitalism, the body is treated as tool—a machine means to be engineered for optimal ends, thus "wring[ing] maximum productivity from the human frame."[240] Frederick Taylor, namesake of the manufacturing management system that tries to achieve perfect efficiency of shop floor labor flow, would've loved sports' metaphorical orientation to minimizing time and maximizing output within spatial constraints.[241] (The Olympic motto itself sounds like something that might have been screamed at an assembly line by a slave-driving factory owner: "Faster! Higher! Stronger!"[242]) And, as demonstrated by the aforementioned Belichickian heartlessness, the athletic body is usually only valued for its future potential, as opposed to past accomplishment—a cruel fate given, as noted earlier, the regularity with which those manly "machines" break down in the heat of battle.[243]

No resting on laurels here: "It doesn't particularly matter what you did last year, or last week, or yesterday; if you are unable to perform at the level your employer expects you to, every single day, they will find someone who will," states sportswriter Will Leitch. "The past is immaterial; you are forced to go out and prove yourself, all the time."[244] The NFL combine is probably the most explicit and visible manifestation of that Foucauldian practice, as experienced by one former NFLer: "[It's] about as much as a human being can be treated like a piece of meat in 21st-century America. You walk onstage in your underwear. You walk room to room, where sometimes five doctors are pulling on different parts of your body while you're in your underwear and [they're] talking about you like you're not there. So, yeah. I mean, it's like cattle. They're in the cattle business. It's how well your body can perform."[245]

In turn, the sports that best expressed that raw physicality of purpose most endeared themselves as familiar to a proletarian fan base and embodied men's *raison d'être*. Early football, in particular, "dramatized working class life," as local teams became symbolic of "blue collar community pride."[246] As feminist critic Varda Burstyn frames it, "Whatever defeats they might regularly have suffered at the hands of upper-class men in their daily lives, working men could regain their lost masculinity on the playing fields, as their professional representatives bested their class opposites."[247]

Certain franchises like the Pittsburgh Steelers came to exude a simultaneously real and media-enhanced toughness in the face of adversity: their name derived from the bitter blue-collar labor that long defined the region; their players and fans proud to endure sub-zero temperatures for the honor of the game; and NFL Films happily marrying these themes together in slow-motion, foggy-breath montages of stars like (the emblematically nicknamed) "Mean" Joe Greene.[248] Moreover, there is a specifically *masculine* masochism to this endurance: The pleasure and glory of football in western Pennsylvania supposedly derives from an apparent "need to absorb punishment in order to prove oneself."[249]

"In certain markets, whether it's Pittsburgh, Boston . . . it's a blue-collar fan base, so they appreciate the effort, because those are the people that are getting up and going to work every day," explains one player agent. "It doesn't matter if you have a cold—I think that resonates with the fan base."[250] Yet Pittsburgh is also a perfectly apt metaphor for the falsity of that residual pretense: a once sooty, gritty city that reinvented and rebranded itself over a generation from manufacturing and industry to health care and the tech sector. A less "masculine" transformation of collective labor identity could scarcely be conjured—from heavy to light, bruising to nurturing. And as the woes of the wider Rust Belt have drained its factories, population, and economic vitality, it has also chipped away at the region's once-vaunted high school football programs; concurrently, the Sun Belt of the American South and West, with its "New Economy" innovation, has arguably displaced it as the center of college football power.[251]

It is perhaps not coincidence, then, that *Atlantic* writer Hanna Rosin could declare *The End of Men* during the same period when the fan and labor experience of sports culture was changing so dramatically.[252] By the start of the decade, women had muscled their way into the majority of the American workforce for the first time in history.[253] "Muscle," though, was precisely *not* a prerequisite for this accomplishment; the post-industrial economy doesn't reward brute force as labor opportunity might have a century (or even generation) ago. It tends to be rather, as Rosin puts it, "indifferent" to men's strength and size, as seen in some of the statistics that define our era.[254]

Seventy-five percent of jobs lost in the aftermath of the Great "Mancession" were held by men (a downturn that was especially acute in explicitly physical fields like manufacturing and construction); in that more "female-friendly" labor market, male wages have either stagnated or plummeted among the less educated.[255] As other blue-collar jobs either shift to robotics or are shipped to foreign workers, the percentage of men in their late teens with high school diplomas who were classified—humiliatingly, within American culture—as "idle" (that is, not employed or enrolled in school) peaked at 16 percent, surpassing that of women.[256] Simultaneously, women have been outgaining men by a ratio of three to two in bachelor's and master's degrees (and earning higher grades throughout); represent an ever-greater share of managerial and professional occupations; and find that the industries projecting most growth have been historically feminized (e.g., nursing, education).[257] One report from some American sperm clinics finds girls being requested three times as often as boys.[258] Thus, for an assortment of reasons—both shown in this hard data of economic indicators and the fuzzy sense of status signifiers morphing—masculinity is said to be again in "crisis."[259] As one sociologist summarizes—taking the long view: "Men's feelings of alienation have roots in . . . the increased social power and independence of women and gays, the neoliberal political economy that has increased the economic insecurity of many working-class and middle-class families, the absence or remoteness of fathers in many

American families today, and especially feelings of national embarrassment and disgust about losing the Vietnam War."[260]

Sport, however—ever patriarchal and patronizing to women—might still represent a rejoinder to some of these trends, just as it did a century ago. As men no longer monopolize the role of breadwinner—and cannot rely upon it as the means to "win" a spouse—they seek alternatives to compensate; what has been "lost" in the labor pool might just be "regain[ed] through their musculature."[261] (Indeed, both men, generally, and those less educated, across genders, tend to report deriving more of a self-esteem boost from their favorite teams succeeding on the field or court.[262]) Yet as brawn comes to matter less than brains within both American work (which is increasingly automated and digitized) and warfare (also undergoing its own post-human, "drone strike," technological transformation), the need to maintain the valorization of the male body as "strong, virile, and powerful" becomes that much more urgent.[263] When women encroached upon male domains of labor and public life in the late 19th century, a similar "cult of manliness" sprung up in sport as the "antidote for [men's] anxieties about effeminacy."[264] Today, too, it might just represent "one of men's last 'chances' to escape from the growing ambiguity of masculinity in daily life."[265]

And, yet, when the male fan flips on the television, what reflected image is he confronted with during the commercial break? A dope; a loser; a bizarre, possessed, dysfunctional nincompoop.[266] A sexual impotent who needs to "ask [his] doctor" about erectile drugs. Simultaneously, sports talk radio has been theorized as an audio space to help men work through the dissolution of their post-feminist power and the anxious uncertainty of their deindustrialized and dematerialized labor—it gives them a "safe haven" in which to bond and to reaffirm that which has been lost to fates supposedly beyond their control.[267]

These are, moreover, not your grandfather's games. Sport itself has undergone a profound digital and data-driven labor disruption—one not unlike that which is reshaping the "real" world of work external to it. Post-*Moneyball* and post-fantasy, there has arguably never been greater obsession with statistically converting the physical experience of athletic activity and venerating those who can manipulate and predict those resultant figures effectively. If, for centuries, sports heroes have been avatars of brawn, today, we find an increasing number whose relationship to and domination of sport—whether professionally in front offices or imaginarily in office pools—is brainy rather than bodily.

There is a longer trajectory to this, of course, as with all trends mapped throughout the book. One of the chief characteristics of modern sport (i.e., of the past 100 years) is its fanatical tendency toward quantification and record keeping; by contrast, the ancient Greeks had neither the technological capacity for—nor, presumably, the interest in—measuring every motion and accomplishment so as to generate useful, cross-historical, comparative data.[268] By contrast, nowadays, data is, in and of itself, the competitive arena for fans and general managers alike. Fantasy sports' steady growth since their inception in the early 1980s by a gang of seamheads at a New York City restaurant exploded upward this decade when daily competition became plausible and lucrative.[269] Today, some 60 million North Americans participate; venture capital has poured a half-billion dollars into the market category; and to capitalize on interest, ESPN staged a 28-hour marathon stunt of fantasy coverage to mark an approaching NFL season kickoff.[270]

Fans' interest in engaging with the games in this utterly postmodern fashion has been a boon to professional leagues and media companies alike. Fantasy functions as a kind of "attention multiplier"—a fan's eyeballs are no longer merely drawn to a single totemic loyalty but scattered across a vaster slate of games (some of which, if blowouts, can still matter for the individual performances).[271] In turn, sports news organizations and broadcasters benefit from the added narrative layer—a meta-storyline, if you will, that now needs covering.[272] As syndicated talk show host Doug Stewart declares: "I can't even put into words how big fantasy sports have been intertwined with sports radio."[273] Nor can the leagues themselves, which benefit from fantasy's gradual seepage into general pop culture consciousness—not unlike the way that filling out an NCAA bracket becomes an office's communal rite of spring even for those apathetic and ignorant about college basketball. Similarly, because of fantasy, one sports consulting executive says, "If you can't come into the office Monday and talk about what happened Sunday, you are out of the loop. So, for a lot of people, the NFL is a social obligation."[274] As shown in the last chapter, that is a valuable position to stake out: squeezing capital out of community.

Yet fantasy gets us to think and feel about sports and athletes very differently than traditional fandom. Chances are many of those halfhearted fantasy duffers (perhaps roped in just to even out odd-number leagues) are adjusting lineups each Sunday morning based upon predicted points alone—the player's name and photo invisible to them, merely a string of data to be optimized and leveraged for competitive advantage. This is perhaps not that dissimilar from how the titans of today's tech industries look upon us all: users whose digital lives make up the Big Data pointillist pattern that produces their profits.

Indeed, those who take up fantasy football—or, for that matter, obsess over the NFL draft or play Electronic Arts' best-selling *Madden* video game in "owner" mode—are being schooled in the pleasures of what one scholar cleverly calls "vicarious management," a new mode of fandom consciousness that "invites audiences to identify with the institutional regimes of the NFL (and the authorities who conduct them) rather than with the athletes . . . [who] are positioned as property, often valuable, but ultimately disposable."[275] Fantasy is, at its core, a simulation of that ownership; a game of who can "best manage human capital."[276] Ideologically, it's perhaps what helps teach fans how to chant "Do! Your! Job!" every Sunday.

As I discovered in conversations with fantasy players for a study a few years back, this is precisely one of the pleasures; pride reflects a sense of managerial success in more of that coldly calculating capacity (e.g., evaluating talent, executing trades) than rooting for one's traditional team in hot-blooded, totemically binding ways.[277] As we "interface" with sports culture differently—with ever more sports talk preoccupied with salary caps and free agent signings and ex-GMs supplanting former players on those TV panel discussions—young fans can daydream less about "coming to the plate in the bottom of the ninth with the bases loaded" and more about "signing the guy who hits the game-winning homer."[278]

That's a peculiar turnabout. And these pervasive fantasy experiences have triggered far more attentiveness to those performing this form of management for "real." Theo Epstein—the boy genius GM who laid low not one, but two, century-old championship curses in Boston and Chicago—was arguably as famous as any player on the 2016 Cubs' roster that he constructed. Sportswriter Will Leitch cleverly contextualizes the appeal of fantasy sports within a "general analytical age" that finds our lives and jobs replete with concern for data, both in terms of attentiveness and anxiety: "The fantasy-sports era has transformed the average fan into a much more sophisticated connoisseur of what really makes teams win than even a general manager might have been a decade or two ago. . . . We're all the Jonah Hill character in *Moneyball*. . . . As in Silicon Valley and on Wall Street, the success of data-driven executives . . . has given us a cult of the general manager to replace, or at least supplement, the hero worship of players."[279]

Silicon Valley—just a bridge ride from the site of *Moneyball*, where Michael Lewis (and, later, Brad Pitt) popularized Billy Beane's sabermetric savvy—offers an apt analogy here: Big Data is reconfiguring sports culture in many of the ways that it is affecting postindustrial work-life writ large. "Twenty years ago, thirty years ago, it would have been inconceivable to have more people who knew the name of the general manager of the Oakland A's than the manager," marvels former *Deadspin* editor-in-chief Tommy Craggs. Moreover, he points out, *Moneyball* offers the perfect late capitalist fable—a paean to that "cult of efficiency" where "there is glory in winning efficiently." "It's the story of . . . a cheapskate owner who didn't want to open up his checkbook and so it forced this really smart guy to underpay talented workers to produce way above their pay grade," Craggs summarizes. "[It's] how a really smart guy used his smarts to suppress the wages of good baseball players."[280] Does that sound somewhat familiar to the wider American labor experience?

Of course, before Beane—whose teams offered a feel-good, meritocratically American, Hollywood-optionable tale of the scrappy upstart competing with profligate big spenders—there was Bill James, "father" of baseball's data revolution, whose writings in the 1970s and 1980s first advanced a positivist approach against the instinctive, gut leanings of the tobacco-chewing "old guard."[281] Yet that approach really exploded in the past decade, as seen in the growth of attendees—from 175 to 3,500—at MIT's annual sports analytics conference.[282]

Subsequent to the wave of quantification that has ensued, much of the league went "overboard" on data, stripping scouting staff and adding analysts, engineers, and software developers to their operations in the hopes of excavating some statistical advantage unseen by the naked, qualitative eye; younger, less experienced managers who are comfortable with those "new-age" metrics and tools have been increasingly supplanting stubborn, older skippers.[283] The world champion Houston Astros front office, for example, included an MBA-credentialed medical risk manager and a former NASA bio-mathematician. Not exactly the "dumb jock" stereotype that hegemonic masculinity has held aloft for decades within sports culture. And those ushering in the brave new data world are as unsentimental as the Zuckerbergs and Bezoses about the skills being rendered obsolete: "There will be two kinds of coaches around the world," predicts the executive at a sports tech firm. "There are going to be coaches that believe in this kind of analytics and engage with it and there are going to be former coaches."[284] Their operating system, in other words, is simply out of date.

Furthermore, as "ubiquitous computing" and data processing have blended "almost imperceptibly into the rhythms and background of social life," they have also become part of the routine of sports production—for those who manage the on-field product, those who package it as mediated spectacle, and those who consume it through those increasingly postmodern lenses.[285] One outgrowth of this trend shows up in labor surveillance—a practice that obviously dates back to Frederick Taylor's 19th-century stopwatch but has burrowed to new depths of granularity given the affordances of the digital era. "Unprecedented" amounts of player performance data and biometrics that are now subjected to regular regression analysis weren't even available a few years earlier, just as questions are raised about the ownership, protection, and distribution of that data.[286]

For example, the dynastic Golden State Warriors became the first NBA team to deploy a "smart court" for practices, wherein multiple HD camera angles are synced into a database system to allow for instantaneous panoptic tracking and statistical calculations.[287] In 2017, Major League Baseball enlisted multiple analytics companies to provide wearable on-field technology, including sensory compression sleeves, bio-harnesses, bat sensors, and swing trackers to help optimize performance.[288] A few years earlier, the NFL began tracking player movements by implanting radio frequency identification tags in shoulder pads—later expanding the tracking chips to footballs, too—which deliver "a seemingly infinite" quantity of data from wideout acceleration to defender separation to quarterback arm strength.[289] A variety of big-time college football programs now report tracking players' sleep data; Clemson, for example, employs a ribbon that can be affixed beneath a subject's mattress.[290] And nearly two dozen professional American franchises—and, now, the U.S. men's national soccer team as well—began analyzing players' DNA sequencing to optimize performance and aid nutritional strategies.[291] As one team's head of player health and performance put it—unknowingly ominously—"I look at it more as a segue to have a conversation with a player. The data is basically saying, 'Looks like you weren't cutting as hard today—is there something going on?'"[292] God help us when all supervisors have the same data-driven capacity to govern our labor thus; that day is surely dawning sooner rather than later.

## THE MORAL (AND MORALE) OF SPORTS LABOR

At some point, for players, it must all come to an end. "Transition" hardly captures the sense of whiplash that accompanies that hard stop. This usually also means finding work that is less taxing on the body and, as they perceive it, earns less respect for that effort. Life after sport is, almost inevitably, less rewarding to macho mentalities—both financially and culturally. Sport scholars Richard Gruneau and David Whitson shrewdly detect broader sociological parallels in that evolution, weaving together assorted themes from this chapter:

What these former players experience is not unlike the ambivalence that a great many working-class men experience when they move from blue-collar to white-collar forms of work. Many men who work with their bodies in industrial settings, often under hard and dangerous conditions, want to be able to find work that leaves danger and physical exhaustion behind. They also want the respect, status, and financial rewards that attach to many forms of white-collar work in Western societies. Yet, ironically, once they get into the office . . . many of them do not feel they are doing much that is worth being proud of. . . . As people who have also done physically demanding, skilled work, many professional athletes find it hard to take the same pride in the kinds of work available to them after retirement.[293]

These are, then, the gendered anxieties that plague the transformation of modern labor—a set of apprehensions in abundance both external to sports culture and on display within it. An information economy does not, culturally, offer those same "macho" jobs, as did the agrarian and industrial eras before it and, yet, that is the direction that labor seems to be pooling. Billy Beane and Theo Epstein—and, for that matter, every Monday morning quarterback swaggering into the office, chest puffed out from his fantasy roster's weekend domination—no longer typify the "rough, manly" sportsmen that Teddy Roosevelt so idealized.[294] They are interacting with sports in a far more bloodless, number-crunching fashion. Athletics have become considerably wonkier and, in juvenile terms, "nerdier" than past incarnations and generations likely could—or would want to—accommodate. What does that portend for American manhood?

To be certain, it's not that contemporary sport has been scrubbed clean of gratuitous violence—far from it, as any cursory glance at the nation's most fanatical pastime, the NFL, will reveal. But even there—at ground zero for both pop culture and masculine performance—there seems increasing unease about the bodily toll that the sport exacts, most notably with the concussion issue and the early retirements it is producing. The solution here, for both sports culture and the norms of American economic life, requires rethinking and reframing the morality that has been long been bestowed upon grueling physical labor. That purported "crisis" of masculinity cannot be addressed until backbreaking work is seen less as a righteous badge of honor and more as historical, geographic, and class-based necessity (and, if we further allow it, an often-dehumanizing form of exploitation). We ought to conjure heartfelt sympathy rather than misty admiration for those whose labor gnarls their bodies—which is, itself, a kind of "feminized" reaction to workplace dictates.

Sports' designation of deeds done amidst danger as "play" has helped frame and perpetuate the obtuseness of this traditional consciousness, but, more so, we idealize in professional sports a performance of labor that is increasingly receding from middle-class American sightlines. Athletes are out there producing with their bodies, doing what—for most of human history—was required and, thus, respected. Such labor had value: materially, morally. For generations of American men in the 20th century who experienced military service and industrial labor, that "accomplishment of rugged and dangerous tasks" on the sports stage reverberated as somehow more "authentic" and "better" than other, softer life alternatives.[295] It need not be that way.

Yet the fewer blue-collar jobs that there are available to the American workforce, the more we will need compensate, culturally, for that lost *moral* force, just as we aim to retrain workers for a digitally disrupted economy. Donald Trump's coarse, reactionary fetish for a particular brand of "rough-hewed American maleness" is nostalgic and (psychically) aspirational for those "dirty-fingernail jobs so revered in the American imagination: coal miners, firefighters, autoworkers."[296] The more people (and, specifically, men) wind up desk-bound, working with computers, the more that pro sports stars will "stand out, and perhaps evoke an appreciation embedded in the human genetic structure for the skills necessary for survival in the wild."[297] At games, when we look up from busying ourselves with work e-mail on smartphones, we see ancestral toil, aestheticized as competitive ballet. But these forefathers got mauled by bears and mangled by industrial machinery. America should stop fetishizing their work as somehow more "righteous," much less "manly"—those are adjectives that can and should be "recoded," more in accordance with the data-driven professions that are overtaking 21st-century life.

Interestingly, of all the topics that I engaged with my interviewees, the production of hegemonic masculinity through sports media seemed to leave them most tongue-tied. To be certain, I did not phrase the question draped in that scholarly jargon—lest their tongues be that much more tied—but any effort to strip down the concept to its basics and elicit some self-reflexivity about what role they might have in representing *what men should be* seemed to trip them up as a puzzling meta-premise: What—me, encode gender norms?

"I certainly don't think about it that way and I haven't—I think it's very much left to the reader," Ben Shpigel, the Jets beat writer for *The New York Times*, emblematically asserts. "It's up to the reader to interpret what they want. I'm certainly not out there trying to go ahead and convince people and tell them what they should feel or think."[298] One creative director similar demurs from the purview of his advertising background: "We didn't make up that narrative. It's in the culture surrounding sports, but they might just visually live up to it. I can't say when it comes to male athletes that we've ever just tried to show power—it's just by the nature of these Adonis-like, superhuman people. They really are that [way] naturally and I think people might form their own narrative around that. Or reflect it, rather. I can't say that we're consciously trying to do that when we work with male athletes."[299]

Such is ideology's invisible power: It's usually like asking a fish about water. A particular vision of masculinity is embedded so deeply in American sports culture that to pose questions about it might as well be asking why there are four downs rather than five in football or a three-point line but not a four-point line in basketball. It's "just" the way it is. And, as the next chapter will show, it's far from the only ideology invisibly "at work" here.

> When people say, "Don't talk about politics in sports," what they're really saying is: "Don't say anything I don't want to hear or I don't agree with."
> —**Bob Costas**, NBC studio host

# FAIR GAME

## The Invisible Ideologies of "Apolitical" Escapism

> The infectious values and myths transmitted by bad sportswriters may be the deadliest words in the paper.
> —**Robert Lipsyte**, *New York Times* sports columnist

# FOR DECADES, AS AMERICAN

# SPORTS AND SPORTS MEDIA HAVE

so seamlessly aligned with commercial objectives, there has been simultaneous pushback—from fans, brands, players, and journalists alike—that sports and politics shouldn't mix.[1] Legendary broadcaster Howard Cosell christened this the cardinal rule of the "jockocracy"—an ironic decree, given his kinship with Muhammad Ali, the greatest transgressor of that rule in sports history.[2] These voices have resisted the intrusion of *explicit* politics into the arena of play—even as implicit ideological messages about economic inequality and militaristic nationalism circulate almost totally unremarked.[3] Most passionately of late, this tension has involved Black Lives Matter activism and exploded into view over the past several NFL seasons. Yet the white-hot visibility of that recent controversy should not be seen as the norm; rather, sports' apolitical inclinations would prefer to extinguish it.

Emblematically, New York Giants quarterback Eli Manning tiptoed around assessing the appropriateness of activism at sports venues: "There's a time and place to make your statements. I don't know if it's always during a game."[4] Coaches and front-office leadership from the NBA's Phil Jackson ("I don't think teams should get involved in the political stuff") to the NFL's Jeff Fisher ("I firmly believe that it's important that I keep sports and politics separate") have similarly parroted this aversion.[5] Ed Snider, the late owner of the Philadelphia Flyers, threatened to reprimand players if they made any (apparently) out-of-bounds statements: "If someone said [then-president George W.] Bush should be impeached, we'd have a problem."[6] And, probably most bafflingly, Ed Rendell, former Pennsylvania governor turned Philadelphia Eagles pregame TV analyst, affirmed "that sports and politics don't mix," seemingly undercutting his own career ambitions.[7]

However misguided, that stance clearly has a fan base behind it. In the fall of 2016, my colleague Emily Thorson and I fielded a nationally representative U.S. survey that asked questions about sports fandom and political attitudes.[8] When presented with the statement "Sports and politics should not mix," less than one in five disagreed or strongly disagreed. When asked, in an open-ended follow-up question, what exactly was problematic about these mixing, fans articulated a variety of concerns. One of the most common themes was that athletes might wield misbegotten power because of their celebrity status; one respondent fretted, for instance, "I don't like it since people are so rabid in their fan-ism that they will blindly follow their favorite team, player, etc." Other clusters of complaints converged, variously, on the perception of athletes being uninformed and therefore unqualified to opine on current affairs; the need for athletes to maintain focus and avoid tangential distraction; the professional mandate to keep political opinions private as uniformed representatives of their employer franchise; and the alienating divisiveness that accompanies political debate (when sports should be a sanctuary for community and escape). These more or less corroborate earlier studies of sports spectating that find little interest among fans in seeing politics intersect with and taint the games that they love.[9]

Beyond survey measurements, that pushback rears up, organically, whenever "outside" politics threaten to intervene. Take, at random, an online article from *Sports Illustrated* about LeBron James advocating gun control (in the aftermath of errant gunfire killing an Ohio infant) and sample the comment section: "Go back to playing ghetto ball LJ and leave the intellectual issues to those that have some common sense. . . . James would do well to focus on putting the round ball through the hoop and leave the heavy thinking to people with knowledge of the subject. . . . LeBron James needs to shut the F up and just play basketball."[10] (Fox News host Laura Ingraham bloviated in much the same way in early 2018, instructing James to "shut up and dribble."[11])

That "stick to sports" brushback seems to be instinctive. In a revealing instance of *self*-censorship, NBA stars Amar'e Stoudemire and Dwight Howard posted social media sympathies for Palestinians in wartime Gaza, circa 2014, before quickly retracting them—the latter appending a chastened *mea culpa* for straying from his assigned "position:" "Previous tweet was a mistake. I have never commented on international politics and never will. I apologize if I offended anyone with my previous tweet, it was a mistake!"[12] To that end, player agents who have the ears of their clients typically whisper restraint: "Politics are very polarizing. It is risky . . . I wouldn't recommend my clients go out and jump on board with that," says Kim Zayotti, a sports consultant.[13] If, however, an athlete overrules that counsel and inserts him- or herself into the political fray, veteran player agent Leigh Steinberg further cautions, "I don't think you should wear something onto the playing field, because people come to games not to see that. If it's outside of the field—you want to take that position, go ahead."[14] Where exactly those boundaries are drawn is central to this chapter—and, in a way, a running theme explored throughout the entire book.

Members of the American sports media seem to be no less wary of this treacherous intersection.[15] The management at *USA Today* reportedly ordered their sports staffers to mute any political commentary on social media (even that which is just shared through personal accounts).[16] Similarly, in the combative run-up to the last U.S. presidential election—facing accusations of liberal bias and an internal study that confirmed nearly a third of viewership thought the network was, indeed, ideologically slanted—ESPN president John Skipper vowed, "We're not trying to espouse a specific political point of view. We don't endorse candidates. We don't take positions on public policy matters or controversial matters that don't cross over into sports."[17] In an interview, Mark Gross, another executive at the network, echoes that trepidation: "We want to stay in our lane and that lane is sports. If there's some venturing out of it because there is some sports angle to a particular political issue, there's a healthy discussion that goes on here before it gets on the air."[18] These edicts to efface any trace of ideological intent trickle down from the C-suite to media practitioners, as one radio host explains:

> One thing we were told when we first started was to stay away from religious conversations and politics. . . . [Politics] comes up a lot and, based on how sensitive the subject is, we may stay away from it . . . totally. Sometimes the issues are just so big that it's almost like the elephant in the room that you can't ignore. . . . We'll touch upon it and then we'll kind of move on and just always reset in saying that this is a sports station. . . . It's a very, very thin line and a delicate topic to talk about, you know, polarizing issues.[19]

Indeed, just as players get the "stick to the game" refrain from fans, so, too, are media members often policed along depoliticized lines, especially on Twitter.[20] In recent years, that blowback was perhaps most acute and aggrieved following the NFL draft of openly gay defensive end Michael Sam and his subsequent kiss on live television. "My e-mail almost crashed after that," says then–ESPN ombudsman

Robert Lipsyte, who would routinely receive the most complaints about "social issues" like gay rights "becoming a continuing story-line on 'SportsCenter' and thus invading the living room during family time."[21]

This imperative to silence political thought ultimately gets internalized by participants in the sports media, without needing explicit orders from inside organizations or hate mail from outside them.[22] Chris Dufresne, college sports columnist for *the Los Angeles Times*, says he is "extremely careful" to excise any appearance of political bias from his copy and social media output.[23] Another network studio host—who requested anonymity on this question—just avoids Twitter altogether because he has liberal sympathies and knows, "I cover a league where there may be a lot of people that don't have those left-leaning political views who are big parts of the fan base." And even when figures inextricably bound to politics cross over into the sports space, they manage to be somehow uncoupled and insulated from them. Take former president George W. Bush, who came on ESPN's *Mike & Mike* morning show on the anniversary of throwing out the first pitch at Yankee Stadium following the World Trade Center attacks; as associate producer Dan Stanczyk recalls: "We were talking about what they wanted to ask him and [Mike and Mike] were like, 'We can't ask him about the [2015] Republican [primary] debates.' I'm like, 'Why not? He was the president. Why can't you ask him about what his thoughts are on the Republican debate? His brother is running for president. You should ask a question about Donald Trump.' They're like, 'No, no, no—we're going to get backlash.'"[24]

That backlash is the point of departure for this chapter. It begins by weighing the genuine social benefits of sports' steering clear of political engagement (e.g., escapism, community) against the less noble motivations extorted by commercial interests. Marxist critics condescendingly liken this evasion to the same "opiate of the masses" brainwashing that religion once supplied, but I will argue that sports, in its veneration of hard-working underdogs and level playing fields, actually embeds, quite openly, a persistent narrative upholding the virtues of capitalist meritocracy—one that bears great relevance to America's current era of pronounced financial inequality. Moreover, as a long-standing geopolitical tool for flexing national identity, sports are equally intertwined with a reflexive militarism financed, quite literally, by millions of dollars from the U.S. Department of Defense. And, yet, as I conclude, there *are* assorted signs of activism reemerging in the aftermath of the Michael Jordan apolitical ideal— protests specifically targeting racial injustice—but that those have to negotiate the default politics of sports culture that have entrenched conservative values as natural and invisible and view any leftist critiques as illegitimate and intrusive.

## THE PRICE OF SILENCE

What, then, compels this aversion? There are, in my estimation, both charitable and cynical explanations to be plumbed here. Thinking charitably, one might take the appeal of escapism, uncritically, at face value. This is the vision of stadia as sanctuary, as conjured succinctly by NBA star Gilbert Arenas on his blog: "When we step inside that court and people into those arenas and sit down, it's not about what they did that day, it's not about their rent, their jobs, how bad their day is going. It's about, 'I'm going to forget about it for two hours.'"[25] This theory holds that we watch sport to cope with "the crippling challenges of daily life"—it is our pop culture palliative, our nightly consolation for suffering, by day, the slings and arrows of outrageous fortune.[26] And there's nothing necessarily wrong with that remedy.

Research on sports fans has confirmed, for example, that such an "escape motive" might, indeed, be driven even more by overstimulation in daily life (e.g., stress) as under-stimulation (e.g., boredom).[27] U.S. presidents have endorsed sports' diversionary value in tough times; during World War II, Franklin D. Roosevelt encouraged professional baseball to continue play to help Americans find some solace and normalcy amid the calamities and burdens of the day.[28] During the 1960s, sport, and football especially, tried to present itself as a "throwback to earlier, simpler days"—a reprieve from the social, political, and racial tumult of the era that furnished a supposed moral clarity of discipline, sacrifice, and tradition.[29] At that time, it preserved and portrayed a tableau of crew-cut, obedient youth—making the most of their bodies, their lives—as opposed to the long-haired, anti-establishment hippies rebelling against those values.

Because of the transcendent allure of this dreamy escapism, politics—at least those that are *openly* acknowledged or contested—represent an oppositional force of gravity within the cultural space, dragging fans back down to shabby, factious reality. "People tune into ESPN and Fox Sports 1 to get away from the political talking heads," posits spin doctor (and political talking head) Frank Luntz.[30] Fans' preference to retreat into an alternative world of simplistic "hagiography," as sport affords, might stem from the complex challenges and intractable problems that do not resolve themselves in an orderly, on-time fashion, as a game clock winds down.[31] Commenting on athletes' recent use of the U.S. national anthem as a platform for protest, one sports business consultant laments, "[That's] working at cross purposes to what the intent of sports is, which is to get relief from the stresses of life. That's what the sports industry has to be concerned about."[32]

Moreover, that divisiveness (an inherent byproduct of cutthroat, zero-sum, irreconcilably polarized politics) does run contrary to our yearning to experience sport as a totemically unifying force. As theorized in chapter 1, this feature is deep, true, and socially necessary, particularly as sport retains mass appeal in an era beset by cultural fragmentation: "Social issues are important, but an NFL stadium is one of the few places where people from all sorts of backgrounds can get together and have fun for a while. There's more racial harmony in the beer line than you'll get in decades of speeches and think tank panel discussions. We can figure all this out if the politicians and organizers just get out of the way, stop trying to turn [sports] into another place for people to dump their baggage."[33]

That sentiment is both naïvely fanciful and genuinely felt: The beer line *can* seem authentically utopic—perhaps because it exists, ostensibly, in a carnival space, outside the cares of the "real" world. And when athletes do confront those contentious politics head on, "community" is often the rhetorical cudgel with which they are beaten back, as when one Maryland state representative rebuked a Baltimore Raven for supporting a gay marriage referendum thus: "I believe [he] should concentrate on football and steer clear of dividing the fan base."[34]

For most athletes, though (as well as teams, leagues, and media partners), escapism and community are just as much a cover-up for the real reason to avoid engaging politics: financial risk. Indeed, that industrial concern—and its accompanying commercial imperatives—makes for the more cynical interpretation of sports culture's political allergy. "Most of the athletes don't want to be polarizing. They want to be unifying. They want everyone to root for them and pull for them and buy the products they endorse," explains Big Ten Network studio host Dave Revsine. "I just don't think that's the right battle for one of those guys to pursue. There's too much at risk for them. They're all their own brand and heaven forbid that they alienate people."[35]

The supposed "safety" of American athletics as an apolitical space for commercial interests traces a long history. Ever since sports sections debuted in newspapers in the 1920s, this content was conceived (and constructed) as ideologically innocuous and unlikely to agitate any segment of the sought-after readership.[36] Sponsors and corporations came to love sports, what with their "risk-free, apolitical message of struggle and triumph."[37] (Struggle and triumph are, however, not at all an "apolitical" message, as I'll argue shortly.) Right around the time that revenues began to flood the coffers of the sports industry—namely, TV money and endorsement deals—the iconic activist athlete receded from view, leaving a "chasmic" gap between the 1960s and today, filled in by a "Nike culture that told athletes there was no higher calling than becoming a brand."[38] This was not mere coincidence.

Recalling the heyday of Bill Russell, Jim Brown, and Arthur Ashe, veteran sportscaster Bob Costas observes, "We're finding less and less of that, as these athletes have become richer and richer."[39] Indeed, one might suspect an inverse correlation here between the lucrativeness of sports and the willingness to confront perceived injustice by name. A corollary might well hold that the more critical that sponsorship is to a given a sport or event, the more sanitized of political controversy the televised image must become.[40] Or, as Pat Sullivan, former general manager of the New England Patriots, simply puts it: "Muhammad Ali didn't have a $60 million a year contract with Nike."[41]

The default imperative is, then, to maximize market share at all costs. And one sports business expert warns of the detrimental effects of political expression, in terms of universality: "If you are the quarterback of the Green Bay Packers, you should not be choosing sides as to who should be the governor of Wisconsin. . . . The team wants Democrats and Republicans to come to their games. It's nondenominational and apolitical."[42] This became conventional wisdom within the sports marketplace: to espouse an opinion of conscience is to repel a potential consumer somewhere. "Why do I [as an athlete] want to piss off half the country by espousing anything?" asks *SportsBusiness Journal* media reporter John Ourand. "I want to bring everybody in. That's what my sponsors that are paying me millions of dollars want. That's what I'm happy to do."[43] Given the brevity of professional playing careers—and, therefore, the narrow window in which to pad personal earnings—the timidity of political voice among athletes for fear of jeopardizing brand luster and ancillary income is certainly understandable.[44] And the reticence is probably even more pronounced among lower-profile sports not swimming in TV contract riches; former figure skater Michelle Kwan, working on behalf of Hillary Clinton's presidential bid, found many fellow Olympians supported her but that their endorsement deals (from which they derive a greater percentage of salary than NBA or NFL stars) precluded them from doing so openly.[45]

Thus, sponsors and their intermediaries have harbored a habit of muzzling political speech. One broadcast consultant outright ordered his clients to avoid activist stances and electoral issues: "There is no benefit for any of my clients to come out publicly and say who they are supporting."[46] Tony Ponturo, the longtime head of sports marketing for Anheuser-Busch—possibly the most powerful patron within the industry—observes, "If [sponsors] pay a lot of money and all they've done is walk into someone else's dialogue of potential negativity, then they're going to start saying, 'Why am I paying millions of dollars for this controversy?'"[47] Some companies apparently opt for team or league sponsorship rights as opposed to affiliating with individual players for precisely this reason—it diversifies and wards off the risk of radicalism—and, moreover, as "the most cautious people imaginable," brand representatives are still scarred by the lessons of Tiger Woods, once squeaky clean but since laid low by lurid scandal.[48] Athletes learn well the enduring message of brand culture: "You have signed away your right to have an opinion beyond your choice of sneaker or sports drink," so, as we heard LeBron James reprimanded earlier, "just 'shut up and play.'"[49]

This certainly proved true for the icon thought most apolitically emblematic in the history of American sports: Michael Jordan. In conversations with interviewees about players' reticence to tackle activist issues, Jordan never seemed far from mind and his now-infamous quote about not opposing a racist U.S. senate nominee—"Republicans buy sneakers, too"—was referenced on multiple occasions. Whether or not Jordan actually, literally, phrased his deference this way probably matters less than the fact he seems to live according to such "principle."[50] Indeed, the almost perfect metaphor for this, given Colin Kaepernick's eventual transgressions, arrived during the 1992 Olympics when the Nike-loyal Jordan draped an American flag over the Reebok logo on his award ceremony outfit; more ironic still was that, some two decades later, Jordan released a *branded* shirt featuring an image of his arm and shoulder cloaked in the flag that paid tribute to that legendary rival sponsor diss.[51] For such slavish corporate fidelity, one media scholar charges Jordan with "abrogat[ing] his basic political and social responsibilities in favor of expensive clothes, commodities, and a megastock portfolio."[52] That said, the police violence and Black Lives Matter activism of recent years got him off the bench, politically speaking, with a generous donation to the cause and an ESPN op-ed headlined, "I Can No Longer Stay Silent."[53] Left unaddressed, of course, in the short, tepidly worded piece was an explanation of what, precisely, had kept his lips sealed all those years.

## LET THEM EAT FOOTBALL

If every rightwing thinktank came up with a scheme to distract the populace from political injustice and compensate them for lives of hard labour, the solution in each case would be the same: football. No finer way of resolving the problems of capitalism has been dreamed up, bar socialism. . . . It is the supreme solution to that age-old dilemma of our political masters: What should we do with them

when they're not working? . . . [F]ootball these days is the opium
of the people, not to speak of their crack cocaine. . . . Nobody serious about political change can shirk the fact that the game has to
be abolished.[54]

For some critics, chiefly those of a Marxist bent (like literary theorist Terry Eagleton, quoted above discussing soccer), all that political
silence—among players, organizations, and media—speaks volumes.
For them, the balm of escapism that sports provide is simply the
opiate of false consciousness by another, sunnier name; if religion
pacified the masses for centuries, today, the spectacle of sport has
the same depoliticizing effect, conditioning workers "against critical thought."[55] Within an ever-secularizing Western world, such
athletic activities supposedly supplement the "narcotic effects" long
attributed, rather cynically, to faith.[56] And from this super-structural
vantage point, sport's great irony is that it offers an entertaining
respite from work while, simultaneously, preparing people to wake
up, trudge off to jobs, and do more of it.[57]

Theoretically, moreover, as that opiate offers temporary diversion
and release, it also distorts working people's frame of identification
and reference.[58] This function (or, to Marxists, dysfunction) explains
how sports allegedly engineer "false solidarity" between groups with
different, incompatible economic positions.[59] In other words, one
winds up cheering in the stands and therefore bonding with those
whose wealth has been accrued from his or her exploited labor: The
minimum-wage fry cook wearing a Cowboys cap at a greasy spoon
Dallas diner absurdly thinks he has something "in common" with the
franchise's billionaire owner, Jerry Jones.

Much as the aforementioned benefits of distraction are inverted
to be read as a conspiracy of consciousness, here the appealing glow
of social unity that fandom affords is equally a trick by the rich and
powerful to align the poor and oppressed with a totem of shared

rooting interest—"winning the hearts and minds of subordinate classes and . . . instilling their respect for and conformity to society's power holders."[60] Marx himself is said (probably apocryphally) to have concluded revolution was unlikely in England after watching a crowd subdued with pleasure at a sedate, bourgeois cricket match; as one cultural studies scholar analyzing Marxist lessons for sport thus suggests, "The working classes must simply be taught to see through the candy spectacle of sports."[61] And, yet, for 150-some-odd years it feels like the scoreboard has remained: Candy Spectacle 1, Marxist Awakening 0.

Arguably the most stinging theorist working in this tradition is the French sociologist Jean-Marie Brohm, whose late 1970s polemic, *Sport: A Prison of Measured Time*, telegraphed in the subtitle just how low his regard was for sports' emancipatory potential: "The spectacle of sport operates as a political economy of licit cruelty which enables, to the advantage of the ruling classes, a fantastic diversion of the aggression of the masses resulting from all the frustrations, disillusions, and disappointments engendered by capitalism. Thus, the masses' capacity for revolt and struggle, instead of being directed against the 'cruel masters' who oppress, repress and culturally impoverish them, is transformed into *organic self-repression.*"[62]

For Brohm, it is the narcotizing abundance of sports content—that quotidian deluge of trivial statistics and box scores—that secures the depoliticization of the proletariat, averting the workers' gaze from the "real political preoccupations" they should be absorbed by (i.e., oppression and revolution).[63] In turn, the thrill of athletics, whether experienced as participants or vicariously as spectators, helps channel dangerous energy to (what Marxists see as) unproductive ends; Brohm calls sport a "mass political safety-valve" for this reason, picturing an approving bourgeoisie watching over the 1968 student agitators as they "work off their aggression on the playing fields. . . . Throw the discus rather than bricks!"[64] Then-congressman

Gerald Ford more or less echoed Brohm's logic when he smiled upon a hippie-devoid college football panorama thus: "I'm glad that thousands of fine Americans can spend this Saturday afternoon 'knocking each other down' in a spirit of clean sportsmanship and keen competition instead of assaulting Pentagon soldiers or policemen with 'peace' placards and filthy words."[65]

One might interject that Ford, himself, was thus mixing politics with sports, but he was hardly the first Oval Office occupant who found athletics a useful domestic resource to that end. Such "political freeloading"—in the sense of feigning fandom to strike a chord with common folk—arguably began with William Taft inaugurating baseball's Opening Day tradition of throwing out the ceremonial first pitch.[66] Courting "hardhat" Democrats who might break for the GOP, Richard Nixon went to even greater fan-boy lengths: releasing photographs of himself bowling and issuing a list of his all-time favorite baseball players.[67] In 2013, the most popular White House blog post of the entire year was Barack Obama's NCAA tournament bracket predictions.[68] And facing doubts about the frailty of their health, John F. Kennedy and Ronald Reagan alike used sports participation as a means of validating virility.[69]

This political "productivity" of sport—because, not in spite, of its apolitical sheen—crystallizes in the reflections of one ESPN reporter who covered George W. Bush's first pitch after September 11: "In that moment, politics were suspended. You watched as an American, as a citizen of the United States, with everyone wounded and grieving over what happened on 9/11 to varying degrees, and President Bush represented all of us that night."[70] For an elected leader, that's an enticing place to be in terms of "winning" bipartisan—indeed, *non*-partisan—goodwill.

But politics are, of course, *never* suspended and ambitions toward and claims about their deferral are usually just indicative of ideological influence submerging itself beneath our radar. This is why, I believe, *New York Times* columnist Robert Lipsyte called sportswriting some of "the deadliest words in the paper," as cited in the chapter's second epigraph. It is precisely *because* sport is instinctively perceived and officiously protected as "separate from the rest of social life" and "neutral when it comes to issues of power and politics"—"cloaked" in an alleged "aura of unreality"—that it can serve power and exercise politics.[71] It is exactly *because* we want to keep these issues out of bounds that we don't notice their consequence within the arena of play.

As sport scholar David Rowe pointedly concludes, "These texts can be especially effective bearers of ideology because they seem so innocuous and can be decoded in such a habituated fashion because of their repetitiveness and familiarity."[72] The remainder of the chapter represents an effort to bring those politics out of the shadows—to make more visible that which has been smuggled in and indict that which has been accepted as outwardly innocent. For the two issues that have arguably *most* defined and dominated U.S. politics in the 21st century—economic inequality at home and military intervention abroad—are also deeply intertwined with sports culture. I turn to the former first.

## THE PROTESTANT SPORTS ETHIC[73]

"A man must prove his faith in sports and the American Way by whipping himself into shape, playing by the rules, being part of the team, and putting out all the way. If his faith is strong enough, he will triumph. It's his own fault if he loses, fails, remains poor."[74] Thus trumpeted the opening pages of Robert Lipsyte's classic *SportsWorld* some four decades ago, a passage that continues to offer a tidy synthesis of the core creed animating American sports culture. For no other form of pop "escapism" so consistently embeds a narrative that explains achievement in terms of meritocracy: Winners succeed *because they work hard.* Think of it—rare is the exultant athlete, hoisting the trophy at the victors' podium, who makes reference to the team's free agency binge in the offseason that helped them buy the championship. Rare is the sportswriter who can resist the heart-warming tale of a superstar born into poverty, hustling his or her way out of the 'hood. Rare is the fan who doesn't swoon for the 16-seed Cinderella story, the underdog slaying Goliaths. As sports sociologist George Sage extrapolates:

> [This] is one of the most powerful contributors to the hegemonic ideology of the openness of American society and its meritocratic social order based upon hard work. Natural ability, self-discipline, hard work, dedication, and sacrifice are all used to explain variations in material success in the American occupational structure. These same attributes are used as explanations for sporting achievements. . . . The work ethic is seen as legitimating achievements and outcomes in sports. . . . It provides convincing symbolic support for the hegemonic ideology that ambitious, dedicated, hardworking individuals, regardless of social origins, can achieve success and ascend in the social hierarchy, obtaining high status and material rewards.[75]

The archetypal hero of sports culture is thus the "self-made man" who, through herculean work ethic alone, attains those heights and suggests—either implicitly or explicitly—that such social advancement is open to all.[76] This is fairy tale catnip that media workers are irresistibly drawn toward: "That's what makes them different," *Boston Globe* hockey beat writer Fluto Shinzawa says, marveling at the otherworldly effort embodied by otherwise mortal men and women. "They're willing to push—physically, mentally, during games or practices or during the summer when they're working out—that these people are pushing themselves to limits that regular people just don't ever get to."[77]

Awestruck, this ideology nudges spectators to see those who have won success in society *beyond sport* as equally deserving by dint of effort; conversely, the "Protestant ethic" (in sports as in life) posits that those condemned to failure are to blame for their chosen indolence.[78] Exertion thus winds up being fetishized not just morally, but even aesthetically: "To me, there is nothing worse, as a player, watching a teammate dog it or not work or not come to work; as a coach, watching that; as a fan, watching your favorite team not come and bring the effort that you expect," says Sarah Kustok, a reporter who covers the Brooklyn Nets for the YES Network. "But there's a beauty in seeing an athlete or seeing a player just bust their ass and play as hard as they possibly can."[79]

The reverence for and righteousness found in men and women committing themselves to unsparing effort pervade sports culture to the point of being a ubiquitous cliché and therefore invisible common sense. It is transmitted to children through shows like Nickelodeon's *NFL Rush Zone*, where in episode 207, Hall of Famer Richard Dent instructs the protagonists, outright, that "through hard work they can succeed."[80] It is how NFL player agent David Canter, breathlessly amped up in an interview, rationalizes the league's best: "They're willing to wake up at 6:00 in the morning—5:00 in the morning, 4:00 in the morning—everyday, 350 days a year. Sacrifice everything—time with family, friends, community—to be the best."[81] It is the semiotic essence of brand messaging that Nike has pushed for decades—churning out commercial "homilies" that reduce the formula for success to two basic ingredients, willpower and discipline, that are allegedly available to all: "Nike provides a language of self-empowerment—no matter who you are, no matter what your physical, economic, or social limitations. Transcendence is not just possible, it is waiting to be called forth. Take control of your life and don't submit to the mundane forces that can so easily weigh us down."[82] And it threads through the vast majority of inspirational quotes slapped up on locker room walls—from Arnold Palmer ("Always make a total effort, even when the odds are against you") to Tommy Lasorda ("The difference between the impossible and the possible lies in a person's determination") to Muhammad Ali ("I hated every minute of training, but I said, 'Don't quit—suffer now and live the rest of your life as a champion'").[83] Through all of these contexts, the sports spectacle covertly smuggles in "Trojan horses" of capitalist consensus—not least because those pacifying paeans to "competitive individualism [represent] the micropolitics of neoliberalism" and obscure the reproduction of inequality under supposedly "just" ideological frames.[84]

For certain, that ostentatious emphasis on hard work deflects our gaze from the powerful role that luck also plays in determining success, in sports as in life. It also telegraphs a message about the failure of laziness and the laziness of failures: "[That] always strikes me as odd," concedes ESPN's college football senior writer Ivan Maisel. "Everyone in sports works hard. I mean, I can tell you I've gone to Indiana's pre-season football training camp now for nine straight years and they're working just as hard as Ohio State is. They just don't have very good players."[85] And, yet, that alternative explanatory narrative (the advantage of *innate talent*) is usually bypassed in favor of more democratic, meritocratic lullabies: "I remember once the great Bill Bradley said, 'The locker room was the ultimate laboratory.' You have people from great poverty; you have people from prep schools," recalls CBS sportscaster Lesley Visser. "It doesn't matter that your father went to college or your mother had a lot of money. It really doesn't matter. It matters if you hit the jumper."[86]

Sports, in short, tell us that the world is a level playing field. They tell us that the source of success is not some pre-existing privilege—whether that be genetic blessings, individually, or Steinbrennerian profligacy on behalf of a team—but rather the blood, sweat, and tears that *anyone* could have committed themselves to, if only they had enough gumption. Pull yourself up by your own Air Jordans, all those Nike advertisements exhort. Because if you don't, you have no one but yourself to blame.

There is something unspeakably cruel about this ideology, catchy and seductive—and, yes, partially true—as it may be. For decades, sport has been sold as one of the rare routes to upward mobility for those hailing from lesser privilege (read: racial and ethnic minorities); historically, a seemingly disproportionate number of football players came from the coal and steel towns of the U.S. Midwest, as English soccer and Canadian hockey often drew from the dregs, geographically and socioeconomically.[87] One study concludes that young men of modest means tend to invest more of their lives to pursue sports dreams than their middle-class counterparts.[88] This despite the fact that, by one measure, two-tenths of 1 percent of high school athletes will reach the professional ranks.[89] As activist and scholar Harry Edwards argues, this "media propaganda" spinning sport as the way out of poverty becomes particularly pernicious when mapped against the backdrop of American race relations: "The athletic accomplishments of blacks are widely construed as confirmation that 'the system works for all citizens'" and that black poverty is somehow simply a product of laziness.[90]

The affirmation of level playing fields within the arena of sport implies an ideological corollary, we'll see shortly, about the fairness of outcomes in free market competition. But, first, a few more words are in order about how venerating the glories of underdogs can serve the political function of confirming some broader class mobility. We hear this, most instinctively, in the language of sports cliché—the default template that casts those Cinderella-slippered sleepers and depicts Davids besting Goliaths, as well as the "new kids on the block who leap rapidly from rags to riches."[91]

The appeal holds equally for individuals as well as teams: "People relate to players and athletes that are closest to them. So, if there is a chubby guy or a guy who doesn't have the most athletic ability in the world . . . the God-given ability like some . . . they relate to those individuals," explains NBA TV host Tas Melas. "They really relate to the blue-collar worker out there."[92] Russ Kenn, who coordinated broadcasts of the Red Sox for NESN, adds why he thinks his audience enjoyed these kind of stories: "[People] can say, 'Nobody expected me to do this and nobody believed in me and look what happened' type-thing."[93] Mike Lynch, a sports anchor for ABC-Boston, actively seeks out those underdog tales not just through segments on the physically unremarkable, but also the geographically unlikely; he loves to spin meritocratic myths by anchoring them in local frameworks. "If you have somebody from your hometown that makes it . . . it becomes something that they can see, feel, hear, and touch—that, 'Yeah, it can happen to me,'" he says, adding later in the interview: "You can be it if you work a little bit harder. It doesn't have to be the guy from Florida, Texas, Ohio, or Pennsylvania. It can happen to you."[94]

These instructional narratives of hard work, level playing fields, and loveable underdogs do not just emerge "naturally" within sports culture; rather, they are constructed by media producers—journalistic or commercial—as evidence from my interviewees suggests. Kenn, for instance, admits to "playing up those things and talking about those kind of things" for the sake of a good, albeit "overblown" storyline and, in part, because "it's not socially acceptable" to attribute success to the good fortune of innate talent.[95] (Research has shown, however, that it *is*, apparently, socially acceptable to valorize white athletes more for their scrappy hustle as compared to black counterparts who, according to stereotypical media depiction, simply waltz in and coast by on "God-given" natural ability.[96]) Similarly, Tina Cervasio, sports reporter for Fox–New York, loves to highlight the benchwarmer hero who makes the game-winning shot, believing that her viewers will infer, "'You know what? This is my dream. Look, it worked out for him. Maybe if I hold on a little bit longer and not give it up.'"[97]

By contrast, sports media hardly ever allocate minutes or column inches to those who "fail to measure up in sports"—the "has-beens, ne'er-do-wells, quitters"—even though they make up the overwhelming majority of those who take up play.[98] ESPN's Maisel contextualizes this impulse from the wider angle on trial here: "I don't know if it's part of the American psyche or the bullshit that we in the media have sent people for a hundred years, but I think the natural inclination is to root for the underdog, because, you know, that's the American storyline. You know, the guys who pull—the whole bootstrap theory of life. It's irresistible to sportswriters, but I think it's irresistible to those who read sportswriters. . . . Long shots make people feel good—it gives them hope."[99]

There is also a marketable advantage to that ideology that sports brands have sought to co-opt over the years. Nike, as noted before, has been one of its chief purveyors, having been hitched to the do-it-yourself, greed-is-good political crosscurrents that Ronald Reagan and Margaret Thatcher first hailed in the 1980s.[100] "'Potential' is the word I'd say that has been [one of] the dominant themes with marketing—it's in you. You can do it," comments Jason Norcross, an advertising creative executive who has worked with Nike in the past. "At the end of any of their marketing, they just want you to feel like you need to get off your couch and go do something."[101] ("Something," first, being a trip to the shoe store.) Another prominent narrative theme, in terms of spinning this ethos, is that of overcoming doubters and haters: Marrying—visually, conceptually—the rare "drive and determination" of the seemingly slighted sports superstar to "how the brand is a contributor to that" can forge a powerful and lucrative connection.[102] As agent Kim Zayotti confirms, "Hard work and perseverance, I think, is a message that almost every brand wants to associate themselves with."[103]

But even brands whose products are non-endemic to the sports arena—like, say, beer, which, in terms of its appeal and effects, would seem to be the bacchanalian antithesis of willpower and discipline— frequently dip into this semiotic font, perhaps precisely to alleviate any guilt about indolence that might accompany its consumption. Take, for instance, Busch, which recently debuted a "Working for Race Day" campaign tie-in to NASCAR (a subset of their wider meritocratic brand slogan, "Here's to Earning It") that features ad images of a deliberate "everyman" pit crew readying a star driver's car, overlaid with a baritone narrator: "Whether you work on race cars or your own car, you know what it's like to work hard with your hands. There's satisfaction in getting the job done. But when you get the job done right? That's when you earn it. That's when a Busch beer never tasted better. Rewarding hard work since 1955."[104] For those burdened with the Protestant ethic, such words are intended to assuage any anxiety that might come from kicking back and cracking open a cold one: *You earned it.*

The most conspicuous commercial capitalization on that theme in recent years, however, has to be Under Armour, which has taken the ideals of hard work and underdog identity to intense, almost sado-masochistic extremes. The apparel brand famously debuted shortly after the turn of the century with a noisy, gritty commercial ode to pre-game training—"Protect This House"—which showcased jacked-up athletes soldiering through an arduous collective regimen: "They weren't pretty but they were tough, and the aspirational athlete looked at that and identified. That message of 'us versus them, and we're the underdog and we're coming' really resonated," explains the ad agency president commissioned to produce the 30-second spot.[105] More than a decade later, their "Rule Yourself" campaign (itself an unknowingly Foucauldian epigram) continues to push the message of disciplined self-improvement, shifting the typical focus within sports advertising from the "end results" (e.g., championships, records) to the tough daily grind. The sweaty means, in other words, *are* the pleasurable ends in Under Armour's moral universe. Adrienne Lofton, senior vice president of global brand marketing, elaborates here on how the brand sees itself (and its interpellated consumer) as the "scrappy outsider":

> What separates us from the clutter is this blue-collar work ethic. We're an underdog brand. We work with athletes who most people wouldn't or didn't draft in the first round, or who they wouldn't traditionally give a prima ballerina title to. We pick that athlete with a chip on their shoulder and their desire to win because it aligns with our own attitude. . . . We want to remind [consumers] that you don't just get this, you have to work to get it. We wanted to show that greatness is showing up every day at 5 a.m. when everyone is asleep. Steph Curry won the NBA championship and MVP because he trained every day, got up when he fell down, continuing to drive with all that unsexy work to achieve his goals. . . . A lot of brands are about that initial motivation—just do it, get up and go—we talk about how sustaining that effort is what makes the difference for an elite athlete, and we want to be the brand to show you how to do it.[106]

There is deliberate, showy self-consciousness about the "lunch-pail mentality" that Under Armour likes to cultivate and advertise of its own corporate culture, even as it has become a $5 billion player, hot on the heels of category leader Nike; the campus cafeteria is, for example, nicknamed "Humble and Hungry" as part of this posturing to employees and outsiders.[107] The narratives that spell out such toilsome effort (and imply a meritocratic vision of the world) continue unabated; most recently, the company rolled out a viral "I Will What I Want" campaign—with such poster taglines as "Will Trumps Fate"—which, according to Droga5, its agency of record, is "based upon a simple insight: You are the sum of all your training. You might not always feel it, but every time you grind out another rep or get up for a 6:00 am run, you build a massive force inside of you. You build your one-man army."[108]

## BOOTSTRAP MYTHS FOR UNEQUAL TIMES

It is hard to see how all of that rhetoric and ideology is *not* a political message at a moment in American history defined by grotesque levels of financial inequality. Such statistics were a familiar refrain of the Occupy Wall Street movement, powered Bernie Sanders's primary campaign, and may well have driven President Donald Trump's electoral success (depending on which part of "white working class" a postmortem chose to emphasize); they similarly propelled French economist Thomas Piketty to the top of global bestseller lists.[109]

To wit: The top one-tenth of 1 percent and bottom 90 percent of Americans now retain about the same share of the nation's wealth.[110] In terms of income, American CEOs now reap about 300 times the salary of their average employee, as compared to just 30 times more in the 1970s.[111] Thanks to a sharp decline in mobility across class brackets in that time, the U.S. now, ironically, lags behind its European social welfare counterparts in terms of the odds of attaining the "American Dream" (i.e., ascending the economic ladder) and, for children of the poorest families, the odds of rising to the top quintile are barely better than 5 percent, compared to those born into it.[112] Finally, with the median household already earning less than it did a quarter-century before (adjusting for inflation), 95 percent of immediate post–Great Recession financial gains had gone to that wealthiest 1 percent.[113]

And, yet, against this litany of evidence, for many decades, optimism in opportunity has not abated in the United States. Pew finds, for instance, that substantial majorities believe that economic success is a product of individual initiative rather than external forces—

documenting widespread agreement with statements like "everyone has it in their own power to succeed" and "most people who want to get ahead can make it if they're willing to work hard."[114] (Indeed, poorer Americans tend to overestimate the likelihood of upward mobility more so than their wealthier counterparts.[115])

Why such discrepancy between the cold reality of deterministic data and the starry-eyed, rags-to-riches, long-shot hopes that circulate within the collective American psyche? For one, sport seems to offer a persuasive script for articulating the capitalist catechism; it may not explain economic inequality in the sense of "cause," but it does perhaps rationalize and legitimize the yawning chasm between haves and have-nots. Sport facilitates a way of viewing the world through that system—a lens that, in turn, "supports, sustains, and reproduces" the ideological framework by naturalizing itself as "inevitable."[116]

By validating competition, ranking, and, above all, productivity as the revered basis for human relations, sports also reflect venerated qualities of culture external to the gameplay; conversely, they render losers "invisible," even though their experience is far more common (in sports as in life).[117] This is also why corporations love to bring in championship coaches for management meeting keynotes (for handsome speaking fees, no less): Jimmy Johnson or Pat Riley is going to ratify the notion "the business world, like sports, is organized so that only the best, brightest, and hardest workers make it to the top."[118] In short, "The sporting event is a pure articulation of the values of a meritocratic system. All players begin the game at the same starting point, but the most talented finish first. The real-world analogue is, of course, capitalist ideology. In the real world, however, all the players, qua laborers, do not begin at the same starting point, teams are not evenly matched, and the scoring system does not necessarily reward skill, training, intelligence, or determination."[119]

However false that premise, there may actually be an empirical relationship between the two in the court of public opinion. Looking again at the national survey that my colleague Emily Thorson and I conducted, a series of standard questions measured respondents' tendency to ascribe economic success to personal effort rather than structural advantages—for example, whether hard work and ambition determine if people get ahead or whether growing up with wealth and high-quality education might explain one's eventual financial position.[120] Controlling for demographic and ideological variables, we found that sports fans are, indeed, more likely than non-fans to believe that economic outcomes reflect meritocratic processes. To be certain, we cannot, at this point, make any claims about causality. Horatio Alger–types might well be attracted to sport as a cultural tableau that affirms their worldview rather than sports discourse necessarily inculcating myths that support a winner-take-all economy. (Notably, however, there was no relationship between reported income level and likelihood of being a fan, so it seems that one-percenters and poverty-liners alike love sports, even as they explain the former's lot in life much more charitably than the latter's.)

"People relate to that, because that's like, inherently, an American thing," notes ESPN Radio associate producer Dan Stanczyk. "You work hard, you can make money, and you outwork everybody, you'll rise to the top. It's a very American ideal. I understand why there's that connection."[121] Myths, of course, have never needed to be true; they've just needed to help us make sense of the world in a way that *feels* right. But myths also have a habit of "naturalizing one group's vested interests at the expense of another's."[122] One need not be a Marxist to see those machinations at work here—be they conspiratorially deliberate or inadvertently organic. And that is perhaps why, for at least one interviewee, the woeful conditions of today's economic reality actually warrant those myths more than ever: "You know, there's so much cynicism in the day-to-day media and there's so many people telling you that you can't do things and income inequality is up—people are worried that social mobility is dying," says

ESPN's Ivan Maisel. "It's not dead. I think seeing that underdog success is more important than ever."[123] Every time a sports superstar emerges from the lower class, the American Dream itself feels somehow validated.[124] It verifies that which Horatio Alger long ago baked into the national subconscious: The bootstraps are there, ready for the taking. "That's what America is all about," *Monday Night Football*'s Jon Gruden once beamed. "A kid comes out of nowhere to become the number one draft pick."[125]

## WINNING NATIONAL IDENTITY

If the second decade of 21st-century American life has been dominated by anxieties of economic upshot—at least as much as any other political issue—then military intervention arguably defined the first decade. The attacks of September 11 beget the War on Terror, which would consume (and, to some extent, devour) George W. Bush's presidency, as the United States launched massive invasions of two Middle Eastern nations to dubious ends. And just as the preceding pages have shown how sports are inextricably intertwined with messages about meritocracy, mobility, and inequality, so, too, have lessons in nationalism, patriotism, and militarism long suffused themselves within sports culture.

National identity can be a tricky thing. Because the notion of a nation is usually too abstract, culturally speaking—"too big to be grasped by individuals"—it requires more concrete, symbolic vessels through which it might express itself and engineer that "we-feeling" of identification with fellow citizens beyond one's perceptual horizon; sport lends perhaps the best space where flags can be hoisted and rituals of patriotism regularly exercised.[126] As British historian Eric Hobsbawm theorizes, sports have become "primary expressions" of this imagined community, fueling "however instantly, a sense of harmony and unity, creating, albeit fleetingly, a homogenizing effect."[127]

This theory has already been well rehearsed throughout the book (and, again, earlier in this chapter), but note here how essential it's been to *national* needs across the sweep of history.

In the late 1800s and early 1900s, when immigration and urbanization first swelled the size of U.S. cities with foreign strangers often packed cheek to jowl, sport was seen as a means to manage that which Durkheim might have identified as "social anomie"—blending and indigenizing anonymous ethnic pockets into a communal rooting soil.[128] More recently, in an era of accelerating globalization and eroding sovereignty, sport's function in cementing "cultural citizenship" takes on renewed urgency as the ideal means for jingoistic dichotomizations of "us" versus "them."[129] With some 60 new states that were established in the last century—many riven by fierce internal factions—sport has been mobilized to meet the challenge of national loyalty.[130] Indeed, besides war—a revealing counterpart to be discussed shortly—few activities *other* than sport can so effectively enable nation building and birth "a strong sense of 'collective conscious,' of being one people."[131]

Examples abound of both the ambition behind and the effectiveness of this nexus. As sport offers a "vehicle through which minority members can learn the value orientation of the dominant culture," immigrant groups' assimilation (especially those of school age) is sometimes charted by how much they embrace the games popular within their adopted homeland.[132] Baseball, in particular, has allegedly "taught generations of immigrants how to become Americans."[133] Likewise, hockey constitutes so much of everyday Canadian life that it solidifies collective identity there—the giant, icy rink literally symbolizing the endless winters and vast, empty spaces of the northern nation.[134] (And the late 1980s deal that sent Wayne Gretzky from the Edmonton Oilers to the Los Angeles Kings ignited a national panic, metaphorically, about free trade and the "Americanization" of their proud cultural heritage.[135]) The sports media obviously plays a central role in linking these identity politics to the performances and even styles of national teams; think here of the simplistic propensity to view, in soccer, Germany's disciplined efficiency or Brazil's rhythmic *jouissance* as reflective of wider stereotypes about national character.[136] And for all of the recent controversy in the U.S. around national anthem posture (or lack thereof), it should be noted that it was not normalized as a pregame song until World War II—and, until 2009, had not even been part of the NFL's routine to feature players on field during its performance.[137]

Thus, as a long-standing platform to project national identity onto the global stage, it is somewhat far-fetched to believe that sport could be immune from politics; rather, as a century's worth of history has shown, sport has served as a powerful weapon in a nation's cultural arsenal. "International sport has always been a battle for national self-pride, a war without weapons," writes sports scholar Garry Whannel, and championships claimed in that space yield an opportunity for "national self-congratulation."[138] (Take, for instance, the smug soccer chant that fetes English national team matches: "Two world wars and one World Cup, doo dah, doo dah. . . .") Officially, the Olympics likes to recuse itself as being somehow "above politics," but reality has demonstrated the exact opposite.[139] At regular intervals—1936, 1968, 1972, and 1980, especially—geopolitical events have intruded and ideological narratives have been overlaid; conversely, host nations have torqued the Games to serve propaganda purposes while indignant visitors have contemplated (and sometimes carried out) boycotts to protest issues far from the field of play.[140]

For decades, sport was especially integral in furnishing a "safe" arena for nuclear rivalries, as communist nations attributed athletic exploits to the superiority of their social engineering (and capitalist competitors constructed claims to the contrary).[141] More recently, sports have served as symbolically validating a nation's rise to power; for the BRIC block, in particular, hosting a global mega-event (as in

Beijing, Sochi, and Rio) is seen "as a sort of coming-out party, signaling that it is now a modernized economy, ready to make its presence felt in world trade and politics."[142] And despite the mythic veneer of a "level playing field" among nations, the medal count disparity typically indexes against the hierarchy of GDP rankings: Rich nations take home gold while smaller states struggle to compete given the resources required to achieve the world's best athletic performances.[143] In turn, defeat on the global stage has sometimes triggered anxieties about national masculinity and virility.[144] And while the Cold War rivalry may have diminished some with the fall of the Soviet empire, in the U.S., sport still comes heavily camouflaged with militaristic pretense.

## THE PENTAGON'S GUERRILLA MARKETING

President Dwight Eisenhower once declared, "The true mission of American sports is to prepare young people for war."[145] Ike was not alone in seeing the parallels and potential in militarizing sport. George Orwell coined it "war minus the shooting"; Ronald Reagan likewise viewed it as "the human activity closest to war that isn't lethal."[146] To some degree, this is linguistic sleight of hand—spiriting in a "military world view" through the words chosen to represent what are, ultimately, merely games.[147] Yet the way that we talk about sports routinely serves to "fuse (and confuse)" any such distinctions between "athletic aggression [and] military destruction."[148] American football appears especially guilty of masquerading as the "war game"—what with its vocabulary of blitzes, long bombs, advance scouts, and men in the trenches that help valorize, rationalize, and desensitize us to the reality of battle.[149]

Sports talk invades journalistic coverage of war just as those military terms are routinely deployed within the sports media.[150] For the former, such "discursive conflation" minimizes the stakes—

"reframing the repercussions . . . from death and destruction to 'winning' and 'losing' and dismissing the reasoning, motivation, and decision for war under a rhetoric of assumed competition that stipulates there is always a game on the horizon"—thereby legitimizing lost limbs and lives, while often obfuscating the rationale for the carnage.[151] On the flip side, military language *raises* the stakes within sport and envelops participants, wrongly, in the same "heroic" glow also cast upon the warrior class.[152] It makes play seem somehow more serious, which is great, financially speaking, for compelling viewers and consumers: How can you fail to attend to a "war" featuring the Patriots and Eagles?

The linkage is, however, more than merely semantic; history is rich with incidences of sport being entangled, literally, with war. Ancient Greek athletics were understood, as Ike diagnosed, as "rehearsals for military action" and, later in Rome, sport had a similar "ulterior" modus; medieval tournaments also mimicked battlefield engagement and the violent folk games of that era aroused peasants with ritualized fighting against rival local factions in an (only slightly) tamer form than open warfare.[153] By the 19th century, physical play had become more civilized but was still seen as an effective "training grounds for war"—particularly for the sort of able-bodied men needed to run the colonial empires spanning the globe.[154] Later, in the United States, military academies positioned sport as a critical part of the college experience: "The better the sports program, they reasoned, the better the solider."[155] And for all the gauzy spin about the Olympics as an incubator of "respect" and "friendship"—two of its three professed cardinal virtues—the modern games were basically born of founder Pierre de Coubertin's grudge against Germany after military defeat, in the hopes that he might shame French youth into toughening up for the wars to come.[156] A half-century later, with the looming national security threat of Soviet Russia bearing down, President John F. Kennedy would similarly transpose a "call for greater physical fitness and preparedness with calls for better military preparedness and missiles."[157] America, it seems, needed to close the track-and-field gap, too.

Today, that militarism continues to saturate American sports culture, with the NFL at the forefront—and not just because, aesthetically, it evokes the infantry warfare of the 1800s.[158] Amidst 1960s peacenik fervor, commissioner Pete Rozelle quite consciously pushed performances of patriotism into the Super Bowl spectacle and his NFL Films division cinematically transformed stars into glamorous warrior heroes.[159] (Sports rhetoric scholar Michael Butterworth has cleverly interpreted the mythos—and timing—of NFL Films' early days as a direct response to America's Vietnam War quagmire.[160]) More recently, a Hall of Fame exhibit on "Pro Football and the American Spirit" that circulated at stadia around the country chronicled the NFL's support for U.S. military action from World War II onward.[161] Such "Gridiron Agitprop" has included everything from the routine (e.g., fighter jet flyovers, remote feeds from soldiers watching games at bases overseas) to the more momentous, as when Super Bowl XXV was turned into a "five hour 'infomercial for war'" in that year's run-up to Operation Desert Storm in the Persian Gulf.[162]

Nevertheless, "it's really ratcheted up since 9/11," says *Around the Horn* panelist Kevin Blackistone. "You're hard-pressed to go to a sporting event these days and not, in some way, be confronted with the marketing of the military."[163] Commercial interests even try to sell through this prism; Blackistone recalls ESPN receiving a promotional kit from Adidas for quarterback Robert Griffin III that arrived in an ammunition box and included camouflage-print cleats, arm sleeve, and cowl.[164] When Under Armour debuted its aforementioned "Protect this House" TV spot in the same wake of 9/11, the advertising community lauded the commercial's ideological synergy: "Protect this house, or home or country, just became an idea that was right for the times, so it resonated," remarked one agency president.[165] Sports media, too, have colluded in conflation—from Fox's animated football robot donning a green army helmet and marching with a General Patton "swagger stick" to their Sunday morning NFL panel broadcasting live, at one point, in fatigues from an Afghanistan base.[166]

Most conspicuous, though, have been the lavish patriotic spectacles coordinated through NFL's "Salute to Service" campaign, when teams devote the whole month of November to military appreciation games and feature special ceremonies, enlistment inductions, color guard presentations, surprise homecomings, and camouflaged ribbons plastered across the live and mediated tableaux.[167] Military brass becomes product placement: General David Petraeus, for example, was trotted out for the opening coin flip at Super Bowl XLIII.[168] Enumerating the many ways that military appreciation is stitched into Jacksonville Jaguars games (e.g., an on-field "Veteran of the Game," a fourth quarter bell-ringing by a recently deployed soldier), the team's senior vice president of fan engagement stresses, "We do everything we can to ensure that people understand and realize how much we appreciate the military and how important we understand they are to the fabric of the community and of Jacksonville."[169]

All of which seduces the apparatus of sports spectacle, as one broadcast producer reports: "It's really good, genuine TV—you know, you don't have to trick that up. You don't have to put a sexy tease on that or anything like that. There's nothing like a flyover or someone in uniform throwing out the first pitch or singing the anthem or 'God Bless America.' It's one of those pure moments that are really easy, because there isn't a bad shot on the cameras and it's really a pure moment that you don't even have to produce—just turn on the camera."[170]

And, yet, the purported purity of those feel-good, organic moments became suspect with the revelation, mid-decade, of the hidden financing behind some of them. According to a report released by two Republican senators, the Department of Defense paid more than $10 million to sports teams over the years to honor service members—including many of those aforementioned "heartwarming displays" that many fans surely perceived as gratis.[171] The New York Jets, for example, took almost a half-million dollars for thanking soldiers on the jumbotron screen.[172] Recruiting was the presumed benefit—as sports fans are thought to be ideal targets for this messaging (being "more physically fit, mentally adept and understand[ing] teamwork and overcoming obstacles," as one army officer put it)—though Congress cut the National Guard's advertising budget when it found that $26 million spent on NASCAR sponsorship failed to generate a single recruit attributable to the campaign.[173] As one scholarly critic discerns, "These types of events become especially important in wartime, when the United States non-conscription based forces struggle to garner new recruits and therefore need to glorify soldiers to help impress upon young men and women the rewards and cultural adulation that awaits them during and after enlistment."[174]

Whether or not that marketing outlay produces actual enlistments, it clearly contributes to a sports culture defined by a militaristic mentality. One does not have to squint when looking at the disciplinary regimen fetishized within sport (and, most especially, football) to see a mirror image of the boot camp ethos—what with "its call-up, roll-calls, troop inspections, uniforms, punishments, deference to superiors, blind obedience and overall respect for hierarchy."[175] Sports spectacle likes to dress players up as soldiers—sometimes through metaphorical discourse, other times literally in special camouflage uniforms—which diminishes and cheapens the commitment of the latter to mere performance and play.[176] The reality of war is, of course, anything but.

Furthermore, the apparatus of valor that greets players (or soldiers) should they be wounded (or killed) in battle (e.g., awards, tributes) "serves to not just honor the individual involved but to legitimize and rationalize away any doubts one might have as to the merit of the act, and ultimately consolidates it in dominant ideology as admirable and manly."[177] In other words, there is no way to "caveat" one's applause for an individual solider being recognized apart from censure reserved for chicken-hawk civilians and politicians who have sent him or her off to the front lines, indefinitely; the Pentagon surely knows this. Fans can be incorporated "by proxy" into the appearance of support for militarized programs and endeavors.[178] Paid patriotism helps "buy" war.

The fumbled story of NFL star turned enlisted "poster boy" Pat Tillman betrayed this appropriation most embarrassingly, with the U.S. military criticized for covering up and misattributing his death to enemy bullets in Afghanistan in what was actually a friendly fire accident—and Tillman's increasingly disillusioned views on the U.S.'s "illegal and unjust" invasion of Iraq were submerged until later.[179] Those revelations ran contrary to the mythology that had been built up around a "hard-bodied patriot who symbolized the ideal patriot-citizen at a time of war."[180] (Tillman even resurfaced as a posthumous foil to the insufficiently patriotic anthem-protestors, as when President Donald Trump retweeted a photo of him, accompanied by a message to boycott the NFL—which Tillman's widow would disavow.[181]) In keeping with sport's aforementioned faith in capitalist meritocracy, his profile was further burnished as the "overlooked and underappreciated overachiever: the American sporting underdog with an indomitable will"—a John Wayne–style "self-determining" man.[182] And his sacrifice, like so many others', was fetishized as the pure object of celebration rather than prompting queries—problematically, at more than a kneejerk, superficial level—as to why exactly that sacrifice needed to be made.[183]

Some have theorized that a key prerequisite for cultivating nationalism is learning to root against an external enemy—a feature of life repeatedly (and metaphorically) socialized within sports culture, what with its basic emphasis on "beating others" rather than "cooperation" with rivals, be they individuals or nations.[184] Few "public spectacles" can match sports in terms of their capacity to explicitly mythologize values like "competition, power, and domination."[185] For all these reasons, lefty critic Noam Chomsky sees sport's authoritarian ethos as "training in irrational jingoism."[186]

Sports culture *is* irrational, especially when it comes to financial outlay (recall the arguments of chapter 1). But more problematic, here, might be the way that the aforementioned intersection of sports and militarism serves to "mainstream war"—channeling patriotic fervor into a contest with unambiguous outcomes and "no unsightly corpses."[187] Neither the invasion of Afghanistan nor Iraq could ultimately deliver on those promises, so sports spectacle has been enlisted in the decade since to airbrush the narrative. And whether from the grandstands or their living room sofas, fans are thus cosseted with a "whitewashed image of military service and of war itself."[188] That is, however, an incomplete portrait.

To maximize marketing potential and maintain the facade of bloodless war, the veterans paraded at sporting events must surely not be missing limbs, PTSD-stricken, or living on the streets; *Deadspin* aptly terms this the "un-earned catharsis" of surprise reunions.[189] It's a camouflage commitment that often feels fashion-deep—a superficial gesture and phony performance of valorizing the honorable in the hopes that some of that valor bounces back and rubs off on the leagues themselves. It is a sanitized act of "remembering" the troops so as to just as quickly forget about their sacrifice—absolving audiences from the burden of being informed beyond what the bloodless spectacle stage circumscribes.[190] Crowds are compelled to rise and salute servicemen and women but too often can't apparently be bothered to contemplate why they serve overseas, in increasingly undefined, indefinite contexts. "Our freedom" is too generic and platitudinous a response from the beneficiaries of that sacrifice.

"To make ourselves feel good, right, we bring out this guy [a soldier] who's had this miserable experience defending our freedoms that we don't know about—that we wouldn't send our kids to be a part of," says Big Ten Network studio host Dave Revsine. "If we give them a standing ovation, somehow we feel like we've washed our— not that we've washed our hands of it, but we've acknowledged it and we've shown them how much we appreciate them. Now—let's get on with the . . . game."[191] For the institutions involved, the symbiosis seems equally cynical: The sports league gets to imagine itself as an American institution on par with the military and the military gets to "sort of tuck themselves under the halo" of the league, as former *Deadspin* editor-in-chief Tommy Craggs suggests.[192] Yet for many of my interviewees for this research, that intersection was utterly unremarkable; few had much to say, beyond automated platitudes, when asked about the context of that military partnership on their media work. Probably befitting his role as a provocative newspaper columnist—tasked with asking critical questions and offering up unpopular opinions—Filip Bondy of *The New York Daily News* evinces a somewhat stronger recoil and hotter take:

> You're touching on a subject that drives me crazy: how these teams drape themselves in the flag and how they drape themselves around the military. . . . The fans will still just lap this shit up and it drives me crazy. And the teams take full advantage of it—you want to get the fans all happy and riled up and thrilled to death? You show yet another guy with a gun on a jumbotron. . . . I got nasty stuff [for writing that]. . . . One guy on the Yankees was threatening to punch me. You kind of have to brace yourself when you write something like that . . . That's probably why I don't write about it.[193]

Such pushback is a byproduct of the fact that militarism has become common sense within sports culture; it is—like the fables of capitalist meritocracy deconstructed earlier—simultaneously ubiquitous and invisible. For sports media professionals, "it's the least we can do" is often the rote cliché trotted out when narrating troop salutes. But, frankly, they might well be speaking on behalf of American society as a whole; the mission drift of endless deployments over the course of two decades of prosecuting the War on Terror has drained military engagement from the forefront of mediated consciousness. In the post-draft era, it's increasingly sacrifice borne by *someone else*'s kids. The U.S. has nearly a quarter-million troops stationed across 172 countries and territories, yet less than 1 percent of the population has served in the military (unlike earlier eras, when conscription made participation widespread and the cost shared).[194] That means that, for many, the only time their efforts are ever even contemplated is within the sports spectacle; this is not enough.

In the aftermath of September 11, recall, American civilians were told their foremost patriotic obligation was to *go shopping*.[195] Similarly, such performances on the field of play become a quick, easy way of "remembering" that sacrifice without ever having to dwell too long on what it is or where and why our troops are making it. It mirrors a foreign policy on "autopilot"—maintaining open-ended missions in the Middle East year after year—that "enable[s] American society to avoid the truly hard questions about war."[196] It's not that American soldiers are undeserving of the fan applause at the games where they are feted; it's that they're deserving of *more* than such applause. And it surely need not be bought with promotional line-item dollars.

Moreover, the opportunistic appropriation of individual soldiers as the empathetic faces of militarism winds up occluding broader strategic questions about the wisdom of wars we have shipped them off to. Americans need less "coverage" of military affairs through the sheen of sports salutes and more through sober and honest news reporting—especially when overseas deployments have slipped further and further from front-page attention with each passing year. This is how perpetual war gets "depoliticized" as an issue and "justified as a non-political enactment of respect and honor" for the armed forces: Spectators are invited to view soldiers' service "as necessary and noble without ever confronting the politics of a given war."[197] You foreground the actors, but detach them from the context—and consequences—of their action.[198] Any set of political interests whose annual budget runs upward of $600 billion—as the U.S. allocates to the Pentagon—clearly needs to buy off that allegiance and good will. But it is, nonetheless, guerrilla marketing in a double sense: marketing war (i.e., *guerra*) and doing so with self-effacing subtlety.[199]

## RETURN OF THE WOKE ATHLETE

"The thing is that, when you are a popular athlete, and you accept the money and the fame, and you become a front person for those who have the power, and they say 'be like this guy' and kids that are coming up say, 'Well, I'll be like him—I won't protest anything. I'll accept everything. I'll just try to be a great athlete and make a lot of money.' So, a culture dies when you do that."[200]

Hall of Fame running back Jim Brown might not have directly referenced fellow sports immortal Michael Jordan when he spoke these words, but his allusive syntax (i.e., "be like [Mike]") certainly conveys an implicit indictment. As sketched earlier, Jordan's studied reluctance to engage in matters political has long been directly correlated—by observers, at least—to his lavish wealth accumulation. And given that racial injustice turned out to be the issue that "woke" long-dormant athlete activism, it is worth recalling that Jordan himself was originally packaged as a transcendent fantasy of post-racial identity—one who could charismatically and unthreateningly tell the tale of metaphorical meritocracy deconstructed earlier.

To do so, though, Jordan's race had to actually be erased: "People don't look at Michael as being black," suggests his agent, David Falk.[201] NBA commissioner David Stern similarly speculates, "It was the Michael Jordan Nike phenomenon that really let people see that . . . black athletes were OK. Defying a previous wisdom—not only that black athletes wouldn't sell in white America, but that the NBA as a predominantly black sport could not sell in white America. And then the sponsors became interested."[202] Simultaneously, the veneration of black stars like Jordan served as an implicit condemnation of African Americans still victim to conditions of inequity; Jordan "proved" that sweat and stick-to-itiveness were all that was needed to soar to the heights of an (apparently colorblind) American Dream, no matter the impediments of class or race.[203]

Today, sports stars are taking on those racial impediments more forcefully and explicitly.[204] This Black Lives Matter activism arguably first emerged in response to the acquittal of Trayvon Martin's killer, when the Miami Heat and other NBA stars donned hoodies—Martin's racially "suspicious" garb the night of his shooting—for photos posted online and scrawled messages on their sneakers demanding justice.[205] A year later, when Eric Garner died in a police chokehold in New York City, Chicago Bull Derrick Rose took the court for warm-ups in an "I Can't Breathe" T-shirt; dozens of athletes followed suit, relaying that message via sartorial or social media means.[206] The WNBA initially fined 30 players who wore similarly political pre-game garb on-court; it later rescinded the punishment as league administration (fittingly) forswore that it was about the offensiveness of the content, but rather the hijacking of a medium reserved for commerce. "My preference would be that players adhere to our uniform rules," NBA commissioner Adam Silver begged out. "As a political forum, I think it's a dangerous road for us to go down. So, I would greatly prefer that the players use the platform they're given—social media, press conferences, media in locker rooms . . . to make their political points of view be known."[207] In other words, just don't occlude the merch—recall here that Silver issued this disavowal only months after announcing that the men's league would begin selling ad space on jerseys. The sports totem is too sacred (and financially valuable) to debase with politicization.

Around the same time, the state of Missouri witnessed two related acts of athlete-driven agitating. Following the death of Michael Brown and the subsequent unrest in Ferguson, five members of the St. Louis Rams took the field with arms held aloft in a "don't shoot" pose of protest; several members of the Congressional Black Caucus mimed the gesture on the House floor and attributed its symbolic spread to the players' efforts.[208] Demanding an apology and disciplinary action, a spokesman for the St. Louis police hinted at a retaliatory boycott: "I'd remind the NFL and their players that it is not the violent thugs burning down buildings [a reference to Ferguson protestors] that buy their advertiser's products."[209] (The team hastened to make a $50,000 donation to a local police charity.[210])

Halfway across the state, the University of Missouri football team would join protests against the school administration over racial offenses on campus with a million-dollar-worthy ultimatum: Resign or they wouldn't take the field for upcoming games.[211] When the president stepped down, one Missouri defensive end proclaimed, "Let this be a testament to all of the athletes across the country that you do have power."[212] To caveat, however, that "power" is entirely predicated upon economic leverage; without big-time sports' capacity to mobilize massive audiences for lucrative shared experiences—to create, in Missouri's case, the "nucleus of campus social life"—the threats of those whose (unpaid) labor is the basis for that money pyramid would be effectively empty.[213] Put differently, the cross-country or volleyball team won't be taking down a college president anytime soon in the same way.

By the fall of 2016, sports' politicization—which had been simmering throughout the aforementioned incidents—exploded into the national consciousness thanks to two provocateurs: Colin Kaepernick and Donald Trump. To be historically certain, there had been "anti-patriotic" protests before—by Muhammad Ali, of course, but also those less remembered, yet equally castigated, by Carlos Delgado and Mahmoud Abdul-Rauf.[214] However, the San Francisco 49ers quarterback's decision to sit, and then subsequently kneel, during the U.S. national anthem was surely the most incendiary and high-profile—particularly as others joined him from across professional and amateur levels of play, sometimes with arms linked or fists raised.[215]

A thousand hot takes bloomed in Kaepernick's wake, but what seems especially relevant here is how the economic consequence of these actions surged to the forefront—as much as the substance and merit of the athletes' calls for justice. Kaepernick openly acknowledged that he might be risking his Beats and Electronic Arts endorsements (and one poll of advertisers found 70 percent saying they would drop him), though it was actually Denver Bronco Brandon Marshall who lost out first, as two sponsors terminated their associations with the protesting linebacker; one noted, tepidly, "While we acknowledge Brandon's right, we also believe that whatever issues we face, we also occasionally must stand together to show our allegiance to our common bond as a nation."[216] Team executives and other business insiders acknowledged, anonymously, that additional sponsors threatened to pull financing if the protests spread and individual deals were apparently scuttled as other players joined the initial uprising in 2016.[217]

Critics variously castigated Kaepernick for his intelligence, his alleged air of entitlement, his wealth, and his apparent trendiness.[218] On YouTube, fans indignantly burned his jerseys; at stadia, vendors hawked shirts with his image in a bull's-eye riflescope. Some press accounts seemed to curiously link his on-field performance to that off-field impudence: "After national anthem protest, Colin Kaepernick is dreadful in loss to Bears," read one *Chicago Tribune* headline, as though the former begat the latter.[219] The American Family Association, a non-profit Christian group, accused "the NFL's true colors emerging as a progressive, left-leaning organization that is . . . enabling activists, individuals and groups that disrespect the U.S.A."—a bizarre contention, given that (as this chapter has taken pains to show) economic and militarized conservatism is the league's, and most sports', naturally occurring political state.[220] Oddly—and notably, too—for most fans, the protests existed more as imagined symbolic slight than actually visible offense: After the first few weeks, TV partners rarely even showed Kaepernick and others' actions on air.[221] The imagery surely wasn't in the financial interests of sport, media, or advertisers.

Indeed, the unexpected early season double-digit ratings plunge for the NFL that year was also pinned on Kaepernick; as *The Sporting News* framed its coverage, "Protests may be hurting the NFL broadcast networks where it hurts them the most: the pocketbook."[222] A #BoycottNFL countermovement arose—stoked by talk radio blowhards like Rush Limbaugh, who noted, "The NFL is sponsored by beer and cars and soft drinks that can easily not be purchased." Various polls conducted around that time showed between one-third and more than one-half of Americans were allegedly watching less football because of the wave of activism, though the NFL issued a memo claiming, of course, "no evidence" for this connection between player protests and the ratings drop.[223] Rather, the NFL sought to pin the disappointment on an unusually engrossing election year, which absorbed much of the oxygen of American attention.[224] At least one—reportedly TV-addicted—analyst found evidence for both: "The NFL is way down in their ratings. Way down. And you know why? Two reasons. Number one is, this politics they're finding is a rougher game than football and more exciting. Honestly, we've taken a lot of people away from the NFL. And the other reason is Kaepernick."[225] That analyst's name was Donald J. Trump.

The untenable prospect of sealing sports off from politics became fully apparent during the 2016 U.S. presidential campaign. Indeed, the vicious and ridiculous twists and turns that unfolded during that electoral battle made sealing *anything* off from politics a somewhat formidable challenge. One ESPN poll found that 35 percent of professional athletes had argued with teammates about the election and at least one NFL coach reportedly banned discussion of Trump during the season.[226] Democratic contender Hillary Clinton had the public support of NBA stars like LeBron James and Magic Johnson; Trump drew endorsement from a more motley crew that included Bobby Knight, John Daly, and Dennis Rodman.[227]

To stump for candidates was, however, financially precarious, as players relearned the enduring lesson of treading lightly on political grounds. The representative of one (unnamed) multinational brand clammed up and backed off from finalizing a major deal with an (also unnamed) celebrity athlete when his support of Trump emerged, going instead with an alternative "who was not publicly political"; former NFL running back turned Trump backer Herschel Walker similarly told TMZ that he was blackballed and disinvited from three speaking engagements because of his allegiance to the former reality TV star.[228] Conversely, one major insurance company sponsor cancelled a photo shoot with an athlete who'd disparaged Trump.[229] And NASCAR CEO Brian France "rattled" that sport's leadership when he threw his support behind the eventual president at a campaign rally, as sports companies from NBC to ESPN to the PGA Tour peeled off from hosting events at Trump properties.[230]

Few felt the heat of the election-season spotlight more intensely than megastar Tom Brady, whose locker room display of a "Make America Great Again" ball cap and apparent personal affection for the real estate mogul set off feverish inquiry from the press about his partisan preferences. Although Trump credited Brady with making "an incredible difference" in his Massachusetts primary victory, he also declined to petition for Brady's outright endorsement, assuming it might endanger millions in sponsorship revenue.[231] Brady himself shook off political questioning from the press with a brand-savvy agility Michael Jordan might have admired in his prime: "I'm not talking politics anymore, guys," he told one Boston radio show. "Just speaking with my family, it's just a bad idea. I know, you guys, I told you I would, then after I told you I would, I changed my mind."[232] (Republicans buy Uggs, too, he might have added.) In that, Brady was pretty much just toeing the company line: Although he was asked thrice at the 2017 Super Bowl media day about Trump, all political references—including teammate Martellus Bennett's announcement that he would skip any White House celebration—were scrubbed clean from the NFL's official transcript of the event.[233]

By that season's end, NFL leadership surely hoped the anthem protests might quietly go away, much as they'd treated Kaepernick himself (who filed a grievance case against the league claiming collusion).[234] For Trump, however, the issue seemed to offer far too juicy "red meat for the base" and at a now-infamous rally in late September 2017, he channeled his swaggering *Apprentice*-era catchphrase: "Wouldn't you love to see one of these NFL owners, when somebody disrespects our flag, to say, 'Get that son of a bitch off the field, right now, out? He's fired.' . . . [That owner will] be the most popular person, for a week. They'll be the most popular person in the country."[235] The rather dormant protest—which had, by then, dwindled to among a dozen or so dissenters—quickly reignited into a widespread national movement, with more 130 players kneeling, sitting, or raising fists in an extraordinary show of defiance; as sportswriter Dave Zirin marveled, "Nothing, literally nothing, in the history of sports and politics can compare to what happened [that] Sunday."[236]

The blowback arrived swiftly and would linger throughout the rest of the season like a political concussion. Some sought to move on, clinging to a familiar shield: "Politicizing the game is damaging and takes the focus off the greatness of the game itself," claimed one NFL owner; "hopefully as we go forward we can begin concentrating on football a little more [and] take the politics out," beseeched another team's head of football operations.[237] Commissioner Roger Goodell, trying to avoid alienating either the producers or consumers of his brand, held aloft the totemic ideal of sports—boasting that "the NFL and our players are at our best when we help create a sense of unity in our country and our culture" (which also, again, reaps them billions)—and ran a sappy, generic PSA during *Sunday Night Football* to "contrast [with] . . . some who practice the politics of division."[238]

The ad—which included montage cutaways to Pat Tillman hugging a black teammate, a U.S. map-shaped football field, and players conspicuously *standing* for what looks like the anthem—clarified a toothless truism no one really asked about: "Inside these lines, we don't have to have to come from the same place to help each other reach the same destination." Indeed, the official spin attempted to affix "solidarity" to the roiling media narrative—eliding the thornier politics of criminal justice—but Trump refused to relent, especially on Twitter; in one (not-at-all racially subtle) contrast of a rebuke, he brayed: "So proud of NASCAR and its supporters and fans. They won't put up with disrespecting our Country and our flag."[239] In response to kneelers at an Indianapolis Colts game, Vice President Mike Pence executed a high-profile walkout stunt, at Trump's apparent behest.[240]

Although the league's partners initially hoped that this latest controversy would simply "blow over"—much as the Ray Rice, Richie

Incognito, and football pressure scandals had earlier deflated without much damaging their bottom line—evidence quickly mounted that, as one consultant diagnosed, "The NFL made the worst branding move in the modern history of sports."[241] The double-digit "ratings erosion" over two seasons continued apace, with nearly half of NFL fans naming the protests as the main reason they were watching fewer NFL games; more illuminating still, negativity toward the NFL tripled among Trump supporters over just several weeks of his offensive, making it one of the 10 most polarizing brands in America.[242]

For the first time since the global economic meltdown of the late 2000s, NFL merchandise licensees reported sales slides—by as much as 20 percent or more—with some customers claiming they wouldn't shop anywhere NFL gear was also sold.[243] DirecTV offered refunds for offended Sunday Ticket subscribers; a coalition of USAA members petitioned the company to drop its contract as the "official military sponsor" of the NFL; and Bud Light's parent corporation received so many angry calls, it set up a special complaint hotline with a pre-recorded declaration of star-spangled fidelity: "We have a long heritage of supporting the nation's armed forces, veterans and military dependents. The national anthem is a point of pride for our company, and for the 1,100 veterans we employ."[244] Even "Papa John" Schnatter—campaign backer of Trump, ubiquitous commercial sidekick to Peyton Manning—carped in an conference call about plummeting pizza revenues due to the unrest, excoriated league leadership, and bailed early on his company's exclusive sponsorship role.[245] By the time the NFL staggered into its 2018 Super Bowl—an event featuring marquee, big-market teams and a compellingly close game, yet that drew the lowest viewership in nine years—team executives were unanimous about the path forward: "We have to get the anthem issue behind us."[246] As one sports marketing consultant summarized: "Sports is unifying and the [NFL] shield is the epitome of that. Politics is a loser's game."[247] It's hard to argue that Trump hadn't won that round.

For all of the aforementioned trolling and mayhem, Trump was named the 2017 "Most Influential Person in Sports Business" by the industry's leading trade journal; beyond the NFL, his second favorite (athletic) punching bag was ESPN, which he derided as "an arm of the failing, liberal media, the sports equivalent of CNN or *The New York Times*—a.k.a., the enemy" and explicitly linked an alleged lefty bias to its subscriber base falloff.[248] That ire was piqued by then–ESPN anchor Jemele Hill's tweet that "Trump is the most ignorant, offensive president of my lifetime" and that "his rise is a direct result of white supremacy"—a slight that the White House press secretary deemed a "fireable offense." Revealingly, Hill was not formally disciplined until she alluded to a potential boycott of the Dallas Cowboys and their advertisers—for owner Jerry Jones's hard-line boast he'd bench protestors—which earned her a two-week suspension. (Note here, once more, the censorious effect of commercial consequence.)

In the wake of the Hill kerfuffle, industry talent agents redoubled their efforts to get clients to "stick to sports" and not "voice opinions other than the ones you're paid to give."[249] ESPN also followed up by amending its employee social media policy to reflect the now-explicit expectation that they be "civil, responsible and without overt political or other biases that would threaten our or your credibility with the public. . . . Do nothing that would undercut your colleagues' work or embroil the company in unwanted controversy."[250] The sincerity of this effort might be plausible if "undercutting" co-panelists and ginning up "unwanted controversy" was not already the hot-take programming mandate for the network's *entire daytime lineup*. Clearly, ESPN was hoping for more of an anodyne Tom Brady–style approach on issues ideological.

In many ways, then, Tom Brady and Colin Kaepernick stand (or, for the latter, kneel) at twin poles of the athlete spectrum when it

comes to political consciousness in the 21st century: the former upholding the traditional diversionary sheen to shield him from off-
the-field issues, the latter forcing those issues ostensibly unrelated to
the game into the American sports conversation. The lessons of 1968
remain relevant here—specifically, Tommie Smith and John Carlos's
protest pose and consequent controversy. Their actions also elicited
backlash because they disrupted the "liberal democratic" pretense of
sports culture—a space that simply wasn't deemed the "proper place"
for such dissent.[251] Similar to those black U.S. sprinters, Kaepernick's
"silent, fundamentally non-violent and politically ambiguous" gesture
won him ferocious rebuke from the American mainstream.[252] He had
violated a sacred context with the "dirty" agenda of politics: despoil-
ing both the purity of play (i.e., escapism) and a compulsory ritual of
nationalism (i.e., community).[253]

Like the bushy Afro he sported later in that initial protest season,
Kaepernick struck many as a throwback; in a *Washington Post* op-
ed defense of his actions, Los Angeles Laker legend Kareem Abdul-
Jabbar's history of athlete activism leaps, abruptly, from the 1968
Olympics to the 2014 NBA season.[254] The four-decade interregnum
was surely not without moments of political intrusion, but collective
memory struggles to quickly conjure them; not insignificantly, these
decades were the same in which television revenues exploded and
American sport found itself awash in money. The 1980s and 1990s
were Jordan's era—on and off the court.[255] Yet something clearly *has*
changed—as Dave Zirin, *The Nation*'s foremost chronicler of sports
activism, tartly puts it, "The opportunity to finally put the Age of
the Apolitical Athlete to bed and reframe their platform as one that
could be used for something other than selling us more crap."[256]

Several factors seem to be prominent in explaining why sports
stars have gotten more "woke" of late. On one hand, substantively,
many black athletes no doubt feel intimately connected to issues
of the criminal justice system, whether through the experiences of

friends and family or the escalation of mass incarceration during the decades in which they came of age, as Zirin suggests.[257] On the other hand, the tools of modern technology—and, once more, social media, in particular—have furnished a "sense of connectivity" such that "they no longer feel alone on an island if they want to demonstrate or speak out about a particular issue," observes *Around the Horn*'s Kevin Blackistone. "When you can see a mass movement, it is much easier to express yourself as part of that mass movement than . . . when you only see yourself as an individual. Then you may be less likely to put your foot in that water."[258]

Twitter feeds and *Players' Tribune* pieces enable athletes, as noted in previous chapters, to narrate their own political consciousness, without a traditional media filter there to truncate and pigeonhole them. For example, a regular group text among NBA stars like James, Carmelo Anthony, Chris Paul, and Dwyane Wade apparently eased the coordination of their activism; similarly, in the NFL, Anquan Boldin initiated his own group text with more than 80 players to talk about backing Kaepernick's actions.[259] Reacting to a widely discussed speech about racial injustice that opened the 2016 ESPY Awards show, Nike's CEO issued a public declaration of support for Black Lives Matter and specifically credited James, Anthony, and Paul for their courageous words there.[260] (Conspicuously, there was no mention of the fourth presenter, Wade, who is no longer a Nike endorser.)

The same forces of fragmentation contextualized in chapter 1 might also apply here. That is, the apolitical profile that Michael Jordan and Tiger Woods struck may have been partly an artifact of a mass media era wherein athletes had to be "all things to all people," inoffensively, and maintaining celebrity meant amassing "as large a group as possible" by biting one's tongue when it came to hot-button issues; in today's environment, however, stars can perhaps narrowcast their causes to still-profitable niches who reward that activism.[261] Brad Brown, who worked as Anheuser-Busch's vice president of sports and entertainment marketing, amusingly analogizes this to the potential alignments for the sub-brands within that portfolio: "If you're a mainstream—like Budweiser's an example—you may not want that [activism] out there. . . . A Shock Top may be able to get by with the product endorser saying what they want on social media a little bit more than Bud Light, just from the simple fact of those demographics. . . . [Protest] may not be offensive for a Shock Top consumer, but it could be really offensive for a Budweiser consumer.[262]

Thus, when UFC president Dana White publicly endorsed Trump for president during the 2016 election, there was probably a coherent and perhaps even justified rationale, given the fan segment that sport consciously cultivates.[263] On the flip side, when Adidas posted a Valentine's Day Instagram photo featuring two female runners in an implied kiss (with the caption, "The love you take is equal to the love you make"), a variety of commenters condemned the ad and announced they'd switch to Nike; rather than backtrack, the social media account instead issued a kiss and goodbye-wave emoji.[264] "There were a lot of haters there in our community that had things to say about not following our brand anymore," admits Lia Stierwalt, Adidas senior director of global communications. "The power of the way [we . . .] really stuck to what the brand believes in and said, 'Go to our competitors. That's fine. We don't need you.' It's a really powerful and bold, provocative statement for a brand to make."[265]

Even Budweiser—that aforementioned paragon of conservative (i.e., safe) mass marketing—courted current events controversy and boycott backlash by airing a Super Bowl spot themed around Adolphus Busch's journey to America, at a moment in the early weeks of the Trump presidency when an immigration was already a flash-point issue.[266] On the other hand, the game itself had to remain, as usual, assiduously off-limits to the incursion of any *explicit* politics: "As far as wedging in political commentary about the immigration situation or President Trump between second and third down, I don't think there's a lot of value in that," demurred Fox play-by-play announcer Joe Buck. "I think people look at the game as a respite from the updates on their phones, the political banter back and forth on CNN and Fox. At some point, you want to turn on the game and watch the game."[267] Yet, as usual before kickoff, a flock of Air Force F-16s still loudly buzzed the stadium—a show of military force apparently exempted from being seen as somehow "political." And Colin Kaepernick, ideologically radioactive, was still looking for work.

## THE ESSENTIAL CONSERVATISM OF SPORTS CULTURE

[Critics] believe—no matter how valid and pertinent a subject may be—that it gets in the way of people's pure enjoyment of the game as an escape. I've always felt that you pick your spots carefully. People have said to me—I think very illogically—"He's interrupted the game by talking about something political." First of all, everything I do in that regard would be at halftime, or in a studio show . . . I would never—no matter how strongly I felt about something—do it in the middle of a game or in the eighth inning with the bases loaded and the game on the line. . . . Some people may say, "Alright, well, do that on HBO" or "do that on ESPN's *Outside the Lines*," and that's all well and good . . . but it's the big events that get the largest audience. An actively crafted two or three minutes on network television in front of tens of millions of people can have a greater impact than a Peabody Award–level thing that goes for twenty minutes on HBO.[268]

For Bob Costas, veteran NBC sportscaster, just such a moment arrived the night of December 2, 2012, during the broadcast of

TV's top-rated *Sunday Night Football*. A day before, Kansas City Chiefs linebacker Jovan Belcher murdered his girlfriend and then shot himself in the head outside the team's stadium. Costas devoted his halftime monologue to a critique of American gun culture and the Orwellian premise that more firearms enhance public safety. The backlash was swift from censuring politicians and fans alike (3,600 of whom liked a "Fire Bob Costas" Facebook page because of his "liberal commentaries"). In defense, Costas notes that he stayed silent on the issue after shootings at Aurora and Newtown but that such an incident involving an NFL star demanded relevant reflection.[269] He further counters that his Olympic-broadcast allusions to the Black September massacre or Soviet suppression were never met with such recoil: "I didn't hear that I was mixing politics with sports [then] because they liked what I said."[270]

The hypocrisy of the backlash against Costas seems richly revealing of an aspect of sports culture less observed: It is, more often than not, an essentially—if not exclusively, but still largely invisibly— conservative space. Calling sports culture "conservative" has a double meaning here. On one hand, sports culture is clearly conservative (as in "cautious") in its aversion to engage explicitly with the political issues and current events of the day. Those controversies and dramas that are splashed across the front pages of newspapers have been historically sealed off from seeping into the "toy department" of the newsroom. Fans, players, and media professionals have, more or less, agreed to bypass problems that polarize en route to revel in ritual that unifies.

Durkheimian theory becomes the dodge here and his insight into the social function of totemic purpose is echoed when NFL commissioner Roger Goodell sidesteps "Media Day" questioning about the Trump administration thus: "I'm singularly focused on the Super Bowl right now. . . . We have a unique position to have an event on Sunday that will bring the world together."[271] The persistence of the pushback against (or, in Goodell's case, outright avoidance of) those instances where politics intrude have been documented throughout these pages—from the testimonies of media professionals to the examples of athletes working, at times, for and, at other times, against that supra-ideology of remaining apolitical, so as to maximize market share.[272]

Yet this chapter has also shown how sports are not just conservative in the sense of remaining circumspect; sports culture also seems to incubate right-leaning values, particularly as they pertain to economic inequality and a militaristic form of patriotism. These are, of course, veiled politics: the politics of common sense or politics unconsciously embedded in the narratives and spectacles of sport. To call them out as "political" probably even strikes some observers as strange. When a championship-winning star attributes his team's good fortune to the meritocratic morality of hard work, he's not *explicitly* explaining why poverty persists (i.e., laziness). He's just talking about—to impishly quote the NBA's Allen Iverson—"*practice, man, practice.*" When fighter jets zip over the crowd during kickoff or troops are trotted out for cheers before a game, they're not *explicitly* propagandizing for this military invasion or that defense budget increase. They're just being honored in the most generic sense imaginable. To read the game naïvely like this is to see it (untenably) as at some kind of a remove from the issues of wealth and war that have dominated American political life in the 21st century. Quite to the contrary, though, sports culture seems to be subtly right-handed on many such subjects; Costas's perception that it's only "politics" if it sounds disagreeable (and it only seems to be disagreeable, for him and others like Kaepernick, when it intrudes from the left) suggests the "natural" ideological tilt that must be maintained therein.

Indeed, one study of Australian sports journalists' attitudes found them more politically aligned with the right (and nearly twice as likely to vote conservative than their non-sports media counterparts).[273] In the United States, sports franchise owners are both well networked in Washington and also generally GOP-leaning, as with those like Phoenix's Jerry Colangelo and New York's Woody Johnson who have been major fundraisers for the party.[274] It is ironic, then, and, again, revealing of *which* politics are allowed, that no one seems to dispute the propriety of *these* sportsmen being politically active—wielding wealth and peddling power, mostly behind the scenes—though their employees dare not step into the spotlight to take a knee or raise a fist on similar grounds.

Ivan Maisel of ESPN recalls administering an informal questionnaire on presidential voting patterns at a college football coaches' meeting some years back and found but one casting a ballot for the Democrats: "I think it's that sort of meritocracy-based thought," he speculates.[275] Another study—this of high school students—found that sports viewership was predictive of a variety of conservative political values like authoritarianism and nationalism.[276] The survey I conducted with my colleague Emily Thorson found that sports fans were not only more likely to attribute economic success to individual effort (as discussed earlier), but also more likely to support increased defense spending, believe that peace is ensured through military strength, and affirm the necessity of maintaining robust armed forces.[277] These findings confirmed the conclusions from another study, a decade ago, that found "masculinist sports" fandom powerfully correlated with several indices of "imperialistic nationalism"—specifically, support for the Iraq invasion and the Bush doctrine of preemptive strikes.[278] If *that's* what the Pentagon has been paying for with its guerrilla marketing troop salutes, it would seem to be getting its money's worth.

Notably, too, our data show that American conservatives are much more likely than liberals or moderates to oppose the intrusion of politics into sports. This is because, as has been argued here, the conservative politics already "inside" of sports are at once invisible and permissible, while those that are "out of bounds" are obtrusive, illegitimate, and left-leaning. And, for that matter, the "keep politics out of sports" crowd protests a bit too much: Most of the actions taken—whether it be John Carlos and Tommie Smith raising their fists in 1968 or NBA and NFL stars donning Black Lives Matter gear and taking a knee in 2016—are happening well *before* or *after* the gameplay itself. Conservative fans might carp about keeping those oppositional politics off the field, but it's not like players are trash talking to each other, in the heat of battle, about whether their favorite Congressperson got a bill through committee that week or the impact a beloved think tank's white paper had on civic debate. Most of these politics are *already* contained out of bounds, for the politics of sport are—as with any other form of popular culture— almost always symbolic. And, yet, even in that state, they are still vigorously policed and, if needed, disallowed from engagement.

The lines thus drawn around where and when and how a player or journalist is allowed to entertain political musings turns out to be unsustainably precarious. The glare of the media spotlight seems to somehow circumscribe the space allotted for activism and, yet, that activism would have little resonance without the media spotlight there to shine upon the injustices illuminated. More bizarrely still, given the ascendance of the "hot-take industrial complex" in sports journalism—where provocative, controversial content is incentivized and increasingly insisted upon—media professionals are expected to bite their collective tongue if thoughts stray too far from the box score. The staged confrontation must apparently be kept to much ado about nothing; for example, one sports media executive's "favorite kind of partisan dispute was one personality rooting for the Patriots to win and another rooting for them to lose—a clash that mimicked the theater of cable news but had none of the baggage."[279]

It is precisely *because* play exists outside of "normal" life—and offers us the appealing and seductive sheen of escape within the boundaries of that alleged diversion—that it can so powerfully smuggle in ideological themes and teach us lessons about the arrangements of power and politics *external* to the amusement. This is because those who hold power shape the "structure and values of sport" in their own interests; they presumably favor forms that "reflect and maintain" those interests and values.[280] It may well be that sport's long-standing reverence for authority, order, tradition, and hierarchy gives it a historically "special, and largely supportive, relationship" with conservative values.[281] The context or label of being "just" a game helps obfuscate these implications and those who militate against the mingling of sports and politics are ignoring all the ways they seem ever inextricable (even as those politics already implicit are somehow uncontroversial).[282] It is, then, "inherently futile" to try to maintain that insulation—an effort that serves to underestimate the immense political power that sports texts do exert.[283] And this power is, in final judgement, sports' defining quality.

I used sports, growing up, to fill a void of low self-esteem. Sports gave me something to look forward to. It made me feel good about myself. . . . It's made me feel fine maybe when things were not fine in other areas of one's life. You know, we always had our team to make us feel everything's going to be okay—win or lose. Because it's kind of like taking us back to our childhood again— where it made us feel okay and comforting.

—**Linda Cohn**, *SportsCenter* anchor

# OUT OF BOUNDS

## The Defining Power of Sports Culture

In the twenty-first century, far too many sports fans have a headache that is rapidly entering migraine territory. . . . The headache comes from the idea that we are loving something that doesn't simply love us in return.

—**Dave Zirin**, *The Nation* sports editor

# It is Both Strange

# AND SAD TO GO TO A WAKE WHEN

you don't yet know whether your loved one is actually gone.[1]

Such was the disorienting melancholy of attending the San Diego Chargers' last game in earthly existence on New Year's Day in 2017. Fans anticipated—and were proven right a dozen days later—that Dean Spanos, the team's owner, would uproot our franchise of five decades and haul it a hundred miles north at season's end.[2] This made the 2017 Chargers calendars, handed out at the stadium gates, a cruel irony—like some paramour preceding a breakup by pegging pictures to all the months you wouldn't get to spend together.

The breakup was about the stadium, as it often is in sports—about saying goodbye to our Brutalist dump ringed by corkscrew ramps and an ocean of parking lot. You always got the feeling, in Qualcomm's later years, that a hunk of stray concrete might shear off its façade and crush some poor sap in a Ryan Leaf jersey. But, still, it was our dump—our repository of memory, both personal and collective. It's well clichéd by now, but nonetheless rings true: Southern California tends to lack those spaces and therefore feelings. The anonymous vibe depicted in movies like *Crash* and

*Magnolia* achingly reflects this. Maybe it's the freeways. Maybe it's the weather.

Whatever the reason, in an era of cultural fragmentation—when we're all streaming TV shows asynchronously, scoffing at each other's (fake) news sources, and burying our consciousness in distracting smartphones—a sports team remains that rare institution that can unify and provide that social glue. It still feels like a *mass* medium amidst a kaleidoscope of niche content. It still demands your attention to what's going on *right now* when so much else seems like it can just be DVR'ed and time-shifted. And it still gives a reason to *hope* and *believe*, unselfconsciously, when the detachment of nihilism and irony remain ever in vogue. A sports team, quite simply, gets us, as fans, to look "up"—literally, metaphorically, spiritually.

Owner Dean Spanos wasn't just making off with a hapless 5–11 ball club. He was making off with the capacity for my hometown to *feel* as one. He was making off with our identity, our community, our memory.

A few rows in front of me in the cheap seats, a burly guy in a Chargers jersey had "Honor" spelled out on the back where a player's last name might otherwise fit. Yeah, right—if only. We like to pretend that our favorite team is just that: ours. Heck, the PA announcer told us as much that day, as at every home game: "Here come *your* San Diego Chargers!"—his jaunty baritone reverberating across the half-empty grandstands. It certainly *feels* true enough, for those who buy into what is, ultimately, a commercialized fiction—this co-ownership of the team totem—in part because that's critical to how it is sold to us as consumers. Could it ever, somehow, be more than that though?

Dave Zirin, sports editor for *The Nation*, suggests, "When a pro sports squad resides in a city for decades, when its triumphs, failures, and even uniform colors become part of how citizens define themselves, then the question of ownership becomes a contested concept.

The owner's name is in the papers, but the community feels a separate sense of possession. A team can feel as much an organic part of the city as the firehouse, the library, or a distinct monument. Fans assume they will have the opportunity to bestow the team on to their children. . . . This can be a powerful, even magical connection."[3]

Early on—and again sprinkled intermittently throughout these pages—I have sought to frame that magic in Durkheimian terms: The religious totem, I believe, best captures the utopian function of these franchises and the fizziness that fandom affords (or what Durkheim called "collective effervescence"). Worshipping the Chargers all those years was, then, but an oblique, socially acceptable way of worshipping my ancestors, my polity, my native soil. Because of that, weirdly, winning didn't *really* matter all that much, at least not according to this theoretical formulation. "We talk about bandwagon fans, but . . . why would you want to be a fan of something that doesn't bring you any joy? Why would you *not* be a bandwagon fan?" puzzles Spike Eskin, program director at WIP Philadelphia. "I have a Sixers podcast and we get 10,000 people a week to listen [during a 10–72 season] and sometimes I think, like, 'Who are you? Why are you doing this?' I don't understand."[4]

His bafflement suggests a "product" other than victory is actually being sought out to bring meaning and joy to those who consume it. The Chicago Cubs—pre-2016, at least—might have been the best example of the irrelevance of futility and the primacy of bonding as the *real* nightly draw when it comes to fan experience.[5] "Sports are just a strange phenomenon," observes Michael Rosenberg, senior writer for *Sports Illustrated*. "Most businesses, if they're failing, you just find another business to help you. If you buy a Volkswagen, then you're mad about this new emissions thing, the next car is not a Volkswagen. Problem solved. In sports, if your team is failing, you just get angry—you don't lose interest in that business. It's just weird, right?"[6]

Weird and fundamentally irrational, as religion is sometimes slighted—the attendance tallies for late-season and perennial bottom-dwellers beg for a more nuanced counterpoint here, but Rosenberg seems, broadly, correct. The annual failures on the field—and, for Chargers fans, these arrived as predictably as clockwork (or timeout mismanagement)—should have long since scattered an unfulfilled tribe, if its social relations were solely dependent upon deliverance to that metaphorical "promised land." But, quite the contrary seems apparent: Our fandom, like so many others', had been made up of a lifetime of accumulated disappointment but never—until January 2017—had we faced a loss so profoundly existential.

What happens on the field, then, must somehow pale in comparison to the importance of the lived culture that is forged in the stands; what matters most, as I have tried to argue throughout the book, is what happens *out of bounds*. "Fans are fans—that's who they are. You're not going to stop loving the Chargers because they disappoint you every year," says Ben Shpigel, *New York Times* sportswriter and Philadelphia native. "I didn't stop loving the Phillies because they were the most dreadful team. It's just who you are."[7]

Because of that, the question of who owns the team can be linked to and framed through a more unsettling inquiry: Who really "owns" our identity as sports fans? Over the course of these pages, I've drawn upon interviews with dozens of professionals involved in sports and sports media: journalists, broadcasters, marketers, and business folks. They may not produce that identity definitively—audiences have the final say in "decoding," as cultural theorist Stuart Hall long ago posited—but they do control the conditions and produce the parameters that make such identity more or less possible and through which means.[8] They dictate the structure of the games and their representation; as shown here, sometimes these various stakeholders play nicely together—other times their interests and tactics are at odds with one another. There is no unified, coordinated pulling of the strings backstage, as political economy sometimes seems to conspiratorially imply, but that's also not to downplay the power of their ownership of and influence over the sports totem. Even if fans delude themselves into conflating the durability of their community with some kind of permanent possessiveness over the object of adoration, you can't pass down something that isn't, ultimately, yours to give. Just ask any Expos fan in Montreal, Sonics fan in Seattle, Whalers fan in Hartford, or fellow San Diegan whose heart has been broken over the years.

The utopian function of sports franchises is, nonetheless, theoretically real enough and often made manifest in (fleeting) empirical form. Sport offers an obvious route to what some scholars call "cultural citizenship," along with education, language, and other forms of material and semiotic heritage. While definitions differ, one way of thinking about this idea is a citizen's right "to partake in essential parts of cultural life that define what it means to belong in an egalitarian society."[9] At present, really only one fan base among the major professional sports leagues in the United States can plausibly lay claim to "cultural citizenship" through their totemic allegiance: the publicly owned Green Bay Packers. Were it not for that anomalous historical arrangement, one has to wonder whether the franchise would have long since beaten a hasty retreat from the 157th largest metro market to, say, Los Angeles sooner than the Chargers could get there. (He says ruefully.)

Zirin thus issues a modest proposal on this front: "In a just universe, there would be a constitutional amendment preventing sports franchises from moving to other cities. Sports teams operate on an entirely different emotional, or even spiritual, plane than any other corporate entity."[10] This is both correct and quixotic. The astral field of sports fandom *is* different and more sacred than other consumer experiences, for all the reasons outlined in chapter 1. Furthermore, sports are "important public goods," deserving of widespread access, and their exclusionary commodification does represent a "pathological" threat to that sublime social potential.[11] As sports scholar Garry Whannel further posits, public ownership of teams might yield more democratic operations of them; at the very least, they surely wouldn't be able to pick up and leave town so impetuously.[12] It seems highly unlikely, however, that a municipality would simply "buy the team"—not given the extent of private ownership in the U.S. and certainly not given the riches to be plundered in those markets.[13] I'll be rooting for this outcome the same way I rooted for the Chargers to win the Super Bowl every year: with my irrational heart and more sober mind diverging.

We are left, instead, with the conundrum of ambivalence announced in opening pages of this book: economics and culture tugging sport in different directions. Sports totems, spaces, and experiences offer fans something sacred, shared, and synchronizing. That magnetism derives from the preservation of institutional vessels that retain collective memory against a zeitgeist of digital fluidity, frayed social relations, and postmodern amnesia.

"What is sacred?" asks Morry Levine, the managing sports editor for CSN–New England. "The old ballparks—Fenway Park, Wrigley Field. Even the fact that the Celtics, after all these years, haven't changed their uniforms—it's still the same uniform that they've had."[14] But that allure is also future-oriented, dependent upon a faith in progress that sports supposedly index: "I grew up in the South Bronx in the late sixties, early seventies. And the Bronx was a terrible place. It was burned down; it was all kinds of things," says Garry Howard, former editor-in-chief for *The Sporting News*. "But what stood there on 161st Street and River Avenue was Yankee Stadium and it was, like, there's a hope for the future—there's change."[15]

Furthermore, those qualities of identity and community proffer the religious texture of sports experience that is central to appreciating its power and functionality: "The idea that people have at least some space where they feel a sense of camaraderie, a sense of connection with other people, a sense of discussion with folks that they otherwise would not be able to talk to—that, to me, is utterly understandable in the way in which needing water and food is utterly understandable," says Zirin. He later adds in our interview, "What sports is actually about, at best, is this idea of doing something memorable . . . making real friendships . . . creating a family unto itself, and creating bonds of connection in an otherwise very alienating world."[16] Increasingly, however, all of those qualities come at a price. Our totem did not survive, despite fervently believing in it. There was too much "brand equity" to be made up Interstate 5.

This is the dystopian ambition of sports franchises and it, too, is real enough. It's not a very original take, but money has been at the root of so many of the ills diagnosed throughout this book—corrupting that which might be imagined and attained with greater purity. Economic imperatives impair the achievement of journalistic ideals: complicating relationships with subjects covered and stooping to grab attention with low-hanging click-bait hot takes. Economic imperatives devalue the contribution of women in sports (i.e., as media professionals, athletes, and fans) in favor of maintaining a hegemonic focus on masculinity and consolidating the wealth that it generates. And economic imperatives muzzle the articulation of dissent, as when organizations and brands shy away from athletes' explicit political engagement (even as politics runs rife—and often rightward—albeit "invisibly" within the sports spectacle). Absent commercialization, I believe, journalists, women, and activists, among others, might find that greater freedom and respect define their sports experience.

Economic imperatives also degrade so much of that cultural essence which sport produces to positive ends—chiefly, once more, identity and community. Our totemic allegiance is as socially powerful as it is increasingly commercially manipulated, as chapter 3 endeavored to show. For decades, brands have evolved from explaining product utility to affecting ethos authenticity—trying to get consumers to believe and repeat, "I am [insert multinational corporation here]." No set of trademarked goods accomplishes that goal more consistently and conspicuously than those that are licensed by athletic teams. The same passion and loyalty that Apple, Coca-Cola, and BMW pray that they might instill in their consumer base is already found, organically, in overflowing abundance among sports fans. As profit-oriented entities, franchises are discovering the value in excavating and exploiting that identity and community as an intangible resource. We might think we "own" it, but that's just how they get us to buy in. The loyalty really only runs one way.

The power of sports is, therefore in final judgment, definitional: It tells us who we are, at the individual, local, and national level, furnishing the character we crave and the status we fetishize.[17] It defines what it time it is—across the arc of seasons-long history, as tradition accumulates, and in the immediate, immersive ephemerality of a single game being played, a single moment that you can't look away from.

"People want to have this collective experience in real time with each other," observes Will Leitch, *Deadspin* founder. "People are lonely; people want to be a part of something—want other people to talk to when something's on . . . Not a lot of things in life [are] something actually happening that the world is watching together and discussing with one another."[18] Sport, however, defines "the now" as much as any facet of contemporary American culture. And sport defines who matters (in terms of its masculine bias) and what's fair in life (in terms of the meritocratic myths it spins). Because it is definitional, sport might be thought of as cultural mirror; that certainly has been a central undercurrent of the book's argument. This makes claims on sport as "diversion" even more untenable:

One of the things that I love about sports . . . is the idea that it's binary. If my team wins, I'm happy; if my team loses, I'm sad. Life is constantly complicated . . . The idea that there's a black-or-white or happy-or-sad in real life? Life is nothing like that whatsoever. Sport is very appealing in that, because it's basic; it's easy; it's a way to escape the insanity of everyday life, the confusion. It's bewildering and terrifying—everyday life is really hard and really complicated and really complex. Sport is a way for people to escape that and to be, like, "I want my team to win—yay! But they lost—argh!"[19]

The bifurcation that Leitch distills here is a compelling façade and seduces with such apparent, appealing simplicity. But while these contests pretend to be an escape from social and political issues, their "defining" cultural power is actually in reflecting and reproducing those contestations, both on-stage and off. Sports are, in fact, revealing rather than diversionary, giving us ways of understanding so many issues and trends in contemporary life across media, culture, and politics that are broader than "mere" games. Sports help us see and say things about America today that need to be seen and said: that journalism's autonomy and critical distance is compromised when technology affords subjects the opportunity to cut out the reporter and speak directly to audiences; that shrillness in the journalistic institutions that survive is no substitute for substance; that commercialism runs rampant and overwhelms any borders that might be temporarily fortified on behalf of values being sold out; that myths about meritocracy erode our empathy for society's economic "losers"; that the performance of patriotism in (paid) spectacle form obfuscates rather than reminds us of the troops and their reality of warfare; and that the recession of blue-collar jobs has shaken the foundations of masculinity in ways both productive and problematic. All of these themes can be identified within sports culture and articulated about the world beyond it. To think that they can be evaded on the field of play is pure folly; rather, play provides a high-profile stage for the performance of these issues—sometimes subtle, sometimes blatant—we'd often prefer to flee.

Because of that, the battle over boundaries—and what should and shouldn't be allowed to "intrude" from the sidelines—runs deep throughout so many of the issues catalogued in these pages. The first step, after all, in making a game involves drawing up the partitions for where play exists and where the "real world" can be kept at bay. The contestation of those boundaries was most fierce and explicit in chapter 5, where overt politics (à la Colin Kaepernick, who kneeled—quite literally and fittingly—at the sideline's edge) threatened to crest over a lucrative cultural form that's already ideologically valenced, albeit invisibly, toward the conservative biases of inequality and militarism.

Yet the issue of boundaries was central to each of the other chapters as well: the boundaries of autonomy, access, and opinionization within the world of sports media; the boundaries of commercial colonization against journalistic process, gameplay structure, and totemic community; and the boundaries of gender roles for journalists, players, and audiences who identify as female in a historically masculine preserve. What I, personally, love about sports is precisely that interplay along the margins: the fact that sports can explain so much about contexts far removed from gameplay like religion, journalism, digitalization, commerce, celebrity, feminism, masculinity, violence, labor, inequality, militarism, activism, and, of course, identity and community. This was a book about sports, but arguably only in a superficial sense; it was really about the dynamics of power as situated across culture, media, and economics. The games themselves might grab the forefront of our attention, but they're really just the backdrop for these other more important realities.

As activist and scholar Harry Edwards concludes, "Sport not only exhibits the same structure and ideological rationalizations of human relations as exist in the larger society, but it plays a fundamental role in sustaining the character of those relations."[20] And, yet, those producing the spectacle, as well as those consuming it, often cling to the hope that these relations can somehow be pushed "out of bounds." I understand and empathize with the impulse here: the divisiveness of political dissent (that I often applaud) could certainly rupture the sense of spiritual community (that I equally treasure). One right-wing pundit articulates this conundrum rather compellingly:

> From television to comedy to sports, politics surrounds and engulfs us, leaving us no space to gather as citizens without giving a thought to it. American culture today is infected with politics to a degree that it hurts our ability to share cultural moments and experiences with people who have different views. . . . When you "stick to sports," you are doing more than confining yourself to the field and the court. You are providing a way for people who may have diametrically opposed politics to share a beer at a bar discussing quarterbacks instead of executive orders.[21]

The problem, as I've tried to articulate, is that sports' "Edenic state," pre-Kaepernick, is not neutral either; those with progressive sympathies have perhaps long felt the alienation about which conservatives now gripe when suddenly confronted with "woke" athletes. For this reason, those with activist ambitions—player, journalist, or fan alike—should keep on the march for the sake of social justice, despite the qualms of those who believe that pursuit will spoil community. The issue of defining boundaries is, after all, an issue of ownership and who has the power and the "right" to delineate identity and circumscribe community. This matters enormously—escapist claims to the contrary.

"The games seem like they should be meaningless," Michael Rosenberg writes in his final column for *The Detroit Free Press*. "But instead they can be the most solid thing we know. They make us feel as alive as we can feel."[22]

I share his faith in this. I believe that it is that animating power that brings to life not just individual experience, but—far more importantly—some kind of collective consciousness. I am appreciative of that "solidity" he describes—and subsequent *solidarity* derived from it—when social experience seems to fray and fragment, when storytelling experience seems culturally kaleidoscopic and chronologically uncoordinated. I am humbled by the way that sports can fill a contemporary spiritual vacuum—how it can make us feel good about ourselves and the world. But I am not naïve about the cost of these benefits—not commercially nor ideologically.

My grandfather was not alive to see the Chargers' last game on San Diego soil. As the final seconds ticked off the clock of their existence, the PA cued up Ben E. King's "Stand by Me" and I lingered awhile in the upper deck, watching the stadium empty out. What an apt dirge; what a false promise. This was the end.

Riding down the escalator and walking back to our car, I kept glancing over my shoulder at the old dump's darkening silhouette, as though memory were already fading along with the twilight. I couldn't tell exactly, but it looked like it was a beautiful sunset out at the beach that night, where people were probably just doing their own thing.

# ACKNOWLEDGMENTS

Any coach will tell you that "there is no *I* in team" and writing a book is no different: The cover accommodates only one name, but everyone knows it takes a village. My gratitude thus spirals outward through concentric circles of familiarity.

First, to those I've yet to meet, save for their scholarly inspiration on the pages that came before: David Rowe, Lawrence Wenner, Garry Whannel, Travis Vogan, George Sage, Michael Messner, Varda Burstyn, Mariah Nelson, Michael Butterworth, and Raymond Boyle, among many others enumerated in the references. The frequency and extensiveness of those endnotes that ensue here is but a testament to my humble genuflection before that teamwork. Likewise, to the anonymous reviewers of this manuscript: I am so appreciative of your time, wisdom, and feedback.

The reader of endnotes will also note this project's heavy dependence on *SportsBusiness Journal* for the raw "data" its coverage supplies and, particularly, the reporting of John Ourand and Terry Lefton. I am similarly indebted to all the other interviewees, cited in the appendix, who generously carved time out from busy schedules; without their thoughts and insights, this book could never have been written. Thanks to the folks associated with NYU Press for their interest in a second go-round together: Eric Zinner, Karen Tongson, Henry Jenkins, Lisha Nadkarni, Dolma Ombadykow, Dan Geist, and others who have assisted.

Thanks to my mentors at all the beloved institutions that I have been fortunate to call "home"—intellectually, professionally, and socially—at various stages of life: CFHS, USF, Sophia, Columbia, the *Houston Press*, Penn, and Fairfield—and especially to Barbie Zelizer, Katherine Sender, Joseph Turow, Joseph Jones, Thierry Robouam, S.J., Stephen Isaacs, Margaret Downing, and David Gudelunas. Thanks to Boston College for offering me the dream gig of a lifetime and for helping support this research and writing—from administration leadership (e.g., President William Leahy, S.J., Dean Gregory Kalscheur, S.J., Chair Lisa Cuklanz) to my wonderful colleagues in the Department of Communication to the undergraduate students (and URF assistants) who provide unparalleled joy both inside and outside of the classroom.

To Mom and Dad, Jules, and all my family and friends that keep me Company: I love you forever and ever and ever and would be nothing without you. And, finally, to Lucy: You bring meaning to our world, brighten our lives every day, and make our hearts overflow with joy; you are, as Papa likes to say, our little gift from heaven.

A running theme of the book is that, because of sports culture, we too often mistakenly attribute life outcomes—especially success or failure—to meritocratic processes. It is why I keep this quote, hanging highest, above my desk: "There, but for the grace of God, go I." I am, in the end, most grateful for that.

# APPENDIX

## INTERVIEWS CITED IN THE TEXT

A brief note on the transcription and use of recorded interview material: I have cleaned up responses for clarity and narrative flow, but have sought to maintain fidelity to the speakers' intent and not fused together sentences from different parts of an interview. Unless noted by the caveat "later in the interview," all quotations are drawn from the same block response to a single question I had posed. A three-period ellipsis indicates that some words from a single spoken sentence were omitted; a four-period ellipsis indicates that more than one sentence has been omitted from that section of the quoted passage.

Bonnie Bernstein, former ESPN reporter. February 15, 2016: 53 minutes.
Greg Bishop, *Sports Illustrated* senior writer. September 23, 2015: 34 minutes.
Kevin Blackistone, *Around the Horn* panelist. January 19, 2016: 55 minutes.
Filip Bondy, *New York Daily News* sports columnist. August 20, 2015: 62 minutes.

Brad Brown, former Anheuser-Busch vice president of sports and entertainment marketing group. March 2, 2016: 51 minutes.

David Canter, NFL player agent. February 15, 2016: 64 minutes.

Tina Cervasio, Fox–New York sports reporter. December 8, 2015: 47 minutes.

Linda Cohn, *SportsCenter* anchor. January 8, 2016: 28 minutes.

David Cornwell, NFL and MLB player agent. March 16, 2016: 46 minutes.

Bob Costas, NBC studio host. November 6, 2015: 29 minutes.

Tommy Craggs, former *Deadspin* editor-in-chief. November 4, 2015: 58 minutes.

Bob Dorfman, Baker Street Advertising executive creative director. February 26, 2015: 42 minutes.

Chris Dufresne, *Los Angeles Times* college sports columnist. September 11, 2015: 53 minutes.

Spike Eskin, WIP Philadelphia program director. November 3, 2015: 48 minutes.

Chad Finn, *Boston Globe* sports media columnist. September 14, 2015: 46 minutes.

Mark Gross, ESPN senior vice president for production and remote events. February 15, 2016: 39 minutes.

Jemele Hill, *SportsCenter* anchor. February 27, 2016: 39 minutes.

Gary Hoenig, *The Players' Tribune* editorial director. August 31, 2015: 38 minutes.

Garry Howard, former *Sporting News Media* editor-in-chief. March 2, 2016: 47 minutes.

Kim Jones, NFL Network reporter. December 1, 2015: 52 minutes.

Russ Kenn, NESN Red Sox coordinating producer. November 24, 2015: 48 minutes.

Sarah Kustok, YES Network Nets reporter. February 24, 2016: 43 minutes.

Terry Lefton, *SportsBusiness Journal* marketing reporter. February 19, 2016: 47 minutes.

Will Leitch, *Deadspin* founder. September 1, 2015: 48 minutes.

Mark Lev, Fenway Sports Management managing director. July 22, 2016: 50 minutes.

Morry Levine, CSN–New England managing sports editor. December 18, 2015: 45 minutes.

Robert Lipsyte, former *New York Times* sports columnist. December 10, 2015: 53 minutes.

Bill Littlefield, NPR *Only a Game* host. September 15, 2015: 25 minutes.

Mike Lynch, ABC-Boston sports anchor. October 6, 2015: 43 minutes.

A. J. Maestas, Navigate Research CEO. April 20, 2016: 54 minutes.

Ivan Maisel, ESPN college football senior writer. August 11, 2015: 72 minutes.

Kim McConnie, Pepsi senior director of sports marketing. June 1, 2016: 27 minutes.

Tas Melas, NBA TV *The Starters* co-host. September 23, 2015: 57 minutes.

Kelly Naqi, ESPN *Outside the Lines* reporter. November 13, 2015: 62 minutes.

Hussain Naqi, Jacksonville Jaguars senior vice president of fan engagement. March 30, 2016: 47 minutes.

Jason Norcross, 72 and Sunny advertising executive creative director. February 3, 2016: 54 minutes.

John Ourand, *SportsBusiness Journal* media reporter. February 26, 2016: 54 minutes.

Bill Rasmussen, ESPN founder. September 2, 2015: 54 minutes.

Dave Revsine, Big Ten Network studio host. October 19, 2015: 51 minutes.

Harry Roman, Droga5 group strategy director. March 3, 2016: 50 minutes.

Michael Rosenberg, *Sports Illustrated* senior writer. September 22, 2015: 58 minutes.

John Rowady, rEvolution president. March 2, 2016: 50 minutes.

Fluto Shinzawa, *Boston Globe* Bruins beat writer. August 24, 2015: 53 minutes.

Ben Shpigel, *New York Times* Jets beat writer. August 24, 2015: 80 minutes.

Marc Spears, Yahoo! Sports NBA writer. December 7, 2015: 43 minutes.

Dan Stanczyk, ESPN Radio associate producer. October 7, 2015: 44 minutes.

Leigh Steinberg, NFL, MLB, and boxing player agent. March 23, 2016: 60 minutes.

David Stern, former NBA commissioner. April 6, 2016: 44 minutes.

Doug Stewart, syndicated sports talk show host. January 20, 2016: 32 minutes.

Lia Stierwalt, Adidas senior director of global communications and media. March 21, 2016: 31 minutes.

Pat Sullivan, New England Patriots general manager. January 21, 2016: 35 minutes.

Lesley Visser, CBS sportscaster. November 14, 2015: 57 minutes.

John Wildhack, ESPN executive vice president for programming and production. November 18, 2015: 29 minutes.

Norby Williamson, ESPN executive vice president of production. February 29, 2016: 39 minutes.

David Wright, former Major League Soccer senior vice president of global sponsorship. May 2, 2016: 37 minutes.

Kim Zayotti, Blue Sky Sports & Entertainment founder and CEO. March 1, 2016: 31 minutes.

Dave Zirin, *The Nation* sports editor. December 16, 2015: 46 minutes.

# NOTES

## CHAPTER 1. KEEPING THE FAITH

1 Following sports scholar Ellis Cashmore, for the sake of stylistic variety, I'll be using "sport" and "sports" interchangeably. Michael R. Real, "MediaSport: Technology and the Commodification of Postmodern Sport," in *MediaSport*, ed. Lawrence A. Wenner (London: Routledge, 1998), 15; Barrie Houlihan, *Sport and International Politics* (New York: Harvester Wheatsheaf, 1994), 2; Ellis Cashmore, *Making Sense of Sports*, 5th ed. (New York: Routledge, 2010), 3.

2 David Stern, personal communication, April 6, 2016.

3 *SportsBusiness Journal*, tallying "advertising, media contracts, gambling facilities, construction projects, operating expenses, transportation, and lodging," pegged it at $213 billion. A. T. Kearney, a global management-consulting firm, takes a more expansive view that includes "sporting goods, apparel, equipment, and health and fitness spending" and which runs as high as $700 million. Andrei S. Markovits and Lars Rensmann, *Gaming the World: How Sports Are Reshaping Global Politics and Culture* (Princeton, NJ: Princeton University Press, 2010), 319; Hervé Collignon and Nicolas Sultan, "Winning in the Business of Sports," A.T. Kearney, 2014, www.atkearney.com.

4 Brett Hutchins and David Rowe, *Sport beyond Television: The Internet, Digital Media and the Rise of Networked Sport* (New York: Routledge, 2012), 6. Given that sport has been central to News Corp's global content strategy, this is also something of a self-fulfilling prophecy. Michael Cieply and Brooks Barnes, "Rivalry Builds off the Field as Talent Agencies Turn to Sports," *New York Times*, September 14, 2015, www.nytimes.com.

5 David Broughton, "Media Rights to Trump Ticket Sales by 2018," *SportsBusiness Journal*, October 19, 2015, www.sportsbusinessdaily.com; Rich Luker, "Sports Spending Not on Pace with Economic Growth," *SportsBusiness Journal*, February 22,

2016, www.sportsbusinessdaily.com; David Broughton, "Media Rights, Labor Peace Push Industry to $69.3B," *SportsBusiness Journal*, December 11, 2017, www.sports-businessdaily.com.

**6** David Broughton, "Slowdown Seen for Media," *SportsBusiness Journal*, October 10, 2016, www.sportsbusinessdaily.com; Broughton, "Media Rights, Labor."

**7** Sports have also "cannibalized" other forms of media culture: Reality TV competitions are obviously not sports in any traditional sense, but they share a competitive texture that makes them difficult to classify wholly separately. Raymond Boyle and Richard Haynes, *Power Play: Sport, the Media, and Popular Culture* (Edinburgh: Edinburgh University Press, 2009), vii; Dan Brown and Jennings Bryant, "Sports Content on U.S. Television," in *Handbook of Sports and Media*, ed. Arthur A. Raney and Jennings Bryant (Mahwah, NJ: Lawrence Erlbaum Associates, 2006), 77; David Rowe, "Sports Media: Beyond Broadcasting, beyond Sports, beyond Societies?," in *Sports Media: Transformation, Integration, Consumption*, ed. Andrew C. Billings (New York: Routledge, 2011), 100.

**8** Andrew C. Billings, "Reaction Time: Assessing the Record and Advancing a Future of Sports Media Scholarship," in *Sports Media: Transformation, Integration, Consumption*, ed. Andrew C. Billings (New York: Routledge, 2011), 187.

**9** Because of this, by 2018, commercial costs to make a Super Bowl appearance had grown to $170,000 per second; the full haul of almost $420 million that NBC was expected to bag from sponsors represented 2.5 percent of the *entire year's* broadcast advertising revenue. Austin Karp and John Ourand, "Sports Leaves Little Room for Debate on Who Rules Viewership," *SportsBusiness Journal*, January 16, 2017, www.sportsbusinessdaily.com; Collingnon and Sultan, "Winning," 6; Bradley Johnson, "Big

Game Punting: Super Bowl Scores $5.4 Billion in Ad Spending over 52 Years," *Ad Age*, January 11, 2018, http://adage.com; Thomas P. Oates and Zack Furness, "Introduction: The Political Football: Culture, Critique, and the NFL," in *The NFL: Critical and Cultural Perspectives*, ed. Thomas P. Oates and Zack Furness (Philadelphia: Temple University Press, 2014), ix.

**10** John Ourand, Austin Karp, and Daniel Kaplan, "Time to Panic over Declining Viewership?," *SportsBusiness Journal*, October 3, 2016, www.sportsbusinessdaily.com; Anthony Crupi, "Scripted TV Is Dying a Slow Death," *Ad Age*, June 9, 2016, http://adage.com.

**11** David Amsden, "Fox Sports 1's 24-Hour Sports Rumble," *Men's Journal*, September 2013, www.mensjournal.com; Nick Summers, "ESPN Is Bigger than Ever—and That Might Not Be a Good Thing," *Newsweek*, January 16, 2012, www.newsweek.com; John Ourand, "NBCSN Stays True to Its Rights, Picks up Subs," *SportsBusiness Journal*, February 27, 2017, www.sportsbusinessdaily.com.

**12** James Andrew Miller, Steve Eder, and Richard Sandomir, "College Football's Most Dominant Player? It's ESPN," *New York Times*, August 25, 2013, www.nytimes.com.

**13** Eric Fisher and John Ourand, "Impasse Ball: Distributor, Channels Still at Odds over Yankees, Dodgers," *SportsBusiness Journal*, March 28, 2016, www.sportsbusinessdaily.com; Anthony Crupi, "Sports Now Accounts for 37% of Broadcast TV Ad Spending," *Ad Age*, September 10, 2015, http://adage.com.

**14** Derek Thompson, "The Global Dominance of ESPN," *Atlantic*, September 2013, www.theatlantic.com.

**15** Daniel Kaplan, "NFL Halfway to $25B Goal," *SportsBusiness Journal*, February 29, 2016, www.sportsbusinessdaily.com.

**16** Mark Leibovitch, "Roger Goodell's Unstoppable Football Machine," *New York Times* Magazine, February 7, 2016, www.nytimes.com; Kurt Badenhausen, "Dallas Cowboys Head the World's 50 Most Valuable Teams of 2016," *Forbes*, July 13, 2016, www.forbes.com.

**17** Markovits and Rensmann, *Gaming*, 279.

**18** Collingnon and Sultan, "Winning," 1; Cashmore, *Making*, 368.

**19** Jeff Phillips and Darren Rovell, "Examining the State of Baseball," ESPN.com, March 19, 2015, http://ESPN.go.com.

**20** David Rowe, *Sport, Culture, and the Media*, 2nd ed. (Berkshire, UK: Open University Press, 2004), 68; Collingnon and Sultan, "Winning," 1.

**21** Boyle and Haynes, *Power*, 68.

**22** Neil DeMause and Joanna Cagan, *Field of Schemes: How the Great Stadium Swindle Turns Public Money into Private Profit* (Lincoln, NE: University of Nebraska Press, 2008), 160.

**23** Garry Whannel, *Fields in Vision: Television Sport and Cultural Transformation* (London: Routledge, 1992), 165.

**24** Miller, Eder, and Sandomir, "College"; Joe Nocera, "At Rutgers, It's Books vs. Ballgames," *New York Times*, May 12, 2015, www.nytimes.com.

**25** DeMause and Cagan, *Field*, 136.

**26** A. J. Maestas, personal communication, April 20, 2016.

**27** Charles C. Euchner, *Playing the Field: Why Sports Teams Move and Cities Fight to Keep Them* (Baltimore: Johns Hopkins University Press, 1993), 66; DeMause and Cagan, *Field*, 28.

**28** Joe Nocera, "Football's L.A. Trick Play," *New York Times*, February 20, 2015, www.nytimes.com; David Broughton, "A Reset, then a Reboot," *SportsBusiness Journal*, January 8, 2018, www.sportsbusinessdaily.com; DeMause and Cagan, *Field*, 29.

**29** Euchner, *Playing*, x.

**30** Mark Rosentraub, "Private Control of a Civic Asset: The Winners and Losers from North America's Experience with Four Major Leagues for Professional Team Sport," in *The Commercialisation of Sport*, ed. Trevor Slack (London: Routledge, 2004), 105.

**31** Ibid., 111, 114; Euchner, *Playing*, 11; George H. Sage, *Power and Ideology in American Sport: A Critical Perspective*, 2nd ed. (Champaign, IL: Human Kinetics, 1998), 107; Paul Hoch, *Rip Off the Big Game: The Exploitation of Sports by the Power Elite* (Garden City, NY: Doubleday, 1972), 49.

**32** Kimberly S. Schimmel, "Take Me out to the Ball Game: The Transformation of Production-Consumption Relations in Professional Team Sport," in *Popular Culture: Production and Consumption*, ed. C. Lee Harrington and Denise D. Bielby (Malden, MA: Blackwell Publishers, 2001), 40.

**33** DeMause and Cagan, *Field*, 3.

**34** Sage, *Power*, 111.

**35** Dave Anderson, "Twelve Vans to Indianapolis," *New York Times*, March 29, 1984, www.nytimes.com.

**36** Dave Zirin, *Bad Sports: How Owners Are Ruining the Games We Love* (New York: Scribner, 2010), 9; DeMause and Cagan, *Field*, 21.

**37** Anouk Belanger, "The Urban Sport Spectacle: Towards a Critical Political Economy of Sports," in *Marxism, Cultural Studies, and Sport*, ed. Ben Carrington and Ian McDonald (New York: Routledge, 2009), 58.

**38** Zirin, *Bad*, 13; Euchner, *Playing*, 60; Kimberly S. Schimmel, "Political Economy: Sport and Urban Development," in *Sociology of Sport and Social Theory*, ed. Earl Smith (Champaign, IL: Human Kinetics, 2010), 63.

**39** Robert A. Baade and Richard F. Dye, "Sports Stadiums and Area Development: A Critical Review," *Economic Development Quarterly* 2, no. 3 (1988). See also DeMause and Cagan, *Field*, 34; Euchner, *Playing*, 71; Andrew Zimbalist, *Circus Maximus: The Economic Gamble behind Hosting the Olympics and the World Cup* (Washington, DC: Brookings Institution Press, 2015), ix.

**40** DeMause and Cagan, *Field*, 230.

**41** Andrew Zimbalist, "Boston Would Be Lucky to Lose the Olympics Competition," *Wall Street Journal*, January 10, 2015.

**42** Zimbalist, *Circus*, 32; Garry Whannel, *Culture, Politics and Sport: Blowing the Whistle, Revisited* (London: Routledge, 2008), 160.

**43** Zimbalist, *Circus*, 54, 55.

**44** Euchner, *Playing*, 12.

**45** Megan Garber, "How Nike Turned Running Shoes into Fashion Objects," Atlantic, July 6, 2015, www.theatlantic.com.

**46** Naomi Klein, *No Logo* (New York: Picador, 2000).

**47** Robert Goldman and Stephen Papson, *Nike Culture: The Sign of the Swoosh* (London: Sage, 1998), 6, 11; George H. Sage, "The Sporting Goods Industry: From Struggling Entrepreneurs to National Businesses to Transnational Corporations," in *The Commercialisation of Sport*, ed. Trevor Slack (London: Routledge, 2004), 29, 38, 45.

**48** Steven Jackson, "Reflections on Communication and Sport: On Advertising and Promotional Culture," *Communication and Sport* 1, no. 1–2 (January 16, 2013): 103; Douglas Kellner, "The Sports Spectacle, Michael Jordan, and Nike: An Unholy Alliance," in *Michael Jordan Inc.: Corporate Sport, Media Culture and Late Modern America* (Albany: State University of New York Press, 2001), 54.

**49** Christopher Ingraham, "The Toll of Human Casualties in Qatar," *Washington Post*, May 27, 2015, www.washingtonpost.com; Owen Gibson and Pete Pattison, "Death Toll Among Qatar's 2022 World Cup Workers Revealed," *Guardian*, December 23, 2014, www.theguardian.com.

**50** Varda Burstyn, *The Rites of Men: Manhood, Politics, and the Culture of Sport* (Toronto: University of Toronto Press, 2000), 17. See also David L. Andrews and Steven J. Jackson, "Introduction: Sports Celebrities, Public Culture, and Private Experience," in *Sports Stars: The Cultural Politics of Sporting Celebrity*, ed. David L. Andrews and Steven J. Jackson (London: Routledge, 2001), 1; Rowe, *Sport*, 70.

**51** Portions of this section of the chapter were earlier featured in a *Communication and Sport* journal article and subsequently excerpted in an *Atlantic* essay. Michael Serazio, "Just How Much Is Sports Fandom like Religion?," *Atlantic*, January 29, 2013, www.theatlantic.com; Michael Serazio, "The Elementary Forms of Sports Fandom: A Durkheimian Exploration of Team Myths, Kinship, and Totemic Rituals," *Communication and Sport* 1, no. 4 (2012).

**52** Garry J. Smith, "The Noble Sports Fan," *Journal of Sport & Social Issues* 12, no. 1 (March 1, 1988): 57.

**53** George Ritzer, *Modern Sociological Theory* (New York: McGraw-Hill, 2008), 20. See also Nick Couldry, *Media Rituals: A Critical Approach* (New York: Routledge, 2003), 4.

**54** Susan Birrell, "Sport as Ritual: Interpretations from Durkheim to Goffman," *Social Forces* 60, no. 2 (1981): 356.

**55** Émile Durkheim, *The Elementary Forms of Religious Life* (Oxford: Oxford University Press, 2001).

**56** Couldry, *Media*, 6, 135.

**57** Durkheim, *The Elementary*, viii.

**58** Robert D. Putnam, *Bowling Alone: The Collapse and Revival of American Community* (New York: Touchstone, 2000), 66.

**59** Durkheim, *The Elementary*, 154.

**60** Ibid., xix.

**61** Ibid., xiii.

**62** In the case of, say, Notre Dame or BYU college football—or, abroad, the soccer rivalry between Rangers and Celtic in Glasgow—the religious metaphor for totemic ritual and team affiliation becomes more literal. Bob Heere and Jeffrey D. James, "Sports Teams and Their Communities: Examining the Influence of External Group Identities on Team Identity," *Journal of Sport Management* 21, no. 3 (2007): 330.

**63** Durkheim, *The Elementary*, 88.

**64** Ibid., 89.

**65** Ibid., 95.

**66** Anthony King, "The Lads: Masculinity and the New Consumption of Football," *Sociology* 31, no. 2 (1997): 333.

**67** Chris Hedges, *War Is a Force That Gives Us Meaning* (New York: Public Affairs, 2002).

**68** Michael Novak, *The Joy of Sports: End Zones, Bases, Baskets, Balls, and the Consecration of the American Spirit*, rev. ed. (Lanham, MD: Madison Books, 1994), 19, 20, 21.

**69** Robert Lipsyte, *SportsWorld: An American Dreamland* (New York: Quadrangle Books, 1975), 15.

**70** Novak, *The Joy*, 144, 145.

**71** Goldman and Papson, *Nike*, 146, 148, 150.

**72** Smith, "The Noble," 56; Mark A. Grey, "Sports and Immigrant, Minority and Anglo Relations in Garden City (Kansas) High School," *Sociology of Sport Journal* 9 (1992): 259.

**73** T. R. Young, "The Sociology of Sport: Structural Marxist and Cultural Marxist Approaches," *Sociological Perspectives* 29, no. 1 (1986): 17; Arthur A. Raney, "Fair Ball?: Exploring the Relationship between Media Sports and Viewer Morality," in *Sports Media: Transformation, Integration, Consumption*, ed. Andrew C. Billings (New York: Routledge, 2011), 82.

**74** Greg Bishop, personal communication, September 23, 2015.

**75** William J. Baker, *Playing with God: Religion and Modern Sport* (Cambridge, MA: Harvard University Press, 2007), 2, 247, 251.

**76** Michael R. Real, "Super Bowl: Mythic Spectacle," *Journal of Communication* 25, no. 1 (1975): 34; Michael R. Real, *Exploring Media Culture: A Guide*, 48.

**77** Daniel Cox and Robert P. Jones, "Nearly One in Three Support Lifetime Ban for Football Players Who Commit Domestic Violence," *PRRI*, January 22, 2015, www.prri.org; Daniel Cox, Juhem Navarro-Rivera, and Robert P. Jones, "Half of American Fans See Supernatural Forces at Play in Sports," *PRRI*, January 16, 2014, www.prri.org.

**78** Houlihan, *Sport*, 113. "Quasi-religious claims" are often made by boosters to justify hosting the "spirit" of the Games and the Olympic flame, creed, and motto were all borrowed specifically from Christianity. Burstyn, *The Rites*, 18–19; John Horne, Alan Tomlinson, Garry Whannel, and Kath Woodward, *Understanding Sport: A Socio-Cultural Analysis*, 2nd ed. (London: Routledge, 2013), 222.

**79** Baker, *Playing*; James A. Mathisen, "Sport."

**80** Baker, *Playing*, 7, 10.

**81** Colin Howell, "A Manly Sport: Baseball and the Social Construction of Masculinity," in *Gender and History in Canada*, ed. Joy Parr (Toronto: Copp Clark, 1996), 194, 201; Baker, *Playing*, 13.

**82** David Yamane, Charles E. Mellies, and Teresa Blake, "Playing for Whom? Sport, Religion, and the Double Movement of Secularization in America," in *Sociology of Sport and Social Theory*, ed. Earl Smith (Champaign, IL: Human Kinetics, 2010), 85; Geoffrey York, "Radical Islamists' Ideology Marks Soccer as Enemy," *Globe and Mail*, June 18, 2014, www.theglobeandmail.com.

**83** Zirin, *Bad*, 76; John Ourand, "Pope Francis Sees Sports as a World Changer," *SportsBusiness Journal*, January 25, 2016, www.sportsbusinessdaily.com; Bill Sutton, "In High-Tech Era, High-Touch Still Counts, No Matter the Market," *SportsBusiness Journal*, May 16, 2016, www.sportsbusinessdaily.com; Samuel G. Freedman, "Author Places Faith at the Center of Circus of Sports," *New York Times*, October 7, 2011, www.nytimes.com; Jay Coakley, *Sports in Society: Issues and Controversies*, 10th ed. (Boston, MA: McGraw-Hill, 2009), 535.

**84** John Ourand, "Big Names Flock to Vatican Event," *SportsBusiness Journal*, October 3, 2016, www.sportsbusinessdaily.com.

**85** Dave Zirin, "Getting God out of Football," *Nation*, September 21, 2015, www.thenation.com.

**86** Yamane, Mellies, and Blake, "Playing," 83; Putnam, *Bowling*, 69.

**87** Putnam, *Bowling*, 71, 74.

**88** Nate Cohn, "Big Drop in Share of Americans Calling Themselves Christian," *New York Times*, May 12, 2015, www.nytimes.com.

**89** Lonnie D. Kliever, "God and Games in Modern Culture," in *From Season to Season: Sport as American Religion*, ed. Joseph L. Price (Macon, GA: Mercer University Press, 2002), 43.

**90** Durkheim, *The Elementary*, vii.

**91** The NFL surely benefits from being scheduled on the "day of rest" in Christianity, which also happens to be U.S. television's most watched day of the week. Norbert Elias and Eric Dunning, *Quest for Excitement: Sport and Leisure in the Civilizing Process* (Oxford: Basil Blackwell, 1986), 222; John Sexton, *Baseball as a Road to God: Seeing beyond the Game* (New York: Gotham Books, 2013), 176; James A. Mathisen, "From Civil Religion to Folk Religion: The Case of American Sport," in *Sport and Religion*, ed. Shirl J. Hoffman (Champaign, IL: Human Kinetics, 1992), 18; Lawrence A. Wenner, Robert V. Bellamy, and James R. Walker, "Selling Out: The Gaming of the Living Room Seat for the US Sports Fan," in *Sport, Public Broadcasting, and Cultural Citizenship: Signal Lost?*, ed. Jay Scherer and David Rowe (New York: Routledge, 2014), 86.

**92** Travis Vogan, *Keepers of the Flame: NFL Films and the Rise of Sports Media* (Urbana: University of Illinois Press, 2014), 35. See also Cox and Jones, "Nearly."

**93** Burstyn, *Rites*, 25, 26.

**94** Steve Almond, *Against Football: One Fan's Reluctant Manifesto* (Brooklyn, NY: Melville House, 2014), 153.

**95** Rowe, *Sport*, 72.

**96** Jeffrey M. Jones, "Confidence in U.S. Institutions Still Below Historical Norms," Gallup, 2015, www.gallup.com.

**97** Putnam, *Bowling*, 16, 18, 25.

**98** Markovits and Rensmann, *Gaming*, 2, 3; Putnam, *Bowling*, 112, 113.

**99** Cornel Sandvoss, *A Game of Two Halves: Football, Television and Globalization* (London: Routledge, 2003), 90, 91.

**100** Carroll Doherty, "7 Things to Know about Polarization in America," *Pew Research Center*, 2014, www.pewresearch.org. See also David Brooks, "The Fragmented Society," *New York Times*, May 20, 2016, www.nytimes.com.

**101** Cass R. Sunstein, *Republic.com 2.0* (Princeton, NJ: Princeton University Press, 2007).

**102** James W. Carey, *Communication as Culture: Essays on Media and Society* (New York: Routledge, 1992), 20.

**103** Sherry Turkle, *Alone Together: Why We Expect More from Technology and Less from Each Other* (New York: Basic Books, 2011); Chris Anderson, *The Long Tail: Why the Future of Business Is Selling Less of More* (New York: Hyperion, 2008).

**104** Joe Nocera, "Can Netflix Survive in the New World It Created?," *New York Times* Magazine, June 15, 2016, www.nytimes.com.

**105** As but one outgrowth of this, a poll among millennials found that, when asked which celebrity they would most like to dine with, the top three vote-getters (Barack Obama, Oprah Winfrey, and Beyoncé Knowles-Carter) received a meager 11, 3, and 2 percent, respectively—a sign that few "gods" are, today, quite as god-like. No star can now claim anything approaching universal adoration as he or she once might have. Farhad Manjoo, "How Netflix Is Deepening Our Cultural Echo Chambers," *New York Times*, January 11, 2017, www.nytimes.com; Alyssa Rosenberg, "What a New Poll Tells Us about Cultural Fragmentation," *Washington Post*, February 4, 2015, www.washingtonpost.com.

**106** Michael Mulvihill, "When Judging World Series, Context Is Paramount," *FoxSports Press Pass*, November 4, 2015, www.foxsports.com.

**107** Lynette Rice, "'Mad Men' Finale Attracts Record Audience," *Entertainment Weekly*, May 22, 2015. http://ew.com; Joe Flint, "Saints' Super Bowl Win Nips 'MASH' Finale for Most-Watched Show Ever," *Los Angeles Times*, February 8, 2010.

**108** Jason Mittell, *Complex TV: The Poetics of Contemporary Television Storytelling* (New York: New York University Press, 2015).

**109** In that sense, sports offer entertainment that is both "serialized" and "self-contained"—a single "episode" can be "enjoyed on its own," but audience engagement obviously escalates with greater familiarity and identification with particular players and teams followed over time. David Whitson, "Circuits of Promotion: Media, Marketing and the Globalization of Sport," in *MediaSport*, ed. Lawrence A. Wenner (London: Routledge, 1998), 61.

**110** Robert Lipsyte, personal communication, December 10, 2015.

**111** Lipsyte, *SportsWorld*, 23.

**112** Garry Whannel, *Media Sport Stars: Masculinities and Moralities* (London: Routledge, 2002), 5.

**113** Jean-François Lyotard, *The Postmodern Condition: A Report on Knowledge* (Manchester, UK: Manchester University Press, 1984).

**114** David Roberts, "America Is Facing an Epistemic Crisis," *Vox*, November 2, 2017, www.vox.com.

**115** Mark Deuze, *Media Work*, 7.

**116** Indeed, the Olympics were born specifically of this spirit—"conceived and developed under the zeitgeist of high modernism, the worldview that believed science, reason, and progress in the classical Renaissance manner would bring humankind increasing health, prosperity, and well-being." Michael R. Real, "The Postmodern Olympics: Technology and the Commodification of the Olympic Movement," *Quest* 48 (1996): 10.

**117** Elias and Dunning, *Quest*, 3.

**118** Ibid., 5; Johan Galtung, "The Sport System as a Metaphor for the World System," in *Sport . . . The Third Millennium*, ed. Fernand Landry, Marc Landry, and Magdeleine Yerles (Sainte-Foy, QC: Presses de l'Université Laval, 1991), 150; Markovits and Rensmann, *Gaming*, 45.

**119** Jeffrey O. Segrave, "The Sports Metaphor in American Cultural Discourse," *Culture, Sport, Society* 3, no. 1 (2000): 48; Whannel, *Culture*, 40.

**120** Richard Gruneau, *Class, Sports, and Social Development* (Champaign, IL: Human Kinetics, 1999), 27, 44.

**121** Billings, "Reaction," 184; Goldman and Papson, *Nike*, 173; David L. Andrews, "Sport in the Late Capitalist Moment," in *The Commercialisation of Sport*, ed. Trevor Slack (London: Routledge, 2004), 3.

**122** David Broughton, "New Research Goes Deep into Minds of Fans," *SportsBusiness Journal*, November 14, 2016.

**123** Vogan, *Keepers*, 55; Almond, *Against*, 19, 85.

**124** Michael R. Real and Robert A. Mechikoff, "Deep Fan: Mythic Identification, Technology, and Advertising in Spectator Sports," *Sociology of Sport Journal* 9 (1992): 324. The Olympics are, moreover, "one of the few remaining opportunities for men and women, both young and old, to watch the same television program" amidst that deepening demographic segmentation. Andrew C. Billings, *Olympic Media: Inside the Biggest Show on Television* (New York: Routledge, 2008), 9.

**125** Cole G. Armstrong, Elizabeth B. Delia, and Michael D. Giardina, "Embracing the Social in Social Media: An Analysis of the Social Media Marketing Strategies of the Los Angeles Kings," *Communication and Sport* 4, no. 2 (2014): 150; Collingnon and Sultan, "Winning."

**126** Lawrence A. Wenner, "Media, Sports, and Society: The Research Agenda," in *Media, Sports, and Society*, ed. Lawrence A. Wenner (London: Sage, 1989), 16. See also Luker, "Sports." The 68 percent figure is drawn from a nationally representative survey that I conducted with Emily Thorson. Emily A. Thorson and Michael Serazio, "Sports Fandom and Political Attitudes," *Public Opinion Quarterly* 82, no. 2 (2018).

**127** Daniel L. Wann, Merrill J. Melnick, Gordon W. Russell, and Dale G. Pease, *Sport Fans: The Psychology and Social Impact of Spectators* (New York: Routledge, 2001), 9.

**128** In addition to this influence from others, a person's inherent (or cultivated) skill and the bounty of opportunities to play (or lack thereof) also determine whether or not he or she takes up sport and sticks with it. Coakley, *Sports*, 54, 55.

**129** Wann et al., *Sport*, 23–28; Merrill J. Melnick and Daniel L. Wann, "An Examination of Sport Fandom in Australia: Socialization, Team Identification, and Fan Behavior," *International Review for the Sociology of Sport* 46, no. 4 (2011): 462.

**130** Wann et al., *Sport*, 31, 45.

**131** Daniel L. Wann, "The Causes and Consequences of Sport Team Identification," in *Handbook of Sports and Media*, ed. Arthur A. Raney and Jennings Bryant (New York: Routledge, 2006), 334, 335.

**132** Benjamin G. Rader, *In Its Own Image: How Television Has Transformed Sports* (New York: Free Press, 1984), 8.

**133** Garry Crawford, *Consuming Sport: Fans, Sport and Culture* (New York: Routledge, 2004), 54; Sandvoss, *A Game*, 92.

**134** Kelly Naqi, personal communication, November 13, 2015.

**135** Rowe, *Sport*, 124.

**136** Sandvoss, *A Game*, 32.

**137** Mack Hagood and Travis Vogan, "The 12th Man: Fan Noise in the Contemporary NFL," *Popular Communication* 14, no. 1 (2016): 33, 34.

**138** Robert B. Cialdini, Richard J. Borden, Avril Thorne, Marcus R. Walker, Stephen Freeman, and Lloyd R. Sloan, "Basking in Reflected Glory: Three (Football) Field Studies," *Journal of Personality and Social Psychology* 34, no. 3 (1976).

**139** Arthur A. Raney, "Why We Watch Sports and Enjoy Mediated Sports," in *Handbook of Sports and Media*, ed. Arthur A. Raney and Jennings Bryant (Mahwah, NJ: Lawrence Erlbaum Associates, 2006), 319.

**140** Young, "The Sociology," 18.

**141** Wayne Wanta, "Reflections on Communication and Sport: On Reporting and Journalists," *Communication and Sport* 1, no. 1–2 (2013): 80.

**142** Adrian J. Walsh and Richard Giulianotti, "This Sporting Mammon: A Normative Critique of the Commodification of Sport," *Journal of the Philosophy of Sport* 28, no. 1 (2001): 14.

**143** Novak, *The Joy*, 150.

**144** To some degree, athletes themselves probably think about the preservation of their "post-self" through the measurement and recording of spectacular feats, seeking a goal of "creative immortality"; various Hall of Fame spaces accommodate these yearnings. Mark Dechesne, Jeff Greenberg, Jamie Arndt, and Jeff Schimel, "Terror Management and the Vicissitudes of Sports Fan Affiliation: The Effects of Mortality Salience on Optimism and Fan Identification," *European Journal of Social Psychology* 30 (2000); Raymond L. Schmitt and Wilbert M. Leonard, "Immortalizing the Self through Sport," *American Journal of Sociology* 91, no. 5 (2014): 1097.

**145** Indeed, studies have shown that—from the U.S. to the UK to Japan—geographic affiliation and parental loyalty were far more important factors in fans' continued support for a team than its actual success on the field of play. Wann et al., *Sport*, 5–7.

**146** Bonnie Bernstein, personal communication, February 15, 2016. Similarly, *Deadspin* founder Will Leitch notes that his two-decades-running fantasy football league "constitutes the closest thing to a constant family atmosphere that I have"—a pattern consistent in my own research discoveries on the social function of fantasy sports. Will Leitch, *God Save the Fan* (New York: HarperCollins, 2008), 241; Michael Serazio, "Virtual Sports Consumption, Authentic Brotherhood: The Reality of Fantasy Football," in *Sports Mania: Essays on Fandom and Media in the 21st Century*, ed. Lawrence W. Hugenberg, Paul M. Haridakis, and Adam C. Earnheardt (Jefferson, NC: McFarland & Company, 2008).

**147** John Rowady, personal communication, March 2, 2016.

**148** "Live" in the form of real-time video is also quickly becoming just as critical to the social media landscape as the mass media era before it; according to a Facebook representative, live video is watched three times longer and receives 10 times as many comments as regular video content. Such are the "engagement" metrics that lure advertiser interest. Michael Serazio, *Your Ad Here: The Cool Sell of Guerrilla Marketing* (New York: New York University Press, 2013), 126; Jeanine Poggi, "CMO's Guide to Live Video," *AdAge*, July 19. 2016. http://adage.com.

**149** Rowe, "Sports Media," 97.

**150** Novak, *The Joy*, 139.

**151** Brian Phillips, "Talking in a Storm: Consuming Sports, Sandy, and Politics in the Digital Age," *Grantland*, October 31, 2012. http://grantland.com.

**152** Johan Huizinga, *Homo Ludens: A Study of the Play Element in Culture* (London: Routledge, 1949), 7–10; Lipsyte, *SportsWorld*, 38.

**153** Smith, "The Noble," 55.

**154** Adam Sternbergh, "The Thrill of Defeat for Sports Fans," *New York Times Magazine*, October 21, 2011, www.nytimes.com.

**155** Kliever, "God," 42.

**156** David B. Sullivan, "Broadcast Television and the Game of Packaging Sport," in *Handbook of Sports and Media*, ed. Arthur A. Raney and Jennings Bryant (Mahwah, NJ: Lawrence Erlbaum Associates, 2006), 135.

**157** Real, "Super," 35.

**158** Novak, *The Joy*, 133.

**159** Sexton, *Baseball*, 214. See also Charles Fruehling Springwood, *Cooperstown to Dyersville: A Geography of Baseball Nostalgia* (Boulder, CO: Westview Press, 1996), 55.

**160** Daniel Dayan and Elihu Katz, *Media Events: The Live Broadcasting of History* (Cambridge, MA: Harvard University Press, 1992).

**161** Couldry, *Media*, 62.

**162** Michael J. Socolow, "Broadcast the Olympics Live. History Demands It," *Boston Globe*, August 9, 2016, www.bostonglobe.com.

**163** Couldry, *Media*, 2, 20, 27, 29, 40. See also Dayan and Katz, *Media*, 1, 15; Edward Shils and Michael Young, "The Meaning of the Coronation," *Sociological Review* 1 (1956).

**164** Couldry, *Media*, 95–97. See also Socolow, "Broadcast."

**165** Graeme Turner, "The Mass Production of Celebrity: 'Celetoids,' Reality TV and the 'Demotic Turn,'" *International Journal of Cultural Studies* 9, no. 2 (2006): 155.

**166** Joseph Epstein, "Obsessed with Sport," *Harper's*, July 1976, 15–16.

**167** Chris Dufresne, personal communication, September 11, 2015.

**168** Notable exceptions include, among others: Hutchins and Rowe, *Sport*; Vogan, *Keepers*; Travis Vogan, *ESPN: The Making of a Sports Media Empire* (Urbana: University of Illinois Press, 2015); Billings, *Olympic*; Mark Douglas Lowes, *Inside the Sports Pages: Work Routines, Professional Ideologies, and the Manufacture of Sports News* (Toronto: University of Toronto Press, 1999).

**169** Lawrence A. Wenner, "Sports and Media through the Super Glass Mirror: Placing Blame, Breast-Beating, and a Gaze to the Future," in *Handbook of Sports and Media*, ed. Arthur A. Raney and Jennings Bryant (Mahwah, NJ: Lawrence Erlbaum Associates, 2006), 46; Vogan, *Keepers*, 5.

**170** Wenner, "Sports," 55, 57. See also Alina Bernstein and Neil Blain, "Sports and the Media: The Emergence of a Major Research Field," *Culture, Sport, Society* 5, no. 3 (2002): 2.

**171** Nick Trujillo, "Machines, Missiles, and Men: Images of the Male Body on ABC's Monday Night Football," *Sociology of Sport Journal* 12 (1995): 405; Wenner, "Media," 43; Wayne Wanta, "The Coverage of Sports in Print Media," in *Handbook of Sports and Media*, ed. Arthur A. Raney and Jennings Bryant (Mahwah, NJ: Lawrence Erlbaum Associates, 2006), 113; Lowes, *Inside*, 5, 6.

**172** Steven J. Jackson, David L. Andrews, and Jay Scherer, "Introduction: The Contemporary Landscape of Sport and Advertising," in *Sport, Culture, and Advertising: Identities, Commodities and the Politics of Representation*, ed. Steven J. Jackson and David L. Andrews (New York: Routledge, 2005), 2. See also Trevor Slack and John Amis, "'Money for Nothing and Your Cheques for Free?': A Critical Perspective on Sports Sponsorship," in *The Commercialisation of Sport*, ed. Trevor Slack (London: Routledge, 2004), 270.

**173** Garry Whannel, "Between Culture and Economy: Understanding the Politics of Media Sport," in *Marxism, Cultural Studies, and Sport*, ed. Ben Carrington and Ian McDonald (New York: Routledge, 2009), 78; Sarah Gee, "'Sexual Ornament' or 'Spiritual Trainer'? Envisioning and Marketing to a Female Audience through the NHL's 'Inside the Warrior' Advertising Campaign," *Communication and Sport* 3, no. 2 (2013): 144.

**174** Sports media production studies can be especially valuable in identifying those "many taken-for-granted assumptions that are implicated in various ways in the production and reproduction of dominant ideologies." David J. Leonard, "New Media and Global Sporting Cultures: Moving Beyond the Clichés and Binaries," *Sociology of Sport Journal* 26 (2009): 11; Margaret Carlisle Duncan, "Gender Warriors in Sport: Women and the Media," in *Handbook of Sports and Media,* ed. Arthur A. Raney and Jennings Bryant (Mahwah, NJ: Lawrence Erlbaum Associates, 2006), 249; Toni Bruce, "Marking the Boundaries of the 'Normal' in Televised Sports: The Play-by-Play of Race," *Media, Culture & Society* 26, no. 6 (2004): 864.

**175** Rowe, *Sport*, 5.

**176** Laurel R. Davis, *The Swimsuit Issue and Sport: Hegemonic Masculinity and Sports Illustrated* (Albany: State University of New York Press, 1997), 32.

**177** Thomas P. Oates, "Shifting Formations: The NFL in Uncertain Times," *Popular Communication* 14, no. 1 (2016): 1. See also Vogan, *Keepers*, 1.

**178** Oates, "Shifting," 1.

**179** Michael Real outlines a set of central questions that inform the media production approach, many of which I borrow here: "Who made this cultural product or practice? Under what conditions was it created and with what purposes? Who owns the product and gains financially from its sales? How is the product distributed, and who benefits from it? Are corporate and financial interests influencing other aspects of the process? Is there a competitive environment and a level playing field among all participants?" He, moreover, links these tactical questions to those of deeper hegemonic consequence (several of which are also pursued here): "Does any special group exert decisive and distorting influence over the shape of the cultural product? Are there particular interests that are served and others that are omitted or opposed through this process of production and distribution? Are certain meanings or ideologies favored? . . . Do women, ethnic groups, workers, minorities, and other populations have a say in how they are represented in the product? . . . What measure or standards of comparison should be used to evaluate the fairness, balance, honesty, representativeness, and justice of the media culture and its products?" Real, *Exploring*, 149.

**180** Wenner, "Sports," 58.

**181** Garry Whannel, "Reflections on Communication and Sport: On Mediatization and Cultural Analysis," *Communication and Sport* 1, no. 1–2 (December 12, 2012): 15.

**182** David L. Andrews, "Michael Jordan Matters," in *Michael Jordan Inc.: Corporate Sport, Media Culture and Late Modern America*, ed. David L. Andrews (Albany: State University of New York Press, 2001), xv. See also Mary G. McDonald and Susan Birrell, "Reading Sport Critically: A Methodology for Interrogating Power," *Sociology of Sport Journal* 16 (1999): 289.

**183** David Rowe, "Media and Sport: The Cultural Dynamics of Global Games," *Sociology Compass* 3/4 (2009): 544.

**184** Rowe, *Sport*, 83.

**185** Brett Hutchins and David Rowe, "From Broadcast Scarcity to Digital Plenitude: The Changing Dynamics of the Media Sport Content Economy," *Television & New Media* 10, no. 4 (2009): 355.

**186** Hutchins and Rowe, *Sport*, 6, 15.

**187** Walter Gantz, "Keeping Score: Reflections and Suggestions for Scholarship in Sports and Media," in *Sports Media: Transformation, Integration, Consumption*, ed. Andrew C. Billings (New York: Routledge, 2011), 8; Nick Trujillo, "Reflections on Communication and Sport: On Ethnography and Organizations," *Communication and Sport* 1, no. 1–2 (December 12, 2012): 71.

**188** Raymond Boyle and Garry Whannel, "Editorial: Sport and the New Media," *Convergence* 16, no. 3 (2010): 261.

**189** Davis, *The Swimsuit*, 6; Richard Gruneau, "Making Spectacle: A Case Study in Television Sports Production," in *Media, Sports, and Society*, ed. Lawrence A. Wenner (London: Sage, 1989), 146.

**190** See appendix for the names, titles, and affiliated organizations of interviewees, as well as the date and length of our conversations.

**191** The work of David Rowe, Garry Whannel, Raymond Boyle, and Brett Hutchins, among others, has been especially instructive on sports outside the U.S. and I could have little hope of contributing much to their successes in this regard.

**192** Whannel, "Reflections," 16.

## CHAPTER 2. POWER PLAY

**1** Michael Hiestand, "Cohn's Memoir Is a Breath of Fresh Air," *USA Today*, July 3, 2008. http://usatoday30.usatoday.com; Jemele Hill, personal communication, February 27, 2016. For more extensive historical background, see also Rowe, *Sport*, 11–36; Boyle and Haynes, *Power*, 19–42; Jennings Bryant and Andrea M. Holt, "A Historical Overview of Sports and Media in the United States," in *Handbook of Sports and Media*, ed. Arthur A. Raney and Jennings Bryant (Mahwah, NJ: Lawrence Erlbaum Associates, 2006).

**2** Boyle and Haynes, *Power*, 20.

**3** Sage, *Power*, 167; Bryant and Holt, "A Historical," 25.

**4** Robert V. Bellamy, "Sports Media: A Modern Institution," in *Handbook of Sports and Media*, ed. Arthur A. Raney and Jennings Bryant (Mahwah, NJ: Lawrence Erlbaum Associates, 2006), 65; Bryant and Holt, "A Historical," 28; Vogan, *ESPN*, 72.

**5** Bellamy, "Sports," 63, 65.

**6** Whannel, *Fields*, 67.

**7** Sullivan, "Broadcast," 133.

**8** David Nylund, "When in Rome: Heterosexism, Homophobia, and Sports Talk Radio," *Journal of Sport & Social Issues* 28, no. 2 (2004): 138; David Theo Goldberg, "Call and Response: Sports, Talk Radio, and the Death of Democracy," *Journal of Sport & Social Issues* 22, no. 2 (1998): 214.

**9** Vogan, *ESPN*.

**10** Ibid., 34.

**11** Billings, "Reaction," 182–83.

**12** Robert W. McChesney, "Media Made Sport: A History of Sports Coverage in the United States," in *Media, Sports, and Society*, ed. Lawrence A. Wenner (London: Sage, 1989), 52.

**13** Sports media have also proven themselves obsequious and boosterish in cheering on the sort of stadium-building shenanigans that, as detailed in chapter 1, muster minimal economic evidence to rationalize costs, with purportedly "objective" coverage often "lifted straight from the teams' PR manuals." DeMause and Cagan, *Field*, 109. See also Sage, *Power*, 170; Lipsyte, *SportsWorld*, 25; Euchner, *Playing*, 172.

**14** Lowes, *Inside*, 11, 12.

**15** The arrangement benefits print demands as well; papers in North America devote more space to sports than any other section or subject of interest. McChesney, "Media," 64; Rowe, *Sport*, 88; Coakley, *Sports*, 409, 411.

**16** Bellamy, "Sports," 66; Rowe, *Sport*, 32; Michael Mondello, "Sports Economics and the Media," in *Handbook of Sports and Media*, ed. Arthur A. Raney and Jennings Bryant (Mahwah, NJ: Lawrence Erlbaum Associates, 2006), 280.

**17** Garry Howard, personal communication, March 2, 2016.

**18** Lowes, *Inside*, 41.

**19** Filip Bondy, personal communication, August 20, 2015.

**20** Lowes, *Inside*, xii, 36, 97, 99.

**21** Summers, "ESPN."

**22** "ESPN's Piano Man," *On The Media*, November, 6, 2015, www.onthemedia.org; Jacob S. Turner, "This Is SportsCenter: A Longitudinal Content Analysis of ESPN's Signature Television Sports-News Program from 1999 and 2009," *Journal of Sports Media* 9, no. 1 (2014), 45.

**23** Sullivan, "Broadcast," 142.

**24** John Koblin, "How ESPN Ditched Journalism and Followed Skip Bayless to the Bottom: A Tim Tebow Story," *Deadspin*, November 12, 2012, http://deadspin.com.

**25** James Andrew Miller and Ken Belson, "N.F.L. Pressure Said to Lead ESPN to Quit Film Project," *New York Times*, August 23, 2013, www.nytimes.com.

**26** Vogan, *ESPN*, 173, 174.

**27** Ibid., 117; Miller and Belson, "N.F.L."

**28** "Chat: ESPN Exec. VP John Wildhack," *ESPN.com*, n.d., http://ESPN.go.com; Josh Krulewitz, "SportsCenter's Executive Producer, Mark Gross, Discusses SC FAQs," *ESPN Front Row*, September 2012, www.ESPNfrontrow.com.

**29** Koblin, "How ESPN."

**30** Linda Cohn, personal communication, January 8, 2016.

**31** Ourand, "NBCSN."

**32** John Wildhack, personal communication, November 18, 2015.

**33** Mark Gross, personal communication, February 15, 2016; Krulewitz, "SportsCenter's."

**34** Bill Rasmussen, personal communication, September 2, 2015.

**35** "ESPN's"; Robert Lipsyte, "Serving Sports Fans through Journalism," *ESPN.com*, December 3, 2014, www.ESPN.com.

**36** Jemele Hill.

**37** Shlomo Sprung, "Michael Smith and Jemele Hill Open Up about His & Hers, The Undefeated, The Roots and Much More," *AwfulAnnouncing.com*, December 8, 2015, http://awfulannouncing.com.

**38** Jemele Hill.

**39** Diana Moskovitz, "This Is Why NFL Star Greg Hardy Was Arrested for Assaulting His Ex-Girlfriend," *Deadspin*, November 6, 2015, https://deadspin.com.

**40** Lesley Visser, personal communication, November 14, 2015.

**41** Mike Lynch, personal communication, October 6, 2015.

**42** McChesney, "Media," 60.

**43** Sarah Kustok, personal communication, February 24, 2016.

**44** Tina Cervasio, personal communication, December 8, 2015.

**45** Russ Kenn, personal communication, November 24, 2015.

**46** Wanta, "Reflections," 77.

**47** John Horne, *Sport in Consumer Culture* (New York: Palgrave Macmillan, 2006), 58.

**48** Wanta, "Reflections," 82; Vogan, *ESPN*, 71.

**49** Ben Shpigel, personal communication, August 24, 2015.

**50** Kevin Blackistone, personal communication, January 19, 2016.

**51** Bryan Curtis, "The Worst Question in Sports: What We Talk about When We Say 'Talk About,'" *Grantland*, January 22, 2015, http://grantland.com.

**52** Raymond Boyle, *Sports Journalism: Context and Issues* (London: Sage, 2006), 97.

**53** Lowes, *Inside*, 100, 101, 103, 104.

**54** Bill Rasmussen.

**55** Leitch, *God*, 188.

**56** Robert Lipsyte. See also Lipsyte, "Serving."

**57** Michael Freeman, *ESPN: The Uncensored History* (Lanham, MD: Taylor Trade, 2000), 276.

**58** John Ourand, "Networks Target Peyton Manning for On-air Role," *SportsBusiness Journal*, February 15, 2016, www.sportsbusinessdaily.com.

**59** Jemele Hill.

**60** Lipsyte, "Serving."

**61** Lowes, *Inside*, 50–53.

**62** Summers, "ESPN"; Vogan, *ESPN*, 100, 144.

**63** Gary Hoenig, personal communication, August 31, 2015.

**64** Bryan Curtis, "Bob Costas's Personality Problem," *New York Times Magazine*, February 5, 2006, www.nytimes.com; Billings, *Olympic*, 82, 83.

**65** Tina Cervasio.

**66** Whannel, *Fields*, 60, 66.

**67** Sullivan, "Broadcast," 138, 140.

**68** Boyle, *Sports*, 130.

**69** Quite unexpectedly, the results of a national survey of American sports fans that I conducted with my colleague, Emily Thorson, suggest that *audiences* might actually want it. Sixty-seven percent of respondents indicated that "journalists and broadcasters should cover teams and games objectively and impartially," as opposed to just 13 percent who want them to "cover sports like a fan" (20 percent expressed no preference).

**70** Bryan Curtis, "On the Peninsula," *Daily Beast*, April 25, 2011, www.thedailybeast.com.

**71** Will Leitch, personal communication, September 1, 2015.

**72** Wanta, "The Coverage," 105.

**73** Garry Howard.

**74** Horne, *Sport*, 50; Boyle and Haynes, *Power*, 167; Cashmore, *Making*, 386.

**75** Boyle and Haynes, *Power*, 164.

**76** Burstyn, *The Rites*, 6.

**77** Boyle, *Sports*, 4, 87.

**78** Eric Morath, "Orthodontists Earn More than CEOs: 10 Facts about Wages," *Wall Street Journal*, April 1, 2014. http://blogs.wsj.com.

**79** Kevin Blackistone.

**80** Bill Littlefield, personal communication, September 15, 2015. See also Boyle, *Sports*, 111.

**81** Gary Hoenig.

**82** Fluto Shinzawa, personal communication, August 24, 2015.

**83** Boyle, *Sports*, 115; Boyle and Haynes, *Power*, 177, 178.

**84** Mike Lynch.

**85** Lowes, *Inside*, 13, 49, 96.

**86** Marc Spears, personal communication, December 7, 2015.

**87** Bryan Curtis, "Distant Thunder: What Did Oklahoma City's Media Do to Piss Off Russell Westbrook and Kevin Durant?," *Grantland*, March 20, 2015, http://grant-land.com.

**88** Kelly Naqi.

**89** Hutchins and Rowe, *Sport*, 137.

**90** Filip Bondy.

**91** Greg Bishop.

**92** Michael Rosenberg, personal communication, September 22, 2015.

**93** Freeman, *ESPN*, 283. See also Lindsey J. Mean, "Sport, Identities, and Consumption: The Construction of Sport at ESPN.com," in *Sports Media: Transformation, Integration, Consumption*, ed. Andrew C. Billings (New York: Routledge, 2011), 172.

**94** Sarah Kustok.

**95** Kelly Naqi.

**96** Fluto Shinzawa.

**97** Robert Lipsyte.

**98** Samantha Grossman, "Top 11 Celebrity Pseudonyms," *Time*, July 23, 2013, http://content.time.com.

**99** Leitch, *God*, 5.

**100** Will Leitch.

**101** Tommy Craggs, personal communication, November 4, 2015.

**102** Curtis, "On the Peninsula"; "Here's What Gawker Media Does" *Gawker*, June 2, 2016, http://gawker.com.

**103** David Carr, "In Ray Rice Scandal, TMZ Scores on a Fumble," *New York Times*, September 14, 2014; Brian Stetler, "TMZ Plans to Expand with Sports Site," *New York Times*, December 27, 2009, www.nytimes.com.

**104** Leonard, "New," 2.

**105** Vogan, *ESPN*, 86.

**106** Serazio, *Your Ad*, 124.

**107** Tas Melas, personal communication, September 23, 2015.

**108** Will Leitch. To some extent (in an older medium), Roone Arledge, the legendary ABC Sports executive, pioneered this logic by formatting *Monday Night Football* with the fan's perspective foremost in mind. Bryant and Holt, "A Historical," 33.

**109** Vogan, *ESPN*, 73, 84, 86.

**110** Tas Melas. See also Vogan, *ESPN*, 84, 166.

**111** Marshall McLuhan, *Understanding Media: The Extensions of Man* (Cambridge, MA: MIT Press, 1994).

**112** Tim Layden, "Homer, Sweet Homer," *Sports Illustrated*, December 18, 2017, www.si.com.

**113** Will Leitch, "Buzz, Bob, Projectile Spittle and Me," *New York*, February 4, 2009, http://nymag.com.

**114** Bob Costas, personal communication, November 6, 2015.

**115** Filip Bondy; Fluto Shinzawa.

**116** Chad Finn, personal communication, September 14, 2015.

**117** Bill Rasmussen.

**118** Summers, "ESPN."

**119** John Ourand, personal communication, February 26, 2016. A similar assumption underscores the retelling of News Corp's story in the United Kingdom—that English Premier League rights were key to the ascent of its BSkyB subsidiary. Andrews, "Sport in the Late," 12.

**120** Vogan, *ESPN*; Freeman, *ESPN*, 133.

**121** Kelly Naqi.

**122** Jay Scherer and David Rowe, "Sport, Public Service Media, and Cultural Citizenship," in *Sport, Public Broadcasting, and Cultural Citizenship: Signal Lost?*, ed. Jay Scherer and David Rowe (New York: Routledge, 2014), 11; David Rowe and Jay Scherer, "Afterword: Sport, Public Service Media, and a 'Red Button,'" in Scherer and Rowe, *Sport*, 300.

**123** John Rowady; Michael McCarthy, "Why Sports Is the Ultimate Winning Play for Engagement," *Ad Age*, January 20, 2014, http://adage.com.

**124** The other 0.6 percent presumably being Pats fans reliving Super Bowl LI, which I have, somewhat bizarrely and regrettably, now experienced twice. Kurt Badenhausen, "Why ESPN Is Worth $40 Billion as the World's Most Valuable Media Property," *Forbes*, November 9, 2012, www.forbes.com.

**125** Jack Neff, "The Big Agenda: What Lies Ahead for Marketing in an Increasingly Ad-Free Future," *Ad Age*, January 11, 2016, http://adage.com.

**126** John Wildhack.

**127** Jason Gay, "A Break from 12 Months of the NFL," *Wall Street Journal*, April 2, 2015, www.wsj.com; Michael Smith and John Ourand, "The Stories behind Selection Sunday," *SportsBusiness Journal*, March 14, 2016, www.sportsbusinessdaily.com.

**128** Gary Hoenig.

**129** Dan Stanczyk, personal communication, October 7, 2015.

**130** Michael Sokolove, "How One Lawyer's Crusade Could Change Football Forever," *New York Times Magazine*, November 6, 2014, www.nytimes.com.

**131** Crupi, "Sports."

**132** Brad Brown, personal communication, March 2, 2016.

**133** Terry Lefton, personal communication, February 19, 2016.

**134** Richard Deitsch, "2017 Year in Sports Media," *Sports Illustrated*, December 18, 2017, www.si.com.

**135** Hutchins and Rowe, *Sport*, 4.

**136** Terry Lefton, "Marketers Aiming to Decipher Shifting Media, Brand Patterns," *SportsBusiness Journal*, December 11, 2017, www.sportsbusinessdaily.com.

**137** Boyle and Haynes, *Power*, 174.

**138** Wanta, "Reflections," 84.

**139** Hutchins and Rowe, "From Broadcast," 358; Hutchins and Rowe, *Sport*, 27.

**140** Gary Hoenig.

**141** Hutchins and Rowe, "From Broadcast," 354; Hutchins and Rowe, *Sport*, 9.

**142** Indeed, that policy commitment to universal access was based upon an understanding of sports' function and benefit as a "public good"; by partaking in a shared, national, non-commercial broadcast, audiences might gain the benefit of "cultural citizenship." Scherer and Rowe, "Sport," 3, 4, 14; Wenner, Bellamy, and Walker, "Selling," 78.

**143** Leigh Steinberg, personal communication, March 23, 2016.

**144** Professional leagues, particularly baseball, are increasingly also scheming the workplace "audience" as a context for sports consumption patterns by targeting them through digital multitasking devices. David Stern; Ethan Tussey, "Desktop Day Games: Workspace Media, Multitasking and the Digital Baseball Fan," in *Digital Media Sport: Technology, Power and Culture in the Network Society*, ed. Brett Hutchins and David Rowe (New York: Routledge, 2013), 41, 42.

**145** David Cornwell, personal communication, March 16, 2016.

**146** Tina Cervasio; Chris Dufresne; Russ Kenn; Doug Stewart, personal communication, January 20, 2016; Mike Lynch.

**147** Leonard, "New," 9.

**148** "Does It Measure Up?," *SportsBusiness Journal*, March 28, 2016, www.sportsbusinessdaily.com; "Forty under 40: How Is Your Generation Changing the Sports Industry?," *SportsBusiness Journal*, April 4, 2016, www.sportsbusinessdaily.com.

**149** Tim Peterson, "Facebook Introduces Live Sports Feed, but It Won't Have Ads Just Yet," *Ad Age*, January 21, 2016, http://adage.com.

**150** Walter Gantz, "Reflections on Communication and Sport: On Fanship and Social Relationships," *Communication and Sport* 1, no. 1–2 (2012): 184; Jimmy Sanderson and Jeffrey W. Kassing, "Tweets and Blogs: Transformative, Adversarial, and Integrative Developments in Sports Media," in *Sports Media: Transformation, Integration, Consumption*, ed. Andrew C. Billings (New York: Routledge, 2011), 115.

**151** Whannel, "Between," 76.

**152** Tom Schreier, "The Top 200 Ways Bleacher Report Screwed Me Over," *Deadspin*, July 22, 2014, http://deadspin.com.

**153** John Wildhack; Mean, "Sport," 173.

**154** Mark Gross; Norby Williamson, personal communication, February 29, 2016. This becomes ever truer as fans act as "sharers and sports content creators," as "pseudo sports journalists," and as "[interpreters of] mediated sports content for other fans." Paul M. Haridakis and Adam C. Earnheardt, "Understanding Fans' Consumption and Dissemination of Sports: An Introduction," in *Sports Fans, Identity, and Socialization: Exploring the Fandemonium*, ed. Adam C. Earnheardt, Paul M. Haridakis, and Barbara S. Hugenberg (Lanham, MD: Rowman & Littlefield, 2012), 4.

**155** Morry Levine, personal communication, December 18, 2015; Dave Revsine, personal communication, October 19, 2015.

**156** Tina Cervasio.

**157** Spike Eskin, personal communication, November 3, 2015.

**158** David Cornwell.

**159** Ben Shpigel.

**160** Fluto Shinzawa.

**161** Portions of this section were featured in an *International Journal of Communication* article that found similar patterns in evidence among the professional experience of political consultants. Michael Serazio, "Managing the Digital News Cyclone: Power, Participation, and Political Production Strategies," *International Journal of Communication* 9 (2015); Eric Klinenberg, "Convergence: News Production in a Digital Age," *Annals of the American Academy of Political and Social Science* 597, no. 1 (2005): 54.

**162** David D. Perlmutter, "Hypericons: Famous News Images in the Internet-Digital-Satellite Age," in *Digital Media: Transformations in Human Communication*, ed. Paul Messaris and Lee Humphreys (New York: Peter Lang, 2006).

**163** Henry Jenkins, Sam Ford, and Joshua Green, *Spreadable Media: Creating Value and Meaning in a Networked Culture* (New York: New York University Press, 2013), 12.

**164** Barry Wellman, "Computer Networks as Social Networks," *Science* 293, no. 5537 (September 14, 2001): 2034.

**165** Raymond Boyle and Richard Haynes, "Sports Journalism and Social Media: A New Conversation?," in *Digital Media Sport: Technology, Power and Culture in the Network Society*, ed. Brett Hutchins and David Rowe (New York: Routledge, 2013), 215.

**166** Horne, *Sport*, 60.

**167** Rowe, *Sport*, 112.

**168** Leigh Steinberg.

**169** David Canter, personal communication, February 15, 2016.

**170** Jemele Hill.

**171** Raymond Boyle and Richard Haynes, "New Media Sport," *Culture, Sport, Society* 5, no. 3 (2002): 96.

**172** Boyle and Haynes, *Power*, 206.

**173** Greg Bishop. Some caution is warranted when hearing tales of the chilled-out "good old days" as contrasted with the frantic present. More than 20 years ago, during his ethnography of a Canadian newspaper's sports page, scholar Mark Lowes "repeatedly" observed the "hectic pace" and "organized chaos" of the newsroom and "a general lack of time" felt by employees there. Our nostalgia tends to often imagine a (subjectively) slower past. Lowes, *Inside*, 26, 30.

**174** Michael Rosenberg.

**175** Jenkins, Ford, and Green, *Spreadable*.

**176** Tina Cervasio.

**177** John Ourand, "ESPN: Van Pelt 'SportsCenter' on Course despite Flat Ratings," *SportsBusiness Journal*, December 7, 2015, www.sportsbusinessdaily.com.

**178** John Ourand, "The Future? Look to Apps, Live-Streaming and Digital Media Firms," *SportsBusiness Journal*, February 29, 2016, www.sportsbusinessdaily.com.

**179** Christopher Clarey, "Every Second Counts in Bid to Keep Sports Fans," *New York Times*, February 28, 2015, www.nytimes.com.

**180** Richard Sandomir, "The Whistle Hopes to Be Sports Media Destination for Children," *New York Times*, January 31, 2012, www.nytimes.com.

**181** Bonnie Bernstein.

**182** Boyle and Haynes, "New," 104.

**183** Ben Volin, "NFL's Twitter Deal Is a Nod to the Future," *Boston Globe*, April 5, 2016, www.bostonglobe.com; John Ourand, "The Eyes Have It," *SportsBusiness Journal*, January 11, 2016, www.sportsbusinessdaily.com.

**184** Hutchins and Rowe, *Sport*, 1, 2; Hutchins and Rowe, "From Broadcast," 355.

**185** Boyle and Haynes, *Power*, 217.

**186** Ian Thomas, "Instagram Sees Itself as Part of Big Picture for Teams, Leagues," *SportsBusiness Journal*, July 11, 2016, www.sportsbusinessdaily.com.

**187** Andrew T. Warren, "What Benefits Do Leagues See by Blocking Content on Twitter?," *SportsBusiness Journal*, September 19, 2016, www.sportsbusinessdaily.com. As one scholar discerns, this is largely about image control: "The tight grip on recorded game content enables the NFL and its partner sports media producers to suppress unpopular, nonconforming narratives for the sake of maintaining a consistent, mainstream (therefore conservative) narrative about itself." Further to that end, the NFL began in 2009 prohibiting even *players* from using social media for 90 minutes before, during, and after games. Jacob Dittmer, "The Ochocinco Brand: Social Media's Impact on the NFL's Institutional Control," in *The NFL: Critical and Cultural Perspectives*, ed. Thomas P. Oates and Zack Furness (Philadelphia: Temple University Press, 2014), 65, 68–69.

**188** David Stern.

**189** By 2018, only the NBA was seen as immune to this "television ratings trend." Ourand, Karp, and Kaplan, "Time?"; John Lombardo and John Ourand, "NBA Beats Odds, Sees Gain in Local Ratings," *SportsBusiness Journal*, February 19, 2018, www.sportsbusinessdaily.com.

**190** Derek Thompson, "How Superstar Economics Is Killing the NFL's Ratings," *Atlantic*, January 10, 2017, www.theatlantic.com.

**191** Phillips and Rovell, "Examining."

**192** Dave Revsine.

**193** Lia Stierwalt, personal communication, March 21, 2016.

**194** John Ourand; Ed Desser, "Handicapping the Netflix of Sports: Win, Place, Show, Scratch," *SportsBusiness Journal*, March 28, 2016, www.sportsbusinessdaily.com.

**195** Volin, "NFL's Twitter"; John Ourand, "Five Things to Know about NFL-Amazon," *SportsBusiness Journal*, April 10, 2017, www.sportsbusinessdaily.com.

**196** Stan Ketterer, John McGuire, and Ray Murray, "Contrasting Desired Sports Journalism Skills in a Convergent Media Environment," *Communication and Sport* 2, no. 3 (2013): 283, 290.

**197** Bonnie Bernstein.

**198** Boyle and Haynes, "Sports," 204.

**199** Hutchins and Rowe, *Sport*, 126.

**200** Greg Bishop; Michael Rosenberg.

**201** Chris Dufresne.

**202** That said, Dufresne himself took a buyout shortly after this interview was conducted.

**203** Marc Spears.

**204** Tommy Craggs.

**205** Filip Bondy.

**206** John Ourand, "'Now, Everybody in My Newsroom Is on Television,'" *SportsBusiness Journal*, February 29, 2016, www.sportsbusinessdaily.com; Boyle and Haynes, "Sports," 208.

**207** Bonnie Bernstein.

**208** Leitch, *God*, 151.

**209** Kevin Blackistone.

**210** Hutchins and Rowe, *Sport*, 126.

**211** Sullivan, "Broadcast," 137.

**212** Wann et al., *Sport*, 15–16.

**213** Spike Eskin.

**214** Dan Stanczyk.

**215** Spike Eskin.

**216** Dan Stanczyk.

**217** Bonnie Bernstein.

**218** "Chat"; Linda Cohn.

**219** For Cohn, the team as a totemic vessel of unity and worship informs her willingness to abandon objective pretense (albeit not in so explicitly Durkheimian terms): "I've always been proud of the fact that I'm a fan first. You have to remember most of my viewers on *SportsCenter* are sports fans to their respective beloved teams. Just like me. I felt it was another way I could connect with them. To make it known I know what it's like to suffer a heartbreaking loss or an exhilarating win." Jeff Pearlman, "Linda Cohn," *JeffPearlman.com*, 2015, www.jeffpearlman.com.

**220** Bill Rasmussen.

**221** Mark Gross; Vogan, *ESPN*, 96, 98.

**222** Leitch, *God*, 155, 161, 186.

**223** Kevin Blackistone.

**224** Leitch, *God*, 151.

**225** Dan Stanczyk.

**226** Michael Rosenberg.

**227** Robert Lipsyte, "Goodbye to Grantland, ESPN's Home for Actual Sports Journalism," *Nation*, November 2, 2015, www.thenation.com.

**228** Bonnie Bernstein.

**229** Turner, "This Is SportsCenter," 62–64.

**230** There is some historical precedence for one sports medium's emergence redrawing the mandate for and format of cultural production in an earlier, now-displaced alternative: When radio came along in the 1920s, newspapers—robbed of their news advantage and "immediacy"—increasingly turned to strategic analysis and personality-driven coverage. The internet may be forcing a similar reorientation of television today. Ourand, "ESPN: Van Pelt"; John Ourand, "ESPN Pushes Back on Negative Critiques of 'SportsCenter,'" *SportsBusiness Journal*, April 25, 2016, www.sportsbusinessdaily.com; Bryant and Holt, "A Historical," 31; Anthony Crupi, "Now This Is SportsCenter," *Ad Age*, April 3, 2017, http://adage.com.

**231** Ben Mathis-Lilley, "Fox Sports 1 Is Amazing! Awful! Fantastic! Execrable!," *Slate*, March 26, 2017, www.slate.com.

**232** John Ourand, "NFL's Twitter 'Experiment' a Glimpse into Sports Media's Future," *SportsBusiness Journal*, October 17, 2016, www.sportsbusinessdaily.com.

**233** Mike Lynch.

**234** Chris Dufresne.

**235** Mark Gross.

**236** Hutchins and Rowe, *Sport*, 141.

**237** Ben Shpigel.

**238** Michael Rosenberg.

**239** As sports media scholar Andrew Billings cautions, however, Twitter is not representative of the public and its role as a gauge for nationwide sentiment can often be "overstated." Nonetheless, the profusion of elite gatekeepers participating there means that it *can* contribute to setting the media agenda. Andrew C. Billings, "Power in the Reverberation: Why Twitter Matters, but Not the Way Most Believe," *Communication & Sport* 2, no. 2 (2014).

**240** Dave Revsine.

**241** Kelly Naqi.

**242** Natalie Jomini Stroud, *Niche News: The Politics of News Choice* (Oxford: Oxford University Press, 2011).

**243** John Wildhack.

**244** Mark Gross.

**245** Richard Deitsch, "An In-Depth Look at ESPN Audio and the Future of Sports Talk Radio," *Sports Illustrated*, May 3, 2015, www.si.com.

**246** Adelle Platon, "Meet the Power Couple Tackling the Culture at ESPN's 'His & Hers,'" *Vibe*, October 21, 2015, www.vibe.com.

**247** Ivan Maisel, personal communication, August 11, 2015.

**248** Schreier, "The Top."

**249** John Wildhack. ·

**250** Chad Finn.

**251** Doug Stewart; "Chat."

**252** Dan Stanczyk.

**253** Norby Williamson.

**254** Mark Gross.

**255** In his interviews with NBC sports executives, sports media scholar Andrew Billings heard much the same deference in claims that Olympic programming strategy was driven by reacting to viewer desire rather than an acknowledged agenda-setting power. Billings, *Olympic*, 36.

**256** Jemele Hill.

**257** John Ourand, "The Moves That Forced ESPN's Cuts," *SportsBusiness Journal*, October 26, 2015, www.sportsbusinessdaily.com.

**258** Two other factors have conspired against ESPN: Those rights deals extending along a longer timeline—from three to five years in the 1980s and 1990s to the (more expensive and less flexible) 10-to-15-year contemporary norm—and NBC and Fox launching cable competitors hungry to bid up those rights to "stratospheric levels" in the early part of the decade. John Ourand, "Inside the ESPN Layoffs and Pay Cuts— and What It Means for TV Sports," *SportsBusiness Journal*, May 4, 2017, www. bizjournals.com; Amsden, "Fox."

**259** Deitsch, "2017."

**260** John Ourand, "Taking the Pulse of ESPN," *SportsBusiness Journal*, June 26, 2017, www.sportsbusinessdaily.com.

**261** Dick Young, "Jackie Robinson, the 1st Black MLB Player, Retires in 1957," *New York Daily News*, January 8, 1957, www.nydailynews.com; Vogan, *Keepers*, 1.

**262** Lesley Visser.

**263** Lipsyte, "Serving."

**264** Chad Finn.

**265** Chris Dufresne.

**266** Sanderson and Kassing, "Tweets," 115.

**267** Ibid., 116; Chris Dufresne; Chad Finn.

**268** Kim McConnie, personal communication, June 1, 2016.

**269** Nina Mandell, "Steph Curry's College Roommate Made Him a New Social Media Platform," *USA Today*, March 1, 2016, http://ftw.usatoday.com. Additionally, whereas before players had to go through the press to get their message out, now they can deliver it "unfiltered" to fans, which, as *Outside the Lines*' Kelly Naqi observes, "Then they have the good fortune of saying, 'I have already addressed it [online]—I want to move on,' even though they haven't addressed it." Kelly Naqi.

**270** Ira Brasen, "Is That an Ad or a News Story—and Does It Matter Which?," *Globe and Mail*, August 3, 2012, https://beta.theglobeandmail.com.

**271** John Ourand, "Dolphins Plow Marketing Budget into Content and Get Results," *SportsBusiness Journal*, March 27, 2017, www.sportsbusinessdaily.com; Serazio, *Your Ad*.

**272** Michael Smith, "Colleges Migrating to Facebook Live," *SportsBusiness Journal*, March 20, 2017, www.sportsbusinessdaily.com.

**273** Hussain Naqi, personal communication, March 30, 2016.

**274** Dave Revsine.

**275** Garry Howard.

**276** Oates, "Shifting," 1. See also Boyle and Haynes, "New," 110.

**277** Terry Lefton.

**278** Richard Sandomir, "Athletes Finding Their Voice in Derek Jeter's Digital Venture," *New York Times*, March 28, 2015, www.nytimes.com.

**279** Alex Silverman, "Sports Business Awards: The Players' Tribune Wins Sports Breakthrough of the Year," *SportsBusiness Journal*, May 19, 2016, www.sportsbusinessdaily.com; Sandomir, "Athletes."

**280** "Derek Jeter Gets Back to Work."

**281** Gary Hoenig.

**282** Ben Shpigel.

**283** Curtis, "Distant?" Filip Bondy of *The New York Daily News* complains about a related behind-the-scenes problem: The team-affiliated TV networks "basically took our interviews public." By this, he means that print reporters might lob the tougher questions in the locker room after the game but can't publish the responses faster than that footage would already be broadcast: "They're having it both ways. Their reporters look like good guys, 'cause they don't ask the questions and then when we ask the tough questions, it's aired hours before we get it into print. . . . They've completely neutralized our interviews in that fashion by basically stealing our stuff." Filip Bondy.

**284** Garry Howard.

**285** Sam Borden, "English Club Shuts Out Journalists with New Kind of Defense," *New York Times*, August 4, 2015, www.nytimes.com.

**286** Ben Shpigel.

**287** Fluto Shinzawa.

**288** Some might counter that lumping together such a wide range of sports media professionals—from the biting print columnist at a daily newspaper to the deferential former player on an expert panel for a team-owned network—stretches too far the banner of a singular "journalism" identity to hold all equally accountable to a common set of standards and ideals. That's a fair rejoinder—and the former would surely disavow the latter's kinship—but I would question whether audiences *themselves* make the distinction that they're not all "journalists" alike.

**289** Coakley, *Sports*, 432.

**290** Sports journalism has evocatively been described as a "leaking craft" for precisely that reason. Boyle and Haynes, "Sports," 207.

## CHAPTER 3. FEVER PITCH

**1** Boyle and Haynes, *Power*, 93; Whannel, *Culture*, 123. I follow sport scholar Michael Real's helpful definition of commodification here: reducing "the value of any act or object only to its monetary exchange value, ignoring historical, artistic, or relational added values." Real, "The Postmodern," 15. See also Walsh and Giulianotti, "This Sporting," 55; Crawford, *Consuming*, 5.

**2** Andrews, "Sport in the Late," 3.

**3** Sut Jhally, "Cultural Studies and the Sports/Media Complex," in *Media, Sports, and Society*, ed. Lawrence A. Wenner (London: Sage, 1989), 80.

**4** McChesney, "Media," 50.

**5** Horne, *Sport*, 76; Houlihan, *Sport*, 163.

**6** Houlihan, *Sport*, 152, 153.

**7** Lawrence A. Wenner, "The Dream Team, Communicative Dirt, and the Marketing of Synergy: USA Basketball and Cross-Merchandising in Television Commercials," *Journal of Sport & Social Issues* 18, no. 1 (1994): 29.

**8** Horne, *Sport*, 21; Wenner, Bellamy, and Walker, "Selling," 80.

**9** Bellamy, "Sports," 65.

**10** Boyle and Haynes, *Power*, 43, 48, 49; Lance Kinney, "Sports Sponsorship," in *Handbook of Sports and Media*, ed. Arthur A. Raney and Jennings Bryant (Mahwah, NJ: Lawrence Erlbaum Associates, 2006), 295.

**11** Horne, *Sport*, 89; Terry Lefton, "Naming-Rights Market Finds More Takers," *SportsBusiness Journal*, February 22, 2016, www.sportsbusinessdaily.com.

**12** Cashmore, *Making*, 401.

**13** Leibovitch, "Roger"; Freeman, *ESPN*, 4.

**14** Rowe, "Media," 546.

**15** Rader, *In Its Own*, 140.

**16** Real, "MediaSport," 16.

**17** For this reason, some have quipped that ESPN "controls" sports as much as it covers them. Whannel, *Culture*, 77; Whannel, *Fields*, 95; Vogan, *ESPN*, 41.

**18** Brad Brown.

**19** Terry Lefton.

**20** "Mike Serazio and Filip Bondy Talk about Sports, the Business of Sports, and Pesky Team Logo," *Annenberg NewsLink*, 2013, https://www.asc.upenn.edu.

**21** Horne, *Sport*, 54; Joe Maguire, "The Media-Sport Production Complex: The Case of American Football in Western European Societies," *European Journal of Communication* 6 (1991): 318; McChesney, "Media," 65.

**22** Boyle and Haynes, *Power*, 94.

**23** Lipsyte, *SportsWorld*, xi; Horne, *Sport*, 60.

**24** Steven J. Jackson, Richard Batty, and Jay Scherer, "Transnational Sport Marketing at the Global/local Nexus: The Adidasification of the New Zealand All

Blacks," *International Journal of Sports Marketing and Sponsorship* 3, no. 2 (2001): 186; Boyle and Haynes, *Power*, 72.

**25** Clarey, "Every."

**26** John Rowady.

**27** Eric M. Leifer, *Making the Majors: The Transformation of Team Sports in America* (Cambridge, MA: Harvard University Press, 1995), 7, 17.

**28** John Ourand, "With Buyouts, Fox Sports Communications Losing Familiar Names," *SportsBusiness Journal*, May 16, 2016, www.sportsbusinessdaily.com.

**29** Thomas J. Moskowitz and L. Jon Wertheim, *Scorecasting: The Hidden Influences behind How Sports Are Played and Games Are Won* (New York: Crown, 2011), 15.

**30** A. J. Maestas.

**31** Ben Fischer and Terry Lefton, "World Congress of Sports: Don't Panic," *SportsBusiness Journal*, April 24, 2017, www.sportsbusinessdaily.com.

**32** John Lombardo and David Broughton, "Going Gray: Sports TV Viewers Skew Older," *SportsBusiness Journal*, June 5, 2017, www.sportsbusinessdaily.com.

**33** Rich Luker, "Cold Reality: Growth No Longer Uncontested," *SportsBusiness Journal*, November 21, 2016, www.sportsbusinessdaily.com.

**34** Anthony Crupi, "Gen Z Punts on the NFL," *Ad Age*, January 24, 2018. http://adage.com. A rebuttal to these fears counters with data showing no difference in fandom between millennials and Generation X for basketball, soccer, college sports, and mixed-martial arts and further attributes the TV-watching gap to most millennials having not yet become parents (which predicts a higher rate of traditional viewing) and also streaming sports, often illegally, at almost twice the rate of their predecessors. Dan Singer, "We Are Wrong about Millennials; They ARE Sports Fans," *SportsBusiness Journal*, September 18, 2017, www.sportsbusinessdaily.com.

**35** Terry Lefton, "Plugged In: Joao Chueiri, A-B InBev," *SportsBusiness Journal*, May 8, 2017, www.sportsbusinessdaily.com. It is ironic, however, to take note of the hand-wringing, back in the *1960s*, that baseball was too slow for "modern" TV attentions, when average game length had then swollen to two-and-a-half hours from its 90-minute norm a few decades prior. Rader, *In Its Own*, 142.

**36** Mark Lev, personal communication, July 22, 2015.

**37** Sullivan, "Broadcast," 137.

**38** Tripp Mickle, "Industry Looks for Right Recipe to Attract Fans among Millennials," *SportsBusiness Journal*, March 24, 2014, www.sportsbusinessdaily.com.

**39** Bill Sutton, "Why Rich Luker and His Insights Keep Me Awake at Night," *SportsBusiness Journal*, October 17, 2016, www.sportsbusinessdaily.com.

**40** Clarey, "Every."

**41** Daniel Kaplan, "Football: Changing Pace," *SportsBusiness Journal*, April 17, 2017, www.sportsbusinessdaily.com.

**42** Russ Kenn.

**43** When it comes to college football, for example, ESPN's stated goal is the "breakfast-to-bedtime fan": Ideally, says one vice president for programming, "have fans sit down in the morning, watch 'College GameDay' and really not be satisfied until the last game, usually from the Pac-12, at the end of the night and into 'SportsCenter.'" Miller, Eder, and Sandomir, "College."

**44** Bill Rasmussen. The perils at the college level in terms of commercialization could occupy a library shelf worth of books rather than the mere footnote here. Suffice to say, those fundamental ideals upon which college sports are theoretically based—"amateurism, education, and not-for-profit status"—often run aground of the reality that "big-time college sport [functions] instead as the booking agents for mass-mediated spectacle while relying on an invisible and unnamed workforce." Ellen J. Staurowsky, "Piercing the Veil of Amateurism: Commercialisation, Corruption and US College Sports," in *The Commercialisation of Sport*, ed. Trevor Slack (London: Routledge, 2004), 143-144, 145.

**45** The bowl season bloat, nonetheless, seems to benefit all parties in that it fills out airtime with low-cost programming and bestows (albeit ever-diminishing) prestige on invitees. Miller, Eder, and Sandomir, "College."

**46** Additionally, Dick Ebersol, head of NBC Sports, lobbied the Chinese Olympic Committee to bump up the 2008 Beijing Games from September to August, so as to avoid football season and baseball pennant race competition for U.S. audiences. John Ourand; Richard Sandomir, "Before Ball Dropped, So Did Viewership of College Football Playoff Semifinals," *New York Times*, January 1, 2016, www.nytimes.com; Markovits and Rensmann, *Gaming*, 125.

**47** John Ourand, "Is Oversaturation Hurting Ratings?," *SportsBusiness Journal*, October 23, 2017, www.sportsbusinessdaily.com.

**48** Hussain Naqi.

**49** Daniel J. Boorstin, *The Image*, 25th anniv. ed. (New York: Vintage, 1992); Gay, "A Break."

**50** John Ourand.

**51** Matthew P. McAllister, *The Commercialization of American Culture: New Advertising, Control and Democracy* (Thousand Oaks, CA: Sage, 1996), 85.

**52** My first book, *Your Ad Here: The Cool Sell of Guerrilla Marketing*, explored this phenomenon in greater detail and portions of this section have been borrowed from it. Serazio, *Your Ad*.

**53** Ibid., 13–14, 16–17.

**54** Bob Costas.

**55** Chris Dufresne.

**56** Brad Brown.

**57** Norby Williamson.

**58** John Ourand, "Fox's Six-Second Ad Decision: How Many to Run?," *SportsBusiness Journal*, December 18, 2017, www.sportsbusinessdaily.com.

**59** Gary Hoenig.

**60** Mike Lynch. In 2014, *The Washington Times* announced a similarly unseemly "content and marketing partnership" with the hometown Redskins whereby the newspaper traded for special access to team personnel in exchange for lending its reporters to in-game scoreboard video features and publishing sponsored content from the franchise. Benjamin Freed, "The Washington Times and the Redskins Are Now 'Content Partners,'" *Washingtonian*, July 28, 2014, www.washingtonian.com.

**61** Bob Dorfman, personal communication, February 26, 2015; Mark Lev.

**62** Dave Revsine.

**63** David Stern.

**64** Freeman, *ESPN*, 24, 93.

**65** Mark Gross.

**66** Dave Revsine.

**67** Miller, Eder, and Sandomir, "College."

**68** Chad Finn; John Ourand and Terry Lefton, "Daily Fantasy Ad Buys Make NFL a Big Winner," *SportsBusiness Journal*, September 14, 2015, www.sportsbusinessdaily.com.

**69** Turner, "This Is SportsCenter," 45.

**70** Russ Kenn. Social media companies are also deploying "live-event tools" for advertisers that give them the opportunity to wrap brand messages "more tightly around the real-time conversation" that often takes place there during sporting events. Facebook can, for example, segment and target clusters of self-identified football fans (based upon status updates and likes) during the hours of big weekend games. Sydney Ember, "Marketing to Sports Fans Online, with Help from Google and Social Networks," *New York Times*, September 8, 2015, www.nytimes.com.

**71** Morry Levine.

**72** Garry Howard.

**73** Nat Ives, "DirecTV's 'Don't Be like This' Push Wraps Sports Illustrated in Freakish Versions of NFL QBs," *Ad Age*, September 2, 2015. http://adage.com.

**74** Tommy Craggs.

**75** See chapter 2 of my first book, *Your Ad Here*, for expanded detail. Serazio, *Your Ad*.

**76** David Wright, personal communication, May 2, 2016.

**77** Bob Dorfman.

**78** Andrew Joseph, "Blake Griffin Was Told That He Had to Jump Over a Kia in the 2011 Dunk Contest," *USA Today*, June 6, 2016, http://ftw.usatoday.com.

**79** John Rowady.

**80** Terry Lefton; Jeff Eccleston, "Technology Adds Critical Value along Its Path of Disruption," *SportsBusiness Journal*, November 13, 2017, www.sportsbusinessdaily.com.

**81** Michael Smith, "Sponsor Offers the Climb That Teams Dream Of," *SportsBusiness Journal*, April 11, 2016, www.sportsbusinessdaily.com.

**82** Rick Burton and Norm O'Reilly, "How Fan, Sponsor Reactions Factor into Team Decisions," *SportsBusiness Journal*, December 10, 2012, www.sportsbusiness-daily.com.

**83** According to one survey, 42 percent of soccer fans confirm that their purchases are swayed by the brand logos that appear on player jerseys—a slightly higher figure than NASCAR fan respondents. Broughton, "New," 10.

**84** Dan Lobring, "A Month without DVR's—Why Marketers Love February," *MediaPost*, February 3, 2016, www.mediapost.com; Terry Lefton and John Lombardo, "Will Jersey Ads Bring Big Bucks?," *SportsBusiness Journal*, April 25, 2016, www.sportsbusinessdaily.com; John Lombardo, "NBA Begins New Season Flush with Cash as Revenue Expected to Hit $8B," *SportsBusiness Journal*, October 24, 2016, www.sportsbusinessdaily.com.

**85** Jeffrey A. Citron, "Jersey Ads Are Low-Hanging Fruit for the NHL," *SportsBusiness Journal*, October 30, 2017, www.sportsbusinessdaily.com.

**86** Terry Lefton, "Movement toward Content Changes Strategy for Sponsors," *SportsBusiness Journal*, October 30, 2017, www.sportsbusinessdaily.com.

**87** E. J. Schultz, "What the NBA's G-League Deal Means for Sports Marketing," *Ad Age*, February 15, 2017, http://adage.com.

**88** "The Jump," *ESPN.com*, 2016, www.ESPN.com.

**89** Serazio, *Your Ad*, 7, 9.

**90** Bill Rasmussen.

**91** Tas Melas; Doug Stewart.

**92** See chapters 4 and 5 of my first book, *Your Ad Here*, for expanded detail. Serazio, *Your Ad*.

**93** Spike Eskin.

**94** Filip Bondy; Boyle, *Sports*, 118.

**95** Terry Lefton, "Leaving a Lasting Impression," *SportsBusiness Journal*, October 17, 2016, www.sportsbusinessdaily.com; Chris Elkins, "Celebrities Team with Big Pharma to Promote Drugs, Disease Awareness," Drugwatch, November 9, 2015, www.drugwatch.com.

**96** "Untenable" if you've ever actually consumed a Bud Light. Eben Novy-Williams, "Peyton Manning Just Gave Budweiser $14 Million in Free Ads," *Bloomberg*, February 8, 2016, www.bloomberg.com.

**97** Mark Gross.

**98** David Wright; Terry Lefton, "Atlantic League Preparing a Visual Feast behind the Plate," *SportsBusiness Journal*, April 18, 2016, www.sportsbusinessdaily.com; "The 2013 Guide to Optimizing Your Sports Sponsorship Portfolio," 2013, *rEvolution* (blog), http://blog.revolutionworld.com; Eric Fisher, "DraftKings Strategy Focuses on Content," *SportsBusiness Journal*, April 18, 2016, www.sportsbusinessdaily.com.

**99** Terry Lefton, "At $30M a Year, Will AT&T Mobilize for Inglewood Stadium?," *SportsBusiness Journal*, May 1, 2017, www.sportsbusinessdaily.com.

**100** Matthew P. McAllister, "College Bowl Sponsorship and the Increased Commercialization of Amateur Sports," *Critical Studies in Mass Communication*, no. 15 (1998): 371.

**101** David Wright.

**102** Lefton, "Movement."

**103** Ben Strauss, "Advertisement Makes Fans' Dreams a Reality."

**104** Lia Stierwalt.

**105** Mark J. Burns, "100+ Sports Business Professionals Discuss Hot Topics, Bold Predictions for 2016," *Forbes*, January 5, 2016, www.forbes.com.

**106** E. J. Schultz, "Hip-Hop and Golf? How Callaway Is Swinging for Millennials," *Ad Age*, August 15, 2016, http://adage.com.

**107** Derrick Heggans, "Why Leagues Connect to Entertainment World," *SportsBusiness Journal*, July 15, 2013, www.sportsbusinessdaily.com.

**108** Jeffrey Montez de Oca, Brandon Meyer, and Jeffrey Scholes, "Reaching the Kids: NFL Youth Marketing and Media," *Popular Communication* 14, no. 1 (2016): 5.

**109** Richard A. Oppel Jr. and Felicity Barringer, "Los Angeles Times Staff Protest Magazine Deal," *New York Times*, October 28, 1999, www.nytimes.com.

**110** Dave Revsine.

**111** Mike Lynch.

**112** Greg Bishop.

**113** Abby Ohlheiser, "Top Gawker Editors Resign after Controversial Story's Removal," *Washington Post*, July 20, 2015, www.washingtonpost.com.

**114** Ivan Maisel. Maisel was not the only interviewee to emphasize the (imagined) savvy of his audiences as license and cover to blend advertiser copy into editorial output; an executive at his network made much the same case. "If we're doing a segment on Steph Curry and all of a sudden, this particular company wants to come in and sponsor that unique analytical assessment of Steph Curry—they're in there with a billboard attach—as long as you're transparent with your audience, that this company is sponsoring the content, I don't have a problem with that," says Norby Williamson. "I think viewers and customers have become much more savvy about that throughout the years. They understand what you're doing. They understand the business model." As I discovered in research for *Your Ad Here*, it is common to make this claim about audience perceptiveness when engaging in schemes that hide the advertiser message among less commercially obvious content. Norby Williamson; Serazio, *Your Ad*.

**115** Bob Costas.

**116** Russ Kenn.

**117** Jemele Hill.

**118** Tina Cervasio.

**119** Ivan Maisel.

**120** Michael Rosenberg.

**121** P. David Marshall, *Celebrity and Power: Fame in Contemporary Culture* (Minneapolis: University of Minnesota Press, 1997).

**122** Boorstin, *The Image*, 45–76.

**123** Whannel, *Fields*, 124.

**124** Andrews and Jackson, "Introduction," 8.

**125** Richard DeCordova, *Picture Personalities: The Emergence of the Star System in America* (Urbana: University of Illinois Press, 1990).

**126** Whannel, *Media*, 31; Whannel, *Fields*, 122.

**127** David Wright.

**128** Andrews and Jackson, "Introduction," 6, 7.

**129** Whannel, *Media*, 34.

**130** Marc Spears; Terry Lefton.

**131** Danny Ecker, "The Challenge of Marketing a Losing Team," *Crain's Chicago Business*, October 31, 2015, www.chicagobusiness.com.

**132** Thompson, "How Superstar."

**133** Whannel, *Fields*, 77.

**134** David Wright.

**135** Ian Thomas, "MLS Updates Media, Player Access Policies," *SportsBusiness Journal*, May 1, 2017, www.sportsbusinessdaily.com.

**136** Ibid.

**137** Marc Spears.

**138** Thompson, "The Global."

**139** Slack and Amis, "'Money,'" 274.

**140** A. J. Maestas.

**141** Andrews and Jackson, "Introduction," xiii. See also Kellner, "The Sports," 46.

**142** Bill Sutton, "Carnival Atmosphere Keeps Big Baller Brand in the Spotlight," *SportsBusiness Journal*, May 22, 2017, www.sportsbusinessdaily.com.

**143** Leigh Steinberg; Ken Belson, "A Battle for Eyes Is Waged via New N.F.L. Players' Ears," *New York Times*, May 1, 2015, www.nytimes.com.

**144** Whannel, *Media*, 49.

**145** Andrews and Jackson, "Introduction," 7; Cieply and Barnes, "Rivalry."

**146** Boyle and Haynes, *Power*, 88.

**147** Bob Dorfman.

**148** Kim McConnie.

149 Cashmore, *Making*, 425.

150 "Borders Sees Social Media as Key to Raising Profile."

151 Bob Dorfman.

152 Rowe, "Sports Media," 101.

153 Dittmer, "The Ochocinco," 74.

154 John Ourand, "Media: Connecting to the Next Generation," *SportsBusiness Journal*, April 17, 2017, www.sportsbusinessdaily.com.

155 Ian Thomas, "NBC Turns 'Summit' Spotlight on NHL," *SportsBusiness Journal*, September 11, 2017, www.sportsbusinessdaily.com.

156 David Stern.

157 Jemele Hill, "The Mailbag: Cam Newton and 'Rocky,'" *ESPN.com*, September 15, 2011, www.ESPN.com.

158 Marc Spears.

159 David Stern.

160 Horne et al., *Understanding*, 102.

161 Michael Rosenberg.

162 Tas Melas.

163 Tim Baysinger, "How Russell Westbrook, NBA Renaissance Man, Is Redefining the Role of Spokesman," *Adweek*, January 26, 2016, www.adweek.com.

164 Christina Cauterucci, "Russell Westbrook Is Turning the NBA Playoffs into a Personal Runaway Show," *Slate*, May 10, 2016, www.slate.com.

165 Kim McConnie.

166 Similar to Stephen Curry's co-founding the social media start-up Slyce (mentioned in chapter 2), LeBron James locked down $16 million from Time Warner for a *Players' Tribune*–style, multi-platform content startup. Burns, "100+ Sports."

167 Chris Dufresne.

168 Liz Mullen, "Agents Finding Deals via Twitter Evolution," *SportsBusiness Journal*, March 28, 2016, www.sportsbusinessdaily.com.

169 Ben Fischer, "NBC Executives Detail Comprehensive Plans for Rio," *SportsBusiness Journal*, May 23, 2016, www.sportsbusinessdaily.com. See also Boyle and Haynes, "Sports," 211.

170 Leigh Steinberg.

171 David Canter.

172 Marty Swant, "5 U.S. Olympians You Should Follow on Social Media during the Summer Games," *Adweek*, June 28, 2016, www.adweek.com; "Case Study: Measuring Value in Social Media Posts for Bose, Kia," *SportsBusiness Journal*, March 28, 2016, www.sportsbusinessdaily.com.

173 "Plugged in: Ty Jones, WhoSay," *SportsBusiness Journal*, April 4, 2016, www.sportsbusinessdaily.com. When asked about the best marriages between corporate brands and athlete endorsers, Brad Brown, former vice president of sports and entertainment marketing for Anheuser-Busch, evokes a similar ideal: "You try to get them in a very relaxed state," he says. "Even if it's an ad. . . . If you can get to the point where it's in a natural setting for them, you're not asking them to be somebody that they're not. . . . Your end product is 99.9 percent of the time so much better than if you put them in a forced situation." Brad Brown.

174 Lia Stierwalt.

175 Jason Norcross, personal communication, February 3, 2016.

**176** Liz Mullen, "Firm's Digital Division Offers Social Media Posts from Athletes," *SportsBusiness Journal*, October 9, 2017, www.sportsbusinessdaily.com.

**177** Indeed, if para-social relationships were once "unilateral" and, for that matter, incidental, they seem to be becoming more "part of the celeb's job definition" in an engagement-defined digital era. Sanderson and Kassing, "Tweets," 122; Cashmore, *Making*, 455.

**178** Whannel, *Fields*, 135.

**179** Jason Norcross; John Rowady.

**180** Crawford, *Consuming*, 81.

**181** Rowe, *Sport*, 73.

**182** Sullivan, "Broadcast," 139.

**183** A. J. Maestas.

**184** Dan Gadd, "Who Tells Your Story? Why Getting Personal Is Key to Great Content," *SportsBusiness Journal*, July 11, 2016, www.sportsbusinessdaily.com.

**185** Crawford, *Consuming*, 113.

**186** Sandvoss, *A Game*, 17, 27.

**187** Mean, "Sport," 163.

**188** Ron Bishop, "Stealing the Signs: A Semiotic Analysis of the Changing Nature of Professional Sports Logos," *Social Semiotics* 11, no. 1 (2001): 25, 32.

**189** Leifer, *Making*, 284; Hagood and Vogan, "The 12th," 32.

**190** "Instant Caps Fans at MedStar, Sports Business Journal, April 25, 2016, www.sportsbusinessdaily.com."

**191** "Stadium Design and Features, https:www.whufc.com."

**192** Mark Lev.

**193** Celia Lury, *Brands: The Logos of the Global Economy* (London: Routledge, 2004); Adam Arvidsson, "Brands: A Critical Perspective," *Journal of Consumer Culture* 5, no. 2 (2005): 237, 245.

**194** Rick Burton, "Teams as Brands: A Review of the Sports Licensing Concept," in *Sports Marketing and the Psychology of Marketing Communication*, ed. Lynn R. Kahle and Chris Riley (Mahwah, NJ: Lawrence Erlbaum Associates, 2004.), 259.

**195** Montez de Oca, Meyer, and Scholes, "Reaching," 8.

**196** Hagood and Vogan, "The 12th," 30, 32. The Cleveland Browns' co-opting and peddling "Dawg Pound" gear back to the very fan subculture that birthed the strange canine sartorial ritual is another apt example of this form of thievery. Crawford, *Consuming*, 87.

**197** A. J. Maestas.

**198** Sutton, "In High-Tech."

**199** Marion E. Hambrick and Sun J. Kang, "Pin It: Exploring How Professional Sports Organizations Use Pinterest as a Communications and Relationship-Marketing Tool," *Communication and Sport* 3, no. 4 (2015): 45, 47, 48.

**200** Douglas B. Holt, "Why Do Brands Cause Trouble? A Dialectical Theory of Consumer Culture and Branding," *Journal of Consumer Research* 29, no. 1 (2002); Serazio, *Your Ad*.

**201** Armstrong, Delia, and Giardina, "Embracing," 146, 150, 160.

**202** Kim McConnie.

**203** Mark Lev.

**204** Terry Lefton, "A-B Pours It On with NFL Team Logo Cans," *SportsBusiness Journal*, July 18, 2016, www.sportsbusinessdaily.com.

**205** On the flip side, Mark Lev reports that some brands in the United Kingdom hesitate to align too closely with a particular Premier League club, for fear it might alienate rivals' supporters: "Companies have said, 'I'm not going to do this sponsorship deal with Manchester United, because . . . we will absolutely alienate Manchester City and Liverpool fans. They'll revolt and won't buy our products." Mark Lev.

**206** Christine Birkner, "Why the San Francisco Giants Are Baseball's Marketing MVPs," *Adweek*, June 27, 2016, www.adweek.com.

**207** Richard Gruneau and David Whitson, *Hockey Night in Canada: Sport, Identities, and Cultural Politics* (Toronto: Garamond Press, 1993), 71.

**208** Bernard Cova and Veronique Cova, "Tribal Marketing: The Tribalization of Society and Its Impact on the Conduct of Marketing," *European Journal of Marketing* 36, no. 5/6 (2002); Albert M. Muniz and Thomas C. O'Guinn, "Brand Community," *Journal of Consumer Research* 27, no. 4 (March 1, 2001).

**209** Bill Sutton, "How Teams Can Use Maslow's Hierarchy to Build Fan Relationship," *SportsBusiness Journal*, January 11, 2016, www.sportsbusinessdaily.com.

**210** Rudi Meir and Don Scott, "Tribalism: Definition, Identification and Relevance to the Marketing of Professional Sports Franchises," *International Journal of Sports Marketing and Sponsorship* 8 (2007): 331, 341.

**211** An article in the *Journal of Sports Management* expressly advises a shift in thinking from "fans as consumers to fans as community members" and suggests leveraging various demographic characteristics or affinity organizations (i.e., "external group identities" like race, sexual identity, and professional vocation) to "foster greater loyalty toward a sports team." Heere and James, "Sports," 319, 321.

**212** Gruneau and Whitson, *Hockey*, 27.

**213** Steven G. Mandis, "Why a Community Brand like Real Madrid Is So Successful," *SportsBusiness Journal*, November 24, 2016, www.sportsbusinessdaily.com.

**214** Terry Lefton, "Nike Goes Big, Broad with New NFL Campaign," *SportsBusiness Journal*, August 28, 2017, www.sportsbusinessdaily.com.

**215** David Stern.

**216** Bob Dorfman.

**217** Hagood and Vogan, "The 12th," 32, 33. Additionally, as detailed in chapter 1, team officials and urban elites often exploit the warm and fuzzy discourse of community and identity to score public financing for venue development. Belanger, "The Urban," 61; Schimmel, "Political," 58.

**218** Jeremiah Oshan, "Bucks Trying to Bring a Bit of MLS to the NBA," *SB Nation*, October 21, 2014, www.sbnation.com.

**219** A. J. Maestas.

**220** Don Muret, "Venues 3.0: Smarter. Smaller. Social," *SportsBusiness Journal*, January 16, 2017, www.sportsbusinessdaily.com; Robert Gray, "Mixing It Up at Venues," *SportsBusiness Journal*, September 18, 2017, www.sportsbusinessdaily.com.

**221** Interestingly, in a case of industrial needs running crossways, broadcasters are actually *opposed* to this communal adaptation of stadia, as it leaves the impression of empty seats and, for TV producers, "implies malaise" about the product on field. Abraham Madkour, "Plenty of Stories to Follow after World Congress," *SportsBusiness Journal*, May 1, 2017, www.sportsbusinessdaily.com.

**222** Adam Stern, "NASCAR Considers Turning down the Volume on Its Cars," *SportsBusiness Journal*, March 6, 2017, www.sportsbusinessdaily.com.

**223** Notably, 56 percent of fans actually live *outside* the market of their favorite team (and the younger the fan, the more likely he or she is geographically distant), which indicates a need to also scheme "social viewing" opportunities for these diasporas. Rich Luker, "Sorting Out Priorities: How Sports Can Improve Standing with Fans," *SportsBusiness Journal*, April 17, 2017, www.sportsbusinessdaily.com.

**224** John Rowady, "Batten Down the Hatches, DraftKings and FanDuel Are Just Getting Started," *MediaPost*, October 6, 2015, www.mediapost.com.

**225** NBC actually faced the reverse challenge when it acquired U.S. rights to the English Premier League—which retains a rich tapestry of history that many American viewers knew little of—and contemplated assembling feature segments that could bring audiences up to speed and "buy into" that collective memory. Ian Thomas, "NBC Touts Stellar Premier League Season," *SportsBusiness Journal*, March 23, 2016, www.sportsbusinessdaily.com.

**226** Hussain Naqi.

**227** Hoch, *Rip*, 46.

**228** McAllister, "College," 359.

**229** Whitson, "Circuits," 59.

**230** King, "The Lads," 335.

**231** Whannel, *Culture*, 133.

**232** Zirin, *Bad*, 2; DeMause and Cagan, *Field*, 49, 141.

**233** Hagood and Vogan, "The 12th," 32.

**234** Goldman and Papson, *Nike Culture*, 61, 62.

**235** To some extent (on an intra-continental scale), this defined the NHL's strategy as franchises migrated from traditional homes in Canada and the northern U.S. states to larger, growing, yet often apathetic markets in the American Sunbelt like Dallas, Phoenix, Atlanta, and Raleigh. Leifer, *Making*, 294; Zirin, *Bad*, 151.

**236** Similar to the dialogue-light action-adventure films that their pace-of-play modifications are modeled after, professional sports also retain the paralinguistic power to cross borders and be read by audiences internationally, sans subtitles: "The appeal is more visceral and universally understood—for good versus evil, right versus wrong, often violent conflict and action, and a lack of moral ambiguity." Bellamy, "Sports," 70. See also Samantha Cooney, "The NFL Should Stop Flirting with a Franchise in London and Go for It," *Mashable*, January 21, 2016, http://mashable.com; Slack and Amis, "'Money,'" 274.

**237** Jeff Zillgitt, "Stern Transformed League; Game's Popularity Up; Revenue, Too," *USA Today*, October 26, 2012, www.usatoday.com; Steven J. Jackson and David L. Andrews, "Between and beyond the Global and the Local," *International Review for the Sociology of Sport* 34, no. 1 (1999): 35; Cashmore, *Making*, 410, 418.

**238** David Stern.

**239** Markovits and Rensmann, *Gaming*, 107.

**240** Leifer, *Making*, 296, 298, 300.

**241** Gruneau and Whitson, *Hockey*, 243.

**242** Bishop, "Stealing," 29.

**243** Gruneau and Whitson, *Hockey*, 233. For instance, teams sometimes "regionalize" their product to the detriment of unequivocal hometown allegiance—whether that be the Orioles dropping "Baltimore" from their jerseys or the NFL Cardinals and

NHL Coyotes opting to represent "Arizona" rather than simply "Phoenix." Euchner, *Playing*, 27.

**244** Walsh and Giulianotti, "This Sporting," 4, 11.

**245** Whannel, *Culture*, 146; Whitson, "Circuits," 71.

## CHAPTER 4. MAN UP

**1** Almond, *Against*, 9; Pearlman, "Linda"; Eric Dunning, "Sport as a Male Preserve: Notes on the Social Sources of Masculine Identity and Its Transformations," *Theory, Culture & Society* 3, no. 1 (1986): 81.

**2** Howell, "A Manly," 187.

**3** Duncan, "Gender," 231.

**4** Michael A. Messner, *Power at Play: Sports and the Problem of Masculinity* (Boston: Beacon Press, 1992), 7.

**5** Steve Almond, "What I Learned in the Locker Room," *New York Times*, September 13, 2015, www.nytimes.com.

**6** Whannel, *Culture*, 50.

**7** Messner, *Power*, 105.

**8** Moskowitz and Wertheim, *Scorecasting*, 134.

**9** Messner, *Power*, 24.

**10** Markovits and Rensmann, *Gaming*, 50.

**11** Whannel, "Between," 77.

**12** Lawrence A. Wenner, "Media, Sports, and Society: The Research Agenda," in *Media, Sports, and Society*, ed. Lawrence A. Wenner (London: Sage, 1989), 15.

**13** Nylund, "When," 149.

**14** Michael A. Messner, *Taking the Field: Women, Men, and Sports* (Minneapolis: University of Minnesota Press, 2002), 123.

**15** Russ Kenn.

**16** The NBA, however, took a stand *for* that gender dynamism when it moved its 2017 All-Star Game from North Carolina to protest that state's discriminatory bathroom law. Susan Birrell, "Feminist Theories for Sport," in *Handbook of Sports Studies*, ed. Jay Coakley and Eric Dunning (London: Sage, 2000), 61; Reeves Wiedeman, "As American as Refusing to Stand for the National Anthem," *New York*, February 21, 2017, http://nymag.com; Mariah Burton Nelson, *The Stronger Women Get, the More Men Love Football: Sexism and the American Culture of Sports* (New York: Harcourt Brace & Company, 1994), 6.

**17** Lawrence A. Wenner, "In Search of the Sports Bar: Masculinity, Alcohol, Sports, and the Mediation of Public Space," in *Voices in the Street: Explorations in Gender, Media, and Public Space*, ed. Susan J. Drucker and Gary Gumpert (Cresskill, NJ: Hampton Press, 1996), 83; Susan Tyer Eastman and Arthur M. Land, "The Best of Both Worlds: Sports Fans Find Good Seats at the Bar," *Journal of Sport & Social Issues* 21, no. 2 (1997): 161.

**18** Lesley Visser. Feminist critic Mariah Burton Nelson similarly observes: "Manly sports do not unite Americans. They unite American men in celebration of male victory." Nelson, *The Stronger*, 6.

**19** Eastman and Land, "The Best," 168; Messner, *Taking*, 51.

**20** Leigh Steinberg.

**21** A cross-national comparison study finds that men in general (and fathers in particular) are the "most influential socialization agent" that introduces and encourages sports fandom. Messner, *Taking*, 51; Melnick and Wann, "An Examination," 464; Springwood, *Cooperstown*, 153.

**22** Almond, *Against*, 93.

**23** Furthermore, the language of sports often seems deeply redolent of male genitalia: talk of "balls, getting it up, thrust, holding, driving onward, and so forth." Novak, *The Joy*, 85. See also Toby Miller, *Sportsex* (Philadelphia: Temple University Press, 2002), 26.

**24** Nelson, *The Stronger*, 118; Davis, *The Swimsuit*, 52, 61.

**25** R. W. Connell and James W. Messerschmidt, "Hegemonic Masculinity: Rethinking the Concept," *Gender & Society* 19, no. 6 (2005).

**26** Toni Bruce, "Reflections on Communication and Sport: On Women and Femininities," *Communication and Sport* 1, no. 1–2 (2012): 128; Bryan E. Denham, "Masculinities and the Sociology of Sport: Issues and Ironies in the 21st Century," in *Sociology of Sport and Social Theory*, ed. Earl Smith (Champaign, IL: Human Kinetics, 2010), 144.

**27** Messner, *Taking*, xviii; Davis, *The Swimsuit*, 59.

**28** Messner, *Taking*, 14.

**29** Robert Lipsyte, "Jocks vs. Pukes," *Nation*, July 27, 2011, www.thenation.com.

**30** Nick Trujillo, "Hegemonic Masculinity on the Mound: Media Representations of Nolan Ryan and American Sports Culture," *Critical Studies in Mass Communication* 8 (1993).

**31** Drew Magary, "Why Your Team Sucks 2012: Tampa Bay Buccaneers," *Deadspin*, September 2012, http://deadspin.com.

**32** Burstyn, *The Rites*, 147.

**33** Leitch, *God*, 94.

**34** Burstyn, *The Rites*, 4.

**35** Messner, *Taking*, xx.

**36** Nelson, *The Stronger*, 12, 55.

**37** Gruneau and Whitson, *Hockey*, 180.

**38** Steven Pinker and Andrew Mack, "The World Is Not Falling Apart," *Slate*, December 22, 2014, www.slate.com.

**39** Dave Revsine, *The Opening Kickoff: The Tumultuous Birth of a Football Nation* (Guilford, CT: Lyons Press, 2014).

**40** Dave Revsine.

**41** Eric Dunning, "Civilizing Sports: Figurational Sociology and the Sociology of Sport," in *Sociology of Sport and Social Theory*, ed. Earl Smith (Champaign, IL: Human Kinetics, 2010), 20, 21; Elias and Eric Dunning, *Quest*, 21.

**42** Elias and Dunning, *Quest*, 132, 140.

**43** Ibid., 41.

**44** Ibid., 66, 89.

**45** Dunning, "Civilizing," 21.

**46** Dunning, "Sport," 87, 88.

**47** Chris Wesseling, "Don Campbell Installs Oklahoma Drill for Dolphins," *NFL.com*, October 7, 2015, www.nfl.com.

**48** Hoch, *Rip*, 8.

**49** Novak, *The Joy*, 83, 90.

**50** Burstyn, *The Rites*, 175.

**51** Steve Fainaru and Mark Fainaru-Wada, "Why Former 49er Chris Borland Is the Most Dangerous Man in Football," *ESPN.com*, August 21, 2015, http://ESPN.go.com. See also Steve Fainaru and Mark Fainaru-Wada, "Inside Borland's Decision to Leave," *ESPN.com*, August 21, 2015, http://ESPN.go.com.

**52** Coakley, *Sports*, 194.

**53** David Canter.

**54** Jean-Marie Brohm, *Sport: A Prison of Measured Time* (London: Ink Links, 1978), 19, 23.

**55** Ibid., 23, 28.

**56** Wenner, "In Search," 81.

**57** Messner, *Power*, 62.

**58** James A. Holstein, Richard S. Jones, and George E. Koonce, *Is There Life after Football? Surviving the NFL* (New York: New York University Press, 2015), 136; Trujillo, "Machines," 412, 413.

**59** Kevin Young, "Violence, Risk, and Liability in Male Sports Culture," *Sociology of Sport Journal* 10 (1993): 373.

**60** Jemele Hill.

**61** Holstein, Jones, and Koonce, *Is There Life*, 222.

**62** Messner, *Taking*, 51.

**63** Timothy Jon Curry, "Fraternal Bonding in the Locker Room: A Profeminist Analysis of Talk about Competition and Women," *Sociology of Sport Journal* 8 (1991): 124.

**64** Bob Dorfman.

**65** Kevin Blackistone.

**66** Holstein, Jones, and Koonce, *Is There Life*, 2.

**67** Fainaru and Fainaru-Wada, "Inside."

**68** Jamil Smith, "The NFL's Macho Culture Must Die," *New Republic*, March 17, 2015, http://newrepublic.com.

**69** Young, "Violence," 382.

**70** Sokolove, "How One"; Daniel Kaplan, "Concussion Settlement Costs Rise," *SportsBusiness Journal*, February 19, 2018, www.sportsbusinessdaily.com.

**71** Zack Furness, "Reframing Concussions, Masculinity, and NFL Mythology in League of Denial," *Popular Communication* 14, no. 1 (2016): 51; Denham, "Masculinities," 147.

**72** Kevin Blackistone.

**73** Leigh Steinberg. Because of this mentality, players downplay anything that stands in the way of that aim. Kim Jones, a reporter for the NFL Network, has heard some openly prefer a concussion to, say, a leg injury, because they can get back on the field quicker. Kim Jones, personal communication, December 1, 2015. Kevin Blackistone of *Around the Horn* recalls much the same of one Chiefs running back who'd been knocked woozy and sent to the sidelines, but, "He's like, 'I'm not going to do anything that's going to suggest to these people that I'm somehow, I've been dinged.' . . . It's, like, more important to play in the game." Kevin Blackistone.

**74** Almond, *Against*, 49.

**75** Fainaru and Fainaru-Wada, "Why Former."

**76** Spike Eskin.

**77** Dave Revsine.

**78** Fluto Shinzawa.

**79** Daniel A. Grano, *The Eternal Present of Sport: Rethinking Sport and Religion* (Philadelphia: Temple University Press, 2017), 151.

**80** Furness, "Reframing," 54.

**81** Aaron Gordon, "When ESPN Cheered Violence," *Salon*, September 15, 2013, www.salon.com.

**82** Michael Kirk, *League of Denial: The NFL's Concussion Crisis,* PBS.org, October 8, 2013, www.pbs.org.

**83** Greg Bishop.

**84** Mike Lynch.

**85** Dave Revsine; Tommy Craggs.

**86** Bob Costas.

**87** Chris Dufresne.

**88** Rick Reilly, "Football Getting Harder to Watch," *ESPN.com*, November 7, 2013, http://ESPN.go.com.

**89** Michael Rosenberg.

**90** John Branch, "ESPN Football Analyst Walks Away, Disturbed by Brain Trauma on Field," *New York Times*, August 30, 2017, www.nytimes.com.

**91** Morry Levine.

**92** Ivan Maisel.

**93** Morry Levine.

**94** Sokolove, "How One"; Fainaru and Fainaru-Wada, "Why Former"; Crupi, "Gen Z."

**95** Montez de Oca, Meyer, and Scholes, "Reaching," 5.

**96** George Dohrmann, "Hooked for Life," *Huffington Post*, December 1, 2016, http://highline.huffingtonpost.com.

**97** Bill Pennington, "Concussions, by the New Book," *New York Times*, November 29, 2014, www.nytimes.com.

**98** Jarrett Bell, "Bell: Surprise Early Retirements Are New Norm in NFL," *USA Today*, April 9, 2016, www.usatoday.com.

**99** Fainaru and Fainaru-Wada, "Inside."

**100** Smith, "The NFL's Macho."

**101** Fainaru and Fainaru-Wada, "Inside."

**102** Holstein, Jones, and Koonce, *Is There Life*, 218, 220.

**103** Ibid., 90, 91.

**104** Leigh Steinberg.

**105** Denham, "Masculinities," 147; Messner, *Power*, 119.

**106** Messner, *Power*, 111; Holstein, Jones, and Koonce, *Is There Life*, 2, 3, 4.

**107** David Canter.

**108** David Cornwell.

**109** Dave Zirin, personal communication, December 16, 2015.

**110** Avery Stone, "Brandon Marshall Opens Up about Mental Illness in New PSA," *USA Today*, January 21, 2015, http://ftw.usatoday.com.

**111** David Canter.

**112** Mark Rosenthal, "Summary of Ted Wells Report on Miami Dolphins," *NFL.com*, February 14, 2014, www.nfl.com.

**113** Ryan Van Bibber, "The Worst of the Richie Incognito/Jonathan Martin Report," *SB Nation*, February 14, 2014, www.sbnation.com.

**114** Ibid.

**115** Doug Farrar, "Report on Richie Incognito–Jonathan Martin Saga: History of 'Persistent Bullying, Harassment and Ridicule' with Dolphins," *Sports Illustrated*, February 14, 2014, www.si.com.

**116** Holstein, Jones, and Koonce, *Is There Life*, 221.

**117** Bryan Curtis, "The Conservative Case for Football," *Grantland*, November 5, 2014, http://grantland.com.

**118** Ibid.

**119** Dave Zirin.

**120** Filip Bondy.

**121** Tina Cervasio.

**122** Michael A. Messner, "Reflections on Communication and Sport: On Men and Masculinities," *Communication and Sport* 1, no. 1–2 (2012): 121; Cheryl Cooky, Michael A. Messner, and Michela Musto, "'It's Dude Time!': A Quarter Century of Excluding Women's Sports in Televised News and Highlight Shows," *Communication and Sport* 3, no. 1 (2015): 278; Ketterer, McGuire, and Murray, "Contrasting," 289.

**123** Nina Mandell, "Lesley Visser: CBS Sports Is 'Taking a Chance' with All-Female Sports Show," *USA Today*, August 26, 2014, http://ftw.usatoday.com. See also John Ourand, "Spain Gets a Spot on ESPN Radio Schedule," *SportsBusiness Journal*, September 12, 2016, www.sportsbusinessdaily.com.

**124** Juliet Macur, "Another Woman at the March Madness Mike? That Only Took 2 Decades," *New York Times*, March 10, 2017, www.nytimes.com.

**125** Brian Horowitz, "So What Do You Do, Lesley Visser, CBS Sports Reporter and Hall of Fame Sportscaster?," *MediaBistro.com*, January 27, 2010, www.mediabistro.com.

**126** Visser recalls, for instance, scrambling to get a quote from quarterback Terry Bradshaw and him snatching away Visser's pen and signing her notebook, assuming she was just an autograph seeker. Freeman, *ESPN*, 216.

**127** Jeff Pearlman, "With Smarts, Grace, This Female Sportscaster Broke Down Barriers," *Sports Illustrated*, July 24, 2009, www.si.com.

**128** Nelson, *The Stronger*, 230.

**129** Kim Jones.

**130** Kelly Naqi.

**131** Charles Curtis, "Men Read Terrible Tweets to Female Sportswriters in Eye-Opening PSA," *USA Today*, April 26, 2016, http://ftw.usatoday.com.

**132** Richard Sandomir and John Branch, "The Dangers of Being a Female Sportscaster," *New York Times*, March 29, 2016, www.nytimes.com.

**133** Marlow Stern, "ESPN: The Worldwide Leader in Pricks," *Daily Beast*, July 29, 2014, www.thedailybeast.com. Other research has reported female sports journalists accepting this disrespect and discrimination from male fans and counterparts as "par for the course" and a "routine part" of professional experience. Freeman, *ESPN*, 137; Marie Hardin and Stacie Shain, "Strength in Numbers? The Experiences and Attitudes of Women in Sports Media Careers," *Journalism & Mass Communication Quarterly* 82, no. 4 (2005): 813; Marie Hardin and Stacie Shain, "Female Sports Journalists: Are We There Yet? 'No,'" *Newspaper Research Journal* 26, no. 4 (2005): 27.

**134** John Ourand, "#MeToo Shakes Sports Industry," *SportsBusiness Journal*, January 22, 2018, www.sportsbusinessdaily.com.

**135** Jon Wertheim and Jessica Luther, "Exclusive: Inside the Corrosive Workplace Culture of the Dallas Mavericks," *Sports Illustrated*, February 20, 2018, www.si.com.

**136** Emma Baccellieri, "NFL Network Suspends Marshall Faulk, Ike Taylor, Heath Evans after Sexual Harassment Lawsuit," *Deadspin*, December 11, 2017. https://deadspin.com.

**137** Jenn Abelson, "At ESPN, the Problems for Women Run Deep," *Boston Globe*, December 14, 2017, www.bostonglobe.com.

**138** Freeman, *ESPN*, 280.

**139** Mark Bechtel, "For Doris Burke, Having Game Is All That Matters," *Sports Illustrated*, December 19, 2017, www.si.com.

**140** Sarah Kustok.

**141** Hiestand, "Cohn's."

**142** Jemele Hill.

**143** Sarah Kustok.

**144** Linda Cohn.

**145** Jessica Wohl, "'Shocked' Dannon Drops Cam Newton after Female Comment," *Ad Age*, October 5, 2017, http://adage.com.

**146** Marie Hardin and Stacie Shain, "'Feeling Much Smaller than You Know You Are': The Fragmented Professional Identity of Female Sports Journalists," *Critical Studies in Media Communication* 23, no. 4 (2006): 324, 334, 335; Hardin and Shain, "Strength," 812.

**147** Hardin and Shain, "'Feeling,'" 335.

**148** Julie DiCaro, "Safest Bet in Sports: Men Complaining about a Female Announcer's Voice," *New York Times*, September 18, 2017, www.nytimes.com.

**149** Jemele Hill.

**150** Bonnie Bernstein; Sarah Kustok.

**151** Deborah Tannen, *You Just Don't Understand: Women and Men in Conversation* (New York: Ballantine Books, 1991).

**152** John Ourand, "TV Pioneer Lesley Visser Combines Grace, Style and Humor," *SportsBusiness Journal*, January 25, 2016, www.sportsbusinessdaily.com. The experience tends to be similar for female sports agents; Kristen Kuliga, an NFL player representative, reports showing up at a conference meeting in the early 2000s and feeling like the "only woman in a room of about 600 guys"—"I remember literally everyone in the room turning around and looking at me." Today, NFLPA statistics suggest that just 5 percent of its certified agents are women. "It was amazing to me how many agents—when I first got into the business—just automatically assumed that because I was a woman, I wouldn't be respected, I wouldn't be taken seriously," says another. Liz Mullen, "Women Make Gains in NFL Agent Business." *Sports Business Journal*, October 2, 2017, www.sportsbusinessdaily.com

**153** Cervasio adds that, because there are so few play-by-play opportunities for female voices to build up their practice and portfolio, she took a freelance opportunity to call games in a Chinese basketball league: "I'm going to have to drive 50 miles and do a game at one in the morning that's in another country with names that are really hard and maybe three American names . . . That's what you have to do, because there's just less opportunity for it." Tina Cervasio.

**154** Hardin and Shain, "Female,'" 24.

**155** Linda Cohn.

**156** Deitsch, "An In-Depth Look."

**157** Jemele Hill.

**158** Garry Howard.

**159** Tina Cervasio.

**160** Cooky, Messner, and Musto, "'It's Dude," 265, 266.

**161** Hardin and Shain, "Strength," 805.

**162** Duncan, "Gender," 234. NBC's Olympics, however, still represent one of the "most progressive" institutions among U.S. sports media on account of its "unprecedented" efforts to showcase female athletics, even as they have yet to reach full parity (making up 48 percent of summer coverage and 38 percent of winter, along with qualitative differences in descriptions). Billings, *Olympic*, 107, 122.

**163** Wanta, "The Coverage," 107.

**164** Mary Louise Adams, "Feminist Politics and Sport," in *Routledge Handbook of Sport and Politics*, ed. Alan Bairner, John Kelly, and Jung Woo Lee (London: Routledge, 2017), 116.

**165** Chuck Schilken, "Are Fans Right to Be Upset That Serena Williams Beat American Pharoah for SI Sportsperson of the Year?," *Los Angeles Times*, December 14, 2015, www.latimes.com; Wanta, "The Coverage," 107.

**166** John Lombardo, "Priority for the New WNBA Leader: Turnout," *SportsBusiness Journal*, February 15, 2016, www.sportsbusinessdaily.com; Richard Sandomir, "After Two Decades, W.N.B.A. Still Struggling for Relevance," *New York Times*, May 28, 2016. www.nytimes.com; Bill Simmons, "Curious Guy: David Stern," Grantland, February 16, 2006, http://grantland.com; Terry Lefton and John Lombardo, "Two Decades of the W," *SportsBusiness Journal*, May 9, 2016, www.sportsbusinessdaily.com.

**167** Angela J. Hattery, "Feminist Theory and the Study of Sport: An Illustration from Title IX," in *Sociology of Sport and Social Theory*, ed. Earl Smith (Champaign, IL: Human Kinetics, 2010), 105, 109.

**168** "U.S. Women's Team Files Wage-Discrimination Action vs. U.S. Soccer," *ESPN.com*, April 1, 2016, www.ESPN.com.

**169** "Canada 2015: Prize Money Doubled for World Cup Winners," *BBC.com*, December 20, 2014, www.bbc.com.

**170** Lena Dubensky, "Closer Look at the Gender Gap from within College Sports," *SportsBusiness Journal*, May 16, 2016, www.sportsbusinessdaily.com. As the head of a trade association for female administrators reports, "A lot of male donors who are on these AD search committees haven't seen women leaders. They just can't picture it. You see the same thing in the corporate world." Michael Smith, "Women Make Progress in Filling Division 1 AD Jobs," *SportsBusiness Journal*, March 27, 2017, www.sportsbusinessdaily.com. See aslo Adams, "Feminist," 115.

**171** "Women and Leadership: Public Says Women Are Equally Qualified, but Barriers Persist," Pew Research Center, January 15, 2015, www.pewsocialtrends.org.

**172** On the other hand, Bruce has also shown that while female audiences might identify those preferred readings, they don't necessarily identify *with* them—actively resisting and interpreting "against the grain" in ways that negotiate pleasure from otherwise retrograde sports texts. Bruce, "Reflections"; Toni Bruce, "Audience Frustration and Pleasure: Women Viewers Confront Televised Women's Basketball," *Journal of Sport & Social Issues* 22, no. 4 (1998): 376.

**173** Markovits and Rensmann, *Gaming*, 195.

**174** Filip Bondy.

**175** Filip Bondy, "Winter Olympics: Russian Beauty Anna Sidorva Brings Tough Competition to Curling Rink," *New York Daily News*, February 11, 2014, www. nydailynews.com; Messner, *Taking*, 95.

**176** John Rowady.

**177** Birrell, "Feminist Theories for Sport," 67.

**178** Messner, *Taking*, 110.

**179** "WNBA Set to Unveil New Marketing Campaign 'Watch Me Work,'" *Sports Illustrated*, January 28, 2016, www.si.com.

**180** One infamous exception was *SI*'s May 1998 cover story ("Where's Daddy?") about the "startling numbers of out-of-wedlock children" that pro athletes were fathering. Grant Wahl and L. Jon Wertheim, "Paternity Ward," *Sports Illustrated*, May 4, 1998, www.si.com.

**181** Cooky, Messner, and Musto, "'It's Dude,'" 261.

**182** Duncan, "Gender," 236. See also Cooky, Messner, and Musto, "'It's Dude,'" 274.

**183** Dave Revsine.

**184** Duncan, "Gender," 237.

**185** Kiley Kroh, "This Is Why the Women's World Cup Got Paid So Much Less," *ThinkProgress.org*, July 20, 2015, https://thinkprogress.org.

**186** John Wildhack.

**187** Hardin and Shain, "Strength," 806.

**188** Marie Hardin, "Stopped at the Gate: Women's Sports, 'Reader Interest,' and Decision Making by Editors," *Journalism & Mass Communication Quarterly* 82, no. 1 (2005): 62.

**189** Garry Howard.

**190** Toni Bruce, "Women, Sport and the Media: A Complex Terrain," in *Outstanding: Research about Women and Sport in New Zealand*, ed. Camilla Obel, Toni Bruce, and Shona Thompson (Hamilton, NZ: Wilf Malcolm Institute, 2008), 55. See also Hardin, "Stopped," 69, 71, 72.

**191** Hardin, "Stopped," 73.

**192** Mike Lynch.

**193** Spike Eskin.

**194** Dan Stanczyk.

**195** Terry Lefton and John Lombardo, "Freedom and a Fast Deadline Created League's Look," *SportsBusiness Journal*, May 9, 2016, www.sportsbusinessdaily.com.

**196** Lefton and Lombardo, "Two Decades."

**197** David Stern.

**198** Adams, "Feminist," 122.

**199** Nelson, *The Stronger*, 11, 30.

**200** Women's soccer may, in fact, offer the best opportunity to achieve symbolic equality, as its marginal status among American *men's* sports means that it has less of a "gendered identity" to overcome as compared to the other three or four team games that dominate domestically. This is also what, conversely, makes a similar ascendance of women's soccer in Europe less plausible. Messner, *Taking*, 137; Messner, "Reflections," 119; Markovits and Rensmann, *Gaming*, 159, 182.

**201** Hutchins and Rowe, *Sport*, 47, 62.

**202** Coakley, *Sports*, 422; Bruce, "Reflections," 130; Bruce, "Women," 53.

**203** Cooky, Messner, and Musto, "'It's Dude," 279.

**204** Terry Lefton.

**205** Vogan, *ESPN*, 25, 26; Lowes, *Inside*, 19.

**206** Mondello, "Sports," 278.

**207** A. J. Maestas.

**208** Thompson, "The Global."

**209** Norby Williamson.

**210** Rowe, *Sport*, 94.

**211** Victoria E. Johnson, "'Together, We Make Football': The NFL's 'Feminine' Discourses," *Popular Communication* 14, no. 1 (2016): 13.

**212** Messner, *Taking*, 86, 87, 88.

**213** "Under Armour: I Will What I Want."

**214** Perhaps not coincidentally, the Olympics are, along with the Kentucky Derby, the rare sports property that consistently draws more female than male viewers. Ben Fischer, "NBC Promos Draw upon Girl Power in Highlighting Women of Team USA," *SportsBusiness Journal*, July 18, 2016, www.sportsbusinessdaily.com.

**215** Johnson, "'Together," 12. Terry Lefton, the marketing reporter for *SportsBusiness Journal*, says he spent considerable time and effort trying to ferret out evidence that the NFL's domestic violence issues had impacted league business but could find none: Revenues only kept going up in the aftermath of scandal. "The sponsorship—they're not going to pull out from the NFL. . . . If they left, there'd be so many more sponsors waiting at the door to get in. Our country is so crazy for football," observes Dan Stanczyk of ESPN Radio. "Sponsors are clamoring to be associated with the NFL. They don't really care about the NFL's issues with domestic violence. They just have to put on a face and pretend that they care about it." Terry Lefton; Dan Stanczyk.

**216** Todd VanDerWerff, "NBC's Coverage of the Olympics Is Atrocious. There's a Simple Reason Why," *Vox.com*, August 12, 2016, www.vox.com. Audience research does suggest different viewing motives and pleasures for different genders. Of seven broad reasons for tuning into sports, women are more driven by the pretext that they encourage spending time with family, while men are more compelled by the excitement and arousal they offer, derive more self-worth from outcomes, and, interestingly, appreciate the aesthetic quality more. Wann et al., *Sport*, 46.

**217** John Ourand. Melodramatic buildup is, moreover, one of NBC's core strategies for its Olympic coverage—which is telling, given its female-tilted viewership. That assumed audience demographic thus informs everything from the "personality-driven formats" to the exclusion of boxing from prime-time scheduling. Billings, *Olympic*, 10, 35; Coakley, *Sports*, 397.

**218** Gee, "'Sexual," 161.

**219** Diana Moskovitz and Jolie Kerr, "The NFL Can't Stop Pandering at Women," *Deadspin*, February 4, 2016, https://deadspin.com.

**220** Ben Mathis-Lilley, "NFL Team That Drafted Jameis Winston Launches Condescending Website Section for Women," *Slate*, August 6, 2015, www.slate.com.

**221** Kristi Dosh, "NFL May Be Hitting Stride with Female Fans," *ESPN.com*, February 3, 2012, www.ESPN.com.

**222** "NFL Scores a Touchdown with Female Fans," *Adweek*, August 24, 2014, www.adweek.com.

**223** Harry Roman, personal communication, March 3, 2016.

**224** Tina Cervasio.

**225** Gee, "'Sexual,'" 145.

**226** Wann et al., *Sport*, 38.

**227** Howell, "A Manly," 192.

**228** Baker, *Playing*, 4.

**229** Messner, *Power*, 14.

**230** Ibid.

**231** Michael A. Messner, "When Bodies Are Weapons: Masculinity and Violence in Sport," *International Review for the Sociology of Sport* 25, no. 3 (1990): 204.

**232** Stephen Hardy, "Sport in Urbanizing America: A Historical Review," *Journal of Urban History* 23, no. 6 (1997): 680.

**233** Gruneau and Whitson, *Hockey*, 192.

**234** Hardy, "Sport," 676.

**235** Springwood, *Cooperstown*, 44, 47; Michael Mandelbaum, *The Meaning of Sports: Why Americans Watch Baseball, Football, and Basketball and What They See When They Do* (New York: PublicAffairs, 2004), 40–54.

**236** Messner, *Power*, 137.

**237** Geoff Schwartz, "Here's What 'Do Your Job' Really Means for the Patriots," *SB Nation*, January 26, 2017, www.sbnation.com.

**238** Burstyn, *The Rites*, 32; Genevieve Rail and Jean Harvey, "Body at Work: Michel Foucault and the Sociology of Sport," *Sociology of Sport Journal* 12 (1995): 165.

**239** Novak, *The Joy*, 339; Goldman and Papson, *Nike*, 66, 157.

**240** Trujillo, "Machines," 407; Whannel, *Fields*, 185.

**241** John Bale, *Landscapes of Modern Sport* (London: Leicester University Press, 1994), 68.

**242** Burstyn, *The Rites*, 23.

**243** Trujillo, "Machines," 410.

**244** Leitch, *God*, 91.

**245** Fainaru and Fainaru-Wada, "Why Former."

**246** Schimmel, "Take," 37-38.

**247** Burstyn, *The Rites,* 107.

**248** Denham, "Masculinities," 147.

**249** Novak, *The Joy*, 241.

**250** Kim Zayotti, personal communication, March 1, 2016.

**251** Ivan Maisel, "How Economic Downturn Has Affected Rust Belt States and College Football Recruiting," *ESPN.com*, May 26, 2010, www.ESPN.com.

**252** Hanna Rosin, *The End of Men: And the Rise of Women* (New York: Riverhead Books, 2012).

**253** Catherine Rampell, "Women Now a Majority in American Workplaces," *New York Times*, February 5, 2010, www.nytimes.com.

**254** Rosin, *The End*, 5.

**255** Richard V. Reeves and Isabel V. Sawhill, "Men's Lib!," *New York Times*, November 15, 2015, www.nytimes.com; Nancy Folbre, "The Declining Demand for Men," *New York Times*, December 13, 2010, https://economix.blogs.nytimes.com.

**256** Katie Johnston, "Young Men Falling to the Bottom of the Income Ladder," *Boston Globe*, May 22, 2017, www.bostonglobe.com.

**257** Reeves and Sawhill, "Men's Lib!"

**258** Rosin, *The End.*

**259** Whannel, *Media,* 46.

**260** Carl Stempel, "Televised Sports, Masculinist Moral Capital, and Support for the U.S. Invasion of Iraq," *Journal of Sport and Social Issues* 30, no. 1 (2006): 85.

**261** Denham, "Masculinities," 145.

**262** Raney, "Why," 319.

**263** Messner, *Power,* 168.

**264** Sage, *Power,* 65.

**265** Bernstein and Blain, "Sports," 10.

**266** Lawrence A. Wenner, "Mocking the Fan for Fun and Profit: Sports Dirt, Fanship Identity, and Commercial Narratives," in *Sports Media: Transformation, Integration, Consumption,* ed. Andrew C. Billings (New York: Routledge, 2011), 61, 64; Michael A. Messner and Jeffrey Montez de Oca, "The Male Consumer as Loser: Beer and Liquor Ads in Mega Sports Media Events," *Signs* 30, no. 3 (2005).

**267** Nylund, "When," 141, 149.

**268** Allen Guttmann, *From Ritual to Record: The Nature of Modern Sport* (New York: Columbia University Press, 2004), 47, 49, 52.

**269** Mandelbaum, *The Meaning,* 61.

**270** Eric Fisher, "Daily Fantasy Sports' Difficult Year Cools Fantasy's Overall Growth," *SportsBusiness Journal,* June 13, 2016, www.sportsbusinessdaily.com; Eric Fisher, "Daily Fantasy Operators Continue Legal, Legislative Wrangling," *SportsBusiness Journal,* February 8, 2016, www.sportsbusinessdaily.com; John Ourand, "ESPN Plans 28-Hour Fantasy Football Primer," *SportsBusiness Journal,* August 8, 2016, www.sportsbusinessdaily.com.

**271** Hutchins and Rowe, *Sport,* 168.

**272** Ibid., 170; Greg Bishop.

**273** Doug Stewart.

**274** Terry Lefton, "What Drives Team Loyalty?," *SportsBusiness Journal,* October 12, 2015, www.sportsbusinessdaily.com.

**275** Thomas Patrick Oates, "New Media and the Repackaging of NFL Fandom," *Sociology of Sport Journal* 26 (2009): 32.

**276** Almond, *Against,* 83.

**277** Serazio, "Virtual," 238.

**278** Neil Pollack, "The Cult of the General Manager," *Slate,* August 29, 2005, www.slate.com;. See also Will Leitch, "Why Fans Are Now More into Free-Agent Negotiations than Games," *New York,* July 27, 2014, http://nymag.com.

**279** Will Leitch.

**280** Tommy Craggs.

**281** Alex Peysakhovich and Seth Stephens-Davidowitz, "How Not to Drown in Numbers," *New York Times,* May 2, 2015, www.nytimes.com.

**282** Alex Speier, "MIT Analytics Conference Probes the Very Future of Sport Itself," *Boston Globe,* February 26, 2018, www.bostonglobe.com.

**283** Peysakhovich and Stephens-Davidowitz, "How Not"; Bill King, "Analyze This!," *SportsBusiness Journal,* October 12, 2015, www.sportsbusinessdaily.com; Eric Fisher and Liz Mullen, "Analytics Fuels Trend toward Younger Managers in MLB," *SportsBusiness Journal,* November 6, 2017, www.sportsbusinessdaily.com.

**284** Speier, "MIT."

**285** Hutchins and Rowe, *Sport*, 11.

**286** Eric Fisher, "Data Flood Brings Push, Pull on What to Share," *SportsBusiness Journal*, October 10, 2016, www.sportsbusinessdaily.com.

**287** Daniel Kaplan and John Lombardo, "Warriors Mine Smart Court Data," *SportsBusiness Journal*, May 9, 2016, www.sportsbusinessdaily.com.

**288** Eric Fisher, "Wearable Tech Wins Over MLB," *SportsBusiness Journal*, March 13, 2017, www.sportsbusinessdaily.com.

**289** Ken Belson, "In a Data-Driven N.F.L., the Pings May Soon Outstrip the X's and O's," *New York Times*, August 22, 2015, www.nytimes.com; Daniel Kaplan, "NFL Slows Sharing of Player Tracking Data," *SportsBusiness Journal*, August 1, 2016, www.sportsbusinessjournal.com.

**290** Marc Tracy, "Technology Used to Track Players' Steps Now Charts Their Sleep, Too," *New York Times*, September 22, 2017, www.nytimes.com.

**291** Ian Thomas, "Will U.S. Soccer Gain Edge with Player DNA?," *SportsBusiness Journal*, May 29, 2017, www.sportsbusinessdaily.com.

**292** Belson, "In a Data-Driven."

**293** Gruneau and Whitson, *Hockey*, 149.

**294** Roosevelt, in fact, explicitly "exploited the occasion [of the 1900 Olympics Games] to pay homage to the virtues of the frontier, westward expansion, and America's policy of manifest destiny." Michael Butterworth, "Sport and Politics in the United States," in *Routledge Handbook of Sport and Politics*, ed. Alan Bairner, John Kelly, and Jung Woo Lee (London: Routledge, 2017), 151.

**295** Wenner, Bellamy, and Walker, "Selling," 85.

**296** It should be noted, of course, that this is the sort of blue-collar work that Trump himself would never deign to stoop to. Jill Filipovic, "What Donald Trump Thinks It Takes to Be a Man," *New York Times*, November 2, 2017, www.nytimes.com.

**297** Mandelbaum, *The Meaning*, 14.

**298** Ben Shpigel.

**299** Jason Norcross.

## CHAPTER 5. FAIR GAME

**1** Bob Costas; Curtis, "On the Peninsula." This impetus to insulate sport as some sort of "apolitical domain" can actually be traced as far back as the British Empire. Whannel, *Fields*, 181.

**2** Dave Zirin, *Game Over: How Politics Has Turned the Sports World Upside Down* (New York: New Press, 2013), 4.

**3** The language of play routinely intrudes upon politics—going as far back as 1836, when newspaper cartoons caricatured presidential candidates as boxers in the ring. Note, too, the extensive use of sports metaphors within other political discourse—most conspicuously in the basic metaphorical framework through which American journalism tends to cover electoral campaigns (to the detriment of substantive policy discussion): the horse race. Critics contend that this particular framing renders citizens, regrettably, as but detached spectators to the process of democratic participation. Segrave, "The Sports," 51; Butterworth, "Sport," 152.

**4** Michael McCarthy, "'I Can't Breathe': Will Sports TV Viewers and Sponsors Be Turned Off by Activist Athletes?," *Sporting News*, December 12, 2014, www.sporting-news.com.

**5** Zirin, *Game*, 128; Nick Wagoner, "Jeff Fisher Chooses to Stick to Football," *ESPN.com*, December 1, 2014, www.ESPN.com.

**6** Zirin, *Bad*, 37.

**7** Ibid. Others who have made the reverse leap from professional sports into political life include MLB owner turned president George W. Bush, NBA star turned U.S. senator Bill Bradley, and NFL quarterback turned congressman Jack Kemp. Anthony Riccobono, "Republican or Democrat? Mayweather, Tebow, Manning among Athletes Linked to Past Elections," *International Business Times*, November 4, 2014, www.ibtimes.com.

**8** Thorson and Serazio, "Sports."

**9** Sandvoss, *A Game*, 51.

**10** Jeremy Woo, "LeBron James Pushes for Tougher Gun Laws after Cleveland Infant Killed," *Sports Illustrated*, October 2, 2015, www.si.com.

**11** Jonah Engel Bromwich, "'To Me, It Was Racist': N.B.A. Players Respond to Laura Ingraham's Comments on LeBron James," *New York Times*, February 16, 2018, www.nytimes.com.

**12** Dave Zirin, "On Dwight Howard and #FreePalestine," *Nation*, July 17, 2014, www.thenation.com.

**13** Kim Zayotti.

**14** Leigh Steinberg.

**15** To be sure, the topical format obviously precludes direct and regular engagement of certain subjects; as one beat writer told me, it would be "ridiculous" for him to ask around the locker room about, say, the Syrian civil war, gay rights, or even presidential-year voting intentions. He's right, of course, but to assume that "natural" genre conventions alone explain the aversion is to miss the deliberate organizational efforts to steer clear of such politics. Ben Shpigel.

**16** Chad Finn, "Should Sports Personalities Stick to Sports on Social Media?," *Boston Globe*, September 17, 2016, www.bostonglobe.com.

**17** John Ourand, "Skipper: There's No Liberal Bias at ESPN," *SportsBusiness Journal*, November 28, 2016, www.sportsbusinessdaily.com. See also Marc Tracy, "Claims of Liberal Bias in Media Now Include Sportscasters, Too," *New York Times*, May 1, 2017, www.nytimes.com.

**18** Mark Gross. A third member of the network's leadership team accused rival upstart Fox Sports of falsely spreading the myth that ESPN harbored those lefty tendencies—amusingly, in the paranoid tradition of Fox's corporate news cousin: "The whole narrative is a false one that was seeded and perpetuated by a direct business competitor," complained Burke Magnus, ESPN's executive vice president of programming and scheduling. "It would be foolish in the business we're in to take sides on the political arena." Magnus was likely referring to any number of recent volleys: a *Wall Street Journal* op-ed griping about ESPN's "strict obedience to political correctness"; a blog posting by another Fox Sports personality lamenting ESPN's "mistake of trying to make liberal social media losers happy and as a result lost millions of viewers"; or *Breitbart News*'s always-subtle, alt-right coverage captured by one telling headline,

"Pro-American Non-PC ESPN Host Sage Steele Removed from NBA Countdown Show." John Ourand, "ESPN Executive Calls Out Competitor for Giving Voice to Claims of Liberal Bias," *SportsBusiness Journal*, June 26, 2017, www.sportsbusinessdaily.com.

**19** Doug Stewart.

**20** Greg Bishop.

**21** Robert Lipsyte; Lipsyte, "Serving."

**22** Two conspicuous exceptions to this rule over the years include right-wing radio blowhard Rush Limbaugh, who dabbled as an ESPN football show analyst, and sportscaster Keith Olbermann, who crossed over to host an MSNBC opinion show for several years. Yet as Dave Zirin—another rare exception and the first sports editor in the 150-year history of *The Nation* magazine—used to joke, you could, until recently, fit the number of political sports media professionals inside a phone booth. Dave Zirin; Will Leitch, "From Mo'ne Davis to Michael Sam, the Culture Wars Have Invaded the Sports World," *New York*, September 8, 2014, http://nymag.com.

**23** Chris Dufresne.

**24** Dan Stanczyk.

**25** Leitch, *God*, 23.

**26** Ibid., 7.

**27** Wann et al., *Sport*, 40.

**28** Ibid., 39.

**29** Baker, *Playing*, 255.

**30** Daniel Kaplan, "Indiana Controversy Shows Sports More Willing to Take a Stand," *SportsBusiness Journal*, April 6, 2015, www.sportsbusinessdaily.com.

**31** Gary Hoenig.

**32** Ben Fischer, "Step Up, Kneel Down: The Athlete Advocate Has Never Been Stronger," *SportsBusiness Journal*, December 5, 2016, www.sportsbusinessdaily.com.

**33** McCarthy, "'I Can't.'"

**34** Zirin, *Game*, 191.

**35** Dave Revsine.

**36** McChesney, "Media," 57.

**37** McAllister, "College," 360.

**38** Dave Zirin, "Hurricane Katrina and the Revival of the Political Athlete," *Nation*, August 14, 2015, www.thenation.com.

**39** Steve Kornacki, "Bob Costas on His Role in Political Sports Commentary," *MSNBC.com*, July 5, 2014, www.msnbc.com.

**40** Boyle and Haynes, *Power*, 60.

**41** Pat Sullivan, personal communication, January 21, 2016. Ali did, however, do pesticide ads in the late 1970s and Under Armour reportedly sold out his branded apparel collection the week after his death. Terry Lefton, "For Ali, 'There Will Always Be a Market,'" *SportsBusiness Journal*, June 13, 2016, www.sportsbusinessdaily.com; Carrie Cummings, "1968," *Adweek*, June 27, 2016, www.adweek.com.

**42** Riccobono, "Republican."

**43** John Ourand.

**44** Doug Stewart.

**45** Wiedeman, "As American."

**46** Liz Mullen, "Election 2016 a Political Minefield," *SportsBusiness Journal*, August 1, 2016, www.sportsbusinessdaily.com.

**47** Fischer, "Step Up."

**48** Bob Dorfman; Terry Lefton.

**49** Zirin, *Game*, 9. Interestingly, retired athletes from Curt Schilling to Kareem Abdul-Jabbar seem to be afforded (or take) more liberty to intervene in political debate. Presumably, they have less to lose at that point. Liz Mullen, "Ex-Athletes More Likely to Take a Political Stand," *SportsBusiness Journal*, August 1, 2016, www.sports-businessdaily.com.

**50** Laura Wagner, "'Republicans Buy Sneakers, Too,'" *Slate*, July 28, 2016, www.slate.com.

**51** Brendan Dunne, "Jordan Shirt Pays Tribute to Michael Jordan's Reebok Diss at Olympics," *Sole Collector*, June 16, 2016, http://solecollector.com; Jeremy Earp, *Not Just a Game: Power, Politics, and American Sports* (Northampton, MA: Media Education Foundation, 2010).

**52** Kellner, "The Sports," 53.

**53** Wagner, "'Republicans.'"

**54** Terry Eagleton, "Football: A Dear Friend to Capitalism," *Guardian*, June 15, 2010, www.theguardian.com.

**55** Sage, *Power*, 12. One scholar succinctly parries this "hackneyed" critique: "The problem with false consciousness as a concept is that it is untestable; there is no way to refute, or verify, its existence. It is akin to a religious faith, one is a believer or a non-believer; either way, it is a sterile scientific concept." Smith, "The Noble," 61.

**56** Jay Coakley, "Sport as an Opiate," in *Sport in Contemporary Society: An Anthology*, ed. D. Stanley Eitzen (New York: St. Martin's Press, 1979), 251.

**57** Cashmore, *Making*, 103.

**58** Hoch, *Rip*, 20.

**59** Young, "The Sociology," 6.

**60** It should also be caveated that, in America, there is (supposedly) no such thing as "class." "Class," according to one critical scholar, is "America's forbidden thought," in part because "individual outcomes are proportional to talent and effort, the resulting rewards are fair and equitable." Sage, *Power*, 31, 40, 43. "Class," on the other hand, is too redolent of an ossified economic determinism. As U.S. presidential candidate Rick Santorum castigated, emblematically, from the stump: "Since when in America do we have classes? Since when in America are people stuck in areas or defined by places called a class? That's Marxism talk . . . . There's no class in America." He is, to be fair, half-right: It *is* textbook Marxism talk. Mollie Reilly, "Rick Santorum on Middle Class: 'That's Marxism Talk,' 'There's No Class in America,'" *Huffington Post*, August 12, 2013, www.huffingtonpost.com.

**61** Ben Carrington, "Sport without Final Guarantees: Cultural Studies/Marxism/Sport," in *Marxism, Cultural Studies, and Sport*, ed. Ben Carrington and Ian McDonald (New York: Routledge, 2009), 20, 21.

**62** Brohm, *Sport*, 28.

**63** Ibid., 168.

**64** Ibid., 51, 114.

**65** Dave Zirin, "The Missouri Tigers and the Hidden History of Black College Football Activists," *Nation*, November 12, 2015, www.thenation.com.

**66** Charles P. Pierce, "Like Chocolate and Tuna Fish: The Uptick in Clumsy Collisions of Politics and Sports," *Grantland*, June 22, 2015, http://grantland.com; Butterworth, "Sport," 152.

**67** Michael Beschloss, "Sports Sharpen the Presidential Image," *New York Times*, February 5, 2016, www.nytimes.com.

**68** Scott Horsely, "In ACA March Madness, Obama's Bracket Is Just a Role Player," *NPR*, March 19, 2014, www.npr.org.

**69** Beschloss, "Sports."

**70** Carrie Kreiswirth, "Olney Revisits Covering President's Visit for Historic Post-9/11 World Series Game," *ESPN Front Row*, September 11, 2015, www.ESPNfrontrow.com.

**71** William J. Morgan, *Leftist Theories of Sport: A Critique and Reconstruction* (Urbana: University of Illinois Press, 1994), 63; Jhally, "Cultural," 76.

**72** Rowe, *Sport*, 127.

**73** Sociologist Steven Overman coined this delicious turn of phrase and outlined several parallels between the Calvinist work ethic and sports culture including the virtues of asceticism, goal orientation, individual responsibility and personal initiative, God's favoring laborious pursuits, and capitalizing on free time. Steven J. Overman, *The Protestant Ethic and the Spirit of Sport: How Calvinism and Capitalism Shaped America's Games* (Macon, GA: Mercer University Press, 2011). See also Coakley, *Sports*, 523–24.

**74** Lipsyte, *SportsWorld*, ix.

**75** Sage, *Power*, 53–54.

**76** Brohm, *Sport*, 55. The opposite of merit—in sports, as in life—is luck, of course, and there is no shortage of athletic superstition and taboo, if only to be on the safe side. For instance, one intriguing study on "baseball magic" found that, as anthropological theory would predict, players maintained the most elaborate rituals for luck in contexts where they could least control the outcome (e.g., hitting, pitching) and very few where fate seemed most in their hands (literally with fielding). George Gmelch, "Baseball Magic," in *Sport in Contemporary Society: An Anthology*, ed. D. Stanley Eitzen (New York: St. Martin's Press, 1979). Elsewhere, a CBS poll found that 69 percent of fans think "good luck" plays a role—be it small or large—in determining who wins a game. With all of that said, it still seems rare that you run into a player or fan willing to ascribe their team's success to capricious luck as opposed to deserved effort; the moral universe of sport is an orderly one. "*CBS News Poll*," Roper Center, 2013, https://ropercenter.cornell.edu.

**77** Fluto Shinzawa.

**78** Coakley, "Sport," 252; Hoch, *Rip*, 101.

**79** Sarah Kustok.

**80** Montez de Oca, Meyer, and Scholes, "Reaching," 6.

**81** David Canter.

**82** Goldman and Papson, *Nike*, 19-20, 99, 146.

**83** "100 Most Inspirational Sports Quotes of All Time," https://www.keepinspiring.me."

**84** David L. Andrews, "Sport, Spectacle and the Politics of Late Capitalism," in *Routledge Handbook of Sport and Politics*, ed. Alan Bairner, John Kelly, and Jung Woo Lee (London: Routledge, 2017), 231, 234.

**85** Ivan Maisel.

**86** Lesley Visser.

**87** Pierre Bourdieu, "Sport and Social Class," *Social Science Information* 17 (1978): 832; Hoch, *Rip*, 20.

**88** Holstein, Jones, and Koonce, *Is There Life*, 14.

**89** Those long odds lead some to conclude that—although sport sometimes offers "opportunities for dramatic and spectacular individual social mobility" to those of underprivileged origins—more often than not, "sport cultures have contributed to the reproduction of existing patterns of social stratification and division, and status inequalities." This is especially insidious when sold to the African American community in the United States, whose numbers are "disproportionately high," percentage-wise, among professional athletes, but for whom "the absolute number of opportunities available relative to the number of aspirants is infinitesimal." Sage, *Power*, 51; Horne et al., *Understanding*, 51; Harry Edwards, "Sport within the Veil: The Triumphs, Tragedies and Challenges of Afro-American Involvement," *Annals of the American Academy of Political and Social Science* 445 (1979): 124.

**90** Edwards marries this to Marxist logic in theorizing sport as "social control" and "ideological indoctrination"—a "mechanism employed by white society to perpetuate its domination over black society." Edwards, "Sport," 119, 120; Harry Edwards, "Crisis of Black Athletes on the Eve of the 21st Century," *Society* 37, no. 3 (2000): 9.

**91** Whannel, *Media*, 60.

**92** Tas Melas.

**93** Kenn adds that his colleague there, the color analyst Jerry Remy (and apparently perfect neoliberal labor role model, in terms of proper supplicating disposition), told him many times that, as a former player, "he felt like he was going to lose his job every day and so that's what drove him—because nothing was handed to him." Russ Kenn.

**94** Mike Lynch.

**95** Russ Kenn.

**96** Bruce, "Marking," 861.

**97** Tina Cervasio.

**98** Donald Sabo and Sue Curry Jansen, "Images of Men in Sport Media: The Social Reproduction of Gender Order," in *Men, Masculinity, and the Media*, ed. Steve Craig (Newbury Park, CA: Sage, 1992), 178.

**99** Ivan Maisel.

**100** Cashmore, *Making*, 425.

**101** Jason Norcross.

**102** Bob Dorfman.

**103** Kim Zayotti.

**104** Adam Stern, "Busch's 'Earning It' Theme Shifts into NASCAR," *SportsBusiness Journal*, January 25, 2016, www.sportsbusinessdaily.com.

**105** Terry Lefton, "'Protect This House' Fired up UA's Marketing," *SportsBusiness Journal*, January 20, 2016, www.sportsbusinessdaily.com.

**106** Jeff Beer, "How Under Armour Uses a Scrappy Outsider Will to Get What It Wants," *Fast Company*, August 31, 2015, www.fastcocreate.com.

**107** Terry Lefton, "The $5 Billion Startup," *SportsBusiness Journal*, June 20, 2016, www.sportsbusinessdaily.com.

**108** "Under Armour: Rule Yourself—Training," Droga5, 2015, https://droga5.com.

**109** Thomas Piketty, *Capital in the Twenty-First Century* (Cambridge, MA: Harvard University Press, 2013).

**110** Tom Kertscher, "Bernie Sanders, in Madison, Claims Top .1% of Americans Have Almost as Much Wealth as Bottom 90%," *Politifact*, July 29, 2015, www.politifact.com.

**111** Alison Griswold, "Robert Reich's 'Saving Capitalism,'" *New York Times* Book Review, November 15, 2015, www.nytimes.com.

**112** Katie Sanders, "Is It Easier to Obtain the American Dream in Europe?," *Politifact*, December 19, 2013, www.politifact.com; Daniel Aaronson and Bhashkar Mazumder, "Intergenerational Economic Mobility in the United States, 1940 to 2000," *Journal of Human Resources* 43, no. 1 (2008); Griswold, "Robert Reich's.'"

**113** Griswold, "Robert Reich's'"; Brenda Cronin, "Some 95% of 2009–2012 Income Gains Went to Wealthiest 1%," *Wall Street Journal*, September 10, 2013, http://blogs.wsj.com.

**114** "For the Public, It's Not about Class Warfare, but Fairness," Pew Research Center, March 2, 2012, www.people-press.org.

**115** Shai Davidai and Thomas Gilovich, "Building a More Mobile America—One Income Quintile at a Time," *Perspectives on Psychological Science* 10, no. 1 (2015).

**116** Whannel, *Culture*, 47; Cashmore, *Making*, 104–5. Sport scholar John Hargreaves further outlines several underlying ways that sport serves capitalism to this end: it disciplines a "docile" workforce to accept the roles demanded of them by industrial production; it converts play and players into replaceable commodities; and it celebrates, rather uncritically, qualities like "aggressive individualism" and "ruthless competitiveness." John Hargreaves, ed., *Sport, Culture and Ideology* (London: Routledge, 1982).

**117** Burstyn, *The Rites*, 28; Whannel, *Culture*, 11. Essayist Steve Almond has an interesting take on sports helping workers cope with capitalism; he sees fandom's function as "a form of surrender to our essential helplessness in the universal order. . . . Backing a team helps Americans, in particular, contend with the unease of living in the most competitive society on earth, a society in which we're *socialized* to feel like losers." Almond, *Against*, 60-61.

**118** Coakley, *Sports*, 320.

**119** Sabo and Jansen, "Images," 183.

**120** Thorson and Serazio, "Sports."

**121** Dan Stanczyk.

**122** Gruneau and Whitson, *Hockey*, 133.

**123** Ivan Maisel.

**124** Goldman and Papson, *Nike*, 48.

**125** Holstein, Jones, and Koonce, *Is There Life*, 34.

**126** Bernstein and Blain, "Sports," 13.

**127** Pablo Alabarces, Alan Tomlinson, and Christopher Young, "Argentina versus England at the France '98 World Cup: Narratives of Nation and the Mythologizing of the Popular," *Media, Culture & Society* 23 (2001): 548, 549.

**128** Hardy, "Sport," 681.

**129** Rowe, "Media," 551.

**130** According to one assessment, two signifiers index the attainment of nationhood in the contemporary world: having a seat at the United Nations and marching in the Olympics' opening ceremonies. Houlihan, *Sport*, 16–17; Horne et al., *Understanding*, 124.

**131** Rowe, *Sport*, 22.

**132** Maria T. Allison, "On the Ethnicity of Ethnic Minorities in Sport," *Quest* 31, no. 1 (1979): 51, 53; Grey, "Sports," 255, 256.

**133** Novak, *The Joy*, 75.

**134** Gruneau and Whitson, *Hockey*, 13, 26.

**135** Steven J. Jackson and Pam Ponic, "Pride and Prejudice: Reflecting on Sport Heroes, National Identity, and Crisis in Canada," in *Sport and Memory in North America*, ed. Stephen G. Wieting (London: Frank Cass, 2001), 49.

**136** Joseph Maguire, Emma Poulton, and Catherine Possamai, "The War of the Words?: Identity Politics in Anglo-German Press Coverage of Euro 96," *European Journal of Communication* 14, no. 1 (1999); Henry Kissinger, "The World Cup according to Character," *Los Angeles Times*, June 29, 1986; Alabarces, Tomlinson, and Young, "Argentina," 563.

**137** Tricia Jenkins, "The Militarization of American Professional Sports: How the Sports-War Intertext Influences Athletic Ritual and Sports Media," *Journal of Sport and Social Issues* 37, no. 3 (2013): 247; Tom E. Curran, "NFL Teams Being on the Field for Anthem Is a Relatively New Practice," *NBCSports.com*, August 29, 2016, www.nbcsports.com.

**138** Whannel, *Culture*, 45.

**139** Houlihan, *Sport*, 111.

**140** Zimbalist, *Circus*, 11; Houlihan, *Sport*, 114.

**141** Houlihan, *Sport*, 6, 203.

**142** Zimbalist, *Circus*, 23.

**143** More broadly, still, organized sport might be thought of as a "luxury item" for rich nations and the richer people who live in them; lacking the discretionary time and money required, those in low-income jobs (or economies) can't work out as often as their higher-income counterparts. Brohm, *Sport*, 117; Coakley, *Sports*, 323.

**144** Howell, "A Manly," 192.

**145** Burstyn, *The Rites*, 187.

**146** Ibid., 165; Maguire, Poulton, and Possamai, "The War," 180.

**147** Hoch, *Rip*, 89.

**148** Messner, *Taking*, 122.

**149** These can be strung together in a single, illustrative sentence: "Quarterback heroes throw bombs under the orders of generals who devise game strategies in war rooms; defense warriors seek to blitz the offensive line; a series of completed passes constitutes an aerial attack; and tied games result in sudden death overtimes." Samantha King, "Offensive Lines: Sport-State Synergy in an Era of Perpetual War," in *The NFL: Critical and Cultural Perspectives*, ed. Thomas P. Oates and Zack Furness (Philadelphia, PA: Temple University Press, 2014), 193. See also Mandelbaum, *The Meaning*, 128–42; Segrave, "The Sports," 50.

**150** Sue Curry Jansen and Don Sabo, "The Sport/War Metaphor: Hegemonic Masculinity, the Persian Gulf War, and the New World Order," *Sociology of Sport Journal* 11, no. 1 (1994): 4. Even political leaders are not immune to this metaphorical slippage; Richard Nixon's secretary of defense once likened the South Vietnamese to an "expansion ball-club" that wouldn't "win every battle or encounter but they will do a very credible job." Lipsyte, *SportsWorld*, 13.

**151** Adam Rugg, "America's Game: The NFL's 'Salute to Service' Campaign, the Diffused Military Presence, and Corporate Social Responsibility," *Popular Communication* 14, no. 1 (2016): 22.

**152** Ibid.

**153** Burstyn, *The Rites*, 29; Allen Guttmann, "The Appeal of Violent Sports," in *Why We Watch: The Attractions of Violent Entertainment*, ed. Jeffrey H. Goldstein (Oxford: Oxford University Press, 1998), 10, 15; Dunning, "Sport," 81.

**154** Dunning, "Sport," 82; Hoch, *Rip*, 89.

**155** Jenkins, "The Militarization," 247.

**156** Indeed, shortly after Coubertin's founding—apparently jacked up on Olympic pride after hosting the 1896 Games—Greece was propelled to launch a war against Turkey. Richard D. Mandell, "The Nazi Olympics," in *Sport in Contemporary Society: An Anthology*, ed. D. Stanley Eitzen (New York: St. Martin's Press, 1979), 261; Hoch, *Rip*, 86; Horne et al., *Understanding*, 123.

**157** Hoch, *Rip*, 78. See also Miller, *Sportsex*, 30.

**158** I draw upon this helpful definition of "militarism" here: "an approach to the world in which global problems are defined primarily as military problems, where the first response of political leadership, and a segment of the population, is the resort to force, and where the pride of place in American life is given to the military and to a culture of violence." Michael Butterworth, "NFL Films and the Militarization of Professional Football," in *The NFL: Critical and Cultural Perspectives*, ed. Thomas P. Oates and Zack Furness (Philadelphia: Temple University Press, 2014), 206.

**159** Vogan, *Keepers*, 57; Michael Butterworth, "Militarism and Memorializing at the Pro Football Hall of Fame," *Communication and Critical/Cultural Studies* 9, no. 3 (2012): 245.

**160** Butterworth, "NFL Films," 207.

**161** Butterworth, "Militarism," 247.

**162** Almond, *Against*, 145. NFL Films auteur Steve Sabol somewhat cavalierly borrowed the now-infamous phrase for the death and destruction the U.S. rained down on Baghdad in 2003 to articulate his wonder of those fighter jets: "Perhaps the most impressive moment of the NFL pregame pageantry is the *shock and awe* of the flyover." Butterworth, "NFL Films," 205.

**163** Kevin Blackistone. Other scholars have observed much the same—ranging from spectacular rituals of flag-rallying found at Super Bowl XXXVI and the Salt Lake City Olympics to the "constant, everyday, and mutually reinforcing character" of sports and war culture. King, "Offensive," 201; Butterworth, "Sport," 156.

**164** Rugg, "America's," 26.

**165** Lefton, "'Protect."

**166** Earp, *Not Just*.

**167** Rugg, "America's," 21, 22. Pro football is not alone in this, of course. In 2016, as one example, MLB staged the first game in the history of professional sports to be played at an active military base in Fort Bragg. "Braves, Marlins to Play at Fort Bragg Military Base July 3," *Sports Illustrated*, March 8, 2016, www.si.com.

**168** Earp, *Not Just*.

**169** Hussain Naqi.

**170** Russ Kenn.

**171** Burgess Everett, "Report: Pentagon Spent Millions on 'Paid Patriotism' with Pro Sports Leagues," *Politico*, November 4, 2015, www.politico.com; John McCain and Jeff Flake, "Tackling Paid Patriotism: A Joint Oversight Report" (Washington, DC, 2015).

**172** Christopher Baxter, "Which NFL Teams Got Your Federal Tax Dollars?," *NJ.com*, May 7, 2015, www.nj.com; Charles P. Pierce, "Veterans Affairs: The Uneasy Marriage of Military Money and the NFL," *Grantland*, May 27, 2015, http://grantland.com.

**173** Tom Vanden Brook, "Congress Cuts Guard's Ad Budget for Racing," *USA Today*, December 15, 2014, www.usatoday.com; "Army Guard Overhauls Sports Marketing and Advertising Program," National Guard, June 19, 2015, www.nationalguard.mil.

**174** Jenkins, "The Militarization," 250.

**175** Brohm, *Sport*, 11.

**176** A range of teams from the San Antonio Spurs to the Toronto Maple Leafs to the Bolton (UK) Wanderers have adopted uniforms featuring such "military iconography"; the San Diego Padres, which sport them regularly for Sunday home games, were the first franchise to establish an "in-house Military Affairs Department." Rhetorically, players occasionally indulge this delusion, too, as when college football star Kellen Winslow flew off the handle following a tough loss: "It's war . . . [and] they're out to kill you, so I'm out there to kill them. . . . I'm a fucking soldier." King, "Offensive," 194. See also Jenkins, "The Militarization," 248; John Kelly, "Western Militarism and the Political Utility of Sport," in *Routledge Handbook of Sport and Politics*, ed. Alan Bairner, John Kelly, and Jung Woo Lee (London: Routledge, 2017), 281.

**177** Young, "Violence," 380.

**178** Kelly, "Western," 278.

**179** Chris McGreal, "New Book Describes Pat Tillman as Increasingly Disillusioned with Iraq War," *Guardian*, September 15, 2009, www.theguardian.com.

**180** Harkening back to themes from chapter 4, some argue that Tillman's body was, in particular, part of a wider, post-feminist, post-industrial "cultural remasculinization project"—appealing to "anxious American white men who feel they have fallen economically, socially, and culturally." By exuding that risky daring and seeking out those long-lost adventures on the natural frontier, he offered a "corrective to the legion of feminized American sensitive guys, victimized white guys, metrosexuals, and boy-men who have increasingly appeared as stock characters in American popular culture over the past two decades." Kyle W. Kusz, "For the Love of National Manhood: Excavating the Cultural Politics and Media Memorializations of Pat Tillman," in *The NFL: Critical and Cultural Perspectives*, ed. Thomas P. Oates and Zack Furness (Philadelphia: Temple University Press, 2014), 227, 235, 244.

**181** "Pat Tillman's Widow: Don't Politicize Pat in Effort to Divide," *USA Today*, September 26, 2017, www.usatoday.com.

**182** Kusz, "For the Love," 234, 236.

**183** King, "Offensive," 198.

**184** Hoch, *Rip*, 83; Real and Mechikoff, "Deep," 333.

**185** Stempel, "Televised," 79.

**186** Sandvoss, *A Game*, 13.

**187** Almond, *Against*, 146.

**188** King, "Offensive," 195.

**189** Dave DeLand, "Paid Patriotism Is Opportunistic Pandering, and Wrong," *St. Cloud Times*, November 5, 2015, www.sctimes.com; Tom Ley, "Surprise Military

Reunions at NFL Games Reach Peak Bullshit," *Deadspin*, September 2, 2015, http://deadspin.com.

**190** Barbie Zelizer, *Remembering to Forget: Holocaust Memory through the Camera's Eye* (Chicago: University of Chicago Press, 2000).

**191** Dave Revsine.

**192** Tommy Craggs.

**193** Filip Bondy.

**194** No doubt sensing that chasm between military culture and civilian life, the U.S. State Department has explicitly sought out "media opportunities . . . for returning soldiers to share their experience with their local communities in an effort to ensure the public maintains a direct connection to today's army." Sport has especially sought to fill that vacuum of opportunity. Kelly, "Western," 278. See also "America's Forever Wars," *New York Times*, October 22, 2017, www.nytimes.com.

**195** King, "Offensive," 199.

**196** Phillip Carter, "Stolen Valor," *Slate*, March 1, 2017, www.slate.com.

**197** Butterworth, "Militarism," 242, 249.

**198** Kelly, "Western," 287.

**199** Serazio, *Your Ad*.

**200** Earp, *Not Just*.

**201** Norman K. Denzin, "Representing Michael," in *Michael Jordan Inc.: Corporate Sport, Media Culture and Late Modern America*, ed. David L. Andrews (Albany: State University of New York Press, 2001), 5.

**202** Simmons, "Curious."

**203** Michael Hoechsmann, "Just Do It: What Michael Jordan Has to Teach Us," in *Michael Jordan Inc.: Corporate Sport, Media Culture and Late Modern America*, ed. David L. Andrews (Albany: State University of New York Press, 2001), 273; Kellner, "The Sports," 48; Cashmore, *Making*, 419, 420.

**204** As for the media covering those issues of injustice, ESPN's Jemele Hill notes that every time she's written a column about race, she inevitably faces the reader question, "Why are you such a racist?" Hill, "The Mailbag."

**205** "Heat Don Hoodies after Teen's Death," *ESPN.com*, March 24, 2012, www.ESPN.com. ESPN initially reprimanded several employees, such as Michael Smith and Trey Wingo, for sporting hoodies in their Twitter avatars, but later accommodated the activism: "At ESPN, typically you tried to avoid the political aspect of things," noted one vice president there, in a familiar refrain. John Ourand, "Veteran Sports Journalists: Politics Is Not Exactly New to the Game," *SportsBusiness Journal*, October 2, 2017, www.sportsbusinessdaily.com.

**206** McCarthy, "'I Can't'"; William C. Rhoden, "University of Missouri Football Players Exercise Power in Racism Protest," *New York Times*, November 8, 2015, www.nytimes.com.

**207** Gary Washburn, "NBA, WNBA Can—and Should—Be Even More Vocal on Social Issues," *Boston Globe*, July 16, 2016, www.bostonglobe.com.

**208** Leslie Larson, "Members of Congress Do 'Hands Up' Gesture on House Floor," *New York Daily News*, December 2, 2014, www.nydailynews.com.

**209** "No Fines for Rams Players' Salute," *ESPN.com*, December 2, 2014, www.ESPN.com.

**210** "St. Louis Rams' 'Hands Up' Players to Attend Ferguson Christmas Party," *FoxSports.com*, December 18, 2014, www.foxsports.com.

**211** Marc Tracy and Ashley Southall, "Black Football Players Lend Heft to Protests at Missouri," *New York Times*, November 8, 2015, www.nytimes.com.

**212** Maxwell Strachan, "Why the Mizzou Football Protests Are a Watershed Moment in Sports Activism," *Huffington Post*, November 10, 2015, www.huffingtonpost.com.

**213** Dave Zirin, "Black Mizzou Football Players Are Going on Strike over Campus Racism," *Nation*, November 8, 2015, www.thenation.com.

**214** Indeed, the experiences of dissenters like Delgado and Abdul-Rauf shows just how "coercive" and "narrowly defined" patriotism can be at times. Jenkins, "The Militarization," 253.

**215** Mark Sandritter, "A Timeline of Colin Kaepernick's National Anthem Protest and the Athletes Who Joined Him," *SB Nation*, November 6, 2016, www.sbnation.com.

**216** Ibid. See also George Slefo, "So You Sponsor Colin Kaepernick, Now What?," *Ad Age*, August 31, 2016, http://adage.com.

**217** Fischer, "Step Up."

**218** Josh Levin, "Colin Kaepernick's Protest Is Working," *Slate*, September 12, 2016, www.slate.com.

**219** John Wawrow, "Colin Kaepernick Kneels for National Anthem amid 'USA' Chants," *Seattle Times*, October 16, 2016, www.seattletimes.com; Chris Kuc, "After National Anthem Protest, Colin Kaepernick Dreadful in Loss to Bears," *Chicago Tribune*, December 4, 2016, www.chicagotribune.com.

**220** Euan McKirdy, "Colin Kaepernick Continues Kneeling Protest ahead of 49ers Opener," *CNN.com*, September 13, 2016, http://edition.cnn.com.

**221** Michael McCarthy, "Is Donald Trump Right about Colin Kaepernick and NFL TV Ratings?," *Sporting News*, October 31, 2016, www.sportingnews.com.

**222** Michael McCarthy, "Kaepernick Effect? Falling Ratings Force NFL TV Networks to Give Back Free Ads," *Sporting News*, October 7, 2016, www.sporting-news.com.

**223** Adam K. Raymond, "Poll: Anger at Colin Kaepernick Is Driving Down NFL Ratings," *New York*, October 20, 2016, http://nymag.com; McCarthy, "Is Donald Trump?"

**224** Michael McCarthy, "League of Denial: How #BoycottNFL Vigilantes Are Targeting NFL Ratings," *Sporting News*, October 11, 2016, www.sportingnews.com.

**225** "Donald Trump: NFL's Ratings Are Down because of Colin Kaepernick," *Sports Illustrated*, October 30, 2016, www.si.com.

**226** Mike Freeman, "Donald Trump Is Tearing the NFL Apart," *B/R Mag*, October 5, 2016, http://thelab.bleacherreport.com; "Politics Confidential: We Ask Athletes to Weigh In on the Election," *ESPN.com*, October 9, 2016, www.ESPN.com.

**227** Donation records from the election cycle prior found that NBA players and coaches threw their weight almost exclusively behind President Barack Obama (although ownership and management split their giving more evenly between the Republican and Democrat contenders). For its part, the Obama campaign team openly chased the endorsement of Cleveland star LeBron James, given his popularity in the swing state of Ohio: "Having him (endorse Obama) was not necessarily going to be the difference between somebody supporting us and not supporting us—but it was going to have a difference in their enthusiasm." Obama also personally sought publicity assistance from James during the White House's health-care enrollment push; the administration attributed impressive Affordable Care Act sign-up numbers in Milwaukee to the outpouring of support from players on the Bucks there. Motez Bishara, "U.S. Elections: Ronda Rousey, Caitlyn Jenner among Those Backing Hopefuls," *CNN.com*, April 20, 2016, http://edition.cnn.com. See also John Solomon, "These 58 Sports Figures Donated Money to Hillary Clinton or Donald Trump," *CBSSports.com*, October 27, 2016, www.cbssports.com; Chris Chase, "List: NBA Players and Coaches Exclusively Donate to Barack Obama's Campaign," *USA Today*, November 5, 2012, www.usatoday.com; Wiedeman, "As American."

**228** Mullen, "Election"; "Herschel Walker Blackballed by Trump Haters," *TMZ.com*, June 25, 2016, www.tmz.com. On the other hand, some stars have spoken out, even directly countering corporate partners about political issues. NBA star Stephen Curry—and the face of Under Armour—rebuked his sponsor CEO's assessment of Trump as a "real asset" to American business, throwing epic shade: "I agree with that description, if you remove the 'et' from asset." Katie Richards, "Under Armour's Star Endorsers Are Coming Out against the CEO's Pro-Trump Statements," *Adweek*, February 9, 2017, www.adweek.com.

**229** Daniel Kaplan, "Are Outspoken Athletes Making Sponsors Nervous?," *SportsBusiness Journal*, April 24, 2017, www.sportsbusinessdaily.com.

**230** Ben Fischer and John Ourand, "Industry Warms to Idea of President Trump," *SportsBusiness Journal*, November 14, 2016, www.sportsbusinessdaily.com; Mullen, "Election."

**231** Freeman, "Donald Trump"; Rachel G. Bowers, "Donald Trump Says Tom Brady Would Endorse Him If He Asked," *Boston Globe*, February 8, 2016, www.bostonglobe.com.

**232** Jason Diamond, "Tom Brady 'Not Talking Politics Anymore,'" *RollingStone.com*, November 14, 2016, www.rollingstone.com.

**233** Benjamin Hoffman and Ken Belson, "No Trump or Goodell at Super Bowl, At Least According to N.F.L. Transcripts," *New York Times*, January 31, 2017, www.nytimes.com.

**234** Part of Kaepernick's case hinged on the abundance of lesser-quality quarterbacks who'd been recruited during his apparent blacklisting; a telling, albeit arcane, statistic noted that he was the only player (of 144 in NFL history) who threw 200 passes at age 29 that didn't make a roster a year later. Others took aim at the seeming hypocrisy of particular owners like John Mara who claimed to have received censuring fan correspondence that precluded offering Kaepernick employment with the New York Giants, even as the team signed kicker Josh Brown, who'd beaten his wife. Dave Zirin, "The NFL's War against Colin Kaepernick," *Nation*, June 8, 2017, www.thenation.com; Ken Belson, "Kaepernick vs. the N.F.L.: A Primer on His Collusion Case," *New York Times*, December 8, 2017, www.nytimes.com.

**235** Megan Garber, "They Took a Knee," *Atlantic*, September 24, 2017, www.theatlantic.com; Glenn Thrush and Maggie Haberman, "Trump's N.F.L. Critique a Calculated Attempt to Shore Up His Base," *New York Times*, September 25, 2017, www.nytimes.com.

**236** Dave Zirin, "For the NFL, It Was 'Choose-Your-Side Sunday,'" *Nation*, September 24, 2017, www.thenation.com.

**237** Daniel Kaplan, "For NFL, Which Way Forward?," *SportsBusiness Journal*, October 2, 2017, www.sportsbusinessdaily.com.

**238** Nick Greene, "How NFL Players Protested Trump throughout Sunday," *Slate*, September 24, 2017, www.slate.com; Garber, "They Took."

**239** Abraham Madkour, "A Controversial Choice, but Trump's Influence Is Undeniable," *SportsBusiness Journal*, December 11, 2017, www.sportsbusinessdaily.com; P. R. Lockhart, "Trump's Reaction to the NFL Protests Shows How He Fights the Culture War," *Vox*, February 4, 2018, www.vox.com.

**240** Cindy Boren, "Trump Says He Directed Pence to Walk Out of Game If 49ers Protested during National Anthem," *Washington Post*, October 8, 2017, www.washingtonpost.com.

**241** Kevin Spain and A. J. Perez, "DirecTV Offering Refunds to Customers Who Want to Cancel over NFL Anthem Protests," *USA Today*, September 26, 2017, www.usatoday.com. See also Kaplan, "For NFL."

**242** Kevin Quealy, "The NFL Is Now One of the Most Divisive Brands in the U.S.," *New York Times*, October 11, 2017, www.nytimes.com; Abraham Madkour, "Can NFL Have Fresh Start after Tumultuous Season?," *SportsBusiness Journal*, February 12, 2018, www.sportsbusinessdaily.com; David Broughton, "The Issue of Unity: Fans," *SportsBusiness Journal*, October 2, 2017, www.sportsbusinessdaily.com.

**243** Terry Lefton, "Licensees See Drop in NFL Sales," *SportsBusiness Journal*, November 27, 2017, www.sportsbusinessdaily.com.

**244** Kristen Mosbrucker, "Some USAA Members Call for Company to Drop NFL Sponsorship after Several Players Take a Knee," *San Antonio Business Journal*, September 25, 2017, www.bizjournals.com; Raymond Bednar, "NFL Current Events Could Mean Profound Changes for Sponsor Relations," *SportsBusiness Journal*, October 23, 2017, www.sportsbusinessdaily.com; Daniel Kaplan, "NFL Sponsors Cite Impact of Anthem Protests," *SportsBusiness Journal*, November 6, 2017, www.sportsbusinessdaily.com.

**245** Terry Lefton, "Pizza Hut Replacing Papa John's as NFL League Sponsor," *SportsBusiness Journal*, 2018, www.sportsbusinessdaily.com.

**246** Madkour, "Can NFL Have a Fresh Start After Tumultuous Season?" *SportsBusiness Journal*, February 12, 2018, www.sportsbusinessdaily.com. See also Darren Rovell, "Eagles-Patriots Super Bowl Watched by Fewer People," *ESPN.com*, February 5, 2018, www.ESPN.com.

**247** Kaplan, "For NFL."

**248** Bryan Curtis, "Deep Six: Jemele Hill and the Fight for the Future of ESPN," *Ringer*, September 13, 2017, www.theringer.com; Madkour, "A Controversial."

**249** John Ourand, "Agents Tell Talent to Stick to Sports," *SportsBusiness Journal*, October 16, 2017, www.sportsbusinessdaily.com.

**250** John Ourand, "ESPN Makes Tweaks in Social Media Policy," *SportsBusiness Journal*, November 6, 2017, www.sportsbusinessdaily.com.

**251** Douglas Hartmann, "The Politics of Race and Sport: Resistance and Domination in the 1968 African American Olympic Protest Movement," *Ethnic and Racial Studies* 19, no. 3 (1996): 548, 558, 559.

**252** Ibid., 557.

**253** Ibid., 561.

**254** Kareem Abdul-Jabbar, "Insulting Colin Kaepernick Says More about Our Patriotism than His," *Washington Post*, August 30, 2016, www.washingtonpost.com.

**255** As one expert summarizes this "tidal shift" in social justice orientation: "For five decades, athletes were universally condemned for taking stands on issues." Kaplan, "Indiana." See also Richard E. Lapchick, "Athletes Rising to the Occasion on Issues of Social Justice," *SportsBusiness Journal*, June 15, 2015, www.sportsbusinessdaily.com.

**256** Zirin, "Hurricane."

**257** Dave Zirin.

**258** Kevin Blackistone.

**259** Wiedeman, "As American."

**260** Ibid.

**261** Will Leitch, "Loud and Clear: Athletes Speaking Up," *Sports on Earth*, December 8, 2014, www.sportsonearth.com; Fischer, "Step Up."

**262** Brad Brown.

**263** Mullen, "Election."

**264** Dominique Mosbergen, "Adidas Shuts Down Homophobic Commenters in the Best Way Possible," *Huffington Post*, February 18, 2016, www.huffingtonpost.com.

**265** Lia Stierwalt. This also symbolizes a rather significant departure from the tradition of brands wooing gay consumers but sidestepping their political identity. Less "powerful and bold," however, was when Adidas North America President Mark King announced at a World Congress of Sports gathering, "To me, [the new activism] will hurt the athletes. We try not to be in social issues, though we are moving toward that because we have to. But we certainly won't associate with athletes that are going to cause our brand something that we don't represent and something we don't stand for. At the end of the day, I think it will significantly hurt athletes in terms of endorsements." Kaplan, "Are Outspoken." See also Katherine Sender, *Business, Not Politics: The Making of the Gay Market* (New York: Columbia University Press, 2004).

**266** Cindy Boren, "A Boycott Budweiser Movement Begins over Super Bowl Immigration Ad," *Washington Post*, February 4, 2017, www.washingtonpost.com.

**267** Ken Belson, "A Different Super Bowl Matchup: Politics vs. the N.F.L.," *New York Times*, February 1, 2017, www.nytimes.com.

**268** Bob Costas.

**269** Bob Costas. Relatedly, the NBA took the unprecedented move—for a professional sports league, at least—of intervening in the fraught American debate about guns with a high-profile PSA militating against gun violence, though its political footing here was still quite cautious; the ads, a spokesperson said, don't "advocate for any change in law or policy," but rather encourage the (hard-to-argue-with) goal of "community safety." Zach Schonbrun and Michael Barbaro, "N.B.A. Lends Its Name and Its Stars to Campaign against Gun Violence," *New York Times*, December 23, 2015, www.nytimes.com.

**270** Kornacki, "Bob Costas." See also Billings, *Olympic*, 57.

**271** Belson, "A Different."

**272** In that, sport is perhaps best conceptualized as "contested . . . terrain," as one scholar terms it—occupying a space that allows for both "resistance and domination, as well as opportunity and constraint," where "images, ideologies, and inequalities are constructed, transformed, and constantly struggled over." Douglas Hartmann, "Rethinking the Relationship between Sport and Race in American Culture: Golden Ghettos and Contested Terrain," *Sociology of Sport Journal* 17 (2000): 229, 230, 243.

**273** Rowe, *Sport*, 50.

**274** Zirin, *Bad*, 33, 40; Mullen, "Election."

**275** Ivan Maisel.

**276** Robert H. Prisuta, "Televised Sports and Political Values," *Journal of Communication* 29, no. 1 (1979).

**277** Thorson and Serazio, "Sports."

**278** Stempel, "Televised," 79, 83.

**279** Bryan Curtis, "The End of 'Stick to Sports,'" *Ringer*, January 30, 2017, www.theringer.com.

**280** Messner, *Power*, 12; Coakley, *Sports*, 317. Conversely, there seems to be little interest in promoting or sponsoring sports "that emphasize partnership, sharing, open participation, nurturance, and mutual support . . . because people with power don't want to promote values that reaffirm equality and horizontal forms of social organization in society." Coakley, *Sports*, 318.

**281** Lincoln Allison, "Sport and Conservatism," in Bairner, Kelly, and Lee, *Routledge Handbook*, 53. Even those who chronicle the sports-sited incidents and organizations that engage in progressive activism—globally, from the Ultras Ahlway fans who joined the Tahrir Square uprising to the millions of Brazilians who took the streets against their nation's FIFA hosting bid to the left-wing traditions of Germany's FC Sankt Pauli followers—acknowledge "the conservative and functional social values that permeate sport and the global neo-liberal economic context within which sport is practiced." Like Kaepernick himself, these are, then, exceptions that I would argue prove the rule. Mick Totten, "Sport Activism and Protest," in *Routledge Handbook of Sport and Politics*, ed. Alan Bairner, John Kelly, and Jung Woo Lee (London: Routledge, 2017), 372, 373. See also Alan Bairner, "Sport and Political Ideology," in Bairner, Kelly, and Lee, *Routledge Handbook*, 42, 46.

**282** For the sake of intellectual consistency, I would certainly defend conservative sports stars' desire to air their political views in public, however disquieting to progressive sensibilities. To that end, ESPN was wrong to fire conservative pitcher turned analyst Curt Schilling for his issuing his social-media takes analogizing Muslims to Nazis and sharing a trans-phobic cartoon. I also applaud NHL goaltender Tim Thomas's protest abstention from his championship team's Obama-era White House visit (whose "beef was the size, scope and power of the federal government"), just as I applaud—with admittedly greater volume—those two dozen members of the New England Patriots who passed on posing with Donald Trump after their Super Bowl victory. Mullen, "Ex-Athletes"; Dugan Arnett, "Curt Schilling Draws Ire, Suspension for Controversial Tweet," *Boston Globe*, August 26, 2015, www.bostonglobe.com; Bill Speros, "LeBron's 'I Can't Breathe' Shirt Offers Profile in Conformity, Not Courage," *Boston.com*, December 17, 2014, www.boston.com.

**283** Rowe, *Sport*, 90, 91.

## CHAPTER 6. OUT OF BOUNDS

**1** Linda Cohn; Zirin, *Bad*, 1. Portions of this section of the chapter were earlier featured in a posting for *Sports Illustrated*'s *The Cauldron* website. Michael Serazio, "A San Diego Fan's Eulogy: Dispatches from the Last Game. Ever," *Cauldron*, January 16, 2017, https://the-cauldron.com.

**2** San Diego is, nonetheless, to be applauded for voting down the taxpayer-funded new stadium measure—making it, as shown in chapter 1, a rare city to do so.

**3** Zirin, *Bad*, 57–58.

**4** Spike Eskin.

**5** Moskowitz and Wertheim, *Scorecasting*, 250, 251.

**6** Michael Rosenberg.

**7** Ben Shpigel.

**8** Stuart Hall, "Encoding/Decoding," in *Culture, Media, Language: Working Papers in Cultural Studies, 1972–1979*, ed. Stuart Hall, Dorothy Hobson, Andrew Lowe, and Paul Willis (London: Hutchinson, 1980).

**9** Wenner, Bellamy, and Walker, "Selling," 74.

**10** Zirin, *Bad*, 57.

**11** Walsh and Giulianotti, "This Sporting," 64.

**12** Whannel, *Culture*, 105.

**13** DeMause and Cagan, *Field*, 187.

**14** Morry Levine.

**15** Garry Howard.

**16** Dave Zirin.

**17** Cashmore, *Making*, 4.

**18** Will Leitch.

**19** Will Leitch.

**20** Edwards, "Sport," 116.

**21** Benjamin Domenech, "The Game Is On. Can You Please Take the Politics Outside?," *New York Times*, February 3, 2017, www.nytimes.com.

**22** Michael Rosenberg, "A Lesson Learned in a Ford Field Elevator," *Detroit Free Press*, May 18, 2012, http://archive.freep.com.

# INDEX

# ABOUT THE AUTHOR

Michael Serazio is a faculty member in the Department of Communication at Boston College who studies media production, advertising, popular culture, and political communication. An award-winning former journalist, he is author of *Your Ad Here: The Cool Sell of Guerrilla Marketing* and writes for both scholarly journals and popular publications.

# POSTMILLENNIAL POP

General Editors: Karen Tongson and Henry Jenkins